BERLITZ®

DISCOVER
CANADA

Design and Cartography by
Visual Image, Street, Somerset.

Although we have made every effort to ensure the accuracy of all the information in this book, changes occur incessantly. We cannot therefore take responsibility for facts, addresses and circumstances in general that are constantly subject to alteration.

If you have any new information, suggestions or corrections to contribute to this guide, we would like to hear from you. Please write to Berlitz Publishing at one of the above addresses.

The Berlitz tick is used to indicate places or events of particular interest.

Photographic Acknowledgements

All photographs by Chris Coe and © Berlitz Publishing Company Ltd. except for the following: Bryan and Cherry Alexander, Dorset, 314, 317, 318, 320, 323, 327, 328, 331, 332, 334, 337, 338, 339.

With thanks to: Bluebird Express/Air Club International; New Brunswick – Inn on the Cove, Saint John, Canadiana Hotel, Moncton; Ontario – Killarney Lodge, Algonquin National Park; British Columbia – Glacier Air Tours, Squamish/Whistler.

Photograph previous page: Totem pole in Stanley Park, Vancouver, British Columbia.

The authors would like to thank the following for their help and support during the most vital stage of any travel book – the research: BC Ferries, Brewster Transportation and Tours, Canadian Tourist Office, London; Cruise Canada, Sandra Gies of Red Deer Lodge Campground, Madawaska, Ontario; Greyhound Lines of Canada, Holiday Inn on King, Toronto; Kampgrounds of America (KOA); Arthur Proudfoot, Vancouver; Patrik and Linda Richardson of Project Partners, Balcombe, West Sussex; ViaRail Canada, and the immensely helpful staff of provincial and city tourism departments throughout Canada.

Phototypeset, originated and printed by C.S. Graphics, Singapore.

Contents

MAPS: Canada 4, 8-9, 35; British Columbia 53; Vancouver Island 55; Alberta 99; Saskatchewan 145; Manitoba 166; Ontario 190; Golden Horseshoe 206; Muskoka Region 215; Quebec 238; Gaspé Peninsula 260; Atlantic Canada 264; Yukon and Northwest Territories 331.
Town Plans: Vieux Montréal 241; Ottawa–Hull 225; Vieux Quebec 252; Downtown Toronto 199; Downtown Vancouver 81.

exploration and settlement began. Montreal and Quebec City have their own unique attractions, and Montreal is often regarded as the New Orleans of the North.

From a tourism point of view, **New Brunswick** is the least well known of Canada's Atlantic Provinces, but it has much to offer – from the beauty of its offshore islands and awesomely high tides of the Bay of Fundy, to the charming and historic cities of Saint John and Fredericton. The province is extensively forested and has a strong French heritage.

As its name suggests, **Nova Scotia** has a strong Hibernian flavour, with Highland Games, Scottish names and roadside mailboxes, not to mention a Gaelic college. Much of the countryside even looks like Scotland, with lochs, forests and open moorland. Halifax, the provincial capital, has a beautifully restored waterfront area and the Citadel, an old colonial fort now a National Historic Site. The province has many fascinating towns and fishing villages, and Cape Breton Island is marvellous for hikers and motorists.

Canada's smallest province, tiny **Prince Edward Island** is largely pastoral, noted for its potatoes, dairy cattle, game fishing, sea food – and *Anne of Green Gables*. The capital, its only city, is Charlottetown. Covering little more than 5,120sq km (2,000sq miles), the island is a rewarding destination for visitors.

Rugged **Newfoundland and Labrador** is largely maritime in character. It has a strong folklore and a firmly established population – 95 percent of its residents are native-born. The people of the capital, St John's, speak with a surprisingly strong Irish accent, and the city is surrounded by a number of quaintly named communities in attractive settings.

The **Yukon** and **Northwest Territories** constitute Canada's Far North, where floatplanes and huskies are a major form of transport. This is the land of Robert Service and the Gold Rush, where there are hundreds of miles of treeless tundra, as well as extensive mountain and forest regions – with the summertime consolation of warm days and the midnight sun. Although conditions are frequently primitive, there are modern cities, notably Dawson City, Whitehorse and Yellowknife.

When to Go

Canadians are proud of their climate, even though they try to play it down. The best line we heard was: 'In the Rockies we have nine months winter and three months damn poor sleigh riding.' There are variations on that all over Canada. However, it is a fact that in most places winter is at least as long as the rest of the seasons put together. So when to go depends on what you want to do.

If theatre, concerts, art exhibitions, museums and culture are your interests then it won't matter which part of the year you choose – there's always something going on. Those involved in outdoor pursuits face some degree of restriction. Canoeists will find the going hard in January. Few skiers will find much satisfaction in August. Anglers will find fish to hook all year round – fly-fishing or spinning in the summer, fishing through holes in the ice in winter.

Climate and Clothing

The most temperate region is the southwestern coastal strip, with rainy winters and sunny but rarely too hot summers.

The warmest winters and mildest summers are to be found in southern British Columbia and western Alberta (though the Rockies can confound statistics). The southwestern part of British Columbia, which includes Vancouver and Vancouver Island, has a relatively mild climate all year – the mildest in Canada. There is, however, a lot of rain and the climate varies greatly from one part of the province to another.

Eastern Alberta, Saskatchewan and Manitoba enjoy short, sunny summers and long winters with light snowfalls but low temperatures. Ontario and Quebec have the greatest contrasts: hot, humid summers and winters that keep deep snow on the ground from December to the end of March. Snow flurries are not uncommon even in early May.

The Atlantic Provinces are said to enjoy relatively mild weather. The key word is 'relatively'. You can find patches of snow on the ground well into spring, and you'll hear coastal foghorns in July – even if you can't see the coast.

So what to pack? In winter you need to assume the attitude and skill of a stripper, dressing in layers that can easily be removed or replaced as temperatures change. You will certainly need a hat, scarf, gloves and a good topcoat, and overshoes will be useful on city streets.

Springtime in the Rockies can be deceptive. Within minutes bright sunshine can give way to a blizzard, and if you are going up the Jasper Tramway, say, you would certainly be wise to take warm clothing. Spring weather elsewhere may be slightly more stable, but the prairie wind can blow hard and cold while sudden storms of rain or snow can blow up anywhere – so your outer clothing will need to be waterproof, too.

*J*oggers make the most of the extensive trails in Vancouver's Stanley Park.

On high ground and in coastal areas you may need a sweater or light jacket on summer evenings. In small towns and rural areas you can stay casual all the time, but rather more formal clothing would be advisable for big city wear in the evenings.

Time Differences

Six time zones operate in Canada: Newfoundland standard time, Atlantic standard time (Labrador, Prince Edward Island, New Brunswick, Nova Scotia), eastern standard time (Quebec, most of Ontario), central standard time (western Ontario,

Manitoba, most of Saskatchewan), mountain standard time (northwestern Saskatchewan, Alberta, eastern British Columbia, the Northwest Territories) and Pacific standard time (the Yukon, most of British Columbia). This means that when it is 7.30am in St John's, it is 6am in Halifax, 5am in Montreal, 4am in Winnipeg, 3am in Edmonton and 2am in Vancouver. Every year, on the first Sunday in April, daylight saving comes into effect in most of the country and clocks are advanced one hour. Standard time is reverted to on the last Sunday in October.

Getting to Canada

By Air
Canada is surprisingly accessible. International airports at Vancouver, Calgary, Edmonton, Winnipeg, Toronto and Montreal have daily flights arriving from the USA, Europe and other parts of the world. St John's, Newfoundland, and Halifax, Nova Scotia, have restricted services from Europe, and travellers to the Maritime Provinces should be aware that careful planning is needed to avoid having to backtrack from Toronto, nearly 1,600km (1,000 miles) inland from the Atlantic coast.

The country's major carriers with international services are Air Canada and Canadian Airlines International, both with daily services from the UK, from where British Airways also offers a range of routes. There are also extensive charter flight services, especially in summer. Lufthansa crosses the Atlantic from its Frankfurt hub and KLM uses Amsterdam's Schipol Airport. Canadian Airlines, Lufthansa and Qantas offer services to and from Australia.

There is an extensive network of flights between Canada and the USA, with services frequent enough to be regarded as a shuttle on the one-hour journey between New York City, Toronto and Montreal. Principal carriers operating on the major US–Canada routes are Air Canada, Canadian Airlines, American Airlines, Continental, Delta, United Airlines and USAir.

By Road
Greyhound's extensive **bus** network enables travellers to get from almost anywhere in the USA to almost anywhere in Canada.

For visitors travelling by **car**, all northbound routes on the US Interstate Highway system lead to the Canadian border, and there are many other crossing points on smaller highways. Car ferry services operate between Seattle and Victoria, on Vancouver Island, and between Bar Harbor and Portland, Maine, and Yarmouth, Nova Scotia.

Foreign driving licences are valid in Canada for varying periods of time depending on the laws of individual provinces and territories. All will accept a one-year International Driving Permit as long as it is supported by a state or national driving licence. Vehicle insurance is compulsory throughout.

It's worth remembering Canadian and visiting motorists are required to produce evidence of financial responsibility in the event of being involved in an accident. US motorists should obtain a Canadian Non-Resident Inter-Provincial Motor Vehicle Liability Insurance Card, that which is available from any American insurance company. The minimum liability requirement is $200,000, except in Quebec where it is $50,000.

A quiet and colourful corner in Ottawa, the nation's capital.

By Rail

Amtrak has services between New York and Montreal, New York, Buffalo and Toronto and Chicago and Toronto. Its crack train, the *Montrealer*, takes a little over 14 hours to cover its overnight journey from New York's Pennsylvania Station to Montreal. Other journey times vary between 10^1/$_2$ and 12 hours. Amtrak services on the west coast terminate at Seattle. From there, passengers can travel to Vancouver and other Canadian destinations by bus.

Customs and Entry Regulations

Citizens and legal residents of the United States do not need a passport or visa to enter Canada, but they may be asked to show proof of citizenship, such

as a birth certificate, valid passport or voter registration form. Proof of identity may also be requested. US residents entering Canada from a third country must be prepared to show a passport, naturalization certificate or 'Green Card'.

Visitors from the UK, countries of the European Union, Australia and New Zealand do not need a visa, provided they have a full passport. Citizens of South Africa must obtain a visa before visiting Canada. Write to the following: Canadian High Commission, Visa Section, PO Box 26016, Arcadia, Pretoria 0007; tel. (27-12) 342-6923; fax (27-12) 342-3839. The street address is 1103 Arcadia Street (corner of Hilda), Hatfield, Pretoria.

All visitors to Canada must have sufficient documentary evidence – a return ticket or evidence of onward transportation – to satisfy an immigration officer that they can return or go on to another country. They must also be able to show that they are genuine visitors and may be required to show that they can maintain themselves during their stay. Unaccompanied persons under the age of 18 must have a letter giving them permission to travel either alone or with a representative or relation.

Visitors to Canada can import goods worth up to a total of $300 free of duty. These can include 200 cigarettes, 50 cigars and 400 grammes of tobacco; 1.14l (40oz) of wine or liquor, or 8^1/$_2$l of beer or ale; gifts worth up to $60 each. Persons importing alcoholic beverages must meet the minimum age requirement of the province in which they arrive.

Cats and dogs must have a vet's certificate showing they have been vaccinated against rabies within the past three years. There are restrictions on the importation of certain agricultural products

T raditional trolleys provide cheap and easy transport for sightseers in many Canadian cities. This is Vancouver.

and livestock and of endangered species of animals and plants and products made from the fur, skin, feathers and bone of endangered species – which means that ivory brooches may be confiscated.

Driving in Canada

Driving is the best way to see Canada. The country has an excellent road system, linked to the TransCanada Highway, the longest in the world. It stretches some 8,000km (5,000 miles) from Nanaimo, on Vancouver Island, to St John's, Newfoundland, with ferry connections to the mainland at each end.

Roads are generally well maintained, but surfaces in some places – especially in the Rockies – may be badly broken up in early spring as a result of frost damage.

Studded tyres are forbidden in Ontario, but allowed without seasonal limitation in Alberta, Saskatchewan, the Northwest Territories and Yukon. The other provinces allow studded tyres only in the winter.

Regulations

Wearing seatbelts is mandatory for all drivers and passengers in Canada, except in Yukon. However, children under the age of six in Yukon must use an approved child restraint. In some provinces vehicles must be driven with headlights on for extended periods after dawn and before sunset. On Yukon highways headlights must be kept on whenever a vehicle is in use. Motorists are not permitted to drive on parking lights.

Speed limits vary from province to province – usually up to 90 or 100kph (55–62mph). Distances are always shown in kilometres (though Canadians almost invariably use miles in conversation) and gasoline is sold in litres.

Automobile Clubs

Full membership services of the Canadian Automobile Association are available to members of the American Automobile Association and to motorists belonging to member clubs of the Alliance Internationale de Tourisme, the Fédération Internationale de l'Automobile, the Federation of InterAmerican Touring and Automobile Clubs, and the Commonwealth Motoring Conference. This means that members of organizations such as Britain's Automobile Association, or the Royal Automobile Club, are entitled to travel information services, itineraries, maps, tour books, road and weather information, emergency and other services on presenting their membership cards. The CAA's address is 1775 Courtwood Crescent, Ottawa, Ontario K2C 3J2; tel. (613) 226-7631; emergency services, 800-336-4357.

Health & Medical Care

Your nose – and any other parts of the body you care to expose – is as susceptible to sunburn in winter as it is in summer, so it's always a good idea to include an appropriate sunscreen in your personal health kit. Frostbite is another winter hazard, especially for the ears, nose and cheeks, which is why the most you'll see of Canadians outdoors on really cold days is their eyes – and not even those if they're wearing sunshields for skiing.

In summer it's a good idea to take an insect repellent with you, especially if you'll be visiting a rural or wilderness area, such as a provincial or national park. Swarms of blackfly can make June a miserable and painful time to be in the Great Outdoors.

If you suffer any of the usual travel ailments during your stay in Canada you'll find supermarkets and drugstores have well-stocked sections selling non-pre-

scription medicines and preparations, with qualified staff on hand to give advice. However, in rural areas the nearest drugstores may be many miles away, so make sure your kit includes such things as analgesics, diarrhoea treatment and antiseptic ointment.

Canadian hospital and medical services are excellent, but can be expensive, so make sure you have adequate medical insurance arranged before you leave home. Visitors taking medicine prescribed by a doctor should take a copy of the prescription in case it needs to be renewed by a doctor in Canada. If you wear glasses take a spare pair – or better still a prescription – with you.

Wilderness Safety Tips

The one important rule in the Canadian wilderness is never to feed wild animals or leave garbage which will attract them. It may seem a nice idea to tempt a bear with a few titbits in the hope of getting a close-up picture, but in the interest of avoiding trouble people are urged to let wild animals stay that way. A wild animal that becomes dependent on handouts from humans is a potentially dangerous one.

Even the amiable moose can turn nasty when it has young. Most wild creatures are too timid to stick around if they are aware of your presence, but if cornered they may attack through fear. Treat them all with respect.

If you are travelling in wilderness areas in the colder months be sure to have your vehicle 'winterised', as the locals do. At any time of year in the north have food, drinks and warm clothing and blankets or sleeping bags available in case you are stranded in an isolated place.

Recreation vehicles and motor homes, in which you carry your everyday living requirements are popular for wilderness travel. Top up with gas whenever the opportunity arises (which may be seldom) and don't run low on heating or cooking fuel or water.

In this friendly country you'll get a greeting from anyone else who happens to be on the road. If you are in trouble, flag down a passing motorist (you may have to wait a while for one). If he can't help, he may well get a message to someone who can.

Disabled Visitors

Many of the larger hotels throughout Canada have rooms and facilities which are specially adapted for disabled travellers. Wheelchair accessibility is also a feature of many restaurants and major attractions.

Facilities for disabled people are widely available. The Canadian Paraplegic Association has an office in every province. The head office address is: Canadian Paraplegic Association, National Office, 1500 Don Mills Road, Suite 201, Don Mills, Toronto, Ontario M3B 3K4; telephone (416) 391-0203.

Advance notice of up to two days is required for wheelchair passengers on ViaRail, and there obviously has to be a limit to the dimensions and weight of a wheelchair because of the width of train corridors. ViaRail staff are extremely helpful to disabled people getting on and off trains and on board. Inquire about roomettes for blind people with guide dogs. Tourist information offices can advise on transport and hotel facilities for disabled travellers.

Children

Canada may not spring to mind immediately as the ideal destination for small children, particularly if a touring holiday is planned, this sector of the population not being noted for its appreciation of spectacular scenery or its tolerance of long journeys.

However, several major cities now offer excellent science centres with the accent on interaction, where youngsters from toddlerhood onwards can have tremendous fun and learn a lot.

Those travelling with tots should consider including such attractions as beaches, water parks, zoos and petting farms in their itineraries. These appeal, too, to children of all ages who may also appreciate mini-golf, electronic games and hands-on museums. Boat trips, horse and buggy rides, miniature railway or steam train excursions may appeal if the opportunity arises and the budget permits.

Mature minded children from the age of about 12 should get as much enjoyment as adults from general sightseeing, watersports, hiking, biking, camping and the other outdoor activities for which Canada is famous. Make sure distances involved aren't too strenuous. Winter sports appeal to most youngsters, and the major ski resorts have good instruction programmes for novices.

Almost all attractions and public transportation systems have lower charges for children and students, while tinies usually get free admission. Cafes and restaurants are accustomed to catering for children, and highchairs are usually available. Many outlets offer special cut-price kiddies' menus. Be warned: burgers and assorted heavily-battered, deepfried fast foods are likely to be to the fore.

Money Matters

Currency

Canadian currency consists of dollars and cents. Bills come in denominations of $2, $5, $10, $20, $50, $100, $500 and $1,000. The $1 bill is no longer in use. It has been replaced by a coin known colloquially as a 'loony' because it bears an engraving of a loon, the distinctively spotted waterfowl. Other coins are 1¢, 5¢, 10¢, 25¢ and 50¢.

Almost every Canadian seems to know the current rate of exchange between the US and Canadian dollar – the American dollar is worth around 25 percent more than its Canadian equivalent. American currency is widely accepted in shops, restaurants and hotels throughout Canada, though it is more advantageous to change it for Canadian dollars.

Credit Cards

International credit cards, such as American Express, MasterCard and VISA, are also readily accepted. Travellers' cheques issued by such companies as American Express, Thomas Cook and the Bank of America are widely recognized. An internationally accepted credit card validated for use in automatic teller machines (ATMs) enables you to obtain cash as and when you need it – on a daily basis if you wish. This improves security because you need only carry relatively small amounts of cash with you, but the cost of obtaining cash from an ATM must be weighed against the cost of buying and cashing travellers' cheques.

Taxes

A Goods and Services Tax (GST), currently 7 percent, is levied on all goods and services. Visitors may reclaim tax on accommodation and goods purchased and taken out of the country, but GST is not reclaimable on food, drink, tobacco, car and motorhome hire or transportation. To claim rebate, visitors must complete a form entitled *Goods and Services Tax Refund for Visitors*, which should be sent with receipts to the address given on the form.

GST must be claimed before applying for rebate on provincial sales tax, except for Quebec and Manitoba, whose sales tax may be reclaimed at the same time on the GST form.

A sales tax is levied on most goods, meals and accommodation in all provinces except Alberta, the Northwest Territories and Yukon. Provincial tax is reclaimable only in Newfoundland, Nova Scotia, Quebec and Manitoba.

Banking Hours

Normal banking hours in Canada are 10am to 3pm, Monday to Friday, with extended hours in some locations.

Crime and Theft

The kind of crime that worries tourists – and tourist authorities – in other parts of the world scarcely exists in Canada, and even cities like Toronto, Montreal and Vancouver have a very safe feel.

However, like everywhere else, Canada does have its black sheep so it pays to take commonsense security precautions at all times. Deposit valuables in hotel safes if you go out for the day, and never leave

Canada is a land of the 'Great Outdoors' where lakes are counted by the million.

precious items in a hotel room. Cameras, camcorders or anything else of value should never be left in view in a parked car. Before you leave home insure adequately against loss, damage or theft.

Electric Current

Canada uses the same electric current as the United States, 110–115 volts, 60 cycles.

Emergencies

In the event of any life-threatening situation, dial **911**.

Accommodation

Hotels
As in the United States, the hotel is a fact of life in Canada and there is generally no shortage of accommodation (though it's obvious that the choice may be restricted at peak holiday times and in remote locations). Many of the world's leading hotel chains are represented in cities across the country, while some home-grown properties – like the grand railway-era establishments of Canadian Pacific Hotels and Resorts – have earned their own international reputation and become national institutions in their own right. For more information consult our list of selected hotels (see p.340), which will help you choose something in your price range.

Bed and Breakfast
Bed and breakfast establishments and country inns are becoming increasingly popular and standards are high. One advantage of such places is that you get to know your hosts – and fellow-travellers – in an informal living-room atmosphere. Coast-to-coast B&B bookings are handled by Capital Bed & Breakfast Reservations Service, 2071 Riverside Drive, Ottawa, Ontario K1H 7X2; tel. (613) 737-4129.

Youth Hostels

Youth hostel membership, available to everyone irrespective of age, offers simple, inexpensive accommodation across Canada, often in rural situations. Information from: Canadian Hostelling Association, 1600 James Naismith Drive, Suite 608, Gloucester, Ontario K1B 5N4; tel. (613) 748-5638; fax. (613) 748-5750.

Camping

Camping is hugely popular and facilities exist in wonderful locations in every province and territory. Facilities range from primitive to luxury. Lists of provincial and privately run campgrounds are available in most provinces. Details of facilities and addresses where lists may be obtained are given where appropriate in the chapters that follow.

Sites operated by Kampgrounds of America (KOA), which has locations all over North America, are to be found in nine provinces, with the greatest concentration in Ontario. KOA facilities are excellent for family camping, often with electricity and water hook-ups for camper trucks or Recreational Vehicles (RVs) as well as tent pitches and log cabins for rent. For information write to Kampgrounds of America Inc, Executive Offices, Billings, MT 59114-0558; tel. (406) 248-7444. In Britain contact KOA, The Project Partnership, The Old House, Balcombe Forest, West Sussex RH15 6JZ; tel. 0144 811027; fax. 0144 811744.

Eating Out

Thanks to an ethnic broth enriched in recent years by the arrival of immigrants from the Indian subcontinent and the Far East, almost everywhere in Canada today offers a wide range of quality cuisine as varied as you will find anywhere in the world.

Fast food ranges from a Harvey's hamburger, available in most cities, to a lobster sandwich – not much dearer than a hamburger – in a downtown diner in Halifax, Nova Scotia. In fact, lobster is so common in Nova Scotia that in times of depression children have been deemed to be undernourished because lobster was all they had to eat.

Seafood is also to be found in abundance in British Columbia, New Brunswick, Prince Edward Island and Newfoundland, where the locals produce some exotic dishes by combining codfish and pork – far tastier than it sounds. Quebec, of course, rests on the laurels of its French heritage, with classic cuisine found in Montreal restaurants and heartier recipes emanating from the voyageurs featured in Quebec City. Ontario produces cheeses, especially the sharp, flavoursome Cheddars that appeal to British palates. The prairie provinces and Alberta are Canada's carnivores, tucking into enormous home-grown steaks.

The Canadians have always made good beer. Now, the range offered by the big names, such as Labatt and Molson, has been extended by the products of microbreweries which are continuing to pop up all over the country. Wine is produced mainly in the Golden Horseshoe region of southwest Ontario. Canadian rye whiskey, of course, is legendary.

Tips and Gratuities

Tips or service charges are not usually added to the bill in Canada. It's usual to allow up to 15 percent of the total as a gratuity for hairdressers, taxi drivers, waiters and waitresses. Porters at airports, railway

stations and hotels should get $1 a bag, and room service maids $1 a day.

City life, Canadian style, at a wine bar in Toronto's BCE Place.

Communications

Telephones

Canada's telephone system is similar to that of the USA, with payphones operating on an initial deposit of 25¢. To place a call to the USA simply dial the area code followed by the number. Most hotels and tourist offices now carry a booklet containing details of how to make international calls.

Postal Services

Postage stamps can be purchased from vending machines in hotel lobbies, airports, bus terminals, railway stations, newsstands and retail stores, as well as post offices. Post Canada has a number of fast delivery services, including Telepost, a next-day-at-the-latest service available 24 hours a day, seven days a week, and Intelpost, which allows documents and photographs to be sent via satellite to addresses in Canada, the USA and Europe. Visitors may have mail delivered to them c/o General Delivery at any post office in Canada, but it must be picked up within 15 days (take some identification with you).

Shopping

Shopping Malls

Canada has a number of renowned shopping centres, notably in Montreal, Toronto and Edmonton. These are massive malls, part underground, totally enclosed as a protection against winter weather, containing hundreds of retail stores as well as restaurants, bars, cinemas and theatres. In Edmonton you can rent an electric scooter if the thought of walking is too daunting.

Speciality Shopping

For **antiques** try browsing along rue Sherbrooke Ouest, rue Notre-Dame and Old Montreal, in Montreal; Toronto's Harbourfront and Lansdowne markets, or anywhere in Vancouver and Victoria, British Columbia.

Arts and crafts thrive all over Canada. Cowichan sweaters originate on Vancouver Island. In Calgary, you'll find Indian ceremonial headdresses, clothing and artefacts. The work of Inuit artists and craftspersons – paintings and soapstone sculpture – is sold all over Canada, but look out for the Canadian government's igloo mark of authenticity. New Brunswick produces sweaters, silver objects, pewter and pottery. Eastern Canada is famous for **maple syrup**, produced by traditional methods in sugarhouses mostly in Quebec.

If you can buy **fur** with a clear conscience – and most people in cold climates can – you'll have no problems in Canada, provided you have the money. Montreal and Toronto are the major centres, but furs can be bought almost anywhere. The Bay, an elegant store found in all major cities, is the modern equivalent of the old Hudson's Bay Company store. January is the best time to buy, especially mink.

Opening Hours

Shops and supermarkets are usually open between 9am and 6pm, Monday to Saturday, with supermarkets in large cities remaining open from 7.30am to 9pm. Many stores stay open longer until 9pm on Thursday and Friday. Drugstores in large cities often stay open until 11pm.

Public (Legal) Holidays

National holidays, celebrated throughout the country, mean that businesses and government offices close for the day. Some large department stores as well as a handful of smaller shops may remain open. If the holiday falls at the weekend, the following Monday is observed instead.

1 January	New Year's Day
March/April	Good Friday/
	Easter Monday
24 May	Victoria Day
1 July	Canada Day
6 September	Labor Day
11 October	Thanksgiving
11 November	Remembrance Day
25 December	Christmas Day
26 December	Boxing Day

Provincial Holidays

British Columbia Day (first Monday in August).

Alberta Family Day (third Monday in February); Heritage Day (first Monday in August).

Manitoba, Northwest Territories, Saskatchewan and Ontario all have the Civic Holiday (first Monday in August).

Yukon Discovery Day (third Monday in August).

Quebec: Epiphany (6 January), Ash Wednesday, Ascension Day, St John the Baptist Day (24 June), All Saints Day (1 November), Day of the Immaculate Conception (8 December).

Newfoundland and Labrador: Commonwealth Day (mid-March), St Patrick's Day (nearest Monday to 17 March), St George's Day (nearest Monday to 23 April), Discovery Day (Monday in late June), Memorial Day (first week in July), Orangemen's Day (around second week in July).

Nova Scotia: Sir John Macdonald's Birthday (11 January).

Piled high and going cheap – a stall in Vancouver's popular Granville Island Market.

Provincial Tourist Information Offices

British Columbia
Discover British Columbia, Parliament Building, Victoria, BC V8V 1X4.

Alberta
Alberta Economic Development and Tourism, City Centre, 10155 102 St, Edmonton, AB T5J 4L6.

Saskatchewan
Tourism Saskatchewan, 1919 Saskatchewan Drive, Regina, SK S4P 3V7.

Manitoba
Travel Manitoba, 155 Carlton Street, Winnipeg, MB RC3 3H8.

Ontario
Ontario Travel, Queen's Park, Toronto, ON M7A 2E5.

Quebec
Tourisme Québec, CP 20000, Quebec City, Quebec G1K 7X2.

New Brunswick
Tourism New Brunswick, PO Box 12345, Fredericton, NB E3B 53C.

Prince Edward Island
Department of Tourism and Parks, PO Box 940, Charlottetown, PEI C1A 7M5.

Nova Scotia
Nova Scotia Department of Tourism, PO Box 456, Halifax, NS B3J 2R5.

Newfoundland/Labrador
Department of Development, PO Box 8700, St John's, NF A1B 4J6.

Northwest Territories

Northwest Territories Economic Development and Tourism, PO Box 1320, Yellowknife, NWT X1A 2L9.

The Yukon

Tourism Yukon, PO Box 2703, Whitehorse, YK Y1A 2C6.

Canadian Consulates

With the exception of the United Kingdom (see below), each of these offices deals with tourism inquiries as well as consular matters.

Australia: Commonwealth Avenue, Canberra, ACT 2600, tel (062) 733-844; 6th Floor, One Collins Street, Melbourne, Victoria 3000, tel (03) 654-1433; AMP Centre, 8th Floor, 50 Bridge Street, Sydney, NSW 2000, tel (02) 231-6522.

Ireland: 65 St Stephen's Green, Dublin 2, Tel (01) 478-1988.

New Zealand: Princess Court, 2 Princes Street, Auckland, tel 393-5161; ICI Building, Molesworth Street, Wellington, tel 739-577.

United Kingdom: Macdonald House, 1 Grosvenor Square, London W1X 0AB, tel (0171) 629-9492. Tourist information: Visit Canada Centre, 62-65 Trafalgar Square, London WC2N 5DT, tel (0171) 839-2299.

United States: Suite 400, South Tower, One CNN Center, Atlanta, GA 30303-2705, tel (404) 577-6810; Suite 400, 3 Copley Place, Boston, MA 02116, tel (617) 262-3760; Suite 1200, 310 South Michegan Avenue, Chicago, IL 60604-4295, tel (312) 427-1031; Suite 1700, St Paul Place, 750 North St Paul, Dallas, TX 75201, tel (214) 922-9806; Suite 1100, 600 Renaissance Center, Detroit, MI 48243-1704, tel (313) 567-2340; Suite 1000, 10th Floor, California Plaza, 300 Grand Avenue, Los Angeles, CA 90071, tel (2130) 687-7432; 1251 Avenue of the Americas, New York, NY 10020-1175, tel (212) 768-2400; Suite 2100, 50 Fremont Street, San Francisco, CA 94105, tel (415) 495-6021; 501 Pennysylvania Avenue NW, Washington DC 20001, tel (202) 682-1740.

Language

Canada has two official languages: English and French. Visitors to Quebec would be wise to brush up on their French. Elsewhere in Canada you could get by with a smattering of German, Icelandic, Ukrainian, Chinese, Korean, Vietnamese, Gujurati, Arabic, Italian, Spanish, Creole… and the languages of the Inuit and Indians.

A little basic French comes in handy in the province of Quebec.

FESTIVALS AND SPECIAL EVENTS

Canada is known for the splendour and number of its festivals. You are likely to happen on a small town throwing itself into a fiddlers' festival or a bustling city where the locals welcome thousands of visitors to a folk or jazz jamboree.

Half the villages in Nova Scotia celebrate summer with a highland fling, clambake, lobster festival ... around 350 events in all. Ethnic communities throughout the country have joyous summer festivals with their own music, dancing, arts and culinary styles available to all.

In spring the maple syrup is tapped and samples are enjoyed in the sugar houses. The Annopolis Valley in Nova Scotia has an apple blossom festival. A small cummunity on Prince Edward Island has a potato blossom festival in late July. Cranberries and field crops are harvested at the end of summer. Even a northern country like Canada produces wine, and British Columbia's ten-day Okanagan Wine Festival takes place in early October.

The long dark months are brightened with winter festivals. Ice sculptures, ice canoeing and other competitive events, illuminated at night, provide glowing memories.

Some of Canada's major festivals, province by province are: **British Columbia** – Whistler Jazz Festival (two days, mid-September); International Jazz Festival, Vancouver (three days, mid-July); International Bathtub Race, Nanaimo, Vancouver Island (late July).

Alberta – Banff Festival of Arts (June-August); Calgary Stampede (ten days, Mid-July); Edmonton Klondike Days (ten days, late July).

Saskatchewan – Royal Canadian Mounted Police Sunset Ceremonies, Regina (July and August).

Manitoba – Folklorama multicultural event in 40 pavilions, Winnipeg (two weeks, end July/early August); Saint Boniface Festival du Voyageur winter celebrations (ten days, mid-February).

Ontario – Winterlude, Ottawa (ten days, early February); Canadian Tulip Festival, Ottawa (mid-May); Festival of Festivals, Toronto (ten days, Mid-September).

Quebec – Montreal Winter Festival (ten days, late-January/early February); Montreal Island cycle tour (one day, early June); Quebec City Winter Carnival (ten days, early to mid-February).

New Brunswick – Festival By the Sea, Saint John (ten days, early August); Harvest Jazz and Blues Festival (mid-September).

Prince Edward Island – Summer Festival/Anne of Green Gables, Charlottetown (June-September).

Nova Scotia – International Tattoo, Halifax (end-June/early July); Craft Festival, Lunenburg (early July).

Newfoundland and Labrador – Folk Festival, St John's (early August); Rowing Regatta - 170th annual contest in 1996 – (first Wednesday in August).

Far North – Yukon Quest, 1000-mile dogsled race (mid-February); Raven Mad Daze, celebration of longest day, Yellowknife (third week in June); Midnight Classic golf tournament, Yellowknife (longest day); Discover Days, Dawson City (annual four-day commemoration of discovery of gold in the Klondike on 17 August, 1896).

A Mosaic of Faces and Cultures

Canadians like to show who they are. They wear maple leaf lapel badges, or baseball caps emblazoned with a maple leaf. They stick their maple leaf flag, with the letters 'CDN', on the bumpers of their cars. They do this not out of excessive nationalism but because they don't want to be taken for Americans.

Not that they have anything against Americans – they just want everyone to know that the Canadians are their own people. They may share a continent with the Americans, they may look like Americans and to the untutored ear they might even sound like them. But that, they'll tell you, is as far as it goes. Canada is a unique nation with a unique heritage, and Canadians are proud of it.

There was a time – in the 1960s and 1970s – when Canadians were said to be seeking a national identity. Canadians even said it of themselves. The trouble was, no one was exactly sure what a national identity is, let alone where you find one. Or what to do with it if you do find one – it doesn't sound like the kind of thing you could possibly slip on like a pair of overshoes.

Now, the Canadians seem to have accepted themselves for what they are: a mixed society of people from different ethnic backgrounds, with different political and religious persuasions and different personal aspirations; a people proud of their parliamentary democracy, of their artists, writers, musicians and of all the things that distinguish them from their southern neighbours, and everyone else for that matter.

If that isn't a national identity – nationhood – then what is?

People

Canada claims to have coined the word 'multiculturalism', a concept in which people of diverse origins and communities remain free to preserve and enhance their own cultural heritage while participating in Canadian society as equal partners. It is a concept you can actually see as you walk down the streets of any Canadian city – all around are faces from all over the world.

It's the same in the United States, of course, but multiculturalists say there is a fundamental difference between the Canadian and American methods. America has tried to achieve homogeneity through the 'melting pot' principle. Canada's approach has created a mosaic.

The First Nations

Let us eavesdrop for a moment in an Ottawa bar frequented by local journalists. Some of the pressmen are discussing their ethnic origins, and the talk degenerates into a disputed league table of whose family has been in Canada the longest. The barman, a solemn-faced member of the Algonquin people, surveys them with a jaundiced eye. 'To me,' he tells them, 'you're all goddam immigrants.'

In truth, of course, the barman himself and every other 'First Nation' Canadian is of immigrant stock.

Canada's first inhabitants, nomadic hunters from Asia, arrived some 25,000 years ago by way of the land bridge that once crossed the Bering Strait between Alaska and the Russian Federation. By 9000BC the nomads had spread throughout North and South America, creating cultures as varied as those of the Inuit in the Arctic north and the Aztecs and Incas of Mexico and Peru.

Three categories of 'aboriginal people' are specified in the Canadian constitution: Indians, Inuit and Métis. The three groups are also referred to collectively as 'Native peoples'. Many Native Canadians prefer the term 'First Nations'.

The Indians

The term 'Indian', derived from Christopher Columbus's mistaken belief that he had reached India, continues to cause confusion, but no one has ever come up with a completely satisfactory alternative word. The largest group of Native peoples, the Indians are divided into five main cultures with widely varying customs and languages.

The Eastern Woodland Indians – Iroquoian and Algonquian – were renowned for their wigwams, not to be confused with the tipis in which the nomadic Plains Indians – Blackfoot, Cree, Ojibwa, Assiniboine, Stoney and Dakota – lived. The Plateau Indians – the Athapascan, Salishan and Kutenai – live between the Rockies and the coastal mountain ranges of British Columbia. The Northwest Coastal Indians – Tlingit and Haida – produce magnificent totem poles. The Sub-Arctic Indians – Dene – live mainly in the forest and tundra belt.

It has been estimated that before the arrival of Europeans the First Nation population was somewhere between 250,000 and one million. By 1867 it had been decimated by smallpox, scarlet fever, tuberculosis and other diseases brought in by the white man. Now, with numbers growing once more, there are 595 Indian Bands – a Band is a formally recognized group – covering all parts of Canada, except the high Arctic. Nearly two-thirds of them live on reserves – areas of land set aside through treaties or the Indian Act for their sole use and benefit.

Indian peoples have managed to maintain a separate identity and culture in spite of numerous attempts in the past to assimilate them into the white man's world. In the 19th century many Indian children were taken away from their families and

*M*usic while you walk:
a busker entertains in the
promenade in Quebec City.

placed in boarding schools where they were forbidden to speak their own language or practise Native traditions. The social costs of this cultural disturbance were high, with high drop-out rates for education, alcohol abuse and disproportionate numbers of Indians in jail.

Now the Federal government is leading rehabilitation efforts. Native language, culture and history programmes have been started in schools; cultural centres are flourishing, and traditional beliefs and practices are being encouraged.

The Inuit

Canada is home to 27,000 Inuit, about a quarter of those inhabiting the entire Arctic region. The word means 'the people'. Previously known as Eskimos, the Inuit live in the tundra and Arctic belt. For many centuries the Inuit were in almost total isolation, living in small family bands, and hunting and fishing for food in a climate which renders the cultivation of crops impossible.

Contact with Europeans was limited until the arrival of the 19th-century whaling fleets. Development of the European fur trade led the Inuit to take up trapping. The second half of the present century has brought rapid economic and social change. The Inuit now live in centrally heated houses, with refrigerators and television sets, in communities linked to the rest of the world by aircraft services and modern communications. The kayak and dog sled have been replaced by canoes

with outboard motors as well as motorized toboggans.

Again, there has been a high social price to pay. The Inuit have been prone to alcohol and other abuses and their suicide rate has been high. Now, they are trying to take control of their own lives and to organize government, education and the economy according to their own traditions and beliefs.

In April 1999 the Inuit take control of 360,000sq km (135,135sq miles) of land awarded to them under a $580 million federal settlement. Representing about one-fifth of Canada's land mass, the area takes in a huge piece of the present Northwest Territories, including Baffin Island. It will be known as Nunavut – 'our land'.

Later Arrivals

The first Europeans to visit Canada were the Vikings in the 10th century. Their settlement, dating from around AD 1000, has

29

A Brief History

Canada's history is the story of people on the move – a restless mosaic of adventurers and refugees, races and religions.

For 20,000 years or so, this vast area was the domain of the First Nations people – descendants of those early Asian nomads who had wandered across the Bering Strait land bridge from Siberia. Generation after generation thrived without the benefits of written language or the wheel, surviving as hunter-gatherers whose only vehicle was the canoe and whose pack or draught animal was the dog.

There are many intriguing legends of early visitors from Europe. In AD 75 the Greek biographer Plutarch wrote of pilgrims sailing from Britain to a shrine which some scholars believe may have been on Cape Breton Island or on Anticosti Island in the Gulf of St. Lawrence. St. Brendan is thought to have crossed the Atlantic from Ireland in a leather boat in the 6th century. Other Irish monks may have travelled along the St Lawrence in the 9th century – a theory which arose when French missionaries found in the 16th century that Micmac Indians made a sign of the cross with their fingers.

Norse sagas of epic voyages beyond Greenland and of settlements in strange lands have been substantiated by archaeological findings at L'Anse aux Meadows on the northern tip of Newfoundland, where the remains of a Viking settlement were unearthed in the 1960s.

Christopher Columbus's 'discovery' of America in 1492 started a gold rush of transatlantic exploration. In June 1497 John Cabot landed at a spot that might have been on Cape Breton Island or Newfoundland and claimed it for his sponsor, King Henry VII of England. No one knows for certain just where it was that Cabot landed, but it is known that on 27 June – the feast day of St. John the Baptist – he sailed into the splendidly sheltered harbour of what is now the city of St. John's.

Cabot, who disappeared on a subsequent voyage to the Americas, failed to find the gold, gemstones and spices he and Henry had been hoping for, but he was able to report that the waters off the Newe Founde Lande were rich in a far more practical treasure. Codfish, he claimed, were so numerous that they could be scooped from the sea in a basket. Soon the waters were teeming with English, French, Spanish and Portuguese fishing boats. The fishermen soon set up bases ashore for drying their catches, but there were few settlers until well into the 17th century.

The French Connection

A rival claim to the land across the Atlantic was established in the summer of 1534 when the French explorer Jacques Cartier sailed with two ships into the Gulf of St. Lawrence and made an uneasy contact with Iroquois Indians. He is believed to have named the land 'Canada' from the Indian word *kanata*, meaning a settlement. When he returned to France before the onset of winter Cartier took with him two sons of the tribal chief who were to be trained as interpreters. The following spring he led an expedition of three ships, this time penetrating as far as Indian communities on the sites of present-day Quebec and Montreal.

Cartier stayed in Canada that winter – and 25 of his men perished from scurvy. Many others were saved when the Indians showed them how to make a brew rich in vitamin C from the bark and leaves of the eastern white cedar tree. The French leader repaid the Indians by kidnapping their chief, Donnacona, and abducting him to France, promising he would be returned the following year.

War between France and Spain prevented Cartier's return until 1541, by which time the chief was dead. The Iroquois were told that Donnacona was enjoying the good life in France, but few believed it. They viewed Cartier and his force – this time totalling some 400 men in five ships – with grave suspicion, and during the following winter kept the Frenchmen in a state of siege in their settlement at Charlesbourg-Royal, near Quebec. To make matters worse, Cartier learned that he was being replaced as leader by a gentleman pirate named Jean-Francois Roberval.

The British

The first English settlements were created in Nova Scotia in 1624, and it was not long before the French and British interests were in conflict over the fish and fur resources – part of the wider clashes between the two nations as they struggled for supremacy in western Europe and other parts of the world.

At first, the British government did little to encourage settlement in Canada, but large numbers of English-speaking colonists – the Loyalists – sought refuge there when the American War of Independence started in 1776. Many of the Loyalists settled in Nova Scotia, New Brunswick and along the Great Lakes.

British migrants began pouring into Canada in the 19th century, hugely outnumbering the Loyalists. A sad feature of this period was child immigration when thousands of orphans were shipped from Britain. The enforced emigration of orphans continued until the 1930s.

German Canadians

Canada has about 1.5 million citizens of German origin, the country's third largest ethnic group. Small groups of Germans were settled near Quebec as early as the first half of the 17th century. The British government actually recruited people suffering from economic difficulty, religious persecution and war in German principalities, and 2,000 such refugees were landed at Halifax, Nova Scotia, between 1750 and 1752.

Many of the Loyalists were German-speaking. Mennonites, facing persecution in America because of their pacifism, bought land in the Waterloo area of Ontario. Others, along with Hutterites, Dukhobors, Amish and Catholics, came directly from Europe. By 1867, some 200,000 people of German origin had settled in Canada. After World War I they were joined by German speakers from the Baltic States, Eastern Europe, Romania, the Balkans, Austria and Hungary.

Afro-Canadians

Canada's first Black people came either as slaves or as refugees from slavery. Thousands of American Blacks escaped from Southern plantations and made their way to Canada after slavery was abolished in

*V*isitors get a glimpse of traditional native life at St Marie Among the Hurons at Midland, Ontario.

1793. They joined other former slaves who had been taken to Canada by the Loyalists.

Liberalization of Canada's immigration laws brought large numbers of West Indian immigrants from the 1960s, bringing the present total up to around 250,000, mostly concentrated in the urban centres of Quebec and Ontario. Canada's Blacks today represent somewhere around 2 percent of the population.

Chinese Canadians

The first Chinese arrived on the west coast at the start of the Fraser River Gold Rush in 1858. Later, they helped to build the Canadian Pacific Railway, working under appalling conditions. By 1885 there were 22,000 Chinese in the west – and an immigration clamp-down was introduced. From 1885 to 1923 Chinese working in Canada had to pay a poll tax, and from 1923 to 1947 they were barred from attaining 'landed immigrant' status.

Immigration restrictions were lifted in 1967 and today's Chinese population is around 500,000. The latest Chinese immigrants – from Hong Kong, South Africa and Asia – speak fluent English and are often successful and rich business people. Chinatowns have grown up in Montreal, Toronto and Vancouver.

Ukrainian Canadians

One of Canada's more flamboyant ethnic groups, Ukrainians first trickled into the country with the Mennonites and other German immigrants in the 1870s. But they did not arrive in significant numbers until after 1896 when Canada began to seek agricultural immigrants from Eastern Europe. Between 1891 and 1914 at least 170,000 peasants arrived from the Ukraine. Another 70,000 made their way between the two world wars, while a further 34,000 displaced persons arrived after World War II.

The Ukrainians settled first in the prairie provinces, then in Ontario. In January 1990 Ray Hnatyshyn was sworn in as Governor-General of Canada and in 1992 a million Ukrainian Canadians celebrated the centenary of their first permanent settlement in Canada.

Italian Canadians

There are about 800,000 Canadians of Italian origin, 65 percent of whom live in Ontario and the remainder in British Columbia and Quebec; 10 percent of Toronto's population is Italian, and in Montreal it is 6 percent.

The Italians arrived in two huge waves. The first came between the turn of the century and 1914 and the second from 1950 to 1970. In 1958 alone, Italy surpassed Britain as a source of immigrants.

Japanese Canadians

Canada has about 40,000 citizens of Japanese origin. Like the Chinese, the first Japanese arrived to work on the west coast and were subject to both intolerance and discrimination.

During World War II 20,881 Canadians of Japanese descent were forcibly relocated more than 160km (100 miles) inland from the Pacific Coast because they were thought to be a security risk. Their property was forcibly sold. After the war they were given the choice of moving again to either Japan or further east. Most chose to go east.

Immigration from Japan did not begin again until 1967. In 1988 the Canadian government formally apologized to Canada's Japanese citizens, and victims were awarded compensation.

Just the Essentials

Canada's bewildering range of attractions will inevitably force you to make difficult decisions. Our shortlist of suggestions for each province will help you set priorities to ensure that you don't miss out on the most important sights.

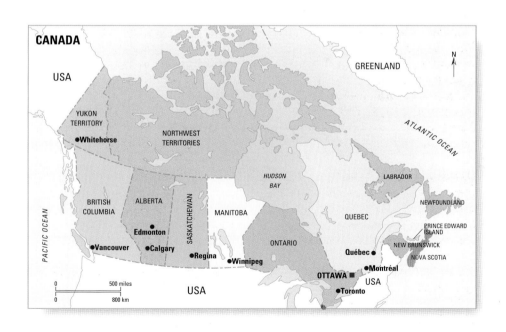

British Columbia

Royal British Columbia Museum, Victoria: from the Ice Age to modern times and from the ocean bed to a coastal rainforest. (See p.60)
Butchart Gardens, Vancouver Island: 21ha (50 acres) of world-famous gardens . Open every day of the year. (See p.62)
Capilano Suspension Bridge, North Vancouver: the 140m (450ft) swaying footbridge high above the Capilano River canyon. (See p.82)
Gastown, Vancouver: the old heart of the city, with cobbled streets, courtyards, passages, gas lamps – and a famous steam clock. (See p.81)
Stanley Park, Vancouver: totem poles, woodlands and a scenic drive. (See p.81)

Alberta

West Edmonton Mall, Edmonton: almost a city in its own right, with 800 shops, 11 leading department stores, 110 restaurants and cafés and 19 cinemas. Rent an electric scooter or take a rickshaw ride. (See p.107)
Stampede Park, Calgary: site of the famous Exhibition and Stampede. (See p.112)
Royal Tyrrell Museum of Palaeontology, Drumheller: 800 fossils from around the world, as well as its local giants, tracing the development of animal life over 3.5 billion years. (See p.116)
Head-Smashed-In Buffalo Jump, Fort MacLeod: one of North America's best buffalo jump sites, a World Heritage Site. (See p.121)
Jasper Tramway, Jasper: a cable car ride of 950m (3,000ft) to the summit of Whistlers Mountain. (See p.128)
Athabasca Glacier, Columbia Icefield: a tongue of ice 6km (4 miles) long and 1km (half-a-mile) wide. (See p.130)

Saskatchewan

Prince Albert National Park: Many visitors make pilgrimages to 'Beaver Lodge', home of the naturalist, Grey Owl. (See p.146)
The Royal Saskatchewan Museum, Regina: see how Saskatchewan evolved from temperate seas to the arrival of man. (See p.155)
Saskatchewan Science Centre, Regina: more than 70 permanent hands-on exhibits, live demonstrations and visiting displays. (See p.157)
RCMP Academy and Museum, Regina: where every Mountie recruit goes through 6 months of rigorous basic training. Sergeant Major's Parade staged daily. (See p.157)
Batoche National Historic Park: site of the last battle fought on Canadian soil. (See p.162)

Manitoba

The Forks, Winnipeg: the city's birthplace has been revitalized as a 23ha (56-acre) waterfront development at the confluence of the Red and Assiniboine Rivers. (See p.180)
Oserodok, Winnipeg: North America's largest repository of Ukrainian historical and cultural artefacts. (See p.182)
Manitoba Museum of Man and Nature, Winnipeg: one of Canada's top museums, with seven galleries which explore mankind's relationship to the environment. (See p.182)
The Royal Canadian Mint, Winnipeg: watch the minting of coins. (See p.185)
Lower Fort Garry, Selkirk: a National Historic Site, the oldest stone fur-trading fort still intact in North America. (See p.186)

Ontario

CN Tower, Toronto: the world's tallest free-standing structure. (See p.196)
BCE Place, Toronto: built in 1992, this stunning building has two towers and a glass gallery of cathedral dimensions. (See p.198)
Royal Ontario Museum, Toronto: North America's second largest after the Metropolitan Museum of Art in New York, with more than 6 million items. (See p.202)
Niagara Falls: an outstanding 155 million litres (34 million gallons) a minute plunging over a 54m (176ft) cliff nearly 1km (half-a-mile) wide. (See p.206)
The National Gallery of Canada, Ottawa: the world's most comprehensive collection of Canadian art. (See p.230)

Quebec
Old Town, Montreal: street entertainment, artists, bistros and cafés. (See p.241)
Old Port, Montreal: delightfully restored waterfront area; popular river cruises aboard the glass-topped *bateau mouche*. (See p.241)
Big O, Montreal: the 1976 Olympic Stadium; on a clear day you see for 80km (50 miles) from the observation deck. (See p.244)

Montreal Biodome: experience four ecosystems – tropical rainforest, the polar world, the Laurentian forest and the marine environment of the St Lawrence. (See p.245)
Quebec City ferry: cross the St Lawrence for a fabulous view of North America's only walled city outside Mexico. (See p.255)
Montmorency Falls, Quebec City: see the falls from a cable car, helicopter or bridge. (See p.256)

New Brunswick
Rockwood Park, Saint John: for a view of the Reversing Falls Rapids. Where the river flows backwards twice daily. (See p.267)
Old City Market, Saint John: a spacious indoor enclave with colourful goods. (See p.267)
Beaverbrook Art Gallery, Fredericton: world-renowned gallery donated by newspaper magnate Lord Beaverbrook, with the works of many prominent Canadian painters. (See p.269)
Kings Landing Historical Settlement: a re-creation of village life 1790 – 1870. (See p.269)
Hopewell Cape: at the mouth of the Petitcodiac River, where everyone flocks to see the world's highest tides, and the flowerpot rocks. (See p.274)

Prince Edward Island
Province House, Charlottetown: considered the actual birthplace of Canada, where the 1864 federal union conference was held. (See p.283)
Fort Amhurst/Port-La-Joye National Historic Site: site of the first French settlement on PEI. The grounds and shoreline attract picnickers. (See p.283)
Green Gables House, Cavendish: 'Anne' fans will be in their element – the house and lots of familiar 'scenes'. (See p.286)
Great Island Adventure Park: a walk-in replica of the space shuttle *Columbia*, and much besides to keep youngsters happy. (See p.287)

Nova Scotia
Halifax Harbour: take a boat tour round the world's second largest and deepest natural harbour, surpassed only by Sydney, Australia. (See p.294)
Historic Properties, Halifax: three blocks of Canada's oldest surviving waterfront warehouses, sensitively restored. (See p.295)
Lunenburg: Nova Scotia's major fishing port and a popular tourism spot. The Old Town area is a National Heritage District. (See p.302)
Cabot Trail, Cape Breton Island: one of North America's most beautiful drives, through Cape Breton Highlands National Park. (See p.312)

Newfoundland and Labrador
Signal Hill, St John's: Site of the final battle of the Seven Years War between English and French forces. (See p.317)
The Newfoundland Museum, St John's: 9,000 years and the lives of six Native groups and European settlers are outlined. (See p.318)
Cape Spear National Historic Site: the easternmost part of North America, with a restored wooden lighthouse. (See p.319)
L'Anse aux Meadows National Historic Site: believed to be where Leif Eiriksson founded a colony 1,000 years ago; a UNESCO World Heritage Site since 1978. (See p.324)

Yukon & Northwest Territories
The Northern Lights: a reward for stalwarts who come here in winter.
The Dempster Highway: the only public road on the continent to cross the Arctic Circle. Never to be forgotten. (See p.335)
Dawson City: where the gooldrush days of a century ago live on. (See p.337)

Going Places with Something Special in Mind

Travellers with special interests can supplement or scrap the standard itineraries, pursuing instead the angles that most appeal to them. Canada has much to offer visitors with special interests, and this section may help you to choose your favourites.

Birdwatching

1 CHURCHILL, MANITOBA
This Arctic port on Hudson Bay is world-famous for the number and variety of its migratory birds, including rare species like the Ross's Gull. Hotel space is at a premium in late spring and early summer when ornithologists gather from around the world.

A steam train crosses a trestle bridge in the British Columbia Forest Park at Duncan, Vancouver Island.

2 RIDING MOUNTAIN NATIONAL PARK, MANITOBA
Boreal forest, open meadowland and moss-filled bogs attract up to 500 varieties, including North America's largest owl, the Great Grey Owl, and many songbirds.

3 OAK HAMMOCK MARSH, MANITOBA
Less than an hour's drive from Winnipeg, this extensive Wildlife Management Area has an excellent new visitor centre and presents first-class opportunities for viewing marshland and wetland species.

4 REDBERRY LAKE, SASKATCHEWAN
The Redberry Pelican Project, near the town of Hafford, has become famous for

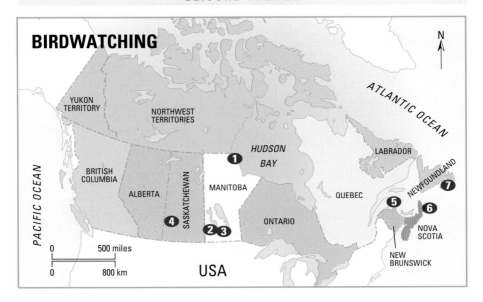

BIRDWATCHING

*D*edicated birdwatchers can choose from numerous sites across Canada, in a wide range of habitats.

protecting white pelicans, piping plovers and about 200 other species.

5 BONAVENTURE ISLAND, QUEBEC

The cliffs of Bonaventure Island, off the rugged Gaspé region coast, are occupied by thousands of gannets. In summer, boats leave frequently on the 45-minute trip from Percé to enable birdwatchers to visit the gannetry.

6 BIRD ISLANDS, NOVA SCOTIA

Atlantic puffins can be seen nesting in this small location off Cape Breton Island. A boat leaves Big Bras d'Or daily with an expert on board.

7 CAPE ST MARY'S, NEWFOUNDLAND

You can stand near the lighthouse at Cape

St Mary's, in Placentia Bay, and see the nesting site for one of North America's largest gannet colonies. The golden-headed birds at the Cape St Mary's Eco-logical Reserve have a 2m (6ft) wingspan, and the cliffs are alive with birds in the summer. The sanctuary may be visited year-round.

Botanical Gardens

1 BUTCHART GARDENS, VANCOUVER ISLAND

A former limestone quarry, a short drive north of Victoria, has been transformed into the world-famous Butchart Gardens. There are blooms to be seen at all times of the year. Hundreds of Japanese cherry trees line the route to the gardens. There are firework shows in July and August.

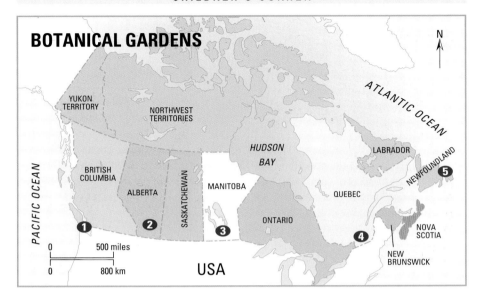

BOTANICAL GARDENS

YUKON TERRITORY

NORTHWEST TERRITORIES

ATLANTIC OCEAN

BRITISH COLUMBIA

ALBERTA

SASKATCHEWAN

MANITOBA

HUDSON BAY

LABRADOR

NEWFOUNDLAND

QUEBEC

ONTARIO

NOVA SCOTIA

NEW BRUNSWICK

PACIFIC OCEAN

0   500 miles

0   800 km

USA

*P*lants from many parts of the world are displayed in botanical gardens from coast to coast.

2 NIKKA YUKO JAPANESE GARDENS, ALBERTA

Built in 1967 as a centennial project symbolizing Canadian–Japanese friendship, these dignified gardens encompass a cypress wood replica of a 16th-century Japanese pavilion.

3 ASSINIBOINE PARK, WINNIPEG

Winnipeg's oldest and largest park has wooded lawns, English Gardens – even cricket pitches – and the largest conservatory in Western Canada with a tropical palm house and a continuous display of flowering and foliage plants.

4 BOTANICAL GARDEN, MONTREAL

More than 26,000 varieties of plants from many parts of the world can be seen here.

It is all impressive, but the bonsai collection is especially admirable. The gardens have been giving pleasure for nearly 65 years.

5 MEMORIAL UNIVERSITY GARDENS, ST JOHN'S

As well as a rock garden, wildlife garden, ericas and alpines, these gardens have a display of plants which grew in Newfoundland before 1940. The gardens are in Pippy Park, St John's.

Children's Corner

1 ALBERTA SCIENCE CENTRE, CALGARY

Laser beams, holograms, frozen shadows and robotic insects contribute to the fun provided by 35 hands-on exhibits – and there's a planetarium with a wrap-around star show.

2 CALAWAY PARK, CALGARY

At one extreme there are lots of white-knuckle rides, including a double-loop roller-coaster. At the other, a petting farm. And in between, three live musical shows, a giant maze and mini-golf. Something for the whole family, in fact.

3 SASKATCHEWAN SCIENCE CENTRE

Located in a former Regina power station, the centre gives visitors the opportunity to make the most of nature – and turn it on its head. Entertaining live demonstrations complement 70 permanent hands-on exhibits.

4 MANITOBA'S CHILDREN MUSEUM

Opened in June 1994, the museum is part of Winnipeg's exciting waterfront rede-

It isn't all amusement parks. Interactive science centres and museums provide a mixture of fun and education.

velopment at The Forks, the junction of the Red and Assiniboine Rivers. Galleries and exhibits cater for children from pre-school age and up.

5 SPACE CAMP CANADA, LAVAL

This is one of Quebec Province's newest projects, part of the Cosmodome space science learning centre on the outskirts of Montreal. Young people from 10 to 14 years can experience simulated life in outer space on a 5-day astronaut training course.

Historic Forts

1 FORT MACLEOD MUSEUM, ALBERTA

In July and August you can witness a stirring musical ride in this convincing replica of the original fort, which has displays featuring the life of Northwest Mounted Police officers and is open year-round.

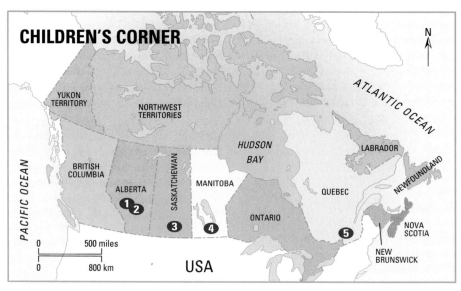

CHILDREN'S CORNER

N

YUKON TERRITORY

NORTHWEST TERRITORIES

ATLANTIC OCEAN

HUDSON BAY

LABRADOR

PACIFIC OCEAN

BRITISH COLUMBIA

SASKATCHEWAN

ALBERTA

MANITOBA

QUEBEC

NEWFOUNDLAND

❶❷

❸

❹

ONTARIO

❺

NOVA SCOTIA

0   500 miles

0   800 km

NEW BRUNSWICK

USA

2 FORT WHOOP-UP, ALBERTA

This is a reconstructed whiskey fort, where illicit liquor was sold to Indians. It stands at Lethbridge on the site of the last great battle between the Cree and Blackfoot.

3 FORT BATTLEFORT, SASKATCHEWAN

Costumed guides conduct tours of this original NWMP post, now a National Historic Site. Visitors can tour the barracks and other buildings with period furnishings.

4 FORT HENRY, KINGSTON, ONTARIO

Daily infantry drills are performed during the summer in this massive fortification, once the principal stronghold of Upper Canada.

5 THE CITADEL, QUEBEC CITY

Built in the shape of a star, the Citadel took more than 30 years to complete. Here in summer the Royal 22nd Regiment maintains the tradition of beating the retreat and changing of the guard.

6 THE CITADEL, HALIFAX, NOVA SCOTIA

Citadel Hill holds a commanding position overlooking the famous harbour. The noonday gun is fired every day at the star-shaped fortification, which is said to be the most visited of all Canada's historic sites.

7 SIGNAL HILL, ST JOHN'S, NEWFOUNDLAND

French and English forces squabbled continually over Signal Hill and it kept changing hands in the 17th and 18th centuries. Today it is a fascinating place to visit.

T imes of conflict are reflected in a number of historic forts around the country.

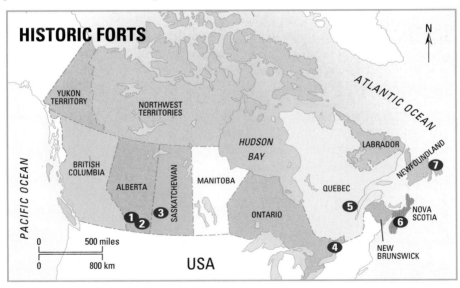

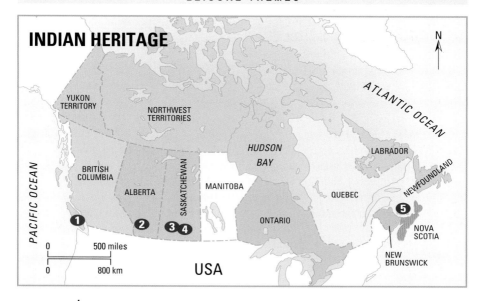

INDIAN HERITAGE

YUKON TERRITORY

NORTHWEST TERRITORIES

BRITISH COLUMBIA

ALBERTA

SASKATCHEWAN

MANITOBA

HUDSON BAY

ATLANTIC OCEAN

LABRADOR

QUEBEC

NEWFOUNDLAND

ONTARIO

NOVA SCOTIA

NEW BRUNSWICK

PACIFIC OCEAN

0 500 miles
0 800 km

USA

A wide range of native history and culture can be experienced throughout the country.

Indian Heritage

1 DUNCAN, VANCOUVER ISLAND
Some 80 totems, mostly carved by members of the Cowichan Band, are on permanent display on the main street and TransCanada Highway, giving Duncan the nickname 'Totem City'.

2 HEAD-SMASHED-IN BUFFALO JUMP, ALBERTA
This magnificent World Heritage Site documents the buffalo-hunting culture of the Plains Indians from ancient times to the arrival of Europeans.

3 WANUSKEWIN HERITAGE PARK, SASKATCHEWAN
Just outside the city of Saskatoon, Wanuskewin contains 19 archaeological sites and an impressive visitor centre in which 6,000 years of history are interpreted.

4 FIRST NATIONS GALLERY, REGINA
Located in the Royal Saskatchewan Museum, this year-round exhibition traces 10,000 years of aboriginal culture.

5 LENNOX ISLAND, PEI
More than 50 Micmac families here are descendants of Prince Edward Island's Native inhabitants. High quality craftware is sold in the village.

Legislative Buildings

1 VICTORIA, VANCOUVER ISLAND
British Columbia's granite and brick Parliament Buildings dominate the harbour and at night are lit by 3,000 twinkling lights. A statue of Captain George Vancouver stands atop the central dome.

LEGISLATIVE BUILDINGS

YUKON TERRITORY

NORTHWEST TERRITORIES

HUDSON BAY

LABRADOR

ATLANTIC OCEAN

NEWFOUNDLAND

PACIFIC OCEAN

BRITISH COLUMBIA

ALBERTA

SASKATCHEWAN

MANITOBA

QUEBEC

ONTARIO

NOVA SCOTIA

NEW BRUNSWICK

USA

0   500 miles

0   800 km

2 REGINA, SASKATCHEWAN
Completed in 1912 and designed to reflect the styles of English Renaissance and the France of Louis XV, Saskatchewan's Legislative Building is grandly located in the city's Wascana Centre.

3 WINNIPEG, MANITOBA
The Manitoba Legislative Building, built in the Beaux-Arts Classical style, features a grand staircase, huge bison statues and a 5-ton statue, the Golden Boy, sheathed in 235 carat gold.

4 PARLIAMENT BUILDINGS, OTTAWA
Superbly located above the Ottawa River, the nation's Parliament Buildings are a neo-Gothic extravaganza of brown stone and green copper roofs.

5 QUEBEC CITY
The most important national historical site in the province, Quebec's Parliament Building is an imposing structure whose architecture was inspired by 16th-century French classicism.

Various grand architectural styles are represented in the nation's legislative buildings.

6 CHARLOTTETOWN, PEI
Province House National Historic Site is known as the birthplace of Canada because the first meeting to discuss federal union was held here in 1864. It houses the provincial legislature.

Living Museums

1 FORT STEELE, KOOTENAY, BRITISH COLUMBIA
Visitors can tour the town's restored Victorian buildings by horse-drawn wagon, take a steam train ride and enjoy music hall shows at the Wild Horse Theatre.

2 FORT EDMONTON PARK, ALBERTA
Three reconstructed streets feature life in

the period between 1885 and 1905. You can visit a newspaper office, a fire station, a saloon and jail.

3 BOOMTOWN 1910, SASKATOON

A branch of the Western Development Museum, Boomtown 1910 is a reconstructed prairie town, with wooden sidewalks and horse-drawn wagons and carriages.

4 UPPER CANADA VILLAGE, MORRISBURG, ONTARIO

More than 150 staff work and play as they would have done 150 years ago in this village of authentic buildings saved from flooding when the St Lawrence Seaway was being constructed.

5 KINGS LANDING HISTORICAL SETTLEMENT, NEW BRUNSWICK

This is one of the province's top ten attractions, where village life of the 19th century is played out among more than 60 restored buildings.

6 ACADIAN HISTORIC VILLAGE, CARAQUET, NEW BRUNSWICK

The village is timelocked in 1755, the year the British expelled the Acadians. Costumed villagers unfold a story of struggle and survival.

7 SHERBROOKE, NOVA SCOTIA

Founded as a fur-trading post in the 1650s, Sherbrooke was in decline when a provincial restoration project saved the village. More than two dozen vintage buildings stand on their original sites.

8 FORTRESS OF LOUISBURG, CAPE BRETON ISLAND

The biggest reconstruction in North America, the fortress's 50 buildings include taverns, a chapel, prison and the King's Bastion which has a Governor's Suite.

Re-enactments which bring the past to life are a great way to learn history.

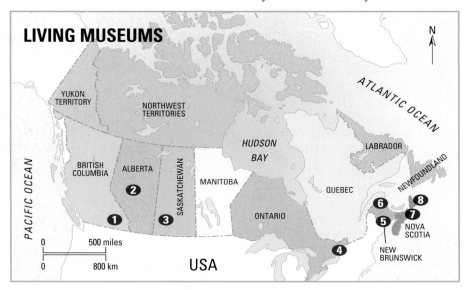

46

*T*he grandeur of the Rockies – Lake Moraine in Alberta.

*A*lthough normally shy, elk graze peacefully among holiday lodges in Jasper National Park.

47

Whale-watching

1 JOHNSTONE STRAIT, VANCOUVER ISLAND

The strait is one of Vancouver Island's best whale-watching locations. Families of minke and killer whales can be observed year round.

2 CHURCHILL, MANITOBA

From early June, white beluga whales make an appearance in the Arctic waters off this Hudson Bay port.

3 GRAND MANAN ISLAND, BAY OF FUNDY

More whale species appear here than at any other location. The rare right whale and the huge finback are among more than 20 species recorded in the area.

W hales may be sighted on the Atlantic and Pacific coasts and in Hudson Bay.

4 NORTHERN CAPE BRETON ISLAND

Whale-watching boat trips start from a number of harbours on the Cabot Trail, including Cheticamp, Capstick and Ingonish.

5 CAPE SPEAR, NEWFOUNDLAND

Whales can frequently be seen from the clifftop lighthouse at Cape Spear, North America's most easterly point.

Wildlife

1 BANFF/JASPER NATIONAL PARKS, ALBERTA

If you see nothing else, you'll certainly see elk – even in the streets of Jasper and Banff. You also stand a good chance of seeing bighorn sheep and mountain goats, with the possibility of catching a glimpse of coyotes and wolves on frozen rivers and lakes.

WHALE WATCHING

N

YUKON TERRITORY

NORTHWEST TERRITORIES

ATLANTIC OCEAN

HUDSON BAY

LABRADOR

PACIFIC OCEAN

BRITISH COLUMBIA

ALBERTA

SASKATCHEWAN

MANITOBA

QUEBEC

NEWFOUNDLAND

ONTARIO

0   500 miles

0   800 km

USA

NOVA SCOTIA

NEW BRUNSWICK

2 ELK ISLAND NATIONAL PARK, ALBERTA

An island surrounded by prairie rather than water, the park has beavers, coyotes, moose, mule deer and about 650 bison. There are some 200 species of waterfowl, great horned owls and chickadees.

3 RIDING MOUNTAIN NATIONAL PARK, MANITOBA

Patient wildlife watchers may sight a cougar, wolf or black bear, but you have a better chance of seeing coyotes, beaver, moose and foxes. Birdwatchers will see bald eagles, ospreys, woodpeckers, grouse and many songbird species.

4 CHURCHILL, MANITOBA

Not for nothing has Churchill been dubbed the 'Polar Bear Capital of the World'. The animals have proven to be such a nuisance as they scavenge for food that the town has had to build a Polar Bear Jail. In addition the area's birdwatching is legendary.

5 NARCISSE, MANITOBA

If you are in Winnipeg in late April or early May you may consider it worthwhile driving 130km (81 miles) north to see the tens of thousands of red-sided garter snakes that pour out of their winter dens to indulge in a frenzy of mating.

6 ALGONQUIN PROVINCIAL PARK, ONTARIO

Traversed by a good highway and reasonably accessible, the park is said to offer the best moose-viewing opportunities in North America. Park staff lead public wolf howlings in August. The park is renowned for its population of timber wolves. Lots of other wildlife is more easily seen.

*F*rom chipmunks to polar bears, Canada's diverse wildlife can be observed in natural habitats.

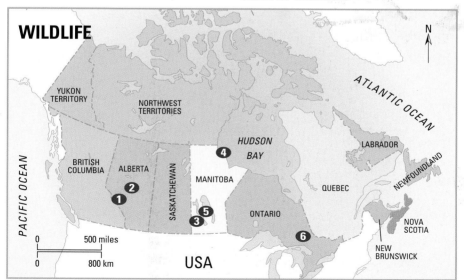

A Land of Extremes

British Columbia is Canada's most geographically diverse province. It has hundreds of miles of deeply indented Pacific coastline, mountains galore, fertile valleys, coastal rainforests, northeastern prairie country and meadowland. It also has 2 million hectares (nearly 5 million acres) of lakes, rivers and streams. Most of the province's 3 million people live in Vancouver and its suburbs and in Metropolitan Victoria, the capital, on Vancouver Island.

Nearly four times the size of Great Britain and twice the size of Japan – both highly populated countries – Canada's most westerly province, British Columbia, has masses of space for its tiny population.

That, and the fact that the province is a beautiful, vast and mainly rural region, may be the reason for the relaxed and easy-going nature of the people. The lifestyle is remarkably laid back, and business tends to be carried out amiably at a leisurely pace even in Vancouver, the largest city in Western Canada, where more than 1 million people live.

British Columbia's population is culturally diverse, with a steady influx of newcomers from other parts of Canada and around the world. The aboriginal people are widely dispersed. Traditional cultures thrive, and great totem poles can be seen in their original surroundings.

Vancouver's largest immigrant groups are British and Chinese. Other groups include Dutch, French, German, Italian, Ukrainian, Greek and Sikhs from Punjab. The Chinese began to arrive in the late 1800s to help build the Canadian Pacific Railway. Having acquired insufficient wealth to return home, they made for the cities.

Vancouver's Chinatown is the third largest in North America (after San

What was once a quarry is now the world famous Butchart Gardens, Vancouver Island.

Francisco and New York). As well as restaurants, there are shops selling herbal remedies, groceries, wood carvings, lacquered pots and richly embroidered dresses. In recent years the Chinese population has been augmented by wealthy Hong Kong business people choosing to set up anew in the west rather than remain in their homeland when it comes under the rule of China in 1997.

Wildlife

British Columbia can claim, among its 144 mammal species, 74 which are found in no other Canadian province. Several species do well here while their populations are diminishing elsewhere in the world, notably Stone sheep, mountain goat, trumpeter swans and blue grouse. A quarter of the world's bald eagles and grizzly bears are in the province. There are substantial numbers of caribou, cougar, moose, mountain sheep, bear, badger, spotted skunk, beaver, marten, muskrat and wolverine, and more than 400 bird species.

Species regarded as endangered even in British Columbia – the white pelican, burrowing owl and sea otter – are maintaining or increasing their numbers.

A Brief History of British Columbia

For 10,000 years before the Europeans arrived in the 1700s, British Columbia's aboriginal people were established in nomadic groups in the northern interior, or in the south, in settled communities where major rivers like those now called the Fraser and the Thompson yielded plenty of fish and the forests lots of meat.

Using primitive tools, they built dugout canoes and totem poles. Their way of life declined considerably, as elsewhere in North America, with the disturbing industries of the white man – mining, logging, fishing, fur trading – and their numbers were decimated by imported diseases, including smallpox.

The Russian, Aleksey Chirkov, explored the province's northwestern coast in 1741, followed by Juan Perez Hernandez, who voyaged from Mexico to Queen Charlotte Islands. In 1778, Britain's James Cook also came here, looking for a Pacific entrance to the Northwest Passage. A man who served under Cook at that time returned in 1792 to carry out a detailed coastline survey. The project was to take him four years. His name? George Vancouver, after whom the city was called.

Settlement and Prosperity

It was the mid-19th century before major settlement of Vancouver began, with an economy based on coal and timber and, later, the building of the Canadian Pacific Railway, with Vancouver the terminus.

In 1858 thousands swarmed into British Columbia, most sailing up the west coast from California, others making their way from US border states, seeking, and finding, gold.

A former sea captain who had taken part in the gold rush moved into town in 1867 with an Indian wife and a barrel of whiskey and opened Vancouver's first tavern. This was 'Gassy' Jack Deighton, whose nickname was given to Gastown, now a fashionable pedestrianized part of the city, with restaurants, lounges and speciality shops.

Today the province's economy is based mainly on forest products, mining – notably copper, gold, silver and zinc –

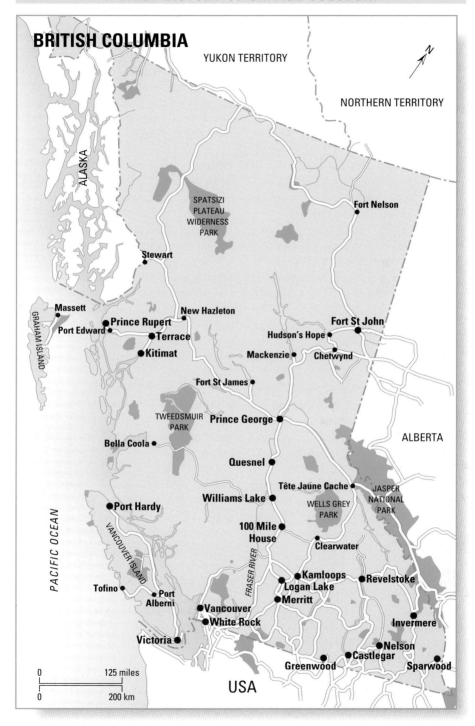

agriculture, fisheries and shipping, as well as tourism.

Sport and Leisure Activities

With its mountains, inland waters, forests, marine parks, six national parks and nearly 400 provincial parks, British Columbia is designed by nature for outdoor recreation, and its people, as well as its visitors, make the most of it.

Activities range from fishing to hang gliding. Vancouver has leisure facilities right on its doorstep. Set between the mountains and the sea, the city has within its boundaries the famous and forested **Stanley Park** – nearly 415ha (1,000 acres) of it – where you can watch float planes taking off and landing in the harbour, and pleasure boats setting off from their moorings.

Public parkland occupies one-twentieth of the province – a larger area than the whole of Switzerland. About one in ten of the parks are in almost untouched wilderness regions, beloved by backpackers and mountain climbers.

Hiking, horse-riding, canoeing or kayaking on inland waterways, wildlife watching, wilderness camping, beachcombing and clam digging are other options, and if you want daredevil action, there's bungee jumping from a bridge near Nanaimo on Vancouver Island.

Camping

Tents can be pitched in wilderness parks. Some hardy campers are satisfied with a bed of fir branches. Those who insist on home comforts choose a recreational vehicle (RV) complete with double bed, microwave oven, shower and flushing toilet.

Campgrounds may have minimal amenities or the lot – electricity, sewer and water hook-ups, fire pit, washing machines and grocery store. When a spell of fine spring weather comes early, the campers may be ready before the campgrounds, and then the choice is to rough it or stay at home.

Skiing

Most of British Columbia is covered by mountains, and in spite of its temperate climate, the province has a long skiing season. After April there is summer glacier skiing, with helicopters setting down avid skiers on mountain tops. Some people make a point of skiing in the morning and swimming in the ocean in the evening.

There are more than 40 downhill skiing resorts, almost 1,500km (830 miles) of groomed Nordic skiing trails and, for the loner, remote skiing in areas accessed by snowcat.

The famous **Whistler Resort** is within a 2-hour drive of Vancouver, but local enthusiasts don't need to leave the city for their sport. The nearest slopes are 20 minutes from downtown – office workers nip out for a lunch-break ski session in midwinter.

Night skiing is enjoyed on three mountains – Cypress, Grouse Mountain and Mount Seymour – at Vancouver's North Shore, with a marvellous view of the city lights. Non-skiers use the gondola to get the view without the exercise.

Visitor Information

British Columbia is divided into nine tourism regions, each offering its own holiday experiences. The regions are: Vancouver Island, Southwest British Columbia, the Cariboo Chilcotin region, the High Country, the Okanagan Silmilkameen region, Kootenay Country, the British Columbia Rockies, North by Northwest and the Peace River region. For more information, contact **Discover British Columbia**, Parliament Building, Victoria, BC, V8V 1X4.

Vancouver Island

Look at the map and you may imagine that a couple of days is enough time to see Vancouver Island and the provincial capital, **Victoria**. Once you get there, you'll find there's a lot more to the island than Butchart Gardens and the world-class Royal British Columbia Museum – two must-see attractions for a start.

Vancouver Island stretches 520km (280 miles) between its southeastern and northwestern tips. A central spine of mountains along its length divides the eastern forests, farmland and sheltered shoreline from the west's peaks and rugged terrain, its deeply indented coastline, logging settlements and fishing communities. Although the is-

land has a mild climate which allows year-round camping (at least for hardy souls), the mountains, some more than 2,200m (7,200ft), trap air masses that produce great snowfalls, with some areas accumulating up to 10m (33ft) each winter.

Many visitors to the island get no further than Victoria and its environs. Pleasant though the capital is, this is a pity because there is dramatic and beautiful scenery to be explored. Activities include swimming, boating, birdwatching, cycling and hiking. Aspects of island history from the days when the Indians had the place to themselves are traced with re-enactments and artefacts, and there are craft centres and art galleries.

Getting There

By ferry: More than 2 million visitors a year arrive in Vancouver Island, most of them crossing by ferry from Vancouver in just over 90 minutes, cruising among the lovely Gulf Islands. Some arrive by ferry from Washington State – Seattle is only 136km (85 miles) from Victoria.

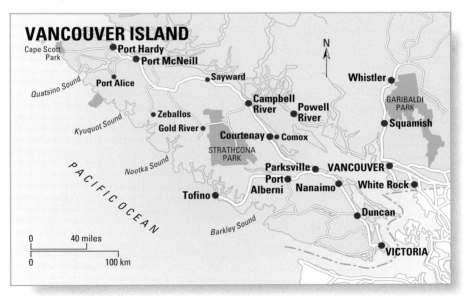

By air: There are air services between Victoria and Vancouver, too, as well as a seaplane service between Seattle and Victoria harbours.

Island Recreation

Because of its mild climate, many outdoor activities, and particularly the most widely practised ones, fishing and golf, can be enjoyed year-round.

Fishing

The Pacific salmon comes in various species, all important quarries for the thousands of fisherfolk who pour into Vancouver Island. There are coho, sockeye and pink salmon, but probably the most coveted is the chinook or king salmon. This fighting fish can grow to more than 23kg (50lb). Boats can be chartered from a wide selection of companies, and chartered float planes can reach even the most remote fishing camp.

Fly fishing in the island's streams is also popular. Trout provide good sport for freshwater anglers.

A licence for all sport fishing is essential. It can be bought from fishing charter companies or from most sporting goods stores.

Golf

In the Victoria area alone there are several public 18-hole golf courses. Almost all have rental facilities, and some are championship courses. There are also private and semi-private courses, including Victoria Golf Club, which is open to members of other clubs.

Hang-gliding

One of Vancouver Island's hang-gliding locations is at Saltspring, the largest and most populated of the Gulf Islands. Pilots launch themselves from the 715m (2,350ft) Bruce Peak into the Fulford Valley. Mount Maxwell (590m/1,900ft) is for the experts, as there is little room for error.

Island Hopping

Vancouver Island's waters vary in character from the peaceful coves of the Gulf Islands to the choppiness of the rugged west coast and the wildness of the Barkley Sound off Ucluelet. Skippered boats will take you sightseeing, or you can charter a sail or power boat and explore independently. Many people hire canoes, kayaks or other small craft for island hopping. Some take bicycles with them for getting about the islands.

Several of the southern islands can be reached by ferry services. From the terminal at Swartz Bay, ferries serve Galiano, Mayne, Saturna, the Pender Islands, Saltspring, Thetis and Kuper, and there are inter-island trips as well. From Nanaimo, a ferry serves Gabriola, the most northerly of the Gulf Islands, and from Buckley Bay, north of Parksville, a ferry goes to Denman and Hornby Islands. Saltspring has trout and bass lakes, mountain peaks and, in Mount Maxwell Provincial Park, limestone caves.

Skiing

Some of the mountains provide good skiing in four ski areas. Of these, **Mount Washington Ski Resort** (PO Box 3069, Courtenay, BC, V9N 5N3, tel. 338-1386) is the largest, with five major lifts including a high-speed quad chair lift, 41 runs and 36km (22 miles) of Nordic trails. It has 480 (1,574ft) of vertical metres and is suitable for all levels of ability.

Mount Arrowsmith (Arrowsmith Ski Hill Ltd, PO Box 266, Port Alberni, BC, V9Y 7M7, tel. 723-1123) is popular with island families learning to ski. The mountain is 460m (1,500ft) high and has three lifts, six runs and 250 vertical metres (825ft).

Ideal for intermediate skiers, **Forbidden Plateau** (Forbidden Plateau Recreation Ltd, PO Box 3268, Courtenay, BC, V9N 5N4) provides a view of mountains to the west and the Strait of Georgia to the east. It is 1,500m (5,000ft) high and has a double chairlift, two T-bars and a practice lift stretching up 300 vertical metres (1,000ft).

Rising out of thickly forested terrain, the **Mount Cain** ski area (PO Box 1225, Port McNeill, BC, V0N 2R0, tel. 949-9496) offers good touring on the higher reaches, and is suited to novice and intermediate skiers.

Watersports

All the popular watersports are available – rowing, windsurfing, snorkelling, water skiing and, at a few locations, including Long Beach in the Pacific Rim National Park, surfing.

There are several highly rated **scuba-diving** sites around Victoria and nearby Sidney, where purple and red hydrocorals, sea anemones in green, red, orange and purple, and brilliant orange sea cucumbers are seen. Nanaimo, too, has some excellent sites.

There are shipwrecks to be explored off Denman Island, such as the 67m (220ft) *Alpha*, an iron steamer which foundered in 1900. Barkley Sound, Ucluelet, also has shipwrecks, and a reputation for a huge variety of rockfish, as well as featherstars, which trap food with their long, plume-like rays. Several professional dive shops in Victoria offer equipment and instruction. All-inclusive dive packages are available from resorts.

Whale-watching

Whale-watching is a growing activity, with organized trips available, some with a naturalist on board to identify what you are seeing and to talk about its lifestyle. Three resident pods, or families, of orcas, known as killer whales, inhabit the Strait of Georgia and the Juan de Fuca Strait around Victoria. They are occasionally seen from the ferry between Vancouver Island and the mainland.

Early spring and late autumn are the times to see migrating grey and humpback whales on the west coast. Dolphins, seals, sealions and many seabird species may also be encountered. Minke whales, as well as orcas, harbour seals, otters and porpoises, are sometimes seen off the craggy coast of Telegraph Cove, near Port Hardy in the north of Vancouver Island.

Victoria

Getting There

By sea: **BC Ferries** (tel. Victoria 386-3431 or Vancouver 669-1211) operates a frequent daily scheduled service for passengers and vehicles through the Georgia Strait between Tsawwassen (south of Vancouver) and Swartz Bay (north of Vancouver). There are also frequent services between Horseshoe Bay (West Vancouver) and Nanaimo (Vancouver Island) and the Gulf Islands.

Altogether the company, which has more than 40 vessels, has 42 ports of call and sailings year-round. In July and August sailings between Vancouver and Vancouver Island are hourly between 7am and 10pm. For the rest of the year sailings are on the odd hours between 7am and 9pm The trip takes just over 90 minutes.

Reservations for vehicles and foot

passengers are unnecessary. Boarding is on a first-come, first-served basis, though drivers of very large recreational vehicles may occasionally have to wait for the next sailing.

More than 20 other BC Ferries routes connect BC coastal communities, including a 15-hour Inland Passage cruise between Port Hardy, on Vancouver Island, and Prince Rupert, on the mainland's northern coast.

Daily sea crossings between Victoria and Port Angeles, Washington State, are operated by **Black Ball Transport**, 430 Belleville Street, Victoria, BC, V8V 1W9, tel. 386-2202.

By bus: Foot passengers wishing to travel between downtown Vancouver and downtown Victoria can take the BC Ferries crossing with **Pacific Coach Lines** (Pacific Central Station, 210-1150, Station Street, Vancouver, BC, V6A 2X3, tel. Vancouver 662-7575 or Victoria 385-4411).

By air: Among airlines flying into Victoria International Airport are **Air BC** (4740 Agar Drive, Richmond, BC, V7B

Victoria's Inner Harbour is a convenient place to start a tour of the city.

1A6, tel. 360-9074), who also have harbour-to-harbour flights daily between Vancouver and Victoria.

There are also daily scheduled flights between Seattle and Victoria operated by **Horizon Air**, PO Box 48309, Seattle, WA 98188, tel. (206) 431-4513, and harbour-to-harbour seaplane flights daily by **Kenmore Air**, 6321 NE 175th, Seattle, WA 98155, tel. (206) 486-1257.

Victoria has a **seaplane** terminal and a waterfront **helijet** landing pad. **Helijet Airways Inc** is at 79 Dallas Road, Victoria, BC, V8V 1A1, tel. 382-6222.

Past and Present

Originally established as a fort and trading post by the Hudson's Bay Company in the 1840s, Victoria was named after the reigning British monarch. Vancouver Island became a British colony in 1849. After nine years of slow growth, it suddenly became a vital stop on the gold rush trail, as fortune-seekers headed north. By the 1860s there were 85 licensed saloons. Gambling parlours, brothels and opium dens were set up.

Now noted for its British characteristics – afternoon tea at the Empress Hotel, shops selling Scottish woollens and tweeds, cricket matches, double-decker buses, even a replica of Anne Hathaway's Cottage at Stratford-upon-Avon, England – Victoria is also famous for its flowers.

Lampposts are festooned with baskets overflowing with blossoms, local residents vie with one another to produce colourful gardens, and every February a day is set aside for a flower census. Everyone counts their blooms as accurately as possible, and the total in billions is announced to the waiting world.

Around Central Victoria

The **Inner Harbour**, with a paved area from which to admire the magnificent yachts and moving traffic, is a convenient place to start a tour of the city. Tourism Victoria's Travel InfoCentre is here, at 812 Wharf Street (tel. 382-2127). You can pick up a street map there.

The central part of Victoria is very attractive, with speciality shops and places of interest in a compact area close to the harbour. The best way to see it is on foot. Guided tours are available, including tours by horse-drawn carriage or limousine. Otherwise you can explore independently, with the freedom to explore shops selling hand-made chocolates, jade and other jewellery, Irish linen or bone china, or simply break for a beer or coffee.

Follow the **waterfront** along Wharf Street, heading inland for Bastion Square and Fort Street, also known for obvious reasons as Antiques Row. This is the site of **Fort Victoria**, built by the Hudson's Bay Company as a trading post and fort in 1843 and demolished at the time of the Cariboo Gold Rush in 1858.

A couple of blocks away are the shops and galleries of Market Square, the heart of the **Old Town**. Licensed saloons burgeoned here in the Naughty Nineties. Now that the 19th-century buildings are restored, there are speciality shops, restaurants and a square where street entertainers often perform.

Close by is a narrow street called **Fan Tan Alley**, where the old opium houses and gambling dens were set up. It now features boutiques and artists' studios. Fan Tan Alley leads to the Gate of Harmonious Interest, the entrance to **Chinatown**. The archway is guarded by a pair of lions, a gift from Victoria's twin town in China, Suzhou.

Victoria claims its Chinatown is the oldest in Canada. By the 1870s, 10,000 Chinese lived there, having arrived in the country to build the railway, dig for coal or seek gold.

Two grand edifices dominate downtown Victoria. They are the granite and brick **Legislative Parliament Buildings** and the **Empress Hotel**. Guided tours of the Parliament Buildings are free. Construction on the site overlooking the Inner Harbour was completed in 1898. An earlier Legislative Building had been destroyed by fire. Standing proudly above the central dome is a statue of Captain George Vancouver. The building is particularly splendid at night when the walls and every turret and dome are outlined in 3,000 twinkling lights.

Victoria's most famous architect, Francis Rattenbury, designed the Parliament Buildings, and many others of similar vintage on Vancouver Island. He came

The Empress

Francis Rattenbury was the architect of the Empress Hotel, which opened in 1908. This is one of the great château hotels built by the Canadian Pacific Hotels Corporation, Canada's largest owner-operated hotel company, with 26 properties.

The Empress, beside the Inner Harbour and recently restored to its original splendour at a cost of $45 million, is very much part of city life. Local people as well as visitors go there for the British-style afternoon tea. More than 80,000 such teas are served in the Palm Court Lobby every year.

Many of the 481 rooms have elegant antique furniture. Some of the larger suites feature turrets and armoires and have ornate fireplaces.

to a sad and early end when he was murdered by a family servant who was his wife's lover.

Next to the Parliament Buildings is the **Royal British Columbia Museum**, in Belleville Street (tel. 387-3701). It depicts 1,200 years of history in such a riveting way that if possible you should set aside several hours for it.

The museum, founded in 1896, was housed in the Parliament Buildings until 1968, when it was moved to its purpose-built premises. Entry is through great doors of carved cedar, and in the lobby are fountains forming a curtain of water.

There are more than 10 million artefacts in the anthropological, biological and historical collections, though only a fraction of these are on public display. Lectures, films and special events are held.

There is much to interest and educate children as well as adults. The sounds and smells appropriate to some exhibits are even reproduced; in the pre-history section, for example, creatures that lived in the forests, mountains, rivers and lakes can be heard baying and roaring.

Industry is graphically illustrated with a fish cannery, a coal-mining shaft, a working gold rush waterwheel and a farmyard diorama of the pioneer days. In the 'Victorian Victoria' section you can watch silent films, walk in a town street admiring the fashionable hats and clothes in the shops and visit the train station. Visitors can step aboard Captain Vancouver's ship *Discovery*, and children are encouraged to examine live marine animals in a pool.

The imposing provincial Parliament Buildings in Victoria were completed in 1898.

Outside is a forest of totem poles in **Thunderbird Park**. You can visit the Carving Shed to see giant totem poles being expertly fashioned by Indian artists, and learn the significance of different features carved in the poles. Carved symbols can be seen in an authentic Indian longhouse built of hand-hewn logs, typical of the coastal homes of Native Indians.

Surrounding the Royal British Columbia Museum are the **Native Plants Gardens**, established in 1968 and containing a wide variety of plants collected by botanists from throughout the province. Take a free guided tour of the gardens. There are six, the Geological Garden, Wetland Garden, Alpine Garden, Coastal Forest Garden, Sand Dune Garden and Dry Interior Garden.

Without leaving the museum grounds, you can visit **Helmcken House**, once the home of the first Speaker of the British Columbia Legislature. He was also a doctor, and the display of 19th-century medical instruments will make you feel thankful for modern technology.

At the back of the Empress Hotel is the **Crystal Garden** (713 Douglas Street). It was originally constructed in the 1920s (another Rattenbury creation) as a covered swimming pool, but in the early 1970s it was converted into a glass-enclosed tropical jungle with waterfalls, lush vegetation, penguins, flamingos, a giant aviary and, among many other creatures, the world's smallest monkeys, some no bigger than a man's finger.

As well as harbour tours and other boat trips, the Inner Harbour offers a submarine theatre experience – the **Pacific Undersea Gardens** (490 Belleville Street, tel. 382-5717). Scuba divers and sea mammals entertain daily at regular intervals in a narrated performance, and marine life in many forms – sea anemones, a giant octopus, wolf-eels and sturgeon – can be seen in their natural habitat.

Directly opposite, at 470 Belleville Street, is the **Royal London Wax Museum**, with over 200 full-size waxen occupants from modern times and history.

In the Land of Lilliput

One of Victoria's newest and highly popular attractions is **Miniature World** (649 Humbold Street, tel. 385-9731). Among the highlights, space travel, the Civil War, Indian conflicts, fairy-tale scenes and an extensive model railway are presented in glorious scaled-down dimensions amid many tiny buildings and scenery. There's a captivating Circus World and fairground with carousels. Among the crowds of miniature people, pickpockets may be spotted by the sharp-eyed.

Historic Houses

Carr House, at James Bay, was built in the 1860s and is the birthplace of the famous painter, Emily Carr. **Pointe Ellice House**, a few minutes from downtown Victoria near the Upper Harbour, is largely unchanged since it was built in 1861. It was lived in until 1975, and a large collection of Victoriana is on view. Its grounds are considered one of the most important garden restorations in North America. A few miles to the west, in View Royal, is Craigflower Farmhouse (1856), restored to its pioneer-era state. The old **Craigflower Schoolhouse** is also open.

Near the centre of Victoria, visible from the top end of Fort Street, the extravagant turreted Victorian pile in stone is **Craigdarroch Castle** at 1050 Joan Crescent. Built for Scots-born coal millionaire Robert Dunsmuir, it took several years to complete and is reputed to have cost

*B*eautiful specimens can be seen at the Butterfly House, a popular Victoria attraction.

children's farm where animals can be petted, and a playground. A band plays on summer Sunday afternoons.

The **Swan Lake Christmas Hill Nature Sanctuary**, a few minutes' drive or bus ride from central Victoria, offers good birdwatching from a floating boardwalk or a pathway.

There are 100 varieties of miniature roses, Oriental lilies, massed rhododendrons, shrubs and perennial plants on display at the **Horticultural Centre of the Pacific** at 505 Quayle Road.

Butchart Gardens are about 20km (12 miles) north of Victoria on the Saanich Peninsula. The 21ha (50 acres) of beautifully kept gardens within a 54ha (130-acre) private estate are open every day of the year.

Incredibly, the place was a blot on the landscape until Jennie Butchart took it in hand. A former limestone quarry supplying the family cement business has been transformed into a visitor's delight, with its sunken garden, formal Japanese garden, Italian garden, English rose garden and many other lovely features.

Musical entertainment is provided daily except on Sunday from June to September. Spectacular fireworks displays set to music are included in the admission charge on Saturday nights in July and August. From mid-June to mid-September the gardens are attractively illuminated after dusk.

Afternoon tea is served all day at **Fable Cottage Estate and World Class Gardens** (5187 Cordova Bay Road, open early March to late October), a modern ocean-front home some 20 minutes from downtown on Scenic Marine Drive. There are guided tours with information about the house and its furnishings, and the gardens are populated by animated gnomes.

$500,000. In 1890, just before it was ready for occupation, Dunsmuir died, leaving his widow to occupy the place for 18 years until her death. The house is now a museum, with a fascinating gift shop.

In the city's Rockland area, some of its grandest houses, with their large, immaculate gardens, are to be found. **Government House** is here – the official residence of British Columbia's Lieutenant-Governor. The house is not open to the public, but visitors may wander in the century-old gardens.

For information on British Columbia Heritage attractions, dial 387-4697.

Parks and Gardens

Victoria is known for its many parks and public gardens. **Beacon Hill Park**, established in the 1880s, is an extensive area of greenery, carriage trails and pathways through formal gardens and wildflower meadows. It is within easy strolling distance eastward of downtown. There's a

Other Victoria Attractions

Canada's largest oceanarium, **Sealand of the Pacific** (1327 Beach Drive), is at Oak Bay, the most English of Greater Victoria's municipalities. Killer whales, seals and sealions entertain, and many other marine creatures can be seen from the viewing gallery. The oceanarium opens daily from March to October, and from Wednesday to Sunday in winter.

A bit of Elizabethan England is authentically reproduced in Esquimalt municipality. **Anne Hathaway's Thatched Cottage** (429 Lampson Street) is a mock-Tudor village complete with inn.

One of the nation's most esteemed art museums is the **Art Gallery of Greater Victoria** (1040 Moss Street). European, Canadian, American, Chinese and Japanese works in various media are displayed, and there is a wide range of work by local artists.

Shopping

A bottomless purse would be useful for anyone confronted by the tempting array of goods in the enticing speciality shops, boutiques and department stores of Greater Victoria.

Arts and crafts cover a wide field, from traditional Native Indian work to up-to-the-minute designs in jade ornaments, polished gemstones and other jewellery. Carved cedar, Irish linen, English woollens, bone china, pottery, hand-made chocolates, spices, woven goods, shops full of collectibles and antiques of many kinds leave the seeker of gifts and souvenirs spoilt for choice.

There are some smart modern shopping malls, the newest being the **Eaton Centre** in Government Street. There are also places where bargains can be found – flea markets, second-hand stores and discount shops. A number of art and craft fairs are held in Greater Victoria.

Entertainment

Music: There are plenty of musical happenings in Victoria. The **Victoria Symphony** is foremost on the classical scene, and special events like the Summer Splash, when the orchestra performs from a barge in the Inner Harbour, are tremendously popular. The much-acclaimed **Pacific Opera Victoria** offers regular productions. Music and arts festivals take place at a variety of well-chosen venues. Clubland offers blues, reggae, jazz, country and rock – you name it – until the small hours.

Drama and dance: Half a dozen theatres stage a wide spectrum of drama and entertainment. Amateur groups as well as professionals display a high standard of performance at the historical McPherson, Royal and Belfry Theatres.

Excursions from Victoria

Sooke

Before setting off from Victoria to places of interest on the eastern side of the island, it's worth taking the 42km (26-mile) journey west to Sooke, a logging, fishing and farming settlement which celebrated its bicentenary in 1990. A visit to East Sooke Park will show that mining also contributed to the local economy at one time. The remains of old copper mines can be seen. There are also some petroglyphs (rock carvings).

The **Sooke Region Museum** (2070 Phillips Road) contains Indian crafts and many artefacts from Sooke's history. A visit to the museum includes a guided tour of Moss Cottage, a small pioneer home of 1870. The museum also has a travel information centre.

All Sooke Day in late July is the showcase for traditional loggers' contests such as log rolling, pole climbing and sawing. The newly established annual International Longboat Race takes place around the same time, when Canadian and American crews in period costume race replica 16th-century longboats in the King of Spain's Cup.

Sidney

Sidney is a 25-minute drive up the eastern coast from Victoria, a seaside town where you can tour the historic area by horse and carriage. In August there's lively annual street entertainment by buskers.

*P*ick your own gems at Mineral World, Port Sidney, or buy them ready polished.

Mineral World (9891 Seaport Place) on the Port Sidney waterfront describes itself as the province's premier gemstone boutique. You buy an empty bag, go to the Scratch Patch of semi-precious stones and shells and get busy, selecting those you want to keep. You can pan for gold, too, and create your own pendants, earrings and bracelets at Mineral World's workbenches. Ready made in the boutique are sculptures and ornaments, polished stone eggs, loose and strung beads, fossils, specimen shells and jewellery.

Sidney **Historical Society Museum** in Beacon Avenue has Indian artefacts and a dugout cedar canoe in a former customs building.

The Saanich Peninsula is the only part of North America where skylarks are heard. The birds are descended from more than 100 pairs brought in by English settlers in the early 20th century. You may also see Christmas holly in the region – it is the only place in Canada where it is grown commercially.

Cowichan Bay

Cowichan Bay is a small fishing village, backed by mountain scenery, built around a natural deep-sea harbour.

For visitors arriving by boat there are good moorings in marinas or at Government Wharf. Most of the accommodation on shore provides a view of the bay, and many of the houses are on stilts, with front doors facing the street and back doors over the water.

Two rivers, the Cowichan and the Koksilah – major salmon spawning grounds – flow into the bay. The village has a busy, nautical air, with freighters loading timber at the harbour, chandleries, five marinas, fishing boats and a fish-processing plant. Boats can be hired, fishing charters,

Tennis

Tennis-playing visitors can, for a fee, use grass courts almost as old as Wimbledon's. South Cowichan Lawn Tennis Club celebrated its centenary in 1987.

whale-watching and nature trips are available and there is plenty of scope for photography and sightseeing.

In 1987 the Cowichan Bay **Maritime Centre** opened on the pier, with the idea of keeping alive the traditional skills involved in building wooden boats. Today the boat-building school offers courses at several levels, and visitors can watch the work in progress.

At the **Marine Ecology Station**, housed in a barge by the Maritime Centre (open to the public daily in summer and at weekends the rest of the year), marine creatures can be examined through a series of microscopes, going about their business.

In June the Cowichan Bay annual **boat festival** takes place, drawing crowds with a display of many types of boat, old and new. A 'Fast and Furious' boat-building team contest adds to the fun.

The Scots-born poet, Robert Service, lived in the village at the turn of the century, working in the Post Office and writing in his spare time.

Duncan

Duncan, midway between Victoria and Nanaimo, is known as the City of Totems.

There are nearly 80 totems in Duncan, most on the TransCanada Highway. They are recent original works of art – post-1985, in fact, when the Totem Poles Project was conceived as a co-operative venture with native carvers, mostly of the Cowichan Band.

When the first white settlers arrived, there were nearly 60,000 Cowichan people in the Cowichan Valley. Now, with fewer than 2,500 members, the Band is the largest in British Columbia. They have a Band Council of 12, and an elected chief.

The Totem Poles Project came into being because most old Indian carvings had been moved from their original sites into museums and private collections. It was felt crucial that the ancient but living native art form should be more accessible, and selected artists were invited to submit models.

Totem poles historically depict a pictorial family background, sometimes with a myth or legend worked in. They were also used as grave markers or memorials. More than 40 totem poles can be seen on a self-guided tour. Informative guided tours are available from the train station with members of the Cowichan Valley Volunteers' Society.

The old station in Canada Avenue, built in 1912, has been converted into the **Cowichan Valley Museum**, run by Cowichan Historical Society. A general store is stocked with countless intriguing items, from a magic lantern to a bear trap,

Native Heritage

Massive totem poles take shape before you at the Native Heritage Centre at 200 Cowichan Way, Duncan, on the banks of the Cowichan River. The Pacific Coast's First People also demonstrate weaving, beadwork and knitting. Don't miss the 'Great Deeds' theatre presentation. Traditional Native food is served, and carvings, masks, prints, hand-crafted jewellery and authentic Cowichan sweaters are on sale. In summer there are 'Feast and Legends' evenings with entertainment and dining. You need to book (tel. 746-8119).

65

and the museum exhibits range from a much-worn hand-made boot to an old kitchen range.

Native arts and crafts, including carved totems and masks and hand-made gold and silver jewellery, are sold at Judy Hill Gallery in Craig Street.

British Columbia Forest Museum Park

Just north of Duncan, on the TransCanada Highway, is the mainly outdoor British Columbia Forest Museum Park, open from May to September, covering native Indian times to the present day on the theme 'Man in the Forest'.

The 40ha (100-acre) park has a 2.5km (1¹/₂-mile) narrow-gauge rail track on which a train hauled by steam locomotive takes people round the park and through the forest, passing over a 92m (285ft) trestle bridge across the Somenos Lake. It passes a sawmill, an 1890 log hauler and early donkey engines. Indoor exhibits show how paper is made and trace the history of the men and machines in the forestry industry. A logging camp depicts the hard life of loggers in the past, when oxen hauled the logs.

The Tree Room displays photographs and historic film of the industry, and demonstrates the lifecycle of forests. The Ranger station illustrates the work of the Forestry Service.

There are walking trails, some ancient totem poles and 25 tree species in the

*T*raditional crafts and costumes are displayed at the Native Heritage Centre in Duncan, known as Totem City.

park. On show is a 35-ton log that is 1,350 years old. Visitors can climb up to the fire look-out for a view of the park.

To the east of Cowichan Bay is **Lake Cowichan**, 45km (30 miles) long, and pleasant to drive around, with dense fir forests. To the north of the Bay is **Maple Bay**, noted for its diving.

Chemainus

Higher up the coast, Chemainus has a population of around 400, yet it attracts some 300,000 visitors a year from around the world. This seems extraordinary in view of the fact that its one industry – timber – founded a few years after the first European settlers arrived in 1862, came to a halt in 1983.

With the aid of a grant, a Downtown Revitalization Project was established and the town became an outdoor art gallery. Painting after painting, each depicting an aspect of Chemainus life and history, appeared on the sides of buildings. More than 30 murals, a massive wood carving and a sculpture, all by talented artists, decorate the town. A self-guided mural tour can be made with the aid of an explanatory map.

Chemainus is open all year, but from the beginning of July to the end of October the town and its visitors celebrate the **Festival of Murals** with a series of events. There's never a dull moment, with street music, folk dancing, puppet shows, art and craft displays and demonstrations, musical events, clowns, street entertainment and outdoor theatre shows. New murals are painted in summer, so that visitors can watch them grow.

This 4-month celebration is augmented in late August by a 3-day art and craft show where the work of more than 80 professional artists and artisans from

A giant circular saw, one of the exhibits in B.C. Forest Museum Park, near Duncan.

many parts of Canada is exhibited at the Pacific Rim Artisan Village Site.

Working exhibits spanning half a century, from the 1870s to the 1920s, can be seen in the Chemainus **Mechanical Music Museum**. The **Chemainus Valley Museum**, opened in 1991 in a state-of-the-art building and run by the local History Society, is open all year (daily in summer) and offers insight into the background of a community which has proved that success can grow out of adversity.

Ladysmith

Further up the TransCanada Highway, Ladysmith is a small town with street names like Kitchener and Baden Powell, betraying its origins at the time of Britain's Boer War victory. It was built as a resort home for the families of miners digging coal in the Nanaimo area by a mine-owner who had ready-made buildings transported from nearby Wellington, forming an instant town.

Ladysmith claims to have the warmest saltwater swimming north of San Francisco, and **Transfer Beach Park** is a great place to put this to the test.

Nanaimo

On the way to Nanaimo, Vancouver Island's second largest city (population 65,000), you may care to stop for a bungee

A reminder of the town's logging history, this waterwheel can be found in a Chemainus park.

jump, leaping into a gorge on the Nanaimo River. Or play safe and watch other people jump. A world first is claimed by the operating company – the first and only specially designed bungee-jumping bridge.

Known as the Harbour City (it has two harbours), Nanaimo has a beautiful **waterfront**. From Fisherman's Wharf – the place for really fresh seafood – to the BC Ferries terminal, you can follow the Waterfront Walkway through **Georgia Park**, where a native canoe and totem poles can be seen. The walkway also takes you to Swy-a-Lana Lagoon, Canada's only man-made tidal pool, and a good swimming spot. **Bowen Park**, in the city centre, has trails, a nature centre and a petting farm.

The name of the city is derived from the Indian word 'Snenymo', which means either 'Meeting place of the tribes' or 'Great and mighty people', depending on which book you read. A heady scent of pine pervades the air on a still day – forestry is a major industry.

Captain George Vancouver arrived at Nanaimo aboard the *Discovery* in 1792, a year after Spain's Captain Narvaez explored the coast in *Saturnina*. Its prosperity was founded on coal, which was discovered in 1851, attracting settlers to the area. Because of attacks on the new

---

Woolly Jumpers

Dairy herds in the Cowichan River Valley supply much of the province's milk. The sheep supply the fleece, heavy with lanolin, from which the undyed wool for the famous Cowichan sweaters is woven. Cowichan sweaters, which bear the patterns on the blankets worn traditionally by the Coast Salish Indians, are heavy, warm and extremely hard wearing.

arrivals by Natives, in 1853 the Hudson's Bay Company built the **Bastion** on the waterfront to protect them. A wooden blockhouse, it is one of the oldest structures of its type in North America.

The Bastion is now a museum on three levels – a ship's ladder leads to the top floor. Be there by midday in summer, when the Bastion Guards, in authentic 19th-century uniform, fire the noonday gun, and the bagpipes play.

Nanaimo's history is traced at the **Centennial Museum** in Cameron Street. The lifestyle of Coastal Salish Indians, before European settlement, is outlined. Coal mining is strongly featured, with early mining work illustrated.

More ancient history can by witnessed in **Petroglyph Provincial Park**, 8km (5 miles) out of town, where rock carvings of men and animals dating back thousands of years can be seen.

In late July the week-long annual **Marine Festival** takes place. It developed from an event started in 1967, the Nanaimo Bathtub Race, in which ocean-going baths powered by outboard motors are steered by intrepid crews towards Vancouver, 48km (30 miles) away across the Strait of Georgia. The race, now an international event, is held on the fourth Sunday in July.

Sport and Leisure Activities

Nanaimo has more than two dozen parks. There is good **sport fishing** for salmon, cod and red snapper – saltwater fishing is year-round – and great **windsurfing**. The city also offers tremendous **shopping** facilities, claiming to have more shops per capita than anywhere else in the whole of North America. Certainly there are plenty of malls with spacious car parks.

For people with **boats**, Nanaimo is a good base from which to explore the Gulf Islands. Alternatively, a ferry operates the few minutes' trip to Gabriola Island, with its sandstone **beaches** enjoyed by clam diggers and beachcombers as well as sunbathers. At Malaspina Point in Gabriola Sands Provincial Park there are jagged rock formations including the curious Galiano Galleries. Gabriola Island has good facilities for scuba diving, sailing, cycling, tennis and golf.

There are many recreation areas in the vicinity where people go **hiking, cycling** and **birdwatching**. One of the provincial parks, **Newcastle Island**, is a 10-minute ferry ride away. Its hiking trails lead to the ruins of a Salish Indian winter fishing settlement, a sandstone quarry and a mineshaft. Natural history displays can be seen in a former 1930s dance hall.

Central Vancouver Island

No boundaries exist, but Vancouver Island is generally regarded as being divided into three. South is roughly from Victoria to Nanaimo, Central from Nanaimo to Campbell River, and North from Campbell River to Port Hardy.

Parksville

Set on a wide bay, Parksville is a family seaside resort with beaches which are ideal for small children, in particular at low tide when the sand stretches into the distance. The sun-warmed sand takes the chill off the water, making it comfortable for paddling and swimming.

With its extensive beach and the texture of its sand, Parksville is the natural venue for the **International Sandcastle Competition** held at the end of July. This is a

*T*he Bastion at Nanaimo was built in 1853 by the Hudson's Bay Company.

serious construction contest. Not only are there classes for tinies, sub-teens, teenagers and families, there is also an executive section in which businesses compete to produce architectural edifices. The international element is there – people from many parts of the world strive to build a respectable castle that will endure until the tide comes in. There's also an annual kite-flying competition on the beach, and a major volleyball championship is held here, too.

Good campgrounds, some of which are open all year, are handy for Parksville and its close neighbour, **Qualicum Beach**. Some campgrounds are at the oceanside. In high summer campers in transit are advised to start early in the morning to seek a site for the night.

Qualicum Beach

Qualicum Beach, which, like Parksville, has extensive beaches, is much quieter than its neighbour, with a more relaxed pace of life. It is a favourite retirement spot, and its visitors include people fishing for salmon. The two communities, which are about 12km (7^1/$_2$ miles) apart, share such amenities as an airport, art gallery and college campus.

The First Nation people in the area had a well-organized lifestyle long before the arrival of European settlers. They fished for coho and sockeye salmon in the Strait of Georgia in summer, and in winter they lived in cedar log bighouses in locations convenient for four prolific salmon waters – Little and Big Qualicum Rivers, Cooks Creek and Englishman River.

The **Old School House** in Qualicum Beach has been restored to its Victorian origins and opened as an art centre, featuring painting, sculpture, carving, pottery and music. It is open to visitors, who can see resident artists at work, demonstrating various techniques.

Coombs

From Parksville you have the chance to leave the TransCanada Highway (which becomes Highway 19, or the Island Highway, north of Nanaimo), to take the beautiful route along Highway 4 to the **west coast**.

Prepare for a surprise at Coombs: the goats browsing on vegetation on the roof of the Old Country Market building are not cardboard cut-outs – watch the kids caper!

Coombs is the home of **Butterfly World**, open daily from April to October. Butterflies from many parts of the world fly freely in the indoor tropical garden.

A small town of around 1,500 people, originally of Yorkshire stock, Coombs has put itself on the summer visitors' map with a rodeo, a bluegrass festival and an old-time fiddlers' contest in the open air. It attracts competitors of a high standard from a wide area.

Cathedral Grove

On the drive west, **Little Qualicum Falls Provincial Park** provides a pleasant woodland stroll to see the falls which crash down 60m (195ft) in three stages. There are camping and picnic sites. Trails lead to nearby Mount Arrowsmith.

Highway 4 hugs Lake Cameron and the Cameron River on the way to **MacMillan Provincial Park** and the awe-inspiring Cathedral Grove. This must be the province's most accessible surviving rainforest. Pull into the lay-by, get out of your car and you're there. To capture the cathedral-like atmosphere beneath intertwined branches, walk among the firs and Western red cedars up to 90m (300ft) tall.

Brant Festival

Brant Festival is a joint venture of Parksville and Qualicum Beach. It celebrates the arrival in spring of the black brant geese (not to be confused with brent geese found in Europe), stopping off to feed and regain strength during migration from their Mexico winter habitat to breeding grounds in Northern Canada, Alaska and Russia.

The brant is a small sea goose, similar in plumage to the Canada goose but scarcely bigger than a mallard duck. The survival of the brant goose has been threatened by diminishing feeding grounds. The type of esturial sites, bays, lagoons and isolated beaches they need are also sites on which developers of marinas, golf courses and resorts cast a covetous eye.

Up to 20,000 brant geese rest and feed at the Parksville–Qualicum Beach sandbars and sheltered beaches every spring. Numbers are at their highest in April. The 3-day festival takes place during the second week.

Viewing sites are set up in Qualicum Beach and Rathtrevor Provincial Park, Parksville. Experts, including Canadian Wildlife Service biologists, share their knowledge with visitors and a local optical company sets up ornithology 'scopes at the Rathtrevor site for the use of brant watchers.

Events during the festival include wildlife art, photography and carving exhibitions and competitions, a Native art display with carvings, silverware, basketry, beadwork and paintings, and salmon barbecued Native-style. Funds are raised for wildlife conservation.

Some are said to be 800 years old or more – they could have been saplings when the Magna Carta was signed.

Horne Lake Caves Provincial Park

Spelunkers will want to turn right about 16km (10 miles) from Cathedral Grove, to Horne Lake Caves Provincial Park. There are six large caves and several smaller ones. Three are permanently open. The others are not for the frail or claustrophobic – explorers must be prepared for much stooping and possibly some crawling. Take a light and wear something warm. The biggest cave, Euclataws, is for scientific groups only. Penetrating Riverbend Cave, which extends for 383m (1,260ft) involves ropes and ladders and, most importantly, a professional guide (tel. 248-3931).

Port Alberni

Return to Highway 4 to Port Alberni, where visiting fishermen are drawn by the chinook, sockeye and coho salmon. At the annual **Salmon Festival** over the Labour Day weekend (early September), enthusiasts compete for thousands of dollars in prize money. The first prize usually goes to the competitor who hauls out a specimen weighing 18–25kg (40–65lb).

Mainly a logging town, Port Alberni (population 20,000) is at the top of the long inlet which stretches from the **Barkley Sound** and the **Pacific Rim National Park**. (A word of caution: those driving on to Ucluelet should check their fuel gauge – filling stations are thin on the ground along the mountainous road.)

Fishing is a big industry at Port Alberni. At least 300 boats operate from the harbour, providing 20 percent of British Columbia's salmon. About 20km (12 miles) northwest of the town at **Robertson Creek** is a fishing hatchery open to visitors where salmon eggs are incubated by the million.

Forestry has been the mainstay of the area since 1860, when the first sawmill opened. The local history of the industry is outlined in the **Alberni Valley Museum**. An old gravel logging road leads from Alberni to **Bamfield**. Watch out for trucks and give them priority. Drive slowly if you don't want your vehicle, especially its fuel tank, to get damaged by flying gravel.

Bamfield and the Broken Group Islands

From Port Alberni, try to make time for a cruise down the inlet to the Broken Group Islands in the Barkley Sound or to the small village of Bamfield, where experienced hikers disembark for the West Coast Trail (see p.75). Others spend time swimming or watching the ships go by until the ferry returns – Bamfield has a long boardwalk along its shoreline.

The service operates with two working freighters, the MV *Frances Barkley* and the MV *Lady Rose*, a stately vessel built in Scotland in 1937. Occasional stops are made to deliver goods and mail.

Many people sail among the Broken Group Islands by kayak or canoe, which can be rented. It take about $4^1/_2$ hours to reach Bamfield, and a little less for the homeward voyage. The service runs on Tuesdays, Thursdays and Saturdays year-round, with Friday and Sunday sailings in July and August. In summer only (early June to late September) a service operates to Ucluelet via the Broken Group Islands on Mondays, Wednesdays and Fridays. All ferries leave Port Alberni's Argyle Pier at 8am. For further information, including canoe and kayak hire, contact Alberni Marine Transportation (1982) Inc, PO Box 188, Port Alberni, BC, V9Y 7M7, tel. 723-8313.

West towards Ucluelet

It is nearly 100km (60 miles) to Ucluelet, through the 1,200m (3,900ft) Mackenzie Mountain Range and through forest, river and lake scenery. Bears and cougars (mountain lions) are among the animals living in this territory.

The biggest trout in British Columbia – cutthroats up to 7kg (15lb) – live in **Sproat Lake Provincial Park**, 13km (9 miles) west of Port Alberni. Sport fishing, water skiing, boating and swimming are enjoyed in the park, which has trails leading to 24m (78ft) limestone cliffs bearing ancient Indian rock carvings of fish and mythological creatures. In the park are two Mars Water Bombers, former World War II troop-carrying aircraft now used in fighting forest fires.

Kennedy Lake is Vancouver Island's largest. The rainforest around it is the home of many bird species.

Soon after you cross the quaintly named **Lost Shoe Creek**, Highway 4 branches right to Long Beach and Tofino. Keep straight on for the logging town of **Ucluelet**, where you come to the end of the road.

Ucluelet's population is under 2,000, multiplied considerably in the season by the arrival of visitors intent on whale-watching, fishing, diving and learning

---

Skunk Cabbage
People from outside Canada may be intrigued by a plant which grows in marshy ground in Cathedral Grove, and other watery spots. Very visible in spring, it has a yellow flower rather like a large tulip blossom, with wide, pale green leaves. The bud forms in autumn and stays dormant until February or March, when it opens to reveal a 'poker'. The plant, called skunk cabbage, generates tremendous heat – up to 15C° (27F°) above the surrounding air temperature.

Broken Group Islands

The Broken Group Islands have accounted for the loss of about 50 vessels in the past 100 years. The wrecks are a mecca for scuba divers. Harbour seals live among the islands, which are in the Pacific Rim National Park. Bald eagles and cormorants nest there, and Pacific grey whales are sometimes seen.

Boating can be hazardous because of reefs and thick morning fog. There are virtually no landing beaches, but Gibraltar, Jacques and Hand Islands have sheltered lagoons. Follow the marine chart.

about the rich marine life in the Pacific Rim National Park.

Small though the town is, it is one of British Columbia's busiest ports. The name comes from the Nu-chal-nulth Indian word for 'safe harbour'. A trading post for fur sealers preceded the first sawmill operation, dating back to the 1880s.

Tofino and the Pacific Rim National Park

Back on Highway 4, the first stop is **Long Beach**, which lives up to its name – 11km (7$^1/_2$ miles) of dazzling pale sand, a paradise for beachcombers, clam diggers and sunbathers, as long as the thick mists to which the area is prone keep away. Boat trips take visitors to watch sealions on rocky outcrops. The **Wickanninish Interpretive Centre** at Long Beach, in the Pacific Rim National Park, has displays and film about the Pacific Ocean, the park's history and its marine life.

Tofino, where tourism, commercial fishing and logging are important, marks the northern end of the national park. The beach provides good walks, with trails leading through rainforest to little coves. Guided sea-kayaking excursions and sailing trips, whale-watching, nature tours and scenic sightseeing are also offered.

The town has a strong Native heritage, with craft shops and galleries, including the **Roy Vickers Gallery** built with hand-hewn cedar logs and named after a noted local artist. The **Whale Centre** has some informative whaling displays, and the **West Coast Maritime Museum** is worth a visit.

In March and April Tofino celebrates the **Grey Whale Festival**, marking the arrival of the whales as they migrate from Mexico and Baja California to summer habitats in Alaska. Some remain in Clayoquot Sound off Tofino, and a local company, James Whaling Station (tel. 725-3919) guarantees sightings of grey whales.

Trips by sea or air go to **Hot Springs Cove**, north of Tofino, where people swim in natural pools with water temperatures of 43°C (109°F). A series of warm waterfalls feeds the pools along the beach.

The **Pacific Rim National Park** is just over 100km (60 miles) long from Tofino to the southern end of the West Coast Trail. It protects ocean beaches, coastal islands and dense coastal rainforest. The park's three sections – Long Beach, Broken Islands and the West Coast Trail – have their own characteristics.

Black-tailed deer may be encountered among the oceanside Sitka spruce trees. Harbour seals, sealions, otters and mink are sometimes seen from the shore, and the sharp-eyed may spot grey whales at migration time.

There is abundant birdlife. The rocky shoreline sustains a wide range of marine flora and fauna, from sponges to sea stars. Cedar, hemlock and fir grow close to the water's edge.

North towards the Comox Valley

Botanical Beach, a rich intertidal area on the coast near Port Renfrew, is accessible only on foot. Go at low tide to see a wide variety of marine life in the tidal pools which are dotted about a sandstone shelf beyond the pebble beach. Leave before the tide turns, as the sandstone gets dangerously slippery.

Returning to the east coast and Highway 19, we reach **Buckley Bay**. From here, **Denman Island** is a 15-minute ferry ride away. Another ferry goes from Denman to **Hornby Island**. There are trails, beaches and cliff walks, and campground, cottage and guest house accommodation.

North of Buckley Bay are the thickly wooded mountains of the Beaufort Range. Three close neighbours, Cumberland, Courtenay and Comox, form the communities of the **Comox Valley**.

Before the turn of the 20th century the Asian population of **Cumberland** was said to be bigger than San Francisco's. With the decline of coal mining in the 1960s, most of the Chinese left. The town's **museum** has a walk-through model of a coal mine.

The urban heart of the Comox Valley is **Courtenay**, where a 1909 locomotive once owned by the Comox Logging and Railway Company is on display at the tourist information centre. Courtenay and District **Historical Museum** has the world's largest vertical log cabin. The museum also traces Cumberland's Chinatown days. Summer music and arts festivals and craft fairs are held at Courtenay. Golfers have a choice of half a dozen courses, all with mountain scenery.

Comox is a seaside town with a large commercial fishing fleet. Its **Air Force Museum** features space technology as well as the history of the Royal Canadian Air Force. Five vintage aircraft stand outside the museum. In alternate years, early and modern aircraft are put through their paces before crowds at an air show in early August.

A car ferry makes the 75-minute trip between Comox and the mainland city of **Powell River**, a year-round trout and salmon fishing area.

The Comox Valley attracts visitors year-round, with its Alpine and cross-country skiing facilities providing good hiking country in summer. **Mount Washington Ski Resort**, Vancouver Island's largest, and **Forbidden Plateau** – Comox Indians believed evil spirits there ate people, and declared it a no-go zone –

The West Coast Trail

The West Coast Trail, in the southwest of Vancouver Island, is not for Sunday strollers. The 77km (48-mile) trail, between Bamfield and Port Renfrew, requires strength, endurance and sure-footedness. A permit is necessary and hikers should be prepared for complete self-sufficiency for the 5 or 6 days' rough trekking.

The only way to follow the trail is on foot. It involves scrambling up and down deep ravines and slipping about on rugged, rain-soaked tracks encumbered with fallen trees.

However, they say the views compensate for it all. No doubt shipwrecked mariners felt the same. The trail was made for them at the turn of the century, providing a route to civilization if they survived the loss of their ships.

are in the Beaufort Range. Mount Washington Ski Resort has a new sled and toboggan area. Summer visitors with a head for heights can go by chairlift to 1.6km (1 mile) above sea level.

Summer hikers can get a great view of the Comox Valley and the mainland beyond the Georgia Strait from the Forbidden Plateau. That is if it's not misty or raining – the central and northern parts of Vancouver Island are particularly susceptible to this type of weather, which accounts for the abundance of lush vegetation. From the Forbidden Plateau Ski Lodge, it's a good 5-hour hike for the fit, strong and agile.

Campbell River and Quadra Island

Highway 19 goes through lush farmland to **Campbell River**, a substantial town (population 26,000) claiming the title 'Salmon Capital of the World' – a title also claimed by Port Alberni. Bob Hope, Bing Crosby and John Wayne have all fished at Campbell River. A freshwater lake and river system yields trout, char and salmon. Guides well acquainted with local waters can be hired – a service advised for visitors because of dangerous fast currents in some areas. For sea fishing without a boat, the town has its Discovery Pier.

A 15-minute ferry ride from Campbell River takes you to **Quadra Island**. At 24km (14 miles) long it is the largest island in the Discovery Passage. At Cape Mudge, on boulders along the shore, you can see petroglyphs of masks and mythological creatures, considered the most important Indian rock carvings of the Pacific Coast.

Nearby is the **Kwakiutl Museum**, housing a wealth of Indian masks, totems and regalia. Native dances are performed in summer, and Kwakiutl feasts served, at the Tsa-Kwa-Luten Lodge, operated by Native people, at Cape Mudge.

Hiking trails and a gravel road lead to lakes and the ruins of the **Lucky Jim Mine**, where gold and copper were found during the laying of a loggers' rail track.

Rebecca Spit Provincial Park, on Quadra Island, has walking trails and boat-launching facilities. A ferry goes to neighbouring **Cortes Island**, which has two provincial parks and a freshwater swimming beach.

Strathcona Provincial Park

Inland from Campbell River, along Highway 28, Strathcona Provincial Park is Vancouver Island's oldest and biggest, at about 222,530ha (550,000 acres). It has the island's highest mountain, **Mount Golden Hinde**, 2,200m (7,218ft) and, in the south of the park, the highest waterfall in Canada, **Della Falls**, with a 440m (1,443ft) drop.

A canoe trail leads from Elk Falls, near Campbell River, through Campbell and Buttle Lakes, to the park. Strathcona Park has drive-in and wilderness campgrounds. For a map and hiking trail guide, get in touch with BC Parks in Victoria (tel. 387-4363).

North Vancouver Island

Return through Strathcona Park to where Highway 28 continues west to **Gold River**, in the North Island. The road and the river which gives the town its name travel together for much of the route. The town appeared in the mid-1960s, being constructed in six months to provide accommodation for employees at a pulp mill. This is wild country which the crowds don't reach, but there is hotel and campground accommodation, and you can get a round of golf on a nine-hole course. Wolves, cougars, bears and elk live in the surrounding dense forests.

Organized **cave tours** are available in Gold River, and an interesting **ferry trip** leaves thrice weekly in summer aboard a converted World War II minesweeper, the Uchuck III. It goes through the Nootka Sound and other scenic waterways, to **Kyuquot**, a 56km (35-mile) voyage with stops to deliver supplies to remote communities. One of these is at Friendly Cove on Nootka Island, where Captain James Cook landed in 1778.

Back to Highway 19, just north of Campbell River, stop at the Ripple Rock **lookout** to see the site of a submerged mountain in the steep-sided Seymour Narrows. More than 100 ships were wrecked by it until a huge controlled explosion blasted it to pieces in 1958.

Inside Passage

The 125m (410ft) *Queen of the North* leaves Port Hardy at 7.30am, docks at Prince Rupert at 10.30pm, and follows a similar timetable in the opposite direction the next day. Check-in time is 6.30am. In winter the sailings are weekly. The ship can carry up to 800 people and more than 150 vehicles.

The scenery will have you constantly reaching for your camera or binoculars. Once the *Queen of the North* cruises behind Calvert Island into FitzHugh Sound, it is in sheltered waters all the way. You pass through virgin wilderness, past the Coast Mountains rising out of the sea and steep, heavily wooded slopes. You may see sealions relaxing on the rocks and bald eagles swooping to grab salmon. Porpoises and humpback whales may even be seen accompanying the ship from time to time.

Whale-watching is a major activity at the **Johnson Strait**, where some of the minke and killer-whale families can be observed all year.

After turning inland for a while, the Island Highway returns to the coast at **Telegraph Cove**, a boardwalk village with buildings raised above the water on piles.

Free forest tours with guided nature walks and steam locomotive rides are offered at the logging centre of **Port McNeill** from June to September, Monday to Friday (tel. 956-3844).

A short ferry ride from Port McNeill is **Alert Bay**, a small island settlement with an airstrip, a wealth of Kwakiutl paintings and totems and a boardwalk.

Port Hardy

The northernmost town on Vancouver Island is Port Hardy, where the Island Highway ends. Beyond it is **Cape Scott Provincial Park**, a wilderness area of lowland bogs and coastal rainforest, with a 30km (19-mile) trek to Cape Scott Lighthouse – a park for the dedicated backpacker.

Port Hardy is where you depart for, or return from, the magnificent BC Ferries cruise through the Inside Passage to **Prince Rupert**, on British Columbia's northern mainland coast. The journey takes 15 hours each way.

A wildlife preserve at Port Hardy, with many animal and bird species, has forest and seashore walks. This village, which has a couple of campgrounds at the shore, is a boardwalk settlemen.

Vancouver

Set between sea and mountains, British Columbia's biggest metropolis has a

*F*rom the top of the Harbour Centre you get a panoramic view of Vancouver and the surrounding area.

natural beauty. Although the city grew up fast, with immigrants from Asia, Europe and elsewhere pouring in, it developed sensitively and managed to avoid any severe architectural blunders.

In the province's southwest coastal area the climate is temperate. Vancouverites talk of their mild winters and point to the daffodils and tulips, in bloom by early April. They turn a blind eye to the rain, which in winter and spring falls by the bucketful. Summers are usually fairly dry.

It is an interesting, stroll-around city, easy on the eye, and if you need a retreat from streets and buildings, you can wander into spacious **Stanley Park**, with its forest and waterfront views, or the only authentic classical Chinese garden outside China. Many of the attractions and communities of Greater Vancouver can be reached by **SkyTrain** or **SeaBus**, and drivers will not find the city difficult to negotiate.

Orientation

For a bird's eye view of Vancouver's downtown area and far beyond, go to The Lookout! at the **Harbour Centre** at Harbour and Seymour Streets. It isn't free but it's an exciting way of getting your bearings, and a 12-minute video on the city goes with it. The glass elevator takes you 170m (581ft) from the lower lobby to The Lookout! in less than a minute, gliding up the side of the building, watched by people in the street below. From the viewing deck, on a clear day, you can see Mount Baker in Washington State, USA, 140km (90 miles) away. Lunch and dinner are served at the Centre's revolving restaurant.

Downtown Vancouver

Now equipped to locate the nearby attractions, start from Cathedral Place where Hornby and Georgia Streets meet. Vancouver Art Gallery, the Canadian Craft Museum and the Sri Lankan Gem Museum are clustered here.

Vancouver Art Gallery is in the old courthouse building. Emily Carr's distinctive paintings of Indian families and forest scenes figure prominently, with work of other members of Canada's Group of Seven, as well as American and European exhibits.

Beautiful hand-crafted objects, both modern and from a bygone era, can be seen at the **Canadian Craft Museum** in Hornby Street. The museum covers a wide range of exquisite traditional and contemporary work.

A new museum with fascinating exhibits is the **Sri Lankan Gem Museum** at Cathedral Place. The precious and semiprecious stones come from around the world, not just Sri Lanka. Visitors can walk into the Jewel Box, where 9,000 pieces of agate form the floor, and the walls are of 24 carat gold.

From Cathedral Place you can walk northwards along Granville Street to **Canada Place**, site of the Vancouver Trade and Conference Centre. The white 'sails' that give the building a nautical air are reminiscent of the Sydney Opera House. Incorporated within the complex are the Pan Pacific Hotel, shops, restaurants and the CN IMAX Theatre. Take the free tour or wander around on your own with a map from the information centre. Cruise ships tie up at the Canada Place terminal. The **pier** provides a good view of Stanley Park across the water, and you can watch seaplanes taking off and landing.

Parks and Gardens

East of Granville Street, at 33rd Avenue and Cambie Street, is **Queen Elizabeth**

Park, 52ha (125 acres) of rose garden, sunken garden, rockeries, flower beds and an arboretum. Now a place of peace and pleasure, men once quarried rock here. In the **Bloedel Conservatory** exotic plants and free-flying tropical birds can be seen. The park has tennis, bowls and pitch and putt.

At Vancouver's western shore are the University of British Columbia **Botanical Gardens**, at Stadium Road off SW Marine Drive, with specimens from many countries as well as a garden of plants native to the province.

Stanley Park

Starting at the foot of West Georgia Street, Stanley Park constitutes 416ha (1,000 acres) of superb recreational facilities northwest of downtown Vancouver. A 10km (6-mile) seawall promenade provides great views for pedestrians and cyclists. Mature woodlands and an extensive freshwater lake attract black squirrels, many bird species and other wildlife – hard to believe that the city is only a few minutes' walk away. Bicycles can be

*T*he city by night. *Vancouver presents a glittering skyline after dark.*

hired, and there are summer rides by 26-seater horse-drawn wagon. Cars can follow the scenic drive. The park has a miniature railway operating from May to September, a free-admission zoo, a children's waterpark and a display of totem poles. Outdoor theatre performances take place in summer.

Also in Stanley Park is the **Public Aquarium** (open daily), one of the ten most visited attractions in Greater Vancouver. Go, and you'll see why. The Aquarium is one of the world's largest marine mammal research and habilitation centres. You marvel over different sea habitats and their occupants – otters, octopus and killer whales of the Pacific Northwest, beluga whales of Arctic Canada – jungle habitat in the Amazon, including a thunderstorm, the endangered coral reefs of Indonesia and, introduced in 1994, a heart-warming exhibit of Habitat Success Stories. Gifts you'd be proud to take home are displayed in the Clamshell Shop.

Chinatown

Chinatown beckons with its spicy smells of the Orient. Vancouver's Chinatown is a three-block enclave of restaurants and stores with enticing goods. Catch a 22 bus from Burrard Street or follow Pender Street to Chinatown, which covers an area from Carrall Street to Gore Street.

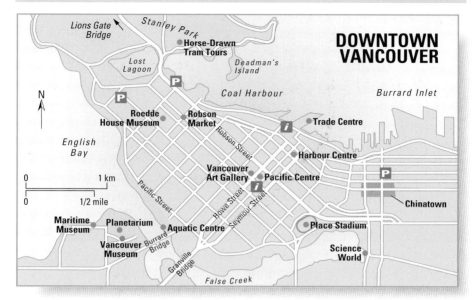

DOWNTOWN VANCOUVER

Lions Gate Bridge
Stanley Park
Horse-Drawn Tram Tours
Lost Lagoon
Deadman's Island
Coal Harbour
Burrard Inlet
N
Roedde House Museum
Robson Market
Robson Street
Trade Centre
English Bay
Harbour Centre
Vancouver Art Gallery
Pacific Centre
0 1 km
0 1/2 mile
Pacific Street
Howe Street
Seymour Street
Chinatown
Maritime Museum
Planetarium
Aquatic Centre
Place Stadium
Vancouver Museum
Burrard Bridge
Granville Bridge
Science World
False Creek

On the way, at Carrall Street, the **Dr Sun Yat-Sen Classical Chinese Garden** is a haven within high white walls. The garden is a place of great beauty and symbolism, graced with elegant buildings such as the Main Hall and Water Pavilion. Plants and shrubs are set among limestone rocks, pools and waterfalls, re-creating a classical garden of the Ming Dynasty (1368-1644). There's also a gift shop selling Oriental items.

Gentrified Gastown

Gastown is Chinatown's neighbour to the north. The SkyTrain station is Waterfront, by the terminus for the SeaBus ferry from the North Shore. Gastown's main thoroughfares are Water Street and Cordova Street. Take a **walking tour** and learn about Blood Alley Square, Gaoler's Mews and the feast and famine history of Gastown. For information dial 683-5650.

'Gassy' Jack Deighton's statue in Maple Tree Square presides over Gastown. In 1867 he set up a saloon and the town, named Gastown in his honour, ma-

terialized around him. In 1886 Gastown was destroyed by fire. Undaunted, Gassy built a new saloon. With the railway came prosperity, and Gastown developed westward. But by the 1930s decline had set in. Demolition squads were about to move in when, in 1971, Gastown was designated a heritage area. Instead of being pulled down, the Victorian buildings were renovated and the whole place was gentrified.

Today Gastown has cobbled streets, courtyards, passages, gas lamps, galleries, lounges, sidewalk cafés, restaurants, shops and boutiques selling Native art, gifts and superb, if pricey, Canadian-made clothes. The famous steam clock – the world's first – draws smiling admirers and whistles cheerfully every 15 minutes.

To the east of Gastown, approached from Hastings Street, is **Playland Family Fun Park**, with more than 35 rides, a petting zoo and live musical revues.

Museums

The University of British Columbia **Museum of Anthropology**, on NW Marine

Horsepower provides a pleasant method of sightseeing for tourists in Vancouver.

Drive, is in an award-winning building and has works in gold, silver, wood and black argillite in its Masterpiece Gallery. Art works and totem poles are shown in one of the world's finest collections of Northwest Coast Native art.

Vancouver Museum in Vanier Park, at the south end of Burrard Bridge, traces the city's history. Exhibits include a replica railcar of an 1897 Canadian Pacific Railway train.

Its neighbour is the **H R MacMillan Planetarium**. You see star shows with spectacular special effects, and astonishing laser imagery set to music – classical and rock.

Also in Vanier Park is the **Maritime Museum**, depicting the port's history, early explorations and the fishing industry. There are some fine old vessels afloat.

Take the SkyTrain to Main Street Station for **Science World**, a fascinating cross between a museum and laboratory where a changing programme of scientific challenges is introduced. Children can explore a beaver lodge, and there's plenty of scope for hands-on experimentation.

North Vancouver

In North Vancouver you can take the SkyRide at the end of Capilano Road and ascend to **Grouse Mountain** by enclosed gondola, travelling 1,138m (3,700ft) in 6 minutes. Vancouver's 'peak' resort offers formal or casual eating at the top, and splendid panoramic views. You can take in one of the hourly multimedia Theatre in the Sky shows covering Vancouver's history, or go for the action and try paragliding. Helicopter tours and horse-drawn sleigh-rides (from December to April) are also available. For children there's a well-equipped adventure playground. In summer, people hike on the slopes enjoyed by skiers day and night in winter.

The **Capilano Suspension Bridge** provides more excitement in North Vancouver. People have been walking 140m (450ft) across the slightly swaying footbridge 70m (230ft) above the Capilano River canyon for more than a century. This is not the original footbridge, but it is said to be the world's highest and longest.

Call at the **Trading Post** for a wonderful display of clothing and crafts, ornate canoe paddles, decoy ducks and geese and a host of goods in natural materials. A garden of totem poles has explanatory plaques and in summer you can see carvers at work. Across the bridge there are nature trails.

From the BC Rail Station in North Vancouver, the 1940s steam locomotive *Royal Hudson*, with restored coaches, sets off for the haul past rugged coastline scenery to **Squamish**, leaving at 10am and returning at 3.30pm. The Coastal Salish Indians originated Squamish. European settlers arrived in the 1880s, establishing a logging industry that continues to this day. Climbers are attracted to Squamish by a 762m (2,476ft) monolith known as Stawamus Chief. A good day trip is to go one way by rail and the other by water.

Greater Vancouver

The towns-within-a-city which make up Greater Vancouver all have spacious parks and a good selection of visitor attractions. **Burnaby** has lakes, forests and a sports stadium in its Central Park. It has the Simon Fraser University, designed with a hint of the Acropolis by Arthur Ericson, and a heritage village with people in 19th-century costume demonstrating work and

*T*he world's largest and highest of it's kind, the Capilano Suspension Bridge provides a thrilling crossing for pedestrians.

Vancouver has many delightful corners behind its modern skyline.

domestic skills as they used to be performed.

Vancouver International Airport is in **Richmond**, a community rich in recreational facilities. These include golf, free year-round tennis and 64km (40 miles) of riverside and ocean-view trails. The historic fishing village of **Steveston**, with its galleries and small speciality shops, is in Richmond.

The seaside villages of **Ambleside** and **Dundarave** are in West Vancouver (turn left after travelling north over the Lion's Gate Bridge). BC Ferries operate from **Horseshoe Bay**. The Canadian Museum of Flight and Transportation is in **Surrey**, an area of undulating farmland and family attractions. South of Surrey is **White Rock**, which has good beaches and a new beachfront promenade. Farther east is **Langley**, where Fort Langley National Historic Park has a full-scale replica of an early Hudson's Bay Trading Post.

Getting Around
Greater Vancouver

Vancouver-based companies provide transport by road, rail, water and air. Coachlines run sightseeing tours and regular services in the region. One of them,

Greyhound Lines Canada, has a daily scheduled service throughout British Columbia and across Canada. From April to October **Vancouver Trolley Company** runs narrated tours covering the main attractions. With a day pass you can get off and on again as you please.

BC Transit runs bus services within Greater Vancouver, the SkyTrain rapid transit system from downtown Vancouver to Surrey and SeaBus ferry services across Vancouver Harbour to North Vancouver.

BC Rail operates the Royal Hudson Steam Train excursion to Squamish and the Cariboo Dayliner to Whistler Resort (see p.89) and the province's interior, as well as scheduled services. A 2-day all-daylight ride through the Canadian Rockies – one of the world's most spectacular train trips – is operated by **Rocky Mountain Railtours**. **VIA Rail Canada** has services right across the country, with booked accommodation in cabins or sleeping cars.

British Columbia Ferry Corporation has regular year-round passenger ferry services on 24 routes, including Vancouver Island, the Gulf Islands, the Inside Passage and Queen Charlotte Islands. **Aquabus Ferry** covers the scenic False Creek, carrying people between downtown Vancouver and Granville Island Market and shops. **Harbour Ferries'** fleet includes the paddlewheeler Constitution. Group functions for up to 500 people can be arranged on board. **Royal Sealink Express** provides speedy passenger-only harbour-to-harbour trips between Vancouver and Victoria.

Tours

Sightseeing tours by helicopter are offered by several companies. A helicopter service between the downtown areas of Vancouver and Victoria is operated by **Helijet**. Seaplane and float plane charters are available for scenic flights, sightseeing, fishing, dinner or picnic trips. Numerous **yacht** and **boat** charters are available. **River-rafting trips** and **wilderness expeditions** with campground accommodation are run by Vancouver-based firms.

Shopping in Vancouver

The city has splendid shops and shopping centres. Fashionable Robson Street in downtown Vancouver has **Eaton's** and some good specialist stores, including **Duthie's** bookshop. The **Hudson's Bay Company** is on George and Seymour Streets. The **Sinclair Centre** is on West Hastings Street.

Communities away from the central core are well served. Vancouver's next-door neighbour, Burnaby, on the SkyTrain line, has **Metrotown**, a bright and jolly retail complex of nearly 400 shops and services. In West Vancouver you'll find shopping by the sea at **Park Royal**, with more than 200 stores, including a wide choice of one-of-a-kind shops.

Markets

Don't miss Vancouver's markets. **Robson Street Market** is open daily. Herbs and spices are offered in bulk, there's an exciting salad bar and buskers provide entertainment.

Granville Island Market is a short bus ride from the downtown area, or by small ferryboat to False Creek. The huge indoor

*O*ne of the irresistible stalls at Vancouver's huge Granville Island Market.

market, which was until a few years ago all warehouses, has irresistible stalls of fruit and vegetables, arts and crafts studios and shops, restaurants, cafés and seafood bars. The market is open daily in summer and from Tuesday to Sunday the rest of the year. At weekends it's as if the entire population of Vancouver has agreed to rendezvous there. There's an Arts Theatre on Granville Island, and a brewery where tours and tastings are available.

New Westminster Quay Public Market is on the shore of the Fraser River at the bottom of 8th Street on the SkyTrain line from downtown Vancouver. You can buy fresh produce, fish, meat, delicatessen fare and browse in specialist shops. Trip boats leave from the Quay in summer. The Samson V, the last steam-powered stern-wheeler on the Fraser River, is now a maritime museum, recalling the days when the river was the main highway.

Another popular waterfront market is at **Lonsdale Quay**, North Vancouver. If you

Just for Kids
In Cartwright Street on Granville Island, the **Kids Only Market** is open daily. About two dozen outlets sell toys, games, kites, puzzles, models, books, clothes, shoes and art supplies; in spite of the name, adults are admitted. A Jack and the Beanstalk sculpture, face painters, storytellers and musicians add to the carnival atmosphere.

go by SeaBus to the north side of Burrard Inlet – it takes about 12 minutes – you have the bonus of a great view of Grouse Mountain from the water. The alternative is to motor over the impressive Lion's Gate Bridge in Stanley Park. Fashions, choice coffees, seafood, an English-style pub, arts and crafts as well as farm produce are among the attractions, and an observation tower provides views of the Vancouver skyline and waterfront.

At weekends a **flea market** with hundreds of stalls opens at 8am in Terminal Avenue, near Main Street Station on the SkyTrain.

Sport and Leisure Activities

Spectator Sports

Hockey, baseball, football and soccer draw the crowds in Vancouver. The BC Lions **football** team plays at the BC Place Stadium in Surrey. It is a 60,000-seat facility with all-weather dome. Major concerts, shows and other events are held

*T*he imposing Lion's Gate Bridge crosses Burrard Inlet from Stanley Park to North Vancouver.

there. Vancouver Eighty Sixers **soccer** club is based at Douglas Road, Burnaby. Vancouver Canadians play professional **baseball** at Ontario Street, near Queen Elizabeth Park, and the Vancouver Canucks **hockey** club's home ground is at the Pacific Coliseum.

Evening Entertainment

Vancouver's performing arts venues cover professional dance presentations at the **Dance Centre** and a range of music, drama and light entertainment shows at theatres around the city and its environs.

Among these is the **Arts Club Theatre** at Granville Island and its neighbouring **Arts Club Review**. The Carousel theatre company and the New Play Centre use the **Waterfront** theatre, also at Granville Island, where new Canadian playwrights get exposure. Between September and June the **Vancouver Playhouse Theatre** stages six plays, both classic and contemporary. Innovative shows which embrace all the performing arts are presented at the **Vancouver East Cultural Centre**, Venables Street.

Vancouver Civic theatre stages a diversity of plays and shows at three downtown venues, the Vancouver Playhouse, the **Queen Elizabeth Theatre** and the **Orpheum**. The Queen Elizabeth, in Hamilton Street, is noted especially for its music recitals and operatic programmes. The internationally acclaimed Vancouver Symphony Orchestra offers programmes from classic to pop at the Orpheum Theatre.

Regular concerts take place at the University of British Columbia and the Simon Fraser University. Vancouver Opera stages major works, and Ballet British Columbia present world-class performances. Shakespeare plays are presented in Vanier Park by **Bard on the Beach** through July and August. During September original and traditional theatre shows are presented at the **Vancouver Fringe Festival**.

For stand-up comedy go to **Yuk Yuk's** on Pacific Boulevard – Wednesday is Pro-Am night – or the **Comedy Punchlines Theatre** in Gastown.

The **Hot Jazz Society** arranges live shows with low charges. **Filmgoers** are well catered for, with high-tech wrap-around, multi-storey screens and numerous cinemas.

Other nightlife options range from nightspots for dancing, cabaret shows, casinos and specialist entertainment provided by the **Soft Rock Supper Club** and other groups.

Southwestern British Columbia

The Sunshine Coast

The name given to this 150km (94-mile) stretch of coastline along Highway 101 by the Strait of Georgia acknowledges the mildness of its climate. Getting there from Vancouver involves a ferry trip across the Howe Sound from Horseshoe Bay to Langdale and another through the Jervis Inlet from Egmont to Saltery Bay. Pleasant seaside towns, fishing, sailing and canoeing locations, plus beaches and campgrounds are encountered on the way.

The last community of any size is **Powell River**, an old logging and pulpmill town noted for the quality of its salmon fishing and scuba diving. There's also a ferry service between Powell River and Vancouver Island. The highway comes to a stop at the small fishing community of **Lund**, at the mouth of Desolation Sound. To the north lies **Desolation**

Sound Marine Park. If you really want to get away from it all, this is the place. The park has no road or any kind of development, but for anglers, canoeists and marine biologists it's heaven.

East towards Harrison Hot Springs

There are **17 regional parks** within an hour's drive of Vancouver as well as many other places of interest and beauty in Southwestern BC. One way to experience several in one trip is to head east. You'll find attractions that are natural, like the Bridal Falls at Chilliwack, some that are man-made, like the Airtram at Hell's Gate, and some that are a combined effort. One of these is the massed blossoms, bonsai and aviaries of the **Minter Gardens**, off Exit 135 on the TransCanada Highway. Another is a daredevil rafting trip on the Fraser and Thompson Rivers.

Chilliwack is a family holiday centre 92km (57 miles) from Vancouver. Drive east a further 50km (30 miles) to reach **Hope**, where museum artefacts tell tales of the gold rush.

Much of Greater Vancouver lives off the Fraser Valley, where the fertile soil yields fruit and vegetables, and fine dairy cattle produce milk, butter and cheese. At **Hell's Gate** you can witness the power and the glory of the Fraser River forcing its way through a gorge 34m (110ft) wide and 180m (585ft) deep. Take the 25-seat **Airtram** 152m (494ft) into the canyon, where at peak levels the water rages through at 200 million gallons a minute. The Airtram operates from mid-April to mid-October. Or you can try the hands-on version and go with the flow as part of a 2- or 3-day **rafting trip**.

To visit the resort of **Harrison Hot Springs**, take Highway 7 east out of

Vancouver to the southern end of the Harrison Lake. Water from two piping hot springs, rich in sulphur and potash, is cooled and fed into two swimming pools. On the way to the springs you pass through **Mission**, with its own Westminster Abbey – a Benedictine monastery where you can 'meet' more than 400 storybook characters through displays on nature walks.

Okanagan Valley

British Columbia has two dozen vineyards and 22 of them are in the Okanagan Valley, where thousands of Canadians and Americans, as well as visitors from other continents, take their holidays. It is one of the leading fruit-growing areas in North America. From late June, when cherry-picking starts, to September and October, when the grapes are harvested, there are crops on sale at roadside stands. Winery tours and tastings are available year-round. The Okanagan Valley has more hours of sunshine every year than any other location in Canada.

There are seven provincial beach parks along Okanagan Lake. The smaller **Osoyoos Lake** to the south is said to be the warmest in the country. It is a popular swimming, windsurfing and waterskiing location. Several of the towns on Okanagan Lake – **Kelowna**, **Westbank**, Penticton – have water parks with slides. There are theme parks, too. Kelowna has the Flintstones' Bedrock City. Old MacDonald's Farm is at Westbank.

Highway 3, which accompanies the Similkameen River through much of the region, goes through the rainforests of **Manning Provincial Park** in Southwestern BC to a mini-desert in **Vaseux Lake Provincial Park**. Very little rain falls here, and there are prickly pear cactuses, horned lizards and burrowing owls in the park. Part of the highway is on the old Dewdney Trail, a mule track which was a gold rush trail in the 1880s.

At the **Nickel Plate Mountain**, just off Highway 3 at Hedley, there are the remains of mines which produced gold, silver and copper for many years until the 1950s. Rockhounds may find agate, jasper and opals in the hills above **Keremeos**, east of Hedley. A restored 1870 grist mill can also be visited here.

Whistler Resort

Two mountains, **Whistler and Blackcomb**, form the world-famous Whistler Resort, 120km (75 miles) **north** of Vancouver on the Sea to Sky Highway, as Highway 99 is known. Developed in the 1980s, it was soon receiving accolades as top ski resort in North America. Almost all the accommodation – and there are over 35,000 guest beds throughout the valley – are located within a few minutes of the slopes and ski lifts. Some of the condominiums have ski-in, ski-out slopeside access.

Blackcomb and Whistler Mountains have between them North America's highest vertical drop – almost a mile at 1,609m (5,280ft); the biggest expanse of terrain – 2,915ha (6,998 acres); and the most high-speed lifts – nine out of a system of 28. There are 200 trails and ten great alpine bowls which include three glaciers. The season usually lasts from November to the end of May.

Winter activities include mountain-top sightseeing and dining, alpine and cross-country skiing, heli-skiing, paragliding, snowshoeing, ice skating, snowmobiling and daytime and evening sleigh-rides with bonfires and singalongs. For tiny tots there are skiing and storytelling programmes.

The Yellowhead Highway

The Yellowhead Highway, which goes from Prince Rupert on Canada's west coast to Manitoba, has a branch, 'the low road', dropping south from Valemount to Kamloops, alongside the Thompson River and the railway. The story goes that the highway was named after an Iroquois Indian hunter and trapper who, in the early 1800s, guided European fur traders through a pass in the Rocky Mountains. What made him remarkable, apart from his skills as a guide, was his blond hair. The Europeans called him Tête Jaune, or Yellowhead.

Summer glacier skiing takes place on Blackcomb Mountain from mid-June to August. Other summer activities are hiking, mountain biking, hot-air ballooning, horse-riding, hayrides, golf, tennis, fishing and walking among wildflowers in alpine meadows. Guided nature tours are also available. Whistler Village has more than 70 shops, a museum, conference centre, restaurants, cafés, bars and nightspots.

High Country

The Fraser and Thompson Rivers merge at **Lytton**, which is close to the southern border of High Country on Highway 1, the TransCanada Highway. You can reach the region by this route or by the Coquihalla Highway (Highway 5) which goes through the Fraser Valley to **Kamloops**. High Country is remarkable for the wide variety of terrain – mountain ranges, undulating ranch country, lakes with beaches and steep, deep river gorges. There are hundreds of lakes and streams beloved by trout anglers.

In and Around Kamloops

A town of 6,900 people where the North and South Thompson Rivers meet, Kamloops has an economy based on forestry,

mining, cattle ranching and tourism. The town originated in 1812 as a fur-trading post, and developed with the arrival of the railway in the 1880s. A **water park** has waterslides, miniature railway rides and a children's zoo. Cruises by old-style sternwheeler – actually built less than 25 years ago – are available on the South Thompson River. Close to Kamloops over the Yellowhead Bridge is the **Sepwepemc Indian Reserve** – open to the public except at weekends – where a museum both outlines the history and beliefs of the Shuswap Indians.

*T*o *cool off in summer,*
fly by light aircraft to a glacier.

Northeast of Kamloops is **Shuswap Lake**, where you can cruise more than 1,000km (625 miles) of placid waterways by hired houseboat. There are sandy beaches and sheltered moorings, some in places accessible only by boat or float plane. The sternwheeler *Phoebe Ann* provides day trips on the lake setting out from **Sicamous**.

For three weeks in October masses of sockeye salmon can be clearly seen returning to their birthplace in a short length of the **Adams River** to lay their eggs in the gravel bed. There are lookout points for a good view of the fish, whose numbers peak at around 2 million every four years. Next peak: 1998.

High Country has seven national and provincial parks. **Mount Robson Provincial Park** has the highest mountain in the Canadian Rockies. At 3,954m (12,850ft) it gives its name to the park. **Wells Gray**

Provincial Park has some spectacular waterfalls, an extinct volcano and more than 100 springs. **Mount Revelstoke Park**, in the Columbia Mountain Range, has trails by permanent ice and through glorious meadows of wild flowers.

Southeastern British Columbia

British Columbia Rockies

Bounded by Yoho, Kootenay and Banff National Parks, the British Columbia Rockies attract millions of visitors, and there's plenty of space for them all. Unsoiled lakes edged with sandy beaches lie between towering mountains. Accommodation ranges from campgrounds to major hotel complexes and hot springs resorts. Skiers, golfers, canoeists, swimmers, horse-riders, anglers, hikers and

bikers, and those touring by car, are well catered for. Heritage towns, waterfalls, museums, even a Bavarian village, can be visited, and there's the constant splendour of the scenery.

Kimberley

The name may not sound Bavarian, but almost everything else about Kimberley is – the town is modelled on the region of southern Germany. Its downtown architecture is Bavarian, band concerts are given in the central square – Der Platz – and there's an outsize cuckoo clock in the town.

Cranbrook and Fort Steele

Cranbrook (population nearly 17,000) is the largest town in the region and has some beautiful 1920s railcars in its Railway Museum. **Fort Steele**, a 20-minute drive away, is an 1890s heritage town originating in the 1860s gold rush days. Buildings have been restored to the late Victorian period. You can tour the town by horse-drawn wagon, take a steam train ride, chat to costumed locals in shops and offices, and applaud the professional music hall shows at the Wild Horse theatre. Go any time of year to Fort Steele, but there's more happening in summer.

For hikers, the **Purcell Wilderness Conservancy** has 61km (38 miles) of trails through mountainous country.

Kootenay Country

Three mountain ranges, the Purcells in the east and the Selkirks and Monashees in

The Tantalus Glacier, above Squamish, is a short flight from Vancouver.

the west, embrace this scenically lovely region. At the southern end of the Kootenay Lake is **Creston**, where birdwatchers can see a variety of waterfowl in the vast marshes and lakes of the **Creston Valley Wildlife Interpretation Centre**, open from April to October. Osprey are seen here in good numbers, and you may spot a tiny calliope humming bird.

Moose, deer, bear, elk and bighorn sheep may also be sighted. Quantities of apples, pears and soft fruit testify to the fertility of the valley. Walleye, sturgeon and some of the world's largest rainbow trout are caught in the Upper and Lower Arrow Lakes and Kootenay Lake.

Kootenay Country is a highly popular tourism area, with attractions ranging from the fascinating to the bizarre. North of Creston is **Ainsworth Hot Springs**, where you can swim in hot mineral water just outside caves glistening with stalactites and stalagmites. The large main chamber in the Cody Caves is known as the Throne Room. The bizarre element is on Highway 3A at **Boswell**, where the building called the Glass House, open from May to October, is constructed from more than half a million embalming fluid bottles.

At **Rossland**, in the south of the region near the US border, summer visitors can take an underground gold mine tour. The town proclaims itself Mountain Bike Capital of Canada, having hosted international championships. Close by is **Trail**, a city founded on silver, which celebrates Silver City Days every May, and a short distance to the north is **Castlegar**, where, at Doukhobor Historic village, you can get a glimpse of Russian life as led by a group of pacifist immigrants in the early 20th century.

Nelson, on the west arm of Kootenay Lake, has one of the largest concentrations

93

of heritage homes and buildings in Canada – some 350. It has a strong art community whose work can be seen in local galleries. A restored trolley – Streetcar 23 – takes tourists along the waterfront.

Lake trips on the SS Moyie paddle-wheeler are available in summer at Kaslo, a pretty town amid mountain scenery. A 45-minute trip on the lake aboard another boat, between **Balfour**, south of Ainsworth Hot Springs, and **Kootenay Bay**, is described as the world's longest free ferry ride.

From **New Denver**, on Slocan Lake, near Valhalla Wilderness Park, you can explore what remains of the ghost town of Sandon, which enjoyed its heyday with the discovery of silver in the 1890s. Its museum tells the story of a fire which destroyed the town in 1901. **Sandon** was rebuilt, only to succumb 50 years later to horrendous flooding which flattened much of it.

Cariboo Chilcotin Coast Region

This is cowboy country. Visitors can stay at guest ranches from the Fraser River to the Coast Mountains, taking part in cattle round-ups and trail rides. Rodeos are held in several locations. The biggest is the **Williams Lake Stampede** in July. There are also ranch resorts, where the accent is on health, fitness and sport.

The region is bounded by the Cariboo wilderness terrain and the foothills of the Rockies in the east, and by the heavily wooded fiords of the Pacific Ocean in the west. Much of the central area is flattish, making it one of Canada's prime cross-country skiing areas.

The Cariboo gold rush days live on in museums and historical displays. Virtually all the communities on the **Cariboo Highway** – Highways 97 and 26 – owe their origin to the early gold rush years. Fortunes were made, but by the 1880s the gold had dwindled. One man who staked a claim and sank a shaft in the right place was Billy Barker, after whom **Barkerville** was named. Today Barkerville Historic Park enables visitors to catch the spirit of the gold rush days. Dozens of buildings, including the Theatre Royal with its 1870s-style shows, drinking saloons and the cemetery, are on view.

At **Quesnel**, the local museum depicts the mining days and other local industries. In July the townfolk celebrate the gold rush with various fun events, including a goldpan-throwing contest.

More than 8,000 lakes in the region provide fishing for the land-locked kokanee salmon and many other species.

Northern British Columbia

North By Northwest

The Great Outdoors is epitomized in this vast region which stretches as far north as the Yukon and has a border with Alaska. The landscape of pine and spruce forests, mountains, lakes and rushing rivers goes on for ever. Hiking, hunting, fishing, rafting, a strong Native culture, with skiing and snowmobiling in season, are some of the attractions. Wildlife is another. Motoring along the lonely road you may see moose, deer, black bear, fox and coyote.

Cities are few. **Prince George** is the biggest, with 70,000 people. Its origins lie in fur trading, with the Fraser and Nechako Rivers handy for transportation. The major industry now is forestry and its products. Formerly known as Fort George, Prince George has the **Fort George Regional Museum** in a park setting. A number of galleries and craft shops display the work of Indian and other artists.

At 'Ksan Indian Village, reconstructed in the 1970s at **Hazelton**, there are six longhouses and some modern totem pole carvings by the Gitksan Indians, including one top-hatted totem. Farther along the Yellowhead highway is **Kitwanga**. Just north of here, at **Kitwancool**, totems more than 100 years old can be seen.

Prince Rupert, about 720km (450 miles) from Prince George, is at the mouth of the Skeena River on British Columbia's northwest coast. The museum of Northern British Columbia at Prince Rupert covers 5,000 years of coastal history.

BC Ferries' *Queen of the North* sails from Prince Rupert through the Inside Passage to Port Hardy on Vancouver Island (see p.77). There is also a year-round ferry service to **Queen Charlotte Islands**, ancestral home of the Haida Indians, whose highly developed culture can be studied at archaeological sites. Beloved by naturalists, the islands form one of the richest biological areas in North America, with a tremendous variety of wildlife, including rare birds.

Peace River Country

Stretching from the Rocky Mountains' foothills in the west to the plains of Alberta in the east, this is a region of peaks and prairies. The John Hart Highway goes north from Prince George to **Dawson Creek**, where the **Mile Zero signpost** marks the start of the **Alaska Highway**. The road, winding through much dramatic scenery, did not exist until World War II,

when a transportation route was urgently needed, and the 2,436km (1,522-mile) highway to Fairbanks, Alaska, was built by Canada and the United States in nine months.

Dawson Creek, about 1,200km (750 miles) north of Vancouver, has fewer than 11,000 people, but it is the biggest community in the region which, until 100 years ago, was home to only a few Indians, fur trappers and seekers of gold.

Summers are short here. July temperatures average 21°C (70°F). Winters are cold: -13°C (8°F) is the January average. There is enough sunshine to ripen grain crops in the Peace River Valley.

Night entertainment in the region is provided by the **Aurora Borealis** – you have a great view from here.

Wildlife includes grizzly and black bears, wolves, elk, moose and caribou. The Stone sheep which you might come across by the highway in **Muncho Lake Provincial Park** are quite unique and can only be found in northern British Columbia.

The Land of Big Surprises

Alberta is by no means the largest of Canada's provinces – that distinction belongs to Quebec – but it certainly has a Big Country feel. This is the land of immense contrasts: of towering mountains, deep lakes, wide rivers and broad horizons; a land of great plains and vast skies. Here, Nature throws big surprises across the path of the modern traveller – herds of elk browsing solemnly through a city's streets, or the massive, green-tinged mystery of a glacier viewed from the highway. Here the Wild West meets the Space Age, and the high-tech cities of Calgary and Edmonton are surrounded by scenery the province's pioneers would recognize.

Some people regard Alberta as Canada's Texas. Like Texas, the province has an economy based largely on oil and beef cattle. With an area of 653,529sq km (255,285sq miles) it's a little smaller than America's largest state, but 2,238,000 Albertans have reason to feel a lot less crowded than 17 million Texans.

Native Americans have inhabited Alberta for some 15,000 years, but European settlement is a very recent development. The first white man to visit the region is

*A*lberta, Canada's Wild West, still willingly gives rein to pioneer spirit.

recorded as Anthony Henday, a fur trader who arrived in 1754. The city of Edmonton was established as a fur-trading post in 1795. Large-scale settlement began 90 years later when the transcontinental railway was completed to provide the first viable all-Canadian route from the Atlantic to the Pacific.

Pioneers from different parts of Europe, but especially from the British Isles, Scandinavia and the Ukraine, settled throughout Alberta, laying the foundations of an agricultural industry which is still a mainstay of the province's economy. Culturally, the different groups also put an indelible stamp on Alberta's social character.

The railway also brought a new industry: tourism. In creating a consumer demand for their new service, the rail barons were inspired by the year-round appeal and success of Switzerland's mountain resorts to build a number of grand hotels in awesome locations among the Rocky Mountains. Their investment continues to pay handsomely today, and the communities which sprang up around the hotels in Jasper, Lake Louise and Banff draw visitors from all parts of the globe.

Accompanied by neighbouring Saskatchewan, Alberta joined the Canadian Confederation in 1905. Edmonton gradually matured as the provincial capital, while 294km (184 miles) to the south Calgary established itself as Stampede City and centre of the oil industry, which began in 1914 with development of the Turner Valley fields.

Alberta's scenic variety is as big an attraction to the film industry as it is to the tourist. The province has played the part of part of the USA in many a big screen and television epic. A gigantic plateau some 670m (2,177ft) above sea level, its features include rugged mountains soaring more than 3,700m (12,000ft), flat prairies, badlands, lakes, streams and forests.

The Great Outdoors

Bordered by the American state of Montana, southern Alberta is an expansive, rolling prairie that merges into a parkland of valleys, wide ridges, lakes, streams and forest. The northern half of the province sees the prairie giving way to a wilderness of forests and lakes crossed by the Peace and Athabasca Rivers. Here in this rugged northern region is Wood Buffalo National Park, Canada's largest.

Extending along Alberta's western edge, straddling the border with British Columbia, the Canadian Rockies encompass the Columbia Icefield, a stunning feature covering more than 340sq km (130sq miles) and reaching a depth of 910m (2,950ft). The icefield is the birthplace of the Athabasca, Saskatchewan and Columbia glaciers, whose melted waters flow into three great river systems: the Mackenzie, which reaches north to the Arctic Ocean; the Saskatchewan, which flows into the Atlantic by way of Hudson Bay, and the Columbia, which plunges westward to the Pacific.

Big City Life

Despite its totally justified Great Outdoors image, Alberta does have an urban side to its character. Half a dozen of its cities have a population in excess of 20,000, while Edmonton and Calgary are among Canada's major cities. **Edmonton**, the provincial capital, has just over 618,000 souls spread over 700sq km (273sq miles). **Calgary** covers an area of 705sq km (275sq miles) and has a population of around 720,000. Both have international airports and are major gateways for foreign visitors. Friendly rivalry between the two cities has inspired each to create a first-rate centre for the performing arts, and both also combine an adventurous frontier spirit with a range of cultural attractions.

National and Provincial Parks

Five national parks and a national historic park lie within Alberta's borders. They are **Banff**, **Elk Island**, **Jasper**, **Waterton Lakes** and **Wood Buffalo National Parks** and **Rocky Mountain House National Historic Park**. Camping facilities are available in each location, with the exception of Rocky Mountain House, which has campgrounds nearby.

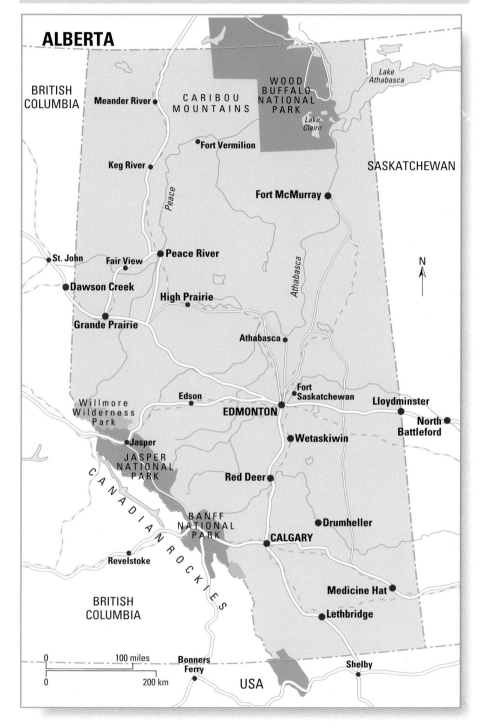

ALBERTA

BRITISH
COLUMBIA

Meander River

CARIBOU
MOUNTAINS

WOOD
BUFFALO
NATIONAL
PARK

Lake
Athabasca

Lake
Claire

Fort Vermilion

Keg River

SASKATCHEWAN

Fort McMurray

Peace

N

Athabasca

St. John

Fair View

Peace River

Dawson Creek

High Prairie

Grande Prairie

Athabasca

Willmore
Wilderness
Park

Edson

Fort
Saskatchewan

Lloydminster

EDMONTON

North
Battleford

Jasper

JASPER
NATIONAL
PARK

Wetaskiwin

Red Deer

CANADIAN ROCKIES

BANFF
NATIONAL
PARK

Drumheller

CALGARY

Revelstoke

BRITISH
COLUMBIA

Medicine Hat

Lethbridge

0   100 miles

0   200 km

Bonners
Ferry

Shelby

USA

Special Attractions

Alberta's 65 provincial parks and more than 200 recreation areas offer a wide range of outdoor recreational opportunities in a variety of settings. Most parks have such facilities as camping, picnicking, boating, canoeing, fishing and swimming, and interpretive hiking trails and programmes are also available at a number of locations.

Special attractions include **Dinosaur Provincial Park**, an extensive United Nations World Heritage site on the banks of the Red Deer River, and **Writing-on-Stone Provincial Park**, where ancient rock paintings and carvings can be seen in a remote location southeast of Lethbridge. **Peter Lougheed Provincial Park**, adjoining Banff National Park in Kananaskis Country, has attracted campers for more than 5,000 years – archaeologists have unearthed a number of ancient campsites throughout the area.

Lesser Slave Lake Provincial Park, 250km (156 miles) north of Edmonton, has bald eagles, wolves, grizzly bears – and white, sandy beaches for sunbathers. Just west of Grande Prairie, **Saskatoon Island Provincial Park** is a nesting area for the rare trumpeter swan, North America's largest native waterfowl.

Winter activities and special winter day events for families are provided in many provincial parks. **Cooking Lake-Blackfoot Recreation Area** and **Kananaskis Country** have extensive cross-country ski trails, and many other locations offer various levels of cross-country trails. Downhill skiing is available at **Strathcona Science** and **Cypress Hills Provincial Parks** and at **Nakiska and Fortress Mountain** in Kananaskis Country. Some parks and recreation areas have limited winter camping services, and lake access for ice-fishing is provided at many locations.

Essential Information

Recreation areas with toilets, picnic tables and garbage containers serve as convenient stopping points for travellers on Alberta's major highways. Many recreation areas also have overnight camping facilities, usually with pump water, fireplaces and firewood provided.

A wheelchair symbol on highway signs shows which provincial parks offer barrier-free access to buildings, facilities and campgrounds, though it is only fair to point out that the degree of access varies from site to site, and it may be best to contact a particular park for specific details.

Information on provincial parks is available from Alberta Tourism, Parks and Recreation, 10155-102 Street, Edmonton, Alberta T5J 4L6; tel. (403) 427-4321 or toll-free 1-800-661-8888.

Camping in National and Provincial Parks

Camping opportunities in the national parks range from trailer sites with full hook-up services to walk-in tenting sites. Most campgrounds have picnic tables, fireplaces, kitchen shelters and flush toilets. Interpretive programmes, with talks and demonstrations from park staff, are offered at most locations.

A daily fee is charged at all campgrounds, and a vehicle licence is required for campers taking a car into the parks. Canadian senior citizens can obtain a complimentary annual vehicle pass from gate attendants on producing proof of age and a vehicle registration.

Campgrounds within the national parks are operated on a first-come-first-served basis. Campsite reservations can be made at a number of provincial park campgrounds from 1 May to Labour Day. Although it is possible to make reservations right up to the day of arrival, as always the advice is to book well in advance.

Fees charged for overnight camping in provincial parks and recreation areas vary according to the standard of facilities and services available. Facilities range from small rustic campgrounds with few amenities to modern, well-developed sites with shower buildings and power and water hook-ups.

Albertan senior citizens receive a discount on camping fees. There is no charge for day use of areas.

Information on national park campgrounds can be obtained from Information Services, Canadian Parks Service, PO Box 2989, Station 'M', Calgary, Alberta T2P 3H8; tel. (403) 292-4401.

Forest Campgrounds

Adventurous campers and hikers will probably be attracted to the abundance of primitive campgrounds located in the dense public forest lands administered by the Alberta Forest Service. There are ten forests covering a total area of 388,500sq km (151,758sq miles), and the western area, where the recreation areas are located, is penetrated by the 1,017km (635-mile) Forestry Trunk Road, mostly gravel, and connected with municipal and provincial roads.

Forest campgrounds accessible to vehicles have from five to 100 pitches and are equipped with picnic tables, fire rings, hand water pumps, toilets, firewood and bear-proof garbage containers. There are no power, water or sewer hook-ups. For information contact: Alberta Forest Service, 6th Floor, 9920-108 Street, Edmonton, Alberta T5K 2C9; tel. (403) 427-3582.

Campgrounds with facilities for tents and recreational vehicles are also maintained by many municipalities and private owners throughout Alberta. Again, standards and fees vary, and amenities range from wilderness conditions to sophisticated resorts with showers, grocery stores and launderettes. Some private operators offer such activities as trail riding, boating, canoeing and mini-golf.

Trail of the Great Bear

Much of southwest Alberta – the prairie lands and foothills region of the Chinook Country, as well as The Rockies – forms a major part of the Trail of the Great Bear, an international tour traversing 3,350km (2,085 miles) of the United States and Canada.

Travelling existing roadways, the Trail links the world's first national park, Yellowstone, in northwest Wyoming, with Canada's first national parks, Banff and Jasper. In the US–Canada border region it passes through Waterton-Glacier, the world's first International Peace Park.

The Trail takes travellers through breathtaking national forests, wilderness areas and colourful local communities whose names are echoes ringing from the Old West. Dubbed the Serengeti of North America, the Trail presents rich wildlife-viewing opportunities for much of the year.

There is also a chance to learn about the heritage of Native Americans at reservations and at centres like the Head-Smashed-In Buffalo Jump, a World Heritage Site documenting the buffalo hunting culture of the Plains Indians at Fort Macleod, Alberta.

Information: Trail of the Great Bear, Box 142, Waterton Park, Alberta T0K 2M0, tel. (403) 859-2663; fax (403) 859-2139.

The Active Life

Alberta is unlikely to appeal to couch potatoes. Its towering peaks and wide open spaces throw out challenges to all those with an active sense of adventure. We've already looked at some of the opportunities for campers, but there's a wide range of pursuits covering many outdoor interests.

Cycling

Cycling is increasing in popularity, thanks to the appropriately named mountain bike, and there are some challenging rides, especially between Banff and Lake Louise. But two of a bike's main features – speed and silence – have thrown up a major problem in the wilderness: there's a chance that a bear won't know you're there until you're too close for comfort – yours as well as his. Or hers – some cyclists have found themselves in trouble by getting between a she-bear and her cubs. Punctured tyres and other breakdowns have also caused rescue problems in remote areas. As a result, cycling in national and provincial parks is often restricted to specified trails and fire roads.

Some tour operators now offer guided cycling tours, often covering rugged backcountry terrain, and bikes can also be rented from well-advertised centres in Banff and Jasper.

Climbing

It goes without saying that the Rocky Mountains make a powerful appeal to climbers, but only the most experienced would be advised to go without a guide. Climbing is a year-round activity, though it tails off during the between-season months of October and November. An eccentric but hardy sub-group of

The aptly-named mountain bike has introduced a new recreation to the Rockies.

mountaineers prefers ice-climbing – scaling glaciers, frozen waterfalls and slippery cliffs in the depth of winter.

Permits for climbing activities within the parks can be obtained from park wardens. Instruction and guided tours are conducted by Banff Alpine Guides, Box 1025, Banff, Alberta T0L 0C0, tel. (403) 762-2791; Canadian School of Mountaineering, Box 723, Canmore, Alberta T0L 0M0, tel. (403) 678-4134; and the Jasper Climbing School, Box 452, Jasper, Alberta T0E 1E0, tel. (403) 852-3964.

Fishing

With so much water around in the shape of streams, rivers and lakes, there's a wealth of opportunity for the rod and line brigade. Trout is the major quarry in the Rockies. Short-term and annual fishing licences are issued in both national and provincial parks, and can be obtained at sports stores and information centres. Information about licences and regulations is available from Fish and Wildlife Division, Department of Forestry, Lands and Wildlife, Main Floor, Bramalea Building, 9920-108 Street, Edmonton, Alberta T5K 2M4.

Hiking

Hikers will have no trouble breaking in their boots. There are some 2,900km (1,750 miles) of hiking trails in the Rockies, and another 1,000km (625 miles) around Jasper, to name just two areas. In southwest Alberta, about 185km (more than 115 miles) of trails in the Waterton Lakes National Park link up with another 1,200km in the adjoining Glacier National Park, across the US border in Montana.

The busiest trails are those in the Banff area, with scenic Lake Louise and Moraine Lake the most popular locations.

Jasper offers the greatest choice of trails, some leading deep into the backcountry, but some routes are so popular that a quota system is operated in high summer. Backpackers must obtain a permit from a park warden before striking out into the wild. This is chiefly in the interests of safety.

A recent development for the well-heeled is **heli-hiking**. Canadian Mountain Holidays, Box 1660, Banff, Alberta T0L 0C0, tel. (403) 762-7100, uses helicopters to lift clients high above the hoi-polloi for tours of 3 to 9 days with accommodation in remote but comfortable lodges. Most of the tours are fairly easy going – suitable for older or less able hikers – but there are routes attractive to hardier souls.

Horse-riding

The horse was made for the Wild West, as the Indians were quick to learn after the animal's introduction to North America by the Spanish Conquistadors. Horse-riding remains a popular pursuit, and although there are restrictions on many national park trails, there are still plenty of opportunities, especially in the Banff, Lake Louise and Jasper areas and in Kananaskis Country. There are lots of pack-trip operators, and numerous guest ranches in the province present another option for the saddle-struck.

Skiing

Some of the world's finest skiing is to be found in Alberta, which has six well-developed mountain ski resorts. Sunshine Village, Lake Louise and Ski Norquay-Banff are in Banff National Park; Marmot Basin is in Jasper National Park; and Kananaskis Country has Fortress Mountain and Nakiska, site of the alpine events during the 1988 Winter Olympics. The Canmore Nordic Centre, where the 1988

Olympic Nordic events took place, has a very extensive cross-country network, with 56km (36 miles) of trails, some of which are lit for night skiing. Many other ski areas and resorts are to be found within the province.

Helicopters, again, have brought a new dimension to the sport in recent years, and heli-skiing, offering the prospect of powder conditions in remote locations, is now featured by a growing number of tour operators, both locally and internationally. Heli-skiing is not cheap, but the demand is great enough to require reservations months ahead.

Watersports

Watersports – everything from gentle canoeing to frenzied whitewater rafting – abound during the summer months. In the Rockies, however, it's worth remembering that the lakes and rivers are fed by glaciers – which means that the water is going to be very cold if you're unfortunate enough to capsize. Make sure you wear the right gear.

Forever Boomtown – Edmonton

Canada's most northerly major city, Edmonton is mocked by its critics as a community of civil servants bolstered by the world's largest shopping mall. In fact, it's a thriving metropolis which seems to have gone from boom to boom since its foundation as a fur-trading post in 1795. The city straddles the North Saskatchewan River, and it was the river that brought those early traders to the Hudson's Bay Company post at Fort Edmonton. The trading post later became the major supply centre for the Canadian North.

More prosperity came in the late 1890s when thousands of fortune-hunters poured through the city, picking up supplies on their way to join the great Klondike Gold Rush. The city still celebrates the excitement of that time with its **Klondike Days**, a 10-day jamboree staged each July.

Edmonton became the capital of Alberta in 1905, and expanded further with the development of the transcontinental railway and the advent of commercial aviation in the 1920s. But the biggest boost to its status and fortune came in 1947 when oil was discovered at Leduc, 40km (25 miles) southwest of the city. The discovery led to the drilling of more than 10,000 wells and the building of dozens of refineries and supply depots. By the mid-1960s Edmonton was justifiably known as Canada's Oil Capital.

The city's wealth has been used wisely, creating an attractive environment which manages to be both relaxed and vibrant. It has green space galore, including Canada's longest stretch of urban parkland, the **Capital City Recreation Park**, a 27km (17-mile) greenbelt with hiking, jogging and cycle trails on both banks of the North Saskatchewan River. There is a skyline of exciting modern buildings. The city stages an acclaimed theatre festival each summer and is home of the renowned Alberta Ballet Company, as well as the second largest university in English-speaking Canada. It also has that mall – 800 shops and enough statistics to stock a supermarket's shelves.

Getting There

By air: Edmonton has two airports. **Edmonton International Airport** is 31km (19 miles) out of town, to the south, which means that taxi rides are an expensive undertaking. However, a cheaper option is the Grey Goose Airporter bus service which runs between the airport and downtown every 45 minutes. It also operates between the international airport and **Edmonton Municipal Airport**, mainly used by short-haul air services and located some 3km (2 miles) north of the city.

Getting Around

Getting around Edmonton is easy and cheap. A comprehensive **bus** service and the **LRT**, a light railway transit system, are run by Edmonton Transit (tel. 421-INFO). Travel on the LRT is free in the downtown area – between Churchill and Grandin stations – from 9am to 3pm weekdays and from 9am to 6pm on Saturdays. **Taxis**, which may be hailed, are relatively expensive.

Orientation

The downtown area is north of the river, between 95th and 109th Streets. The city is laid out on a conventional North American grid, with numbered streets running north and south and numbered avenues running east and west. Edmonton's main street is Jasper Avenue, located between 100 and 102 Avenues.

The best place to start a tour of the city – and pick up some maps and leaflets at the same time – is the **Edmonton Tourism Information Centre** at 97th Street and Jasper Avenue (tel. 496-8400 or 463-4667). The office, open daily, 8.30am to 4.30pm, from mid-May to September and weekdays only from September to mid-May, is part of the striking **Edmonton Convention Centre**, a tourist attraction in itself. Built into the bluffs above the North Saskatchewan River, with terraces looking out over the valley, it also houses Canada's Aviation Hall of Fame, with displays and model air-

craft, and the Canadian Country Music Hall of Honour.

Another good spot for orientation is **Vista 33**, the 33rd floor of the Alberta Government Telephone headquarters at 10020 100th Street. There are splendid views of the surrounding city and countryside, and the history of the telephone is told in the Telecommunications Museum located at Vista 33.

Around Edmonton

Also overlooking the river valley – at 100th Street and Jasper Avenue – is the château-style **Hotel Macdonald**, an Edmonton institution now restored to its old glory. It was built in 1915 by the Grand Trunk Railway Company and closed in 1983. In 1988 it was acquired by Canadian Pacific Hotels and Resorts and after extensive restoration opened again in 1991.

Canada's largest theatre complex, the **Citadel Theatre**, is to be found on the corner of 99th Street and 101A Avenue. A glass and wood structure, originally built in 1976 and enlarged in 1984, it houses five theatres, with rehearsal rooms, workshops, offices and a reference library. It also has an indoor garden complete with waterfall. The largest by far, the Citadel is nevertheless only one of 13 professional theatre companies in the city.

Another major entertainment centre is the **Northern Alberta Jubilee Auditorium** at the University of Alberta, 87 Avenue and 114th Street. This is where performances by the Edmonton Opera, the Edmonton Symphony Orchestra and the Alberta Ballet Company are staged.

For art lovers, a programme of exhibitions is held regularly at the **Edmonton Public Library**, just across the street from the Citadel, at 7 Sir Winston Churchill

Square, but the city's major art centre is the **Edmonton Art Gallery** at 2 Sir Winston Churchill Square. Alberta's largest gallery, it features works by the Group of Seven, and each year stages at least 30 exhibitions of Canadian and international works, both classical and contemporary.

A Step into the Past

The search for local history will take you away from downtown Edmonton. The **Provincial Museum of Alberta** is in a large building constructed in the grounds of the old Government House as a Centennial project in 1967. It has four main galleries illustrating the province's wildlife, geology, Indians, fur traders and pioneers. You will find the museum located at 12845 102 Avenue.

Looking farther back in time, the **Strathcona Archeological Centre** is on the site of an encampment where tools were made some 4,000 years ago. Visitors can join an interpreter on a guided boardwalk tour, watching archaeologists digging and sifting through topsoil in search of evidence of the activities of ancient craftsmen. The centre, which is closed during winter months, is on the city's eastern edge, located on the eastern bank of the North Saskatchewan River, between Highway 16 and 17th Street.

Southwest of the city centre, at Whitemud and Fox Drives, is **Fort Edmonton Park**, an outdoor museum featuring the period between 1885 and 1905 in three reconstructed streets. Among the buildings are a reconstruction of Fort Edmonton, the original offices of the Edmonton Bulletin – western Canada's first newspaper – a saloon, fire station and jail. The park also contains the John Janzen Nature Centre, with natural history exhibits and more than 4km (2¹/₂ miles) of trails. There are rides on horse-drawn wagons, a streetcar and stagecoach, and there is a farmers' market on Sundays during the summer.

There are more restored buildings in the **Old Strathcona Historic Area**, around 82 Avenue and 104th Street, south of the downtown area. This is the old commercial sector of the city, dating from around 1912, and the ambience of the Pioneer West is preserved in its wide streets and low-rise buildings.

Those who are happy wandering around stately homes will doubtless want to head for **Rutherford House**, the elegant Edwardian dwelling of Alberta's first premier, Alexander Rutherford. Costumed interpreters recreate daily household activities and re-enact important events in Rutherford's life as they lead guided tours. The house has a tea room and gift shop, and is located on the University of Alberta Campus at 11153 Saskatchewan Drive (tel. 427-3995 or 427-2022).

Other Attractions

Looking to the future, the **Edmonton Space and Science Centre** explores the universe in a stunning mix of high-tech exhibits, laser shows and big screen IMAX film shows. The centre is at 11211 142nd Street (tel. 451-7722). Rather more down-to-earth displays will be found at

Klondike Days
Gold fever hits Edmonton each July when the whole city goes a little crazy and relives its Klondike Days. In a 10-day festival of log-chopping, rock-lifting and raft-racing, Edmontonians strut around in Victorian finery, gambling (legally) in the Silver Slipper Saloon, singing (raucously) to the music of straw-hatted piano players, and panning (hopefully) for gold in a stream created for the occasion.

the **Muttart Conservatory** at 9626 96A
Street. Plants from different climatic en-
vironments are displayed in three glass
pyramids. A fourth pyramid features special floral displays.

Shopping

Edmonton is more likely to tug on the
purse strings than the heart strings, especially when you bear in mind that Alberta
has no provincial sales tax. The city's
principal shopping attraction, large
enough to gain a place in the Guinness
Book of Records, is the **West Edmonton
Mall**, at 87th Avenue and 170th Street.
With 800 shops, 11 leading department
stores, 110 restaurants and cafés and 19
cinemas it is almost a city in its own right.
Shoppers daunted by the thought of walking can rent an electric scooter, or take a
rickshaw ride. And with its own 18-hole
miniature golf course, ice-skating rink,
two indoor lakes (one offering submarine
rides), a dolphin show, casino and luxury

*West Edmonton Mall
has 500 shops and a range of
amenities, entertainments and
recreational activities.*

resort hotel, the mall rivals the amenities
of a Florida theme park.

Downtown, the **Eaton Centre**, **Edmonton Centre** and **Manulife Place**
muster a mere 325 stores between them,
but they and such department stores as
The Bay, Woodwards and Eaton's are all
connected by tunnels and bridges. A lively
area of indoor and outdoor stalls and street
entertainers is the **Boardwalk Market**, at
102nd Avenue and 103rd Street, and another charming marketplace is to be found
in the former Edwardian post office in
Strathcona Square, in the Old Strathcona
Historic Area.

Excursions from Edmonton

About 25km (16 miles) northeast of Edmonton, **Fort Saskatchewan** has a museum in which the story of the region is told from 1754 when the Hudson's Bay fur trader Anthony Henday first explored into Blackfoot country. Restored buildings include a red-brick courthouse, a school and a two-storey log farmhouse.

Just outside the park's eastern gate, on Highway 16, the **Ukrainian Cultural Heritage Village** is a 'settlement' of restored buildings moved from sites in surrounding communities. These include a church, community hall, hardware store, farmsteads, railway station, blacksmith's shop and a school. Costumed characters recreate turn-of-the century pioneer life, and a farmers' market is held at weekends.

Animals from other continents can be viewed in open-air settings at **Polar Park**, a 6sq km (2sq mile) safari park at Cooking Lake, 18km (11 miles) south on Highway 824, a side road off the Yellowhead Highway west of Elk Island. Among 100 species are Siberian tigers, cheetahs, lions and rhinoceroses, as well as a pair of mountain gorillas.

Elk Island National Park

Easily reached in a day's outing from Edmonton, a mere 50km (31 miles) to the west, Elk Island National Park is unusual in that it is surrounded by a 2m (6ft) fence, but with an area of more than 190sq km (75sq miles) nobody will feel hemmed in. The fence is there to protect endangered species from wolves and other predators.

Among the threatened mammals and birds that inhabit the park are plains and wood bison, elk, of course, and trumpeter swans. An island surrounded by prairie, rather than water, the park got its name from the large herds of elk which once roamed the area, and had been all but exterminated by hunters when the refuge was set aside in 1906.

A herd of about 450 plains bison now roams north of Highway 16 – the Yellowhead Highway – which passes through the park, and 200 or so wood bison are to be found to the south.

Elk Island's hilly terrain – it is situated in the northern section of the Beaver Hills – is in contrast to the surrounding plains. Here, there are stands of spruce and poplar, birch and trembling aspen, and in summer months wild flowers grow in profusion. The park's lakes and ponds attract more than 200 species of waterfowl, while great horned owls and black-capped chickadees are to be found among the

Calgary, where the average age is 30, rises dramatically from the surrounding prairie.

Canada's Cowtown – Calgary

Calgary got its name from a Gaelic word describing a farmstead located near calm, clear water. But the image almost certain to spring into most people's minds when they hear the word is of chuckwagons careering around the track in a noisy, dusty, crazy race during the city's annual **Stampede**. And you'd better spell that with a capital 'S', pardner!

trees. Other wildlife include beavers, coyotes, moose and mule deer.

The park serves as a recreation area, as well as a wildlife refuge. There is a beach at Astotin Lake, and there are campgrounds and a nine-hole golf course as well as facilities for canoeing, sailing, swimming and picnicking. In winter the park is a firm favourite with both skiers and snowshoers.

Elk Island can be fitted into a compact and interesting round trip from Edmonton, using Highways 15, 831 and 16.

The Stampede takes up only 10 days of each year, in the first half of July, but Calgary trades heavily on its Cowtown image for the remaining 355. Historically, it's justified, for the city's early development depended largely on ranching and the meat industry. The rich pasturelands of the prairies were ideal for rearing beef cattle, and the coming of the transcontinental railway helped Calgary to become the focal point of Canadian meat production.

Meat is no longer the city's main economic preoccupation. Major discoveries of oil and gas in Alberta since 1914 have placed energy in the premier position, and some 83 percent of Canadian oil and gas producers and 60 percent of coal companies now have their headquarters in the city. Nevertheless, agricultural commodities – wheat and small grains, as well as cattle – remain important and Calgary is the marketing, service and processing centre for a vast agricultural region.

Modern Calgary is a high-tech community, with expanding manufacturing industries, especially in computers and telecommunications, and a rapidly growing financial services sector. Tourism is the city's fastest growing industry, contributing well over $50 million a year in taxes and employing some 50,000 Calgarians in 2,400 tourism-related businesses.

The largest city on the TransCanada Highway, Calgary rises like a pilgrim's vision from the foothills of southwestern Alberta. It stands at the junction of the Bow and Elbow Rivers, lots of glass and glitter at an altitude of 1,048m (3,406ft) above sea level. To the west is the stunning backdrop of the Canadian Rockies, 100km (62 miles) away, but looking much nearer in the clean, clear air. This is a young city, where the average age is a stripling 30.

Getting There

By air: **Calgary International Airport** is 12km (7 miles) northeast of the city centre – about 25 minutes by road. An

---

The Stampede – a Runaway Success

Calgary's tourism statistics would make Guy Weadick throw his hat in the air. He was the man who first saw Calgary as home of the world's biggest frontier days show. Already established as a ranching centre, the city staged its first agricultural fair in 1886, and it was so successful that three years later the organizers bought the land now known as Stampede Park. Then came a slump in ranching and people begin to look around for something else to keep the dollars rolling in.

Guy Weadick, an itinerant trick-roper, came up with the idea of a super rodeo, and persuaded four local cattlemen to stump up $100,000 to get the show on the road. The first show, staged in September 1912, was a huge success. In 1923 the Stampede rodeo combined with the agricultural fair, and the first-ever competitive chuckwagon races were held. Now known as the Calgary Exhibition and Stampede, affectionately abbreviated as 'the CE & S', it went on growing in size and popularity.

The Stampede gets off to a spectacular start each year with a grand parade of bands, floats, cowboys, Indians and Mounted Police. Each afternoon is taken up with competitions in bronco-riding, calf-roping, steer wrestling and bull riding. Each evening the chuckwagon teams roll out to compete for the championship title and $337,000 prize money in the ever-exciting Rangeland Derby. As well as the competitions, there are singers, dancers and musicians, and each evening closes with a breathtaking fireworks display.

The Stampede takes place at Stampede Park, a few blocks south of downtown, but you don't have to move far to capture the spirit. Everyone goes western crazy, and big hats, boots and spurs are the order of the day even for bank clerks. There's dancing in the streets and free breakfasts of pancakes and syrup are served at the roadside.

Airporter bus departs for downtown hotels on the hour and half hour between 6.30am and 11.30pm. A taxi ride downtown costs about three times as much as the bus fare.

Getting Around

The city is covered by a comprehensive **bus** service, and a light rail transit system – the **C-Train** or LRT – has lines running northeast (Whitehorn), northwest (Brentwood) and south (Anderson) from downtown. One fare covers a trip of any length on the C-Train and a book of ten tickets saves around 20 percent. An even better bargain is the CT **Day Pass**, offering unlimited travel for about a third of the cost of ten tickets. Travel on the 7th Avenue line in the downtown shopping district is free.

Five major **taxi** companies operate in the city, charging moderate fares. Those driving their own cars will encounter the usual big city problem for motorists: parking. However, visitors can obtain a free 3-day **Visitor Car Park permit** for use on street level meters. The permits are available between June and September from the Calgary Convention and Visitors Bureau, 237 8th Avenue SE (tel. 263-8510 or 800-661-1678).

Orientation

Calgary's grid pattern can be maddening for strangers. Numbered streets run north–south in both directions from Centre Street, and numbered avenues east–west in both directions from Centre Avenue. In theory, it should be easy to know exactly where you are. In fact, it's easy for a lost driver to confuse avenues with streets and get southwests and northeasts all mixed up with northwests and southeasts. Try to study the street map before you set out on a journey – and stay cool!

Many of the city's attractions are to be found within walking distance in the downtown area, and here at least everything falls sensibly into place, thanks largely to **Plus 15**, a neat planning idea in which most of the buildings are connected by enclosed walkways 4.5m (15ft) above street level.

In any event, if you do get lost, either on foot or in the car, just ask. Calgarians are a friendly, helpful people.

Downtown Calgary

As with Edmonton, you can take an orientation look at the city from a high building. In this case it's the **Calgary Tower**, most prominent part of the Tower Centre at 9th Avenue and Centre Street S. It is 190m (626ft) high and topped with the Olympic Flame, recalling the 1988 Winter Olympics and lit on special occasions. There is a staircase of 762 steps, but an elevator will take you to the observation deck in no time. Right at the top is the Panorama Dining Room, a revolving restaurant serving breakfast, lunch and dinner. Tower Centre has a number of restaurants, as well as shops, banks, a post office and Calgary Visitor Information Centre.

Cross 9th Avenue SE on the Plus 15 walkway to reach the **Glenbow Museum** (free admission Saturdays), which houses archives and a library as well as exhibition space for art shows and historical displays. The museum's permanent exhibition features the history of Western Canada, native history and culture, European exploration and settlement, the Northwest Mounted Police and the building of the Canadian Pacific Railway. There is an extensive military collection. The museum is at 130 9th Avenue SE (tel. 264-8300).

Another Plus 15 walkway leads across 1st Street SE to the **Calgary Centre for**

Performing Arts at 205 8th Avenue SE. Opened in 1985 and recycled from two older buildings, the centre encompasses three theatres, a 1,800-seat concert hall (home of the Calgary Philharmonic Orchestra) and a shopping mall. Conducted tours of the centre take place at 11am, Monday to Saturday. Free organ recitals are performed at noon on Tuesdays throughout July and August.

The area surrounding the Performing Arts Centre is the beating heart of downtown Calgary. **Olympic Plaza**, created for medal presentations during the 1988 Winter Olympics, is the scene of concerts and special events throughout the year, and is a popular lunchtime spot for city office workers. The huge mirror-building standing across Macleod Trail from Olympic Plaza is the **Municipal Building**, where many of them work.

Toronto Dominion Square, at the heart of the downtown shopping area between 2nd and 3rd Streets and 7th and 8th Avenues, is topped by the 1ha (2-acre) **Devonian Gardens**, an indoor cornucopia of 20,000 plants, fountains, waterfalls and reflecting pools. There are musical performances and art exhibitions, and a playground is available for children. Beneath the gardens, which are reached by a glass-walled elevator, is a complex of more than 100 shops. Other shopping centres, including the Eaton Centre, Stephen Avenue Mall, Scotia Centre, and Penny Lane, are nearby. Remember, there's no charge for travelling on the C-Train 7th Avenue Downtown line.

Beyond Downtown

Moving away from downtown, **Fort Calgary**, where the city was born, is on 9th Avenue SE, at the confluence of the Bow and Elbow Rivers. This was where the Northwest Mounted Police established a post in 1875 after trouble between Indians and whiskey traders. The fort itself is now no more than an outline of foundations marked by logs, but the area's history is graphically told in the excellent interpretive centre. The Fort can be reached by bus numbers 1 (Forest Lawn) or 14 (East Calgary) from 7th Avenue.

Across the 9th Avenue Bridge, on the opposite bank of the Elbow River, is the **Deane House**, built in 1906 as a residence for the post commander. There are conducted tours, and a tea room serves lunch and afternoon tea daily from 11am to 5pm with brunch served at weekends between 11am and 2pm. Murder mystery nights are usually organized in the house on Fridays (tel. 269-7747).

Calgary Zoo and Prehistoric Park

From downtown, the C-Train's Whitehorn line will take you to Calgary Zoo and Prehistoric Park on St George's Island in the Bow River. Established in 1920, and one of the world's major zoos, it houses about 1,500 animals in natural settings, including rare and endangered species. There are complexes for polar bears, reptiles and amphibians, primates and exotic birds, and special sections for nocturnal creatures and for the wildlife of Australia and North America. Aspen Woodlands, which opened in 1992, is the first phase of a presentation area dealing with the Canadian Wilds. Young visitors can do a little petting in the Children's Zoo, and the Prehistoric Park recreates the world of dinosaurs.

Stampede Park

Where the famous Exhibition and Stampede take place each July, is south of downtown. You can get there on the

Anderson C-Train to Victoria Park/Stampede or Stampede/Erlton stations. When they are not being used in connection with the big event, the Roundup Centre, Big Four Building and Agriculture Building host trade shows and exhibitions. Concerts and Calgary Flames hockey games are staged in the distinctive Saddledome which may be toured on non-event days.

The **Grain Academy**, an offbeat museum located in the Roundup Centre, tells the story of grains and their contribution to daily life. Built as a Centennial gift to Calgary from the Alberta Wheat Pool, the academy has a working model grain elevator, a replica country elevator office of the 1940s, a display of historical farm artefacts, and a mini-cinema in which the audience sit on tractor seats. An extensive model railway demonstrates how grain is moved from the prairies, through the Rockies, to the ocean shipping terminal at Vancouver. Entry to the Grain Academy (tel. 263-4594) is free.

Heritage Park Historical Village

Southwest of the city, on the shores of Glenmore Reservoir, more than 100 buildings have been assembled to recreate a pre-1915 village of Western Canada. Visitors to Heritage Park Historical Village can board a steam train, take a paddle wheeler voyage, and ride horse-drawn buses to visit the only antique fairground in North America and the different 'neighbourhoods', where costumed guides tell the story of pioneer and settler life in Victorian and Edwardian times. To reach the village, take the Anderson C-Train to Heritage station, then transfer to Bus 20 (Northmount).

Calgary Museums

Military buffs will be in their glory on the Crowchild Trail in this southwest corner of the city. Just north of the Heritage Park is the **Museum of the Regiments**, the largest military museum in Western Canada. Different sections pay tribute to Lord Strathcona's Horse (Royal Canadians), the Calgary Highlanders, Princess Patricia's Canadian Light Infantry, The King's Own Calgary Regiment and the Royal Canadian Corps of Signals. Bus 13 advances on the museum from The Bay on 8th Avenue SW, but the journey involves a march of five blocks north from 50th Avenue.

The **Naval Museum of Alberta** is at 1820 24th Street (Bus 2 Killarney from 7th Avenue and 8th Street SW). It tells the story of the Royal Canadian Navy and the Royal Canadian Naval Volunteer Reserve from 1910 and has real fighter aircraft, including the Supermarine Seafire, the Hawker Sea Fury and the McDonnell F2H3 Banshee. There are displays of uniforms, paintings, model ships, flags and photographs.

Those interested in aviation history might prefer to head northeast from downtown, towards the airport. Here, at 64 McTavish Place NE, off McKnight Boulevard, is the **Aero Space Museum of Calgary**, which traces Western Canada's aviation heritage from the 1913 flight of the *West Wind*, one of Calgary's first aircraft, to the sleek jetliners of today. It features a collection of aircraft, aeronautical engines and artefacts. To get there, take the C-Train to Whitehorn, then transfer to Bus 57.

Film fans who find themselves in this northeast corner of Calgary will certainly want to visit the **Museum of Movie Art,** where some 4,000 cinema posters from the 1920s to the present day are displayed. Among the exhibits are giant billboard posters advertising such classics as *Gone With the Wind*. There is also a shop stocked with 10,000 different film and film star posters and stills, with prices ranging from $2 to $1,000. The museum is at 9, 3600-21st Street; to get there take the Whitehorn C-Train to Barlow/Max Bell station then Bus 33 (Vista Heights/Mayland).

A one-block walk from the 10th Street SW station, on the C-Train's 7th Avenue line, takes you to the **Alberta Science Centre and Planetarium** at 701 11th Street SW. Lots of fun to be had here, with 35 hands-on exhibits featuring laser beams, holograms, frozen shadows and other Space Age wonders, and walkabouts by robotic insects, reptiles and dinosaurs. The planetarium has a 360-degree theatre in which Star Shows are presented.

Olympic Park

Calgary's high spot, literally, is the 90m (290ft) ski jump tower in the Canada Olympic Park. The 115ha (275-acre) park was the site of the 1988 Winter Olympic Games, but is now a year-round attraction, where visitors can watch world-class athletes in training – and experience bobsleighing and ski jumping for themselves in authentic simulators, or take a real luge ride on the Olympic track at speeds up to 40kph (25mph). There are tours of the ski jump tower, and the Olympic Hall of Fame has three floors of exhibits, videos and films featuring highlights of Calgary's Winter Olympics. There are separate charges for the Hall of Fame, ski tower and rides. The park's Naturbahn Teahouse has become a fashionable Sunday brunch spot and reservations are a must (tel. 247-5465).

The Olympic Park is on Highway 1 West, a 10-minute drive from downtown.

Sporting Activities in and around Calgary

From July to November, spectator sports fans can watch the Calgary Stampeders

playing their **Canadian Football League** home games in McMahon Stadium, at 2225 Macleod Trail SW (tel. 289-0205), while the Calgary Flames can be seen fulfilling their **National Hockey League** fixtures at the Olympic Saddledome in Stampede Park from October to April. There's **horse-racing** year-round – except March – in Stampede Park, and world-class **show-jumping** events are held from June to September at Spruce Meadows, southwest of the city boundary on Marquis of Lorne Trail. Training and breeding facilities are maintained at Spruce Meadows, which is open daily. Visitors are welcome to come along free of charge on non-event days.

For those who like to do their own thing, Calgary has some 200km (105 miles) of **jogging** paths and **cycle** trails winding through city parks and along the banks of the Bow and Elbow Rivers. **Golfers** have a choice of more than 40 courses in the greater Calgary area, ranging from spectacular mountain terrain to winding, riverside undulations. There are half a dozen municipal courses. For health and fitness freaks there are three **water parks** with wave pools, slides, gymnasiums and training facilities. The parks are as follows: Family Leisure Centre, 11150 Bonaventure Drive NE (tel. 278-7542); Southland Leisure Centre, 2000 Southland Drive SW (tel. 251-3505); and Village Square Leisure Centre, 2623 56th Street NE (tel. 280-9714). Family and Southland centres both have **racquetball** and **squash** courts.

*W*inter games are a year-round activity in Calgary's Olympic Park.

Entertainment

Family fun: for a family outing, **Calaway Park**, the largest outdoor amusement park in Western Canada, has 19 white-knuckle rides, including the double-loop roller-coaster, three live musical shows daily, a huge maze, 17 cafés and restaurants, mini-golf, a driving range and a petting farm. There is an adjoining RV park and campground. Calaway Park is 10km (6 miles) west on the TransCanada Highway (tel. 240-3822, or 240-3824 for recorded information).

Music, dance and **theatre**: Calgary offers a wide spectrum of entertainment when the sun goes down. In addition to the Centre for the Performing Arts, concerts ranging from classical music, opera, ballet and rock are staged at the **Southern Alberta Jubilee Auditorium** at 1415 14th Avenue NE (tel. 297-8000). Known affectionately as 'the Jube', it houses a 2,713-seat auditorium and the Dr Betty Mitchell Theatre, seating 231, as well as meeting and banquet rooms. Another concert venue is the **University of Calgary Theatres**, 2500 University Drive NW (tel. 220-4900), a complex which includes the Reeve Theatre where productions of contemporary and classical drama are staged. **The Pumphouse Theatre** at 2140 9th Avenue SW (tel. 263-0079) features the work of more than 20 local companies.

Not surprisingly, **Country and Western** music is big. Here, the top spots are the **Longhorn Dance Hall**, 9631 Macleod Trail S (tel. 258-0528), **Ranchman's,** 9615 Macleod Trail S (tel. 253-1100) and the **Rocking Horse Saloon**, 24-7400 Macleod Trail S (tel. 255-4646).

For jazz try the **Café Calabash** at 107 10A Street NW (tel. 270-2266). **Sparky's Live**, 1006 11th Avenue SW (tel. 244-

4888) offers blues, folk, rock and big-band sounds.

Comedy: for comedy you can choose between **Yuk Yuk's**, at the Blackfoot Inn, 5940 Blackfoot Trail (tel. 258-2028), or **Jester's**, 239 10th Avenue SE (tel. 269-6669). Top of the bars and clubs circuit – at least, it is if you enjoy audience participation – is the **Loose Moose**, 2003 McKnight Boulevard NE (tel. 291-5682), but there are many pubs catering for all tastes.

Casinos: gamblers have a choice of four casinos: **Cash Casino Place**, 4040B Blackfoot Trail SE (tel. 287-1635), **Frontier Casino** in the Big Four Building in Stampede Park (tel. 261-0101), the **River Park Casino**, 1919 Macleod Trail S (tel. 269-6761), and the **Tower Casino** in the Tower Centre downtown (tel. 266-7171).

The Dinosaur Tour

Drumheller

The bridge that carries Highway 9 across the Red Deer River at Drumheller is guarded by a dinosaur – a Tyrannosaurus Rex, if you want to be precise, although the craftsman who made it took a few liberties in the interests of tourism and souvenir photographs.

Dinosaurs mean a lot to Drumheller. In fact, if it wasn't for the prehistoric monsters the place would probably be no more than just another coal-mining town in the middle of nowhere. As it happens, it is home to one of the world's largest fossil museums and the centre of a thriving and unusual branch of tourism.

It all began in 1884 when Dr Joseph Tyrrell, a geologist and explorer, found the petrified head of a fierce beast named Albertosauros – a discovery which revealed the 'Valley of the Dinosaurs', a vast prehistoric graveyard. Whole skeletons of dinosaurs have been uncovered there, and more than 40 of them have been reconstructed in the **Royal Tyrrell Museum of Palaeontology** in Dinosaur Provincial Park, 6km (4 miles) west of Drumheller (see p.117).

The museum has 800 fossils from throughout the world, as well as its local giants, and its exhibits trace the development of animal life over 3.5 billion years. There are interactive exhibits, computer simulations and a prehistoric garden. Interpretive programmes are available, and there are guided tours in which you can see fossil formations in natural settings.

Drumheller is about 130km (81 miles) northeast of Calgary, and you get there by way of the TransCanada Highway and Highway 9. At first, the terrain is flat, open prairie, then the badlands start – a stark lunar landscape of windswept hoodoos – eroded pillars of rock – rugged bluffs and gullies. This is dinosaur country, though it didn't look like this in their day. Then it was an area of sub-tropical marshlands. Everything changed when enormous subterranean pressures created the Rockies 70 million years ago.

Not surprisingly, Drumheller has gone a bit dinosaur daft. There's the **Drumheller Dinosaur and Fossil Museum** at 335 1st Street East and the **Drumheller Prehistoric Park**, where children can play among life-size dinosaur reproductions and everyone can buy fossils, petrified wood, ammonite souvenirs and bits of dinosaur bone at Ollie's Rock and Fossil Shop. The park is 1km (half a mile) along the South Dinosaur Trail and is signposted from the city centre, where there are other fossil shops.

The Dinosaur Trail

The Dinosaur Trail is a 55km (35-mile) loop that takes you west of Drumheller on the north side of the Red Deer River into Midland Provincial Park and the Valley of the Dinosaurs. The provincial park was once the site of the first two mines in the valley. An interpretive centre is housed in a former mine office, and there are picnic tables and walking trails.

About 18km (11 miles) west of the Royal Tyrrell, on the North Dinosaur Trail, **Horsethief Canyon** presents a spectacular view of the badlands valley and its layered canyon walls. It got its name in the early 1900s when thieves and their stolen horses hid among the hills and bends.

The Bleriot Ferry transports vehicles across the Red Deer River to the southern section of the Dinosaur Trail. Operated by cables and pulleys, the ferry was established in 1913 and is one of the oldest of its kind still working in Alberta. There were once 13 like it on the Red Deer River.

The route back to Drumheller overlooks **Horseshoe Canyon**, 200ha (480 acres) of badlands, 1.6km (1 mile) across. The canyon floor, which can be reached by footpaths, is strewn with dinosaur bones, and petrified shells and wood.

Dinosaur Provincial Park

Continuing the dinosaur theme, it's worth travelling a further 150km (93 miles) to visit Dinosaur Provincial Park, a 2,650ha (15,000-acre) World Heritage Site, about 48km (30 miles) northeast of the town of **Brooks**. You get there from Drumheller by taking Highway 56 south, then east on Highway 1, or by driving north on Highway 56 from Drumheller then east on Highway 9 and south on Highway 36.

Covering areas of badlands and prairie, the park stretches some 27km (17 miles) along the banks of the Red Deer River and is one of the most extensive dinosaur graveyards in the world.

Much damage was done in the first half of the 20th century by people digging up bones and fossils to sell to museums or use as garden ornaments. As a safeguard it was established as a provincial park in 1955 and later became a World Heritage Site. Now, the fossilized plants, fish, shellfish, turtles, crocodiles and dinosaurs are protected from vandalism in a restricted zone.

The Royal Tyrrell Museum of Palaeontology has a field station in the park where scale models of dinosaurs and other exhibits are displayed.

During the summer months, visitors can join bus tours or take conducted hikes which will take them into otherwise restricted areas. The park has excellent camping and RV facilities, but space is limited, so make an early reservation (tel. 378-4342) if you plan to stay overnight.

Medicine Hat and Southeast Alberta

The province's fifth largest city – and the only community of any substance in eastern Alberta – **Medicine Hat** lies about 112km (70 miles) southeast of Brooks along the TransCanada Highway, and only 40km (25 miles) from the border with Saskatchewan. It's a busy but attractive place with a population of around 43,000, and it occupies a scenic position astride the winding South Saskatchewan River.

Around Medicine Hat

Much of Medicine Hat's prosperity comes from its underground resources: vast reserves of natural gas and an unlimited supply of cool water. Some of the gas is used to light the old-fashioned streetlamps in the Edwardian downtown area. A shining contrast to all this quaintness is the glass-walled **City Hall** at 1st Street SE and 6th Avenue SE, where visitors may take either a self-guided or guided group tour.

The city's **tourist information centre** is at 8 Gehring Road SW (tel. 527-6422).

Medicine Hat has made the most of its wealth and location by creating a series of pleasant **parks** and environmental areas along the banks of the South Saskatchewan River and Seven Persons Creek, which crosses the city from southwest to northeast. Some 60km (38 miles) of trails enable walkers, cyclists and in winter skiers to move from park to park. **Echo Dale Regional Park**, on the western outskirts, has facilities for swimming, boating and fishing.

South of Medicine Hat, the vast treeless prairie gives way to the forests, meadows and valleys of the **Cypress Hills**, reaching an elevation of 1,372m (4,459ft) above sea level. Ten thousand years ago a sheet of ice 1km (half-a-mile) thick covered Canada between the Laurentians and the Rockies, scouring the western prairies, but the high Cypress Hills remained uncovered.

The first organized exploration of the area was in 1859 when a British survey team was led there by John Palliser of the Hudson's Bay Company. Palliser described the hills as 'an island in a sea of grass'. Settlement inevitably changed the region's character, but the best of it remains as the Cypress Hills Provincial Park.

Cypress Hills Provincial Park

Cypress Hills, a protected area of 200sq km (80sq miles), spilling into neighbouring Saskatchewan, is Alberta's second largest provincial park. It has a wealth of plant and animal life. Crocuses, daisies, harebells and phlox flourish in the meadows in spring and summer, and on the higher ground mountain flowers and 14 varieties of orchid are to be found. There are forests of trembling aspen, white spruce and lodgepole pine. About 200 bird species have been recorded in the hills, including mourning doves, McGillivray's warblers, red-breasted nuthatches, red-tailed hawks and great horned owls. Bobcats, red foxes and coyotes prowl the countryside, and there are moose, wapiti, prong-horned antelope and white-tailed and mule deer.

There are three major expanses of

The Hat that Lost a Battle

They argue long and loud in Medicine Hat over the origin of their city's name, but the story that is most widely accepted tells how the Cree and Blackfoot fought a fierce battle beside the South Saskatchewan River.

The Cree were doing well until their medicine man fled across the river, losing his elaborate headdress in midstream. Disheartened by this bad omen, the Cree warriors were slaughtered.

The Blackfoot named the battle site 'Saamis', meaning 'Medicine Man's Hat'. White settlers later translated this as 'medicine hat' and gave the name to the settlement that sprang up in the 1880s.

Massive buffalo herds once roamed Canada. Only a few remain, some now 'living' in local museums.

water in the park: Spruce Coulee Reservoir and Elkwater and Reesor Lakes, and there are facilities for fishing, swimming and boating.

Campers and RV tourists should have no difficulty finding somewhere to pitch up. The park encompasses 13 individual campgrounds with a total of more than 440 sites. Another three campgrounds, with a total of 74 sites, are located in the **Michele Reservoir Provincial Recreation Area**, 8km (5 miles) south of Cypress Hills Provincial Park. Reservations and information about the park and recreation area from Box 12, Elkwater, Alberta T0J 1C0 (tel. 893-3777).

Cypress Hills Provincial Park is reached from Medicine Hat by travelling east on the TransCanada Highway for about 16km (10 miles) then south on Highway 41 for 34km (21 miles).

Writing-on-Stone Provincial Park

Adventurous travellers with a penchant for Native American culture might like to head south from **Elkwater**, picking up the secondary highways 889 and 501 to travel first south for about 55km (35 miles) then west for another 80km (50 miles) or so to reach Writing-on-Stone Provincial Park.

The park, 32km (20 miles) east of the town of **Milk River** and less than 20km (12 miles) from the border with the American state of Montana, is the home of ancient rock paintings and carvings on sandstone. Among the petroglyphs,

carved over a period of three centuries, is one showing dozens of armed warriors in battle. Others depict a buffalo hunt, deer and other animals.

The Indians who once lived in the area believed it to be haunted, doubtless because of its weird landscape, sculpted by wind, frost and water.

The park contains a reconstruction of buildings from a Northwest Mounted Police outpost which was established nearby in 1899 to halt the illicit trade in whiskey.

Writing-on-Stone Provincial Park, PO Box 297 Milk River, Alberta T0K 1M0 (tel. 647-2364) has a campground with 75 sites for RVs and tents. There are interpretive programmes and organized tours, as well as facilities for picnicking, canoeing, fishing, swimming and hiking.

Lethbridge and Southwest Alberta

Alberta's third largest city, **Lethbridge** (population 61,000) is 216km (135 miles) south of Calgary and 164km (102 miles) west of Medicine Hat on Highway 3, also known as Crowsnest Highway. Lethbridge was founded as a coal-mining town in the 1870s, when it was known as Coalbanks, but its economy now is based on livestock, grain, sugar beet, oil and natural gas.

The city boasts that its annual total of sunshine hours is the highest in Alberta, but turn the statistic on its head and you get the driest place in the province – a fact borne out by all those sprinklers, reservoirs, canals and culverts that work so hard to irrigate the area's 400,000ha (960,000 acres) of agricultural land.

Lethbridge has another unique claim to gain a mention in the Great Book of Statistics. Its **High Level Bridge**, built in 1909 to span the Oldman River, is the world's longest for its height: more than 1km (half-a-mile) long and at its highest point 95.7m (311ft) above the river bed.

What to See in Lethbridge

The city's major attraction is **Fort Whoop-up**. The name alone demands attention. It's a reconstruction of the whiskey fort of that name that was established at the junction of the Oldman and St Mary Rivers at about the same time as the city's foundation. A whiskey fort was a riotous trading post – they flourished throughout southwestern Alberta in the late 19th century – where whiskey was sold illegally to the Indians. Whoop-up summed it up. The liquor certainly would not have met today's consumer protection standards, but it earned a lot of money for its vendors – and led to a lot of trouble. In the end, the Northwest Mounted Police had to come in and sort it all out. By 1874 the party was over for Fort Whoop-up.

The reconstructed fort is in **Indian Battle Park**, Whoop-up Drive, site of a great battle fought between the Blackfoot and the Cree in 1870. The fort includes an interpretive centre and display gallery, with weapons, relics and an audiovisual presentation. Visitors can take wagon-train tours of the area.

Every year, in late July or early August, Lethbridge citizens let their hair down during their **Whoop-up Days**, a combined rodeo, agricultural fair and festival. It captures some of the spirit of the old days.

When they've finished whooping it up, Lethbridgers like to relax in the **Nikka Yuko Japanese Gardens**, a tranquil oasis of ordered horticulture with coiffured trees, colourful shrubs, pools, miniature waterfalls and a 16th-century tea house in replica. Located in Henderson Lake Park, 3km (2 miles) east of downtown, the gardens were created in 1967 as a symbol of Japanese–Canadian friendship.

Fort Macleod

A drive of 51km (32 miles) west along Crowsnest Highway (Highway 3) leads to Fort Macleod, a small and quiet town (population, 3,123) of wide streets and low buildings. Its downtown streets of pre-1900 wood-frame buildings and more recent structures in sandstone and brick were declared Alberta's first Provincial Historic Area, and the town is a classic North American community in the Norman Rockwell mould. It was named after Colonel J F Macleod, who built the first Northwest Mounted Police post in the west here on an island in the Oldman River in 1874.

Fort Macleod Museum overlooks the river and is a convincing replica of the old fort, with displays showing the life of NWMP officers, the Indians and pioneers of the area, and the role of the present-day Royal Canadian Mounted Police (RCMP). Four times a day during July and August riders in period costume perform the stirring RCMP Musical Ride.

Head-Smashed-In Buffalo Jump

Murray Small Legs is emphatic. 'You have to understand,' he says, 'that the people who used this site in the old days didn't just wake up one morning and say, "Hey, let's go hunt some buffalo." What they did was a carefully planned operation – a patient hunt that lasted for days.'

Murray, a powerfully built six-footer in spite of his name, is a guide at Head-Smashed-In Buffalo Jump, an interpretive

A stirring musical ride is performed at Fort Macleod Museum, which depicts 19th-century frontier life.

centre and World Heritage Site documenting the buffalo-hunting culture of the Plains Indians from ancient times to the arrival of the Europeans. The centre is imaginatively built into the steep side of a hill with majestic views of the surrounding prairie 18km (11 miles) northwest of Fort Macleod. You reach it by way of Secondary Highway 785, off Highway 2.

The buffalo was profoundly important – sacred, even – to the people of the Plains. It was a source of fresh meat, and its flesh, dried as pemmican, would feed the tribes through the harsh prairie winter. Its hide served as clothing, blankets and the coverings for tipis. Its bones could be made into tools and implements. The horns were frequently used to decorate ceremonial bonnets.

The popular image of a buffalo hunt is of whooping tribesmen on galloping mustangs, shooting the stampeding beasts with rifles. That was the high-tech way to do it – the white man's way. You have to remember that there were no horses on the prairies before the 18th century, and the crack of a rifle was not heard in Alberta much before the mid-1800s.

Yet the Blackfoot people and their forbears were successfully hunting buffalo for thousands of years – perhaps as early as 8000BC at Head-Smashed-In – before the white man turned up to decimate the herds.

The idea was simple. The animals could be herded and driven over a cliff to their death – safer, more efficient and yielding far greater rewards than attempting to stalk the great beasts and kill them with rudimentary weapons. But it needed a great deal of organization.

After a period of sacred pre-hunt ceremonies, a group of 30 or so young braves would set out on foot to select the animals destined to be herded over the cliff. One would imitate the sound of a lost calf to attract the herd's attention, and another, wearing the hide of a dead calf, would act as a decoy to draw the animals into the drive lanes. These were a complex network of cairns, extending as far as 8km (5 miles) and funnelling the buffalo toward the kill site.

Meanwhile, the base of the 10m (30ft) jump was a scene of intense activity as meat-drying racks were prepared and boiling and roasting pits dug. Finally, the dogs were muzzled and silence fell as ears strained for the sound of the driven herd.

At first it was a gentle process, nudging the animals away from the gathering area. Then more pressure would be applied and hunters would emerge from hiding behind the cairns, waving robes and shouting to stampede the animals deeper into the narrowing lane.

The whole process – and the lifestyle of the Plains Indians – is graphically illustrated in the interpretive centre, which is on six levels and includes a film theatre, cafeteria and gift shop stocked with native arts and crafts and souvenir items. From the upper level a trail leads to a spectacular viewpoint at the site of the actual jump.

Covering some 625ha (1,500 acres), Head-Smashed-In is one of the oldest, largest and best-preserved buffalo jump sites in North America. Its archaeological, historical and ethnological value was recognized in 1981 when it was officially designated a World Heritage Site, joining such exclusive places as Machu Picchu in Peru, India's Taj Mahal, the Palace of Versailles in France, and the Egyptian Pyramids.

And the origin of its gory name? Legend has it that about 150 years ago a young brave stood under the shelter of a ledge to witness the death plunge of the buffalo. But the hunt was especially good that day, and he became trapped by the mounting bodies. When these were removed for butchering, the young man was found dead – his skull crushed by the weight of the animals.

Crowsnest Pass

From Fort Macleod, Highway 3 continues west towards British Columbia, passing through some of southern Alberta's most varied – and windiest – countryside. With the wind against them, the drivers of RVs and other high-sided vehicles may find it difficult on occasions to drive as fast as 50kph (30mph). But who would want to hurry through scenery that shifts from prairie to rolling cattle country, from foothills to the soaring Rockies, with rivers and forests thrown in?

In the past, this was an area of industrial development – and disaster – and now the small communities are conveniently spaced out for resting or sightseeing. The little township of **Lundbreck** (population 261) impressively marks the eastern end of the Crowsnest Pass. Here, the Crowsnest River plummets 18m (60ft) as the Lundbreck Falls.

Less than 10km (6 miles) farther west, the rather larger town of **Bellevue** acclaims through its name the vista it enjoys from its lofty position. This was the first of the south Alberta coal towns that supplied fuel for the early steam trains. **Leitch Colliery Provincial Historic Site**, 9km (6 miles) east of the town, tells the story of its mining days. **Hillcrest**, Bellevue's neighbour, saw Canada's worst mining tragedy in June, 1914, when 189 men died in a gas explosion. Their remains lie in a mass grave marked only by a picket fence.

Another disaster site, this time the result of a natural phenomenon, is to be found at the little town of **Frank**. Disaster struck here at 4.10am on 29 April 1903 when a massive chunk of limestone 640m (2,080ft) high, 915m (2,970ft) wide and 150m (487ft) thick slid down Turtle Mountain, engulfing part of the sleeping community. In less than two minutes 70 people died. The **Frank Slide Interpre-**

*F*eeding a chipmunk can be fun, but the general rule is: don't feed the animals.

tive Centre, located 1.5km (1 mile) off Highway 3, tells the story of the disaster and portrays the history of the Crowsnest Valley in an award-winning multimedia presentation.

The western end of the pass is watched over by **Crowsnest Mountain**. This is where those winds reach their highest velocity – sometimes as much as 160kph (100mph) – and local yarns have it that freight wagons have been blown along the rails for distances up to 24km (15 miles). The Municipality of Crowsnest Pass, nudging the BC border, was founded in 1979, an amalgamation of all the communities on the Alberta side of the Crowsnest Valley.

Waterton Lakes National Park

Waterton Lakes National Park, in the extreme southwest corner of Alberta, is the iceberg tip of a vast wilderness area that straddles the border between the United States and Canada and is known jointly as the Waterton-Glacier International Peace Park. Established in 1895, the Canadian park was united with Montana's Glacier National Park in 1931 to form the world's first international peace park.

The park offers stunning contrasts, with a sudden and dramatic meeting of prairie and mountain. In an abrupt shift, the land elevates through four botanical zones. The lowest level, up to 1,370m (4,450ft), sees plants such as the prairie crocus and Red Indian paintbrush thriving among aspen groves and prairie grasses. Next, up to an elevation of 1,830m (5,950ft), comes a heavily forested zone covered by lodgepole pine, white spruce and Douglas maple. The Hudsonian zone, rising to around 2,250m (7,300ft), is the home of evergreens, though these will probably be stunted by cold winds. Above them all is the Arctic/Alpine zone, with tundra emerging above the tree line and Arctic poppies and moss campion growing close to the ground.

There are three Waterton lakes, connected by the whimsically named Bosporus and Dardanelles straits and separating the Lewis and Clark mountain ranges. Visitors may cruise the length of Upper Waterton Lake aboard the vessel *International*. For the more energetic there are 160km (100 miles) of hiking trails within the park, linking a cornucopia of topographical features: rivers, lakes, waterfalls, canyons and peaks.

A favourite trail follows Blakiston Creek into the colourful **Red Rock Canyon**, whose 20m (65ft) walls are a blaze of red, green, purple and yellow as a result of chemical reactions in the rock. **Mount Blakiston**, the park's highest peak at 2,940m (9,550ft), glowers over the canyon.

Among the many wildlife species roaming the Waterton landscape are deer, moose, plains bison and both the black and grizzly bear. Wildlife-viewing and birdwatching opportunities abound in the spring and autumn, and day trips and explorations led by naturalists are available.

Campers – with tents or RVs – have a choice of five grounds. Three of them – two within the park and the third in the township of Waterton – are managed by Canada Parks Service. The other two, both privately owned, are located on the approaches to the park gate.

The national park is reached by Highway 5 south from Lethbridge or Highway 6, which strikes south from Highway 3 at the tiny settlement of Pincher, 44km (27 miles) east of Fort Macleod. From Lethbridge to the park gate is a journey of 114km (71 miles).

The Porcupine Hills

Highway 2 is the quick route between Fort Macleod and Calgary, but a more interesting and scenically more satisfying return trip from southwest Alberta can be made by way of Secondary Highways 940 and 532 then Highway 22 or 2A. The secondary road strikes north from **Coleman**, part of the Municipality of Crowsnest Pass, on Highway 3.

Scenery apart, there isn't much to Coleman. But it does have one attraction: **'Ten Ton Toots'**, claimed by residents to be the world's biggest piggy bank. 'Toots' is an old locomotive, and visitors are invited to pitch in their loose change. Every now and then a whole loco-full of money is donated to a worthy charity.

This quiet route to Calgary takes you through the **Porcupine Hills**, the rolling foothills of the Rockies. Here, Alberta's finest beef cattle are raised on rich grassland. Thanks to the chinook – the warm wind that sweeps down from the mountains, melting the snow at the end of winter – the nourishing feed is available to the herds much earlier than elsewhere. Cattle ranching began in the Porcupine Hills in the 1870s, soon after the Northwest Mounted Police arrived to curb the rough and ready ways of the pioneers. The first herds came across the Rockies from British Columbia, but later stock came from Montana and the East.

According to a legend going back to those early days of settlement, there's gold in them thar hills – somewhere. It was struck in the 1880s by two men – one named Blackjack, the other Lemon – somewhere near The Hump, a 2,000m (6,500ft) mountain, now accessible from Highway 532. The two prospectors quarrelled, Lemon killing Blackjack with an axe. The murder was witnessed by two Indians whose chief cast a spell on the place, rendering it invisible. Lemon went crazy trying to find it, and no one else has so far uncovered the lost lode.

A better prospect for travellers in the region today is a stop at **Chain Lakes Provincial Park**, on Highway 22. It's a small park, barely 4sq km (1^1/$_2$sq miles), but it's a tranquil spot set around an 11km (7-mile) long reservoir richly stocked with trout. There are excellent picnic facilities and wonderful views. The reservoir, formed from three small lakes in the 1960s, is part of Willow Creek, which subsequently joins the Oldman River. Canoeists can follow the creek to **Willow Creek Provincial Park**, an idyllic waterside location just off Secondary Highway 527, about 12km (7 miles) west of Stavely on Highway 2. Here, there are 150 well-spaced-out pitches for tents and RVs. Motorists can get to Willow Creek Provincial Park by following 527 east from Highway 22. It's a spectacularly beautiful route through ranch country.

From Chain Lakes Provincial Park you can continue north along Highway 22 to the town of **Black Diamond** – a route of broad vistas – or follow Secondary Highway 533 east to the town of **Nanton**, renowned for its piped Porcupine Hills spring water, then head north on Highway 2A. This will bring you to the very pleasant town of **Okotoks**, near which is the **Big Rock**, a massive rock standing out like a sore thumb in the gentle undulations of the surrounding countryside. The rock, said to weigh around 18,000 tons, is an Erratic – the biggest of thousands of such loners found among the foothills of the Rockies. The Erratics are believed to have been created in a giant rockslide onto a moving glacier. As the glacier melted the rocks were dumped like markers across the land.

A lone canoe emphasises the splendid isolation of the Rockies.

Okotoks – it's the Blackfoot word for 'big rock' – has an attractive, riverside park with woodland walks, a bird sanctuary and a restful campground run by the local Lions Club, as well as some useful stores, boutiques and restaurants. The old Canadian Pacific railroad station has been turned into a cultural centre and art gallery, and a number of exhibitions and antiques fairs are held in the town throughout the year. Add to those amenities the facts that it has three first-class golf courses, a brand new liquor store and is only a 30-minute drive south from Calgary and it's no surprise that Okotoks is a favourite with the city dwellers.

The Canadian Rockies

The majority of travellers to Alberta fly in from the east, arriving at either Calgary or Edmonton, but an increasingly popular – and far more dramatic – route is to take VIA Rail's crack train *The Canadian* from Vancouver to Jasper, then travel by motor coach along the Icefields Parkway through Jasper and Banff National Parks. The rail and road combination allows you to see the best of the Canadian Rockies and to stop over in the region's best resort areas.

The train journey takes about 17 hours, and although it involves some overnight travel you still get to see more of the mountains than most other travellers would, enjoying awesome panoramas from the air-conditioned comfort of a dome car or while enjoying a drink in the lounge. In the winter, the view through the train's picture windows is a kaleidoscopic composition in white, silver, blue and green.

126

Jasper National Park

Jasper does not have the feel of a leading mountain resort. It's a fairly small town (population 3,270) dominated by the railway line, which is probably reasonable since it owes its very existence to the railway. There was a settlement of sorts here in the late 19th century when it served as a focal point for such wilderness travellers as trappers, prospectors, explorers and missionaries. It was originally named Fitzhugh, but the name was later changed to honour Jasper Hawes, who ran the local Northwest Company office. The railroad arrived in 1907, and the federal government wisely decided to preserve the area – some 10,800sq km (4,200sq miles) – as a national park.

Jasper Park Lodge

One way and another, a lot of forward thinking went on in the Jasper area in those early years of the 20th century. In 1911 the Grand Trunk Pacific Railway started looking for sites which could be developed as hotels, but plans to build a grand property near Jasper were shelved when the company ran into financial difficulties in 1914. But the demands of tourism were becoming strident, and led a year later to the founding of Tent City. It was a modest beginning to what would become one of the most fashionable year-round resorts in North America.

The 'city' consisted of ten tents, each with wooden floors and walls. The sleeping accommodation for guests was furnished with 'comfortable beds and all the accessories that go to make up a modern bedroom'. A large marquee served as a dining room and lounge. The development was the result of efforts by the railway company – now scaling down its original ambitions – the owner of an Edmonton tent-making company, and brothers Fred and Jack Brewster, pioneer outfitters in the area. It was the Brewsters who found the perfect location: the shores of Lac Beauvert, ringed by The Whistlers, Signal Mountain, Pyramid Mountain, Roche Bonhomme – the rocky profile of a supine Old Man – and a dramatic peak that would later commemorate the name of the World War heroine, Nurse Edith Cavell.

Tent City opened on 15 June 1915, charging an all-in rate of $15 to $18 a week, plus a $1 charge for the round trip between station and resort in the Brewsters' horse-drawn carriages. Guests could enjoy fishing, climbing, boating and 'no mud' canoeing. Well over 250 visitors from throughout Canada, the United States and abroad were registered during that first season. But it was not to last. World War I closed Tent City. It reopened in 1919, an instant success, and in 1922, now owned by the newly formed Canadian National Railways, upgraded to a property with about a dozen four-bedroom log bungalows, dining hall, dance pavilion, and a trophy-hung central lounge with a stone fireplace of baronial hall proportions. From now on, Tent City was known as Jasper Park Lodge.

The resort began to spread. More cabins were built along the shores of Lac Beauvert, joined by connecting paths and miniature roadways. Some of the cabins are still in use today, when the total room count is 442. That may sound like high-density living, but bear in mind that those cedar chalets and log cabins are spread over a spacious 375ha (900 acres) in which herds of elk tread daintily, and room service waiters deliver club sandwiches and the like on bicycles. An 18-hole golf course, opened in 1925, has been rated one of Canada's top ten. There are also four hard surface tennis courts, as well as facilities for trail riding, fishing, boating and cycling.

Over the years Jasper Park Lodge has become polished to the point of luxury and for decades now has attracted the rich and famous – including Bing Crosby, Marilyn Monroe, Pierre Trudeau, Anthony Hopkins and British royalty – but it has managed to retain its country camp ambience, even though its main lodge contains a basement shopping promenade with 13 boutiques, a nightclub, lounge, café and formal dining room – to say nothing of 13 meeting rooms with convention facilities for up to 1,000 people, a health spa and ballroom.

The Wild Side

The Canadian Rockies are home to lots of wildlife, much of which can frequently be viewed from the roadside – but please don't approach too closely and don't attempt to feed animals. Remember, they are wild – however cute they may appear – and are susceptible to stress. Some of them are also likely to turn nasty if they feel threatened.

Winter is the best viewing time, when there is less cover and snow provides a contrasting background. At this time coyotes and wolves may be seen on frozen rivers and lakes, where travel is easier. Rocky Mountain bighorn sheep, which thrive in steep rocky habitats, often venture down to the roads to lick the salt used to keep the roads clear. They are particularly numerous on Tangle Ridge in the Columbia Icefield area. Mountain goats are more difficult to see as they scamper along the narrow ledges of the high rocky walls.

Mule deer and elk are frequently seen. The mule deer are a little shy, preferring to keep close to woodland as they browse in sunny spots, but the bolder elk will wander haughtily along town streets.

Around Jasper

Jasper Park Lodge is not the only place where you can eat and sleep in Jasper. Restaurants and motels are to be found along Connaught Drive, running alongside the rail tracks, and there are a number of bars, lounges and night spots. Most people use the town as a jumping-off spot for exploring some of the 1,000km (625 miles) of hiking and cross-country skiing trails in the surrounding national park or as a centre for sightseeing. Summer and winter, the accent in Jasper is very much on the outdoor life.

The area's principal downhill skiing centre is **Marmot Basin**, a 20-minute drive from Jasper via the Icefields Parkway south and Marmot Basin Road west. There's a shuttle bus service from hotels in town during the season. With more than 400ha (1,000 acres) of terrain, Marmot has skiing for all levels of expertise. Snowboarders and telemark skiers are welcome, and facilities include a ski shop, ski school and nursery. Base and mid-mountain day lodges with sun decks serve food and drink.

Information on activities year-round, as well as events, amenities and accommodation, can be obtained from Jasper Tourism and Commerce, 632 Connaught Drive (tel. 852-3858). The Jasper Information Centre run by Parks Canada is at 500 Connaught Drive (tel. 852-6176).

The town's nearest attraction is the **Jasper Tramway**, 3km (2 miles) to the south off Highway 93. The tramway is a cable car ride of 950m (3,000ft) to the summit of Whistlers Mountain, with superb views (weather permitting) of Mount Robson, 80km (50 miles) to the west, and the Miette and Athabasca Valleys which converge on Jasper. There is a licensed restaurant at the summit. The

tramway is open from mid-April to mid-October. Early and late in the season it can be very cold at the top and sudden snowstorms are not uncommon, so take warm clothing. Whistlers Mountain gets its name from its population of hoary marmots, the curious rodents that make an eerie whistling sound.

Excursions from Jasper

Another easy outing takes in **Pyramid** and **Patricia Lakes**, 4km (2½ miles) northwest of town on Pyramid Avenue. There are good cross-country skiing trails here, and in the summer you can rent boats, canoes and motorized surfboards. You can also rent a boat or join a guided cruise to explore emerald-green **Maligne Lake**, 22km (14 miles) long and 46km (29 miles) east of Jasper along Maligne Lake Road. Passengers on the cruise vessel visit Spirit Island, beautifully located in the middle of the lake.

Between the town and the lake, the road passes **Maligne Canyon**, a twisting, narrow fissure, some 15m (50ft) deep and carrying the Maligne River for about 2km

Alberta's lively rivers provide exhilarating sport for whitewater rafters – but be prepared for an icy ducking.

(1¼ miles). In the summer it's a roaring torrent of water, but in winter it's a wonderland of pale blue and green, where an icy floor weaves between limestone walls hung with frozen waterfalls. Canyon crawling is a popular and relatively easy pursuit here, though it would be wise to join a guided tour, available in most hotel lobbies in Jasper or directly through Maligne Tours (tel. 852-3370) or Mountain Meadow Tours (tel. 852-5595). Those too timid or too short of time to join the crawlers might prefer to follow the footpath that traces the canyon, frequently crossing it on bridges. Afterwards, everyone can warm up in the nearby tea house.

Another sight on the way to Maligne Lake is **Medicine Lake**, a dry stretch of

*T*ough vehicles take visitors on to the Athabasca Glacier on the Columbia Icefield.

gravel for most of the year, but during the summer run-off from the mountains and glacial meltwater turn it into a lake 8km (5 miles) wide and up to 25m (80ft) deep. Even then it frequently dries out, drained by a complex system of underground channels.

The Icefields Parkway

Between Jasper and Lake Louise, the 230km (144-mile) stretch of Highway 93 is known as the Icefields Parkway. It traverses some of the most awesome scenery in the Rockies, winding along the shoulder of the Great Divide, and is one of the world's great highway experiences. With a panorama of peaks, canyons,

glaciers and waterfalls, it follows five major rivers, including the Athabasca, Sunwapta and North Saskatchewan, and crosses the **Columbia Icefield**, the largest accumulation of ice in the Rockies, covering about 325sq km (126sq miles) to a depth of 300m (1,000ft).

Started as a work project for the unemployed during the 1930s depression, the highway was completed in 1960, and spectacular though it is, it can be dangerous in the winter. At that time it's wise to drive with a survival kit – blankets or sleeping bags, food, snow shovels, tyre chains and SOS flares. Before setting out, get a road and weather report from the RCMP (tel. 762-1450).

A short detour off the highway some 32km (20 miles) south of Jasper leads to **Athabasca Falls**, where the Athabasca River plunges dramatically over a 25m (80ft) cliff, then charges through a narrow gorge before reaching a line of steep rapids. The water's milky green appearance is the result of sediment. Another 24km (15 miles) to the south the Athabasca River is joined by the green waters of the Sunwapta, which is huddled by the highway as far back as its headwaters at the foot of the Athabasca Glacier.

The Columbia Icefield marks the boundary between Jasper and Banff National Parks and is one of the largest areas of ice and snow south of the Arctic Circle. The continuing accumulation of snow continuously feeds eight major glaciers, including the **Athabasca**, **Dome and Stutfield Glaciers** which are visible from the Parkway. The meltwater of the Columbia Icefield feeds streams and rivers that pour into three different oceans – the Arctic to the north, Atlantic to the east and the Pacific in the west.

There's no chance of missing the place to stop to see the icefield at its best: the Columbia Icefield **Visitors' Centre** makes sure of that. And facing it, stretching towards the Parkway, lies the Athabasca Glacier, a tongue of ice 6km (nearly 4 miles) long and 1km (half-a-mile) wide. The urge to walk on it is irresistible, and in the summer months visitors can ride across it in a SnoCoach, a huge comfortable vehicle on massive wheels that travels to the middle of the glacier on a 5km (3-mile) round trip that includes an opportunity to step out on to ice formed from snow that fell four centuries ago.

Banff National Park

Established in 1885 as Canada's first national reserve, Banff National Park extends over 6,600sq km (2,578sq miles) of protected wilderness. From the north, it starts where Jasper National Park ends – at the Sunwapta Pass, less than 5km (3 miles) from the Icefield Visitors' Centre. The pass marks the divide between the headwaters of the North Saskatchewan and Sunwapta Rivers. The waters of the North Saskatchewan flow south, cross the prairies and eventually enter Hudson Bay. The Sunwapta waters flow north and reach the Arctic Ocean by way of the Mackenzie River. The Icefield Parkway's elevation at the point where it crosses the divide is 2,035m (6,614ft) above sea level. You can find snow banks here even in the height of summer.

Saskatchewan River Crossing, where Highway 11 – the David Thompson Highway, named after an early 19th-century explorer – strikes eastwards to the city of Red Deer, is the only place between Jasper and Lake Louise where you can refuel your car summer and winter. There is also

a cafeteria. Just north of the crossing a 3km (2-mile) loop road – the Parker Ridge Trail – gives a view of the Saskatchewan Glacier, birthplace of the river. Several viewpoints near the crossing show the river valleys and glaciers extending from the Columbia Icefield.

Some 4km ($2^{1}/_{2}$ miles) from the crossing, you can park in a roadside pull-out and follow a short nature trail down to **Mistaya Canyon**, where the rushing waters of the Mistaya River have gouged deeply into the limestone bedrock, forming a narrow, snaking gorge. The canyon is spanned by a footbridge, and hikers can follow trails from here to **Sarbach Lookout,** 5km (3 miles) away, and **Howse Pass,** 27km (17 miles) distant. Howse Pass and Howse River, which joins the North Saskatchewan at the crossing, were named after Joseph Howse, a Hudson's Bay Company trader who passed this way in 1810.

The Icefields Parkway passes a number of impressive lakes formed by glacial streams. The **Upper** and **Lower Waterfowl Lakes,** through which the Mistaya River journeys, are shallow, marshy stretches of water which attract much wildlife, including moose. **Peyto Lake**, seen from a viewpoint just off the highway at Bow Pass, is fed by the meltwaters of Peyto Glacier and named after Bill Peyto, a mountain guide who subsequently became a national park warden. Hanging above **Bow Lake** is Crowfoot Glacier, and behind that is the start of the Waputik Icefield. **Hector Lake**, brilliantly turquoise, and the neighbouring **Mount Hector,** honour the name of Dr James Hector, a geologist who in 1858 was the first white man to pass this way. Hector also played a part in the naming of **Kicking Horse Pass**, 8km (5 miles) west on

Highway 1, the TransCanada Highway, which joined the Icefields Parkway just before the town of Lake Louise. The explorer was travelling through the pass in 1858 when he was kicked unconscious by a packhorse, and almost buried by his distraught Indian guides.

Lake Louise

The lake from which the town gets its name was originally called Emerald Lake because of its milky green sedimentary hue – when it isn't blanched by ice and snow, of course. It was first named in 1882 by Tom Wilson, a surveyor with Canadian Pacific Railways, but later renamed in honour of Queen Victoria's daughter. In the course of the past century, the view enjoyed by Tom Wilson has become one of the world's most famous mountain scenes. And it really is a classic – straight off the lid of a chocolate box: an oval-shaped lake surrounded by fairy-tale forests and a ring of majestic mountains, with the neo-Gothic grandeur of the **Château Lake Louise Hotel** faced by the natural splendour of the Victoria Glacier. The lake is 2.5km (1¹/₂ miles) long, over 1km (³/₄ mile) wide, and 85m (273ft) deep. It is around 1,750m (5,700ft) above sea level and in the winter is great for skating. In the summer it is not so good for swimming – the water's temperature never rises above 5°C (41°F).

As elsewhere in the Canadian Rockies, the major activities in the Lake Louise area revolve around the Great Outdoors:

hiking, cycling, horse-riding and the like in the summer months; skiing, skating, tobogganing for the rest of the year. The town is tiny, with a resident population of 355, and at any one time there are likely to be more people staying at Chateau Lake Louise, with its 513 guest rooms, than there are in the community.

Around Lake Louise

The focal point of life in the town is the crossroads where Lake Louise Drive and Village Way meet, with the railway tracks and the Bow and Pipestone Rivers also converging in more or less the same place. Here you'll find a handful of hotels, a small shopping centre and the new Lake Louise **Visitor Centre** (tel. 522-3833), a striking building whose contours pick up the shapes of the surrounding mountains. The centre encompasses exhibition galleries and a multimedia show, which tells in 25 minutes how the Canadian Rockies were formed over a period of 600 million years. There are also exhibits on the area's natural and human history.

During the summer, visitors can take a ride on the Lake Louise **Gondola**, which is used by skiers in the winter. It's a popular excursion, with a tea house at the

*R*elaxation in Banff National Park. Even the loveliest spots (far right) are likely to be deserted.

Lake Louise has become one of the world's most famous mountain scenes.

summit from where a number of hiking trails lead. Chateau Lake Louise, 6km (4 miles) out of town, is the starting point for another network of trails. One of the most popular is a hike of just over 3km (2 miles) to **Lake Agnes**, where a petite tea house serves home-baked bread, cookies and soup and affords a stupendous view.

The vast chateau, embracing five restaurants, a Western saloon and an Alpine lounge, as well as a recreation centre and shops – to say nothing of all those rooms and a lobby big enough to land a helicopter in – is the centre for a variety of activities, not least of which are horse-riding, canoeing, rock-climbing and mountaineering.

About 11km (7 miles) south of Lake Louise is the area known as the **Valley of the Ten Peaks**, where another sheet of turquoise water, Moraine Lake, lies before the stunning spectacle of the Wenkchemna Peaks. A lakeside lodge, open from 1 June to 30 September, offers accommodation and refreshment, and canoe rentals are available. More hiking trails lead from the lake, the most popular being **Eiffel Lake** trail, a 5.5km (3^1/2-mile) climb through sub-alpine meadows, and the 3km (2-mile) **Larch Valley** trek, a favourite in the colourful autumn.

Banff

From Lake Louise, Highway 1 – the TransCanada Highway – follows the Bow River for 56km (35 miles) to Banff. This is the quick route. Highway 1A, a two-lane road known as the Bow Valley Parkway, follows a parallel route for much of the way but is rather more scenic, and there are plenty of places where you can stop and drink in the view. There are also opportunities to see wildlife, including elk, moose, mountain sheep and even the occasional wolf.

Halfway between Jasper and Banff, on the west side of the TransCanada

Highway, is the **Sunshine Village** ski resort, perched on the Continental Divide at an altitude of 2,730m (9,000ft). Nearly 9m (30ft) of soft, natural snow falls here each season, and there are 62 runs, most of them eventually converging in the village area. From late June to early September visitors can take a 25-minute gondola ride to reach the village inn – the only on-hill accommodation in Banff National Park – restaurant and interpretive centre. From here a short chair-lift ride continues to the starting point for nature walks through sub-alpine meadows which are carpeted with wildflowers from late July to mid-August.

About the same distance from Banff as Sunshine Village, but located off the Bow River Parkway, is **Johnston Canyon**, where seven waterfalls drop through a

T he Banff Springs Hotel was the largest in the world when it opened in 1888.

canyon that reaches 30m (100ft) deep. In some places the walls are only 6m (20ft) apart. In winter the falls are dramatically frozen.

Banff owes its existence to the discovery of hot sulphur springs in 1883, and so indeed does the national park. The springs were discovered by three adventurous CPR workers who had climbed down a tree trunk ladder to see what might lie in a cave after noticing wisps of steam rising from a fissure. This was they heyday of

the European spa, and the workmen staked a claim to what could clearly be a money-spinner by building a cabin nearby. Within a year, two or three small hotels had been built, attracting clients who believed the hot springs could cure them of everything from rheumatism to gunshot wounds.

To safeguard the area against exploitation, the federal government stepped in and created a national park around the springs. It was Canada's first national reserve, a modest area not much more than 2.5sq km (1sq mile), but it soon grew. Today it spans the Continental Divide for 240km (150 miles) and covers an area of about 6,650sq km (2,600sq miles).

Around Banff

The story of Banff's beginnings is told at the **Cave and Basin Centennial Centre** on Cave Avenue. The European-style spa which was built in 1887 has been restored, and summer visitors can 'take the waters' in a replica of the original pool. There are interpretive exhibits and films, and historical and geological displays. A Marsh and Discovery boardwalk gives an insight into the area's flora and fauna. A guided tour leaves daily at 11am.

Banff today is a lively little town in a super location. During peak holiday times its resident population of less than 5,000 is swollen many times over and its main street – Banff Avenue – becomes choked with tour buses and RVs, and the sidewalks are crowded with tourists. There are plenty of hotels, shopping malls, stores, restaurants and pubs – and even the occasional elk wandering along the side streets. There's an amiable commercialism about the place that is summed up in this handwritten notice in a shop window on Banff Avenue: 'If we're closed, just push your money under the door.'

The town's most striking building is the **Banff Springs Hotel**, with its green roofs and rock walls, hanging above the Bow River Valley like a mad baron's castle. The largest hotel in the world when it opened in June 1888, it has 846 guest rooms, 17 restaurants and lounges, shops, a health club, a $23 million convention centre – and a maze of corridors and staircases that sometimes seem to lead into the fourth dimension. It has a ghost, too, so they say – one Sam McCauley who drove the coach between hotel and railway station in the 1930s. The 'Springs' is so much a part of the town's tourism scene that it has become something of an attraction in its own right, and there is a guided tour daily at 2.30pm.

The Banff **Visitor Centre** at 224 Banff Avenue (tel. 762-1550) is a good place to get one's bearings and to learn something about the area. National Parks staff are on hand to answer questions, and a theatre features continuous videos showing the attractions of Banff National Park. There is also a souvenir shop. The **Banff Park Museum**, built in 1903 and now a designated historic site, houses a comprehensive collection of artefacts and wildlife species mounted in turn-of-the-century style. A reading room contains books on natural history and the park as well as a display of prints by the wildlife artist, Robert Bateman. The museum is at 93 Banff Avenue.

The geological evolution of the Rockies is featured in dioramas, models, diagrams and audiovisual presentations at the **Natural History Museum** at 112 Banff Avenue. There are displays of rocks, minerals, fossils, dinosaur bones, flowers and plants. There is also a life-sized model of 'Big Foot', the legendary ape-like giant said to live in mountain regions. The museum is upstairs in the Clock Tower Mall.

Across the Bow River bridge, on Cave Avenue, the **Luxton Museum** looks into the heritage of the Natives of the Northern Plains and Canadian Rockies. Native arts and daily life before the arrival of the

*P*opular Banff was *founded after the discovery of hot sulphur springs in 1833.*

white man are depicted in life-sized scenes, and there are displays featuring ornamental costumes and ceremonies. There's a wider view of the past at the **Whyte Museum of the Canadian Rockies** at 111 Bear Street. Here there are art galleries, a heritage collection and six historic homes in wooded grounds. Contemporary and historic art exhibitions change monthly.

The town's cultural heart is the **Banff Centre**, said to be one of North America's foremost schools of the visual and performing arts. There is a continuing programme of exhibitions, concerts, drama, film, ballet and poetry readings. The centre is on St Julien Road (tel. 762-6300).

Excursions from Banff
There are a half-dozen or so attractions within easy reach of Banff, most of them served by tour bus, if you don't have a vehicle of your own.

Upper Hot Springs, about 2km (1¹/₄ miles) south of the town, along winding Mountain Avenue, is the place to go for a soak in Banff's mineral waters. The average water temperature is 38°C (100°F). Locker, swimsuit and towel rentals are available. Also on Mountain Road is the **Sulphur Mountain Gondola**, a ride of 2,285m (7,500ft) in eight minutes. On a clear day you can see for 150km (90 miles) from the top, and there are two short trails for wildlife viewing. At the summit is Canada's highest restaurant, with theatre-style seating to make the most of the mountain panorama.

At the western end of town, just off Highway 1, is the **Vermilion Lakes Drive**, a 9km (5¹/₂-mile) route skirting the shores of the three Vermilion Lakes. This marshy area is rich in wildlife, and discreet visitors may be rewarded with sight-

ings of beaver, muskrat, elk, bighorn sheep and the odd moose. The lakes are ringed by Mount Rundle, Sulphur Mountain and the Sundance Range of peaks.

Tunnel Mountain Drive, on the eastern side, is a scenic 5km (3-mile) loop that passes the Banff Centre and leads to the **Hoodoos**, curious rock formations shaped like gnarled fingers, the result of erosion.

Some 10km (6 miles) northeast of Banff, off Highway 1, is **Lake Minnewanka**, at 27km (19 miles) long the largest in the national park and the only lake on which power boats are permitted. Glass-enclosed tour boats cruise the lake, and there are guided fishing trips. Lake Minnewanka is noted for its trout, weighing up to 13.5kg (30lb). The road from Banff to the lake passes the old coal-mining town of **Bankhead**, at the foot of Cascade Mountain. In Banff's early days, the seams of Cascade Mountain were mined to fuel the new railway's steam trains. But Bankhead died as quickly as it had grown up when mining was banned in the national park. Today, visitors can follow a self-guided trail through the ghost mine.

Kananaskis Country
From Banff a drive of 30km (20 miles) east along the TransCanada Highway leads to **Canmore**, a picturesque mountain town which was established as a coal-mining centre in 1883. Its present population of around 4,500 is mainly concerned with such outdoor activities as fishing, climbing, canoeing, golf – the town has a magnificent 18-hole course bordering the Bow River – and, of course, hiking and skiing. It's an active place, keen on festivals, especially its Canada Day Celebrations in July, Heritage Day Folk Festival in early August and its Scottish

Folk Festival, with Highland Games, pipe bands and dancing in September.

The Canmore **Nordic Centre**, less than 2km (1¼ miles) out of town, was the site of the cross-country skiing and biathlon events during the 1988 Olympic Winter Games. It offers skiers some 56km (35 miles) of cross-country trails and in summer months welcomes hikers and mountain bikers.

Canmore marks the northwest corner of Kananaskis Country, more than 4,000sq km (1,600sq miles) of spectacular scenery set aside by the Alberta government for year-round recreational use and nature conservation. The region encompasses three provincial parks – **Peter Lougheed**, **Bragg Creek** and **Bow Valley** – and has facilities for hiking, horse-back riding, even the motorcycles and all-terrain vehicles that are strictly banned in the nearby national parks.

From Canmore the **Smith-Dorrien/**

Spray Trail leads south through the Spray Lakes area to join Highway 40 in Peter Lougheed Provincial Park, the largest in Alberta and named after a former provincial premier. The park's 500sq km (200sq miles) include mountain wilderness, crystalline lakes and beautiful valleys. Highway 40, also known as the **Kananaskis Trail**, leads south from the TransCanada Highway about 35km (21 miles) east of Canmore. After passing through the Peter Lougheed park, it climbs over **Highwood Pass**, the highest pass in Canada accessible to motor vehicles.

Much of Highway 40 is closed during the winter, but you can drive from the TransCanada turnoff to the **Nakiska** ski area and **Kananaskis Village** at any time of the year. Nakiska was the venue for alpine events during the 1988 Winter Olympics. Kananaskis Village, another Olympics development, has year-round hotel and restaurant facilities.

Where The River Flows Swiftly

Saskatchewan's flag is green and yellow, symbolizing the province's forests and grain areas, and in a way it also symbolizes the inadequate image of the place held in the minds of many people, because there is so much more to Saskatchewan than forests or fields of wheat, however huge they may be. In fact, the province splits up into half a dozen distinctly different regions, and its name comes from the Plains Indian word 'kisiskatchewan' – the river that flows swiftly.

Saskatchewan's Regions

The South: Prairies and Mountains

In the south, the great plains present everyone's image: mile upon golden mile of waving wheat separated from a brilliant blue sky by shimmering horizons far, far away. Brightly painted grain elevators stand guard over railway lines that reach arrow-straight across the prairie-flat earth.

Saskatchewan's western heritage is celebrated during Buffalo Days, staged in Regina each summer.

However, the land here is not entirely flat. Here and there, high country punctuates the southern plain. In the southwest, the **Cypress Hills** reach a height of 1,392m (4,520ft), the highest point of land between Labrador and the Rocky Mountains, exceeding the altitude of Banff, Alberta. Untouched by the glaciers of the last Ice Age, the area has an abundant cover of lodgepole pines and white spruce trees. The Duck Mountain and Moose Mountain areas of the south east also stand in sharp contrast to surrounding plains. All three forested highlands contain provincial parks, indigenous wildlife and glorious landscapes.

More or less in the centre of Saskatchewan's extreme southern strip are the **Badlands**, a wildly beautiful landscape of sheer cliffs, huge hogback-shaped rocks and eroded sandstone buttes. The Killdeer Badlands and some stunning sections of the Frenchman River Valley are preserved in **Grasslands National Park**. The Big Muddy Badlands, reaching south to the border with Montana, are an inextricable part of Western folklore, an area of forbidding terrain where outlaws of the calibre of Butch Cassidy, Dutch Henry, Sam Kelly and the Wild Bunch holed up when they were not stealing horses or robbing trains and stagecoaches. Tours are available of the old outlaw caves.

Stretching across two-thirds of southern Saskatchewan, the **Qu'Appelle Valley** is the province's playground, a vast sunken garden shaped millennia ago by rushing rivers of ice-cold water. The Qu'Appelle River links a string of eight lakes – from Buffalo Pound, west of Regina, to Crooked and Round Lakes, about 230km (144 miles) to the east, and the area embraces attractive resort villages, provincial parks and golf courses. Access points to some of the valley's most beautiful sections are signposted along the Trans-Canada Highway.

Deserts and Dunes

You might expect to find camels in the **Great Sand Hills**, a 1,900sq km (742sq mile) area north of Maple Creek, in the triangle formed by the TransCanada Highway and Highways 21 and 32. But the active sand dunes and semi-arid vegetation are home instead to antelope, mule deer, kangaroo rats and Saskatchewan's emblem bird, the sharp-tailed grouse. Other desert areas are to be found at **Douglas Provincial Park** on the eastern shores of Lake Diefenbaker, northeast of Moose Jaw, and along the southeast end of Good Spirit Lake near Yorkton in the east.

The **Athabasca Sand Dunes**, on the south shore of Lake Athabasca in the northwest corner of the province, are the world's most northerly major dunes. Covering 2,000sq km (781sq miles), they are the largest in North America, up to 30m (100ft) high and 1,500m (4,875ft) long.

More than 50 rare species of plants grow there, ten of them unique to the area. The sand dunes were designated a provincial wilderness park in 1992.

Central Region:
Provincial Parks

A strip across the lower middle of the province marks Saskatchewan's parkland region, a transition zone of farmland and forest merging the open prairies of the south with the rugged wilderness of the north. Here are some of Saskatchewan's finest parks, including the vast **Prince Albert National Park**, where the celebrated 'Indian' naturalist Grey Owl lived in the 1930s, hiding his true identity. Here, too, the mighty North and South Saskatchewan Rivers gradually converge, meeting at last just east of the city of Prince Albert.

The North: Lakes and Forest

You can fish in a different lake every day in Northern Saskatchewan, but to complete the course you would have to set aside 270 years. That means there are close on 100,000 lakes, to say nothing of 33 million ha (80 million acres) of forest. This is the land of wilderness adventure, with remote fishing and hunting camps hidden among a Pre-Cambrian landscape, accessible only by floatplane, where the canoe comes into its own.

A Brief Background

Little is known of Saskatchewan's human inhabitants prior to historic times, but evidence suggests that mankind has been there for at least 10,000 years. When the first fur traders and explorers arrived, Chipewyan Indians wintered in the northern fringes, moving into the tundra during the summer to hunt caribou. The Blackfoot and Assiniboine roamed the parklands and the plains, hunting buffalo. Later, the Cree moved in from the east to become the dominant tribe.

Hudson's Bay Company and
the Fur Trade

The first European to explore the area was Henry Kelsey, of the Hudson's Bay Company, who arrived around 1690. He had been sent to encourage the Indians to make the long journey north for trade. Other adventurers followed, making their way inland from Hudson Bay or the Great Lakes far to the east. Gradually, the area was opened up to the growing fur trade. Trade routes such as the Carlton

*G*rain silos are a standard feature of the landscape in the prairies – Canada's bread basket.

Trail were established overland and on waterways such as the Clearwater and Churchill Rivers.

Remnants of the fur-trade era can be seen in a number of provincial parks, notably at Cumberland House, near the Manitoba border due east of Prince Albert National Park, and Fort Carlton on Highway 12, about 60km (37 miles) north of Saskatoon. Cumberland House Provincial Park is the site of the Hudson's Bay Company's first inland fur-trading post, established in 1774 by the explorer Samuel Hearne. Preserved there are the remains of the HBC sternwheeler *Northcote* which sailed the Saskatchewan River more than a century ago. The fur-trading days of the 1860s are re-created at Fort Carlton, a reconstructed post on the banks of the North Saskatchewan River. The stockade encompasses the clerk's quarters, trade shop and fur and provision stores, all authentically furnished.

The Era of 'Mass Settlement'

Rupert's Land, as Saskatchewan was first known, was owned and ruled for 200 years by the giant Hudson's Bay Company, but in 1870 the government of Canada recognized the region's agricultural and settlement potential and bought it for £300,000. The price included much of what is now the three prairie provinces. The first permanent capital of this vast region, which became known as the Northwest Territories, was established at Battleford in 1877. In 1883 the seat of government was moved to Regina.

The formation of the mounted police, construction of the transcontinental railway and the Canadian government's offer of 66ha (160-acre) quarter-sections of land for $10 encouraged mass settlement. 'Mass settlement' is a relative term. In 1885 the population of what is now Saskatchewan was a little over 32,000 – most newcomers in the early days were Canadians born in the settled east. Even today, there are barely a million people living in an area of 644,352sq km (251,700sq miles). They are a mix of British, German, Ukrainian, Scandinavian, French, Native American, Dutch, Polish, Russian and non-European origins.

Home of The Mounties

The development of Saskatchewan runs parallel with the history of the Royal Canadian Mounted Police. The story begins in July 1874, when 300 recruits of the Northwest Mounted Police, as the force was first known, were sent from Manitoba to establish law and order in the Northwest. It was an epic march, covering some 1,300km (800 miles). Today, the route taken by those six 50-man troops of scarlet-coated horsemen, accompanied by a cavalcade of horses, cattle, machinery and provision wagons, is more or less followed by the interprovincial highway known as the **Red Coat Trail** (Highway 13 in Saskatchewan).

A number of early Mounted Police posts have been resurrected as national historic sites in various locations throughout the province. Fort Walsh in the Cypress Hills was established in 1875 to ensure peaceful settlement and control the illegal whiskey trade with the Indians. Nearby is Farwell's Trading Post, where whiskey and guns were traded for furs. Fort Battleford reflects the life of a NWMP post and details the role the fort played in the 1885 Northwest Rebellion. Wood Mountain Post, near the US border, is where Chief Sitting Bull and 5,000 Sioux followers crossed into Canada after the Battle of the Little Big Horn in 1876.

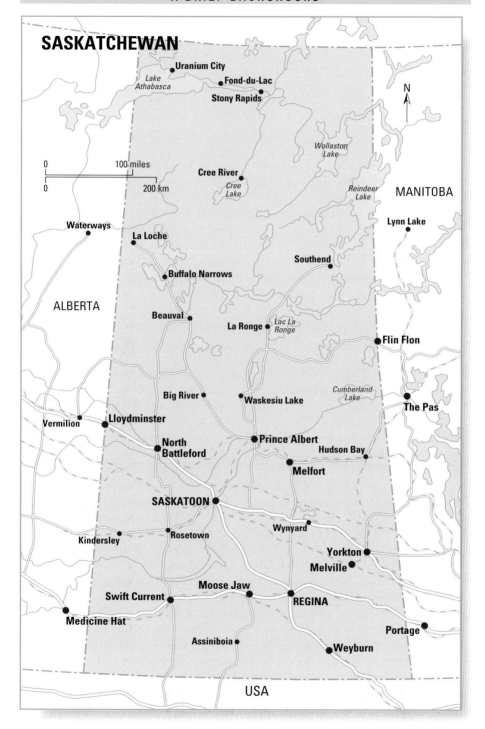

SASKATCHEWAN

Uranium City
Lake Athabasca
Fond-du-Lac
Stony Rapids

N

Wollaston Lake

0 100 miles
0 200 km

Cree River
Cree Lake

Reindeer Lake

MANITOBA

Waterways

Lynn Lake

La Loche

Southend

Buffalo Narrows

ALBERTA

Beauval

La Ronge
Lac La Ronge

Flin Flon

Big River

Waskesiu Lake

Cumberland Lake

The Pas

Vermilion
Lloydminster

North Battleford

Prince Albert

Hudson Bay

Melfort

SASKATOON

Wynyard

Kindersley
Rosetown

Yorkton

Melville

Moose Jaw

Swift Current

REGINA

Medicine Hat

Portage

Assiniboia

Weyburn

USA

145

Mounties Museum

The RCMP Centennial Museum in Regina (free admission) reflects the background and work of the force in relics, photographs and memorabilia. There are derring-do tales of the Mounties' stout efforts to get their man that are just as sensational as the incidents portrayed in the museum's collection of Hollywood posters.

The museum is at the RCMP's national training academy in west Regina, which also contains the city's oldest building, the RCMP Chapel. The colourful Sergeant Major's Parade, when the recruits are put through their paces, is staged daily and draws large, admiring crowds.

After negotiating with Major James Walsh of the NWMP, Sitting Bull and his people were allowed to stay in relative peace in Canada for the next five years.

Modern Times

In 1905 Saskatchewan became a fully fledged province, with Regina as its capital city. The new province prospered until the 1929 stock market crash was followed by a worldwide depression and a decade of drought and crop failure. The Saskatchewan Wheat Pool, which grew from humble beginnings in 1924, has become one of the world's largest grain-handling co-operatives, and is the leading company in the province.

There have been many changes in Saskatchewan in the last half century. Vast mineral riches were uncovered, and modern pioneers developed the continent's first arts board and Canada's first medical care insurance scheme. The exploration continues today – in the arts, business and space research.

Saskatchewan's progress is traced in four branches of the **Western Development Museum**, each of which has its own theme. The story of the people of the province is told in the branch at Yorkton. Transportation is the theme in Moose Jaw, where visitors can see how settlers travelled across the prairies in the Red River ox cart, covering 24km (15 miles) a day at best. In Saskatoon you can take a walk

through the past in Boomtown 1910, a living museum with a reconstructed prairie town main street. The theme is agriculture at North Battleford, where a working farm grows and harvests its crops using the methods and machinery of the early 20th century. Special events are staged at all four branches during the summer.

National and Provincial Parks

There's no shortage of open space in Saskatchewan. The province has more than 200 national, provincial and regional parks and nearly 2 million ha (4.8 million acres) of parkland.

Prince Albert National Park

Halfway up the province on the southern edge of the great northern forest, this is one of Saskatchewan's most popular destinations. Here you can experience wilderness adventures and the comforts of a lakeside resort.

Established more than 60 years ago, the park covers some 388,000ha (nearly 1 million acres) and has three distinct environmental regions. Its wide open grassland region, in the southwest, supports prairie animals, including bison. Elk, deer and badgers are to be found in the rolling parklands; while wolves, elk, moose and bears inhabit the northern forests. Canada's second largest pelican colony nests at **Lavallee Lake** in the far north. One-fifth of the park is water, with some 1,500 lakes and streams supporting 23 species of fish.

The park's extensive **trail** system encompasses all grades of hiking, from short self-guided walks to day-long and overnight treks. Some of the longer trails have also been designated for mountain bike use. Visitors seeking a real getaway experience will head for the backcountry. The **Elk Trail** and the **Hunters Lake Trail** lead to seldom visited lakes. **Canoe routes** range from the pleasant Bagwa course adjoining Kingsmere Lake to the demanding Bladebone route with its many portages. There are three major **campgrounds**, with more than 500 pitches, and many rustic and primitive campgrounds in remote areas.

The gateway to the park is the bustling little town of **Waskesiu** – it means 'red deer' in the Cree language – which has more than 300 hotel and motel rooms and cabins and two major campgrounds. It also offers a superb 18-hole golf course, outdoor theatres, sternwheel cruises and other activities. Maps and information are available at the park visitor centre in Waskesiu – tel. (306) 663-5322 – and you can learn about the area's wildlife through films and exhibits in the nature centre there.

There is a charge for vehicles entering Prince Albert National Park, which is off Highway 2, about 85km (53 miles) north of the city of Prince Albert.

Grasslands National Park

Opened in 1991, Grasslands National Park in southwest Saskatchewan is still being developed. Eventually, it will cover a total of some 900sq km (350sq miles). Interpretive and visitor services are still limited, but tent camping is available.

Located in two blocks between **Val Marie** and **Killdeer**, the park is surrounded by ranching country and preserves a variety of native mixed grasses in some of the last untouched prairie in North America. But the park holds more than rolling grasslands of western wheat grass, snowberry and silver sage. Its rugged landscape includes eroded cliffs, ravines and stark badlands linked by the meandering Frenchmen River. The most dominant feature is **70 Mile Butte**, named after Mile 70 on the old Northwest Mounted Police Trail.

Wildlife is abundant. In addition to golden eagles, pronghorn antelope, prairie rattlesnakes, sage grouse, prairie falcons, bobcats and porcupines, there are 12 endangered and threatened species, including ferruginous hawks, burrowing owls and short-horned lizards. Colonies of black-tailed prairie dogs thrive in the Frenchman River Valley, the only place in Canada where they are still found in their natural habitat.

There is much evidence of human habitation. Here, the Plains Indians hunted buffalo, and more than 2,500 prehistoric sites have been identified, including several major drive lanes, cairns and tipi rings, where rocks were laid to hold down the edge of a tipi. The Northwest Mounted Police travelled extensively in the area from 1874 to 1918, and many of the markers along their trail can still be seen. There are also the remains of pioneer homesteads, including the shack of the cowboy author and artist Will James.

The park's information centre, at **Val Marie**, is open daily from late May to early September (tel. 306/298-2257). On Sunday mornings in July and August interpreters lead hikes into the park.

Tale of an Empty Cabin

Many visitors to Prince Albert National Park make a 20km (12 1/2-mile) pilgrimage on foot or by canoe to a simple log cabin on the shores of Ajawaan Lake. But this is no ordinary cabin – it is 'Beaver Lodge', home for the last seven years of his life of the man the world knew as Grey Owl.

In the 1930s he was the world's most celebrated naturalist – a writer and lecturer who preached the message of conservation long before the word 'ecology' entered common usage. A colourful figure, tall and spare with plaited hair and buckskin clothing, he claimed to be the son of an Apache mother and a Scottish father.

After his death in 1938 it was learned that he was, in fact, Archibald Stansfield Belaney, born in Hastings, England, in 1888. As a child he had been fascinated by legends of the Wild West and Indian rituals. At 17 he left home for Canada.

After two unsuccessful marriages and service in France in World War I, he returned to Ontario where he met and married a Mohawk girl named Anahareo. Archibald Belaney had found a new life. In buckskins and braided hair, he was now known as Wa-Sha-Quon-Asin (He Who Walks By Night).

In 1929 he wrote his first nature article, and the publishers demanded more. His first book, published in 1931, was Men of the Last Frontier, an instant success. Later that year he and Anahareo moved to Prince Albert National Park and built Beaver Lodge. Here he wrote Pilgrims of the Wild, Sajo and the Beaver People and Tales of an Empty Cabin.

Now known internationally as Grey Owl, he lectured in the United States and Britain, where he was invited to Buckingham Palace by King George VI. In 1937, after a hectic tour of England, he returned exhausted to Ajawaan Lake. The following year, on 13 April, he died of pneumonia.

Grey Owl's image was tarnished for a time by the revelation of his true background, but his writings have survived and there is now a new respect for the man who told people: 'Remember, you belong to nature, not it to you.'

He and Anahareo and their daughter Shirley Dawn lie in a grave overlooking Beaver Lodge.

Provincial Parks

Saskatchewan has 24 provincial parks offering a range of activities in scenic wilderness areas, popular recreation areas and historic sites.

Southern parks include such favourites as Cypress Hills, Moose Mountain and the tourist playgrounds of the Qu'Appelle Valley. In the central parklands are the wooded hills and lakes of Duck Mountain, Greenwater Lake and Narrow Hills – ideal natural environment parks. In the rugged north are wilderness parks like Lac La Ronge and Clearwater River.

Rental cabins, horseback riding, golf, swimming pools and beaches, boat rentals, tennis courts and waterslides can be found in the more developed parks. In others, an electric torch will be the last word in technology. Many provincial parks have special staff to help visitors understand more about the great outdoors, leading hikes, giving campfire talks and operating interpretive centres.

There are daily entrance fees for vehicles entering provincial parks, most of which are open year-round. Provincial historic parks are open during the summer months. Some parks offer outdoor packages combining adventurous experiences with recreational skill development through such activities as whitewater canoeing, off-road mountain biking, fishing and hiking.

Regional Parks

A network of 101 regional parks, established by communities and municipalities throughout Saskatchewan, offers a range of outdoor experiences, including camping, boating and golf. Many are to be found along the province's backroads, giving a taste of rural life. Some have special events or attractions, such as **Wood Mountain Regional Park**, site of Canada's oldest continuous rodeo and home of the Wood Mountain Rodeo and Ranching Museum, and **Redberry Lake Regional Park**, part of an important bird sanctuary.

Sports and Leisure Activities

In and On the Water

Nearly 100,000 freshwater lakes cover about 12 percent of Saskatchewan, the majority in the rugged Precambrian Shield zone up north. But there are endless opportunities for watersports enthusiasts in more accessible locations. Most recreational waters in the south are in or near parks. Among the favourites are such lakes as Waskesiu, in Prince Albert National Park, Kenosee in Moose Mountain Provincial Park, and Good Spirit Lake, near Yorkton. Turtle Lake, near Glaslyn in central west Saskatchewan, is said to have a Loch Ness-type monster lurking in its depths.

Boating and **water-skiing** is big on Buffalo Pound Lake and the chain of lakes in the Qu'Appelle Valley, while **sailing** and **windsurfing** are popular on Last Mountain Lake north of Regina, Jackfish Lake near North Battleford, and Greig Lake at Meadow Lake Provincial Park. The damming of part of the South Saskatchewan River in 1967 created Lake Diefenbaker, with 800km (500 miles) of prairie shoreline, northwest of Moose Jaw. Eight parks border the lake, including Elbow Harbour Recreation Site, which has an impressive yacht marina.

Lake Diefenbaker is one of several expansive stretches of water, including a number in the north, where holidaymakers can take the helm in a chartered self-skippered **houseboat**. These are large self-contained craft, comfortably furnished, well-equipped and easy to handle. This is one way for a family to answer the call of the wild without going to rugged extremes.

Canoeing and Whitewater Rafting

For those who do want to follow the rougher routes, the province has more than 50 mapped and documented **canoe** routes, most of them accessible by road and several suitable for novices. Avid canoeists agree that northern Saskatchewan is one of the great adventure destinations. The Churchill River, north of the 55th parallel, provides some of North America's most exhilarating whitewater canoeing as it surges through rapids and tumbles over many falls. The river also has large stretches of smooth water as it links dozens of quiet lakes on its way from Alberta to Hudson Bay – the historic route used by the early *voyageurs* and fur traders.

The Clearwater River, endowed with limestone cliffs and majestic canyons as well as lots of whitewater, is another favourite with experienced canoeists. Because of its natural features and historical associations – it has numerous Indian pictographs and the Methye Portage from fur-trading days along its route – it was officially declared a Canadian Heritage River in 1986.

The Clearwater also offers big adrenalin challenges to **whitewater rafting** enthusiasts. In one section you go through 28 sets of rapids and run through Skull Canyon with 45m (145ft) cliffs rising on either side of the foaming water. The Foster River north of La Ronge dodges through 43 sets of rapids in unspoiled wilderness.

Fishing

Wherever you can paddle, sail or cruise you can almost certainly fish. Saskatchewan has 68 species of fish in its lakes, rivers and streams, with northern pike and walleye the most evenly distributed. Trout include rainbow, brook, brown and the laker, the province's only native trout. In the north anglers face a vigorous challenge against the elusive Arctic grayling.

Keen northern anglers use the facilities of outfitting camps, with full fly-in and drive-in packages from outfitters offering qualified guides, boat and motor rentals.

Fishing licences are available at most sporting goods stores, resorts and fishing camps. Part of the licence fee goes towards improving and diversifying fishing in the province.

Hunting

Sportsmen from across North America are attracted to Saskatchewan for big game, waterfowl and game bird hunting. Many hunters use the services of outfitters for accommodation, guides and organized expeditions, such as goose hunting in the southwest or going after black bear in the north.

Most outfitting camp operators in the province belong to the Saskatchewan Outfitters Association, Box 2016, Prince Albert, Saskatchewan S6V 6K1, tel. (306) 763-5434, fax (306) 922-6044. A complete listing of all licensed Saskatchewan outfitters – and information on the range of outdoor activities in the province – is given in *The Saskatchewan Outdoor*

Saskatchewan's extensive waters provide ample space for watersports, even in the heart of Saskatoon.

Adventure guide available from **Tourism Saskatchewan**, Saskatchewan Trade and Convention Centre, 1919 Saskatchewan Drive, Regina, Saskatchewan S4P 3V7; tel. 1-800-7191 (toll-free in Canada and USA) or (306) 787-2300; fax (306) 787-5744.

First-time hunters and those aged under 18 must have completed a hunter education course before they are allowed to buy a hunting licence. All regulations apply equally to resident and non-resident hunters, but there are a few additional restrictions for visitors.

The province has 76 hunting zones and restrictions vary from one to another, so hunters are advised to obtain a copy of the current *Saskatchewan Hunting and Trapping Guide* when they buy a licence, or to get one in advance from Tourism Saskatchewan. The guide is usually available by mid-August.

One out of every four ducks bagged on the continent originates in Saskatchewan, which is located along one of North America's major waterfowl migration routes. Ducks, geese, coots and common snipe may all be hunted by non-residents.

Upland game bird hunting for sharp-tailed grouse, Hungarian partridge, ruffed grouse and spruce grouse usually begins in late September. Good upland game bird hunting is to be found in the grasslands area of the southwest and in large areas of the farmland and parkland habitats.

The major big game hunting territory is in the extensive northern forests, although trophies may be pursued in other parts of the province. Over the years, Saskatchewan has yielded world-class trophies for both black bear and white-tailed deer. Dozens of outfitting camps cater for big game hunters. Non-residents of Canada are required to use the services of licensed guides or outfitters to hunt big game, including white-tailed deer, moose and bear.

Watching Wildlife

For those who would rather hunt wildlife with binoculars or a camera, the opportunities are limitless. Wildlife attractions are numerous, ranging from museums with natural history collections to scheduled naturalist-guided walks, 'wolf howls', 'bison caravans' and 'owl hoots'. There are wild animal parks in Moose Jaw and Saskatoon, bison herds at Buffalo Pound Provincial Park and Prince Albert National Park, and bird sanctuaries at Regina, Redberry Lake, Last Mountain Lake and elsewhere.

Saskatchewan is a great place to see the rare whooping crane, a magnificent white bird with a wingspan of around 2m (6ft), and standing almost as tall as a man. They are frequently seen during migration between their nesting grounds in **Wood Buffalo National Park** and their wintering grounds in Texas.

From late August to November geese, ducks, swans and sandhill cranes swim into Saskatchewan in their millions, congregating on shallow lakes and marshes – as good a reason as any for bird lovers to visit the province in the autumn.

North America's oldest bird sanctuary is **Last Mountain Lake National Wildlife Area**, north of Regina. It was established in 1887 and offers two nature trails, an observation tower and a picnic area. As many as 40,000 sandhill cranes and hundreds of thousands of other waterfowl gather at the sanctuary before flying south for the winter.

On Redberry Lake, near the town of Hafford about an hour's drive northwest of Saskatoon, a group of local wildlife enthusiasts has won a number of conservation prizes for an ecotourism project which preserves a fragile environment while allowing visitors a close look at some of nature's most magnificent birds.

The **Redberry Pelican Project** protects some 200 bird species – including white-winged scoters, cormorants and piping plovers, as well as the white pelicans for which it has become famous. With advance notice, visitors can tour past nesting islands in a patrol boat.

An interpretive centre features exhibits on the lake's special qualities, its flora and fauna, with a special focus on pelicans. Its highlight is a video monitoring system in which remote cameras located on nesting islands enable visitors to get a close-up view of the pelicans' current behaviour.

There are birdwatching opportunities even in the province's two largest cities. In Regina, the marshes and islands of the Wascana Centre are a refuge for hundreds of Canada geese, while ducks, geese, swans and pelicans shelter on display ponds near the Saskatchewan Centre of the Arts. From the viewing area at Saskatoon's Mendel Art Gallery you can watch geese, pelicans and other birds on the **South Saskatchewan River**, and nesting and migratory birds can be observed at the **Beaver Creek Conservation** area just south of the city.

Taking the Waters

Saskatchewan has its own equivalent of the Dead Sea. In fact, the specific density of **Little Manitou Lake** is even greater than that of the Dead Sea, and its mineral content is similar to that of the leading European spas.

Little Manitou Lake is about 120km (70 miles) southeast of Saskatoon (take Highway 16 east then 365 south). The early Indians knew it as 'The Place of Healing Waters', and 50 years ago it was known to visitors from throughout North America as 'The Carlsbad of Canada'.

Today, the community of Manitou Beach is enjoying a comeback as holidaymakers, as well as sufferers from arthritis, rheumatism and other ailments, flock to the **Manitou Springs Mineral Spa**, opened in 1988. The spa has Canada's largest indoor mineral pool, in which people bob like corks, unable to sink.

The spa is linked to a 60-room hotel and convention centre, and a mini-mall includes a gift shop specializing in Saskatchewan crafts. Another village amenity is the 1930s Danceland, which has a dance floor padded with horsehair.

Accommodation

The Country Life

More than 70 families offer visitors the chance to experience Saskatchewan's rural lifestyle by staying as guests on **farms** and **country homes**. Guests can stay for bed and breakfast or linger for an extended period.

Staying on a farm is an attractive and restful holiday option. You can share in the work – feeding chickens, perhaps, or bringing the cows in for milking – or you can do your own thing. And there is the considerable bonus of home-cooking: freshly baked bread and buns, fruit pies,

FESTIVALS AND EVENTS

With some 500 special events taking place in the province each year, there's no shortage of things to do in Saskatchewan. Celebrations range from the big and spectacular – like the Big Valley Jamboree, Agribition and Folkfest – to the small and eccentric, among which are the Duck Derby at Lumsden, near Regina, the World Chicken Chariot Races at Wynard, south of Quill Lakes, and the World Championship Gopher Derby at Eston, in southwest Saskatchewan.

Rodeos and Frontier Festivals

About 50 rough and tumble rodeos are staged annually, including Canada's oldest, first launched by the Mounties at Wood Mountain in 1890. To see the best bronco busting, bull riding and calf roping there's a choice of the **Frontier Days Rodeo** in Swift Current, Maple Creek's **Cowtown Rodeo**, and the **Stampede** at Meadow Lake. There is also a full calendar of frontier festivals, exhibitions and pioneer days celebrating Saskatchewan's past. Best-known of these is Regina's **Buffalo Days**, held in late July. Other popular events are the Saskatoon Exhibition, the Hometown Fair at Moose Jaw, the Yorkton Exhibition and the Melfort Summer Fair.

Pow Wows

Authentic Indian pow wows, complete with traditional food, costumes and dancing, take place at many reserves in the province. These are not events staged for tourists, but celebrations organized by the Indians as an important part of their cultural heritage. However, visitors are welcome to attend.

Summer pow wows are normally staged over a weekend, with people usually arriving on Friday to set up camp. Saturday and Sunday are given over mainly to the songs and dances.

Some of the better known pow wows are held on the Sakimay, Poundmaker, Piapot, Standing Buffalo and Onion Lake reserves. Times and locations are listed in the *Saskatchewan Events Calendar* obtainable from Tourism Saskatchewan.

home-cured hams, and vegetables grown right outside the window.

Compared with hotel prices, the cost of staying on a farm is extraordinarily reasonable. Some farms have special packages for families, campers and hunters. Most vacation farms in the province are members of the **Saskatchewan Country Vacations Association**, Box 654, Gull Lake, Saskatchewan S0N 1A0; tel. (306) 672-3970.

Vacation farms are indicated by a barn symbol on highway signs and located on the official Saskatchewan highway map.

Camping

Saskatchewan has more than 450 campgrounds, many of them operated by the provincial government in conjunction with national and provincial parks. Other well-serviced operations can be found at private resorts and regional parks, in towns and cities, along major highway routes and on farms. They are to be found, also, in the remotest locations – even in the wildernesses of the far north.

Sites with electricity are available in many places, with the exception of some in the far north. Standard fees are charged at provincial government campgrounds across the province, and rates charged reflect the level of service offered. Discounted fees may be available in some locations and at certain times of the year. Many provincial parks offer designated group camping areas, where a number of sites are linked to form small camping communities.

Regina

Saskatchewan's capital city, fair Regina, was first known, rather less gloriously, as Pile O' Bones. It was an apt name for an insignificant prairie settlement whose principal feature was a mound of buffalo bones 2m (6ft) high and about 12m (40ft) in diameter. The bones had been placed there, at the intersection of a well-trodden buffalo trail and a small creek, by generations of Cree Indians who believed they would attract more buffalo to the slaughter site.

A Brief Background

'Pile O' Bones' was the white man's interpretation of Oskunah-Iasis-Take, which was the prettier Cree way of saying more or less the same thing. In 1882 the rather dreary little settlement suddenly turned respectable. It became a rail terminal. The Northwest Mounted Police established its headquarters there, and the capital of the Northwest Territories was moved from Battleford. Pile O' Bones was renamed Regina in honour of Queen Victoria.

Settlers poured into the treeless but fertile plains, and the infant city began to grow. Stores, banks, hotels and churches were built, a school opened and hospital services began. In 1905, when Regina was named capital of the new province of Saskatchewan, its leaders determined to create a city worthy of its name. Wascana Creek, once dominated by all those buffalo bones, was dammed to form a reservoir which later became an attractive lake. Land was prepared for a grand Legislative Building, and more was set aside as a public park which over the years has grown to become the city's showpiece, the 959ha (2,300-acre) **Wascana Centre**, encompassing cultural and educational buildings and enviable recreational facilities.

From Depression to Boom

Like many other places, Regina had a

tough time during the 1930s. Thousands found themselves on relief as extreme drought on the prairies added to the economic hardship caused by worldwide depression. Oil and gas exploration brought rewards after World War II, and in 1951 an oil pipeline linked Regina with the oil fields of Alberta and the refineries in the east.

The 1960s were a boom time. The city annexed new areas to accommodate a population which was growing at the rate of 4,500 a year. Old industries were extended and new ones established. Newcomers found excellent employment opportunities. Buoyancy continued in the 1970s, but the economic character of the city began to change as its dependence on agriculture gave way to industrial and commercial activities. Nevertheless, the rich farmland of its hinterland continues to produce wheat, oats, flax, barley and mustard. The area also has oil, gas and potash deposits. Today, Regina is a major financial, business, industrial and cultural centre with a population of around 180,000.

Getting There

By air: Regina Airport, served by Air Canada, Canadian Airlines International and a number of commuter airlines, is about 6km (4 miles) southwest of the city centre. Taxis are plentiful and the 15-minute ride into town is inexpensive.

Getting Around

Regina Transit (tel. 777-7777) operates 19 bus routes throughout the metropolitan area. There are no buses on Sundays. Regina has no passenger rail services.

Orientation

Tourism Regina (tel. 789-5099) maintains an information centre on the Trans-

Canada Highway east of the city (the highway bypasses Regina), and an information booth is in Wascana Centre, off Lakeshore Drive, near the Diefenbaker Homestead. Streets in the city run north–south, with avenues running east–west. Albert Street (Highway 6) is the major north–south route and Victoria Avenue the main east–west artery.

The city's major attractions are to be found in **Wascana Centre**. You can take a **tour** on a double-decker bus to get your bearings, and bicycles can be rented in the park, together with helmets and child carriers. You will need plenty of time if you feel like walking, but a booklet obtained from the information centre maps out six walks, each lasting 20 or 25 minutes.

City Highlights

The **Royal Saskatchewan Museum** on the corner of Albert Street and College Avenue is in the northwest section of the Centre, one of the first areas to be developed. The museum's Earth Sciences Gallery shows how Saskatchewan evolved from temperate seas, through the age of dinosaurs, to the arrival of man, presenting the origin of landscapes, mineral resources and life in modern, multimedia exhibits. An exciting time tunnel takes visitors on a walk through $2\frac{1}{2}$ billion years of geological history, and there's a chance to meet Megamunch, a robotic dinosaur who comes to life with realistic roars.

The **First Nations Gallery**, opened in 1993, traces the history and traditions of aboriginal societies over a period of some 10,000 years, showing how the lives of Native Americans were closely linked with the plants, animals and other natural resources around them. The gallery also presents an outstanding collection of murals, sculptures and background paintings

by Saskatchewan native and non-native artists, complementing artefacts from the museum's extensive archaeological and ethnological collections.

South of the Royal Saskatchewan, Albert Street continues to **Speakers' Corner**, where the right of free speech is expressed as vigorously as it is in London's Hyde Park. In fact, the gas lamps at the entrance once stood near the original Speakers' Corner. Another import from England are the birch trees, brought from the meadow at Runnymede, where the Magna Carta was signed by King John in 1215.

Beyond Speakers' Corner, Legislative Drive leads to the Saskatchewan **Legislative Building**, the most impressive structure in Wascana Centre. Designed to reflect the architecture of the English Renaissance and the France of Louis XVI, the building was completed in 1912 and accommodates 265 rooms. The interior gleams with 34 different types of marble, and pastel prints of tribal chiefs of old are hung in the Assiniboine Gallery. Admission to the Legislative Building is free and there are guided tours.

The **Mackenzie Art Gallery** is south of the Legislative Building, on Saskatchewan Road. It houses a collection ranging from historical to contemporary works by Canadian, American and international artists and places particular emphasis on the works of emerging Saskatchewan artists.

A former power station houses the **Saskatchewan Science Centre** on Winnipeg Street and Wascana Drive. The centre features more than 70 permanent hands-on exhibits, live demonstrations and visiting displays. Visitors can blow giant bubbles, make hot-air balloons rise and fall, freeze their own shadows, change their appearance with the aid of a computer and fool around with nature to their heart's content. Also located in the centre is the Kramer IMAX Theatre, where exciting films are shown on a five-storey screen with 11,000 watts of six-channel all-round sound.

Opposite the science centre, on the other side of Wascana Lake, are the **Wascana Waterfowl Park Display Ponds**. You can stroll along a boardwalk constructed over a marsh and identify more than 60 species of geese, ducks, pelicans, swans and other waterfowl with the help of display panels.

Along Lakeshore Drive, north of the Mackenzie Art Gallery, is the **Diefenbaker Homestead**, the boyhood home of John G Diefenbaker, Canada's thirteenth Prime Minister. As a youngster, the future politician helped his father to build the house at Borden, Saskatchewan, in 1905. It was moved to Regina in 1967 and now contains many family artefacts and memorabilia from the early 1900s.

Tour guides in period costumes escort visitors through **Government House**, an elegant mansion which was the official residence of Saskatchewan's Lieutenant Governors from 1891 to 1945. It reflects the period of Lieutenant Governor Amédeé Forget, with large, regal rooms restored to their turn-of-the-century grandeur. Government House is at 4607 Dewdney Avenue.

The most popular tourist attraction in Regina is the **Royal Canadian Mounted Police Academy and Museum** at 6101

T he fountain in front of Saskatchewan Legislative Building originally came from Trafalgar Square in London.

Dewdney Avenue, about 2km (1 mile) west of Government House. Every recruit to the Mounties must go through 6 months of rigorous basic training at the academy.

The Mounties arrived in Regina in 1882, when they made their headquarters here. The city's oldest building – a former cookhouse built in 1883 – is now the non-denominational chapel, a simple but dignified structure with original pews and brilliant stained-glass windows which relate incidents in the history of the force. A daily event is the stirring Sergeant Major's Parade, held on the parade square in summer and in the drill hall in winter and during inclement weather. Tours of the academy are conducted by recruits.

Some 25,000 artefacts are on show in the RCMP **Centennial Museum** – everything from the cannons dragged across the prairies by men of the Northwest Mounted Police in 1874 to the clandestine kit of a Nazi spy captured in 1942. Many exhibits illustrate incidents that seem to come straight out of the pages of *The Boy's Own Paper* – pure Robert Service. There is the story of the Mad Trapper of Rat River. There is the 1885 Rebellion and the crucifix worn by the Métis leader Louis Riel as he went to the gallows. And there is the beaded rifle case and tobacco pouch presented to Chief Sitting Bull by Superintendent James Walsh, who looked after the Sioux leader and his followers when they sought refuge in Canada after Custer's Last Stand at the Battle of the Big Horn.

The city's early days are brought into sharp focus in the **Regina Plains Museum** at 1801 Scarth Street – a building known as 'the old post office'. Exhibits include a primitive sod hut and rooms furnished in turn-of-the-century styles. There are also displays showing the his-

*T*he Mounties' headquarters have been in Regina since 1882. Their museum is a leading attraction.

tory of the Plains Indians and of the 1885 Northwest Rebellion, a conflict involving federal forces and the Métis, a mixed-race people descended from French-Canadian *voyageurs* and Cree and Saulteaux women.

Another attraction in the old post office is the **Globe Theatre**, a 400-seat theatre-in-the-round where classic drama and contemporary Saskatchewan productions are presented by professional players. Original productions are also presented at the Regina Little Theatre in the **Regina Performing Arts Centre** at 1077 Angus Street. The **Saskatchewan Centre of the Arts**, at 200 Lakeshore Drive, in Wascana Centre, has two theatres which stage Broadway shows, plays, dance performances, pop concerts and performances by the Regina Symphony Orchestra.

Nightlife

Compared with some other provincial capitals, Regina's nightlife is limited. The chief night spot is **Capers** in the Ramada Renaissance Hotel on Saskatchewan Drive. Blackjack, roulette and other games are played at the **Buffalo Buck Casino** in Regina Exhibition Park. The casino is open Thursday, Friday and Saturday.

Country and Western music fans can try the **Longbranch Saloon**, 1400 McIntyre Street, and **W H Shooters**, 2075 Broad Street. **Delbert's**, 1433 Hamilton Street, is a rock 'n' roll place.

The city's **restaurants**, mostly in the low to middle price range, offer fast food, home cooking, ethnic dishes and *haute cuisine*.

Shopping

Two major shopping complexes are to be found in Regina's Market Square, an area bordered by Saskatchewan Drive, Victoria Avenue, Albert Street and Broad Street. These are the **Cornwall Centre**, 11th Avenue and Scarth Street, and **The Galleria** at Scotia Centre, 11th Avenue and Hamilton Street. **Northgate Mall** is about 20 blocks north of Market Square, at Albert Street and 9th Avenue North. The **Regina Antique Mall**, at 1175 Rose Street, is claimed as the finest centre of its kind in Western Canada, with 28 dealers offering a wide assortment of antiques and collectibles. The mall is open 7 days a week, with late shopping on Wednesday and Thursday nights and Sunday opening noon to 5pm.

Saskatoon – City of Bridges

With seven bridges spanning the South Saskatchewan River, Saskatoon is an attractive, lively city, and the largest in the province with a population of around 186,000. Its founders were a group of Methodists from Ontario who arrived in 1883 determined to build a teetotal Utopia. Today, the only reminder of their vision is Temperance Street. Nevertheless, those pious pioneers would no doubt be as proud of the city as their successors are.

'Saskatoon' is the Cree word for a sweet and tasty purple berry that thrives in the area and turns up in a number of desserts, notably as a breakfast pancake filling, and in Saskatoon Pie, which has almost become the official provincial dish.

Like many Canadian cities, Saskatoon sprang into prominence with the arrival of the transcontinental railroad in 1890. Commerce began to grow as entrepreneurs and shopkeepers provided for the needs of settlers – the temperance ideal did not last long – and the city expanded with the exploitation of wheat, potash and oil. Now it is the service centre for a vast agricultural area and for Saskatchewan's mining industry. The technological needs of these two major industries have made the city into a leading high-tech hub. It is the home of the University of Saskatchewan.

Getting There

By air: **Saskatoon Airport** is 8km (5 miles) from the city centre. **Taxis** and airport **limos** are reasonably priced.

By train: **VIA Rail** passenger trains arrive and depart at the station, off 11th Street, about 15 minutes west of downtown.

By bus: **Greyhound Canada** operates long-distance bus services to various parts of the country from the bus terminal on 23rd Street East, downtown. The **Saskatchewan Transportation Company** provides frequent daily services between Saskatoon and Regina and to most points throughout the province.

Getting Around

All parts of the city are served by **Saskatoon Transit System** buses.

Visitor Information

Tourism Saskatoon's main information centre is at 6-305 Idylwyld Drive North (tel. 242-1206), and from mid-May to the end of August other centres are operated at Avenue C and 47th Street, Highway 7 at 11th Street, and Highway 11 South at Grasswood Road.

What to Do

There's plenty to keep the visitor occupied: museums, art galleries, theatres; golf courses galore, curling rinks, bowling alleys, swimming pools, and racquetball and tennis courts. There are plenty of restaurants. The South Saskatchewan River, which divides the city diagonally, is an area of activity summer and winter. Shakespeare is performed in a bankside festival tent in July, and gentle cruises along the river take place several times a day from June to August. There is a 16km (10-mile) hiking and cycling trail along both banks and in the winter there are riverside ski trails.

Orientation

The downtown area is on the west bank of the river, between Victoria and University Bridges, and spreads westwards to Idylwyld Drive. The best place to get acquainted with the city is the **Meewasin Valley Centre**, a small but entertaining museum with hands-on exhibits that tell the story of Saskatoon and the river. The centre is at 402 Third Avenue South, near the Victoria Bridge. It marks the start of the Meewasin Valley Trail and offers information on hiking, cycling, canoeing and birdwatching opportunities as well as general sightseeing. 'Meewasin' is the apt Cree word for 'beautiful valley'.

Around the City

From the Meewasin Valley Centre, Spadina Crescent follows the river north, passing the **Delta Bessborough**, one of Canada's great château-style hotels and a major feature of the Saskatoon skyline. At 910 Spadina Crescent East is the **Ukrainian Museum of Canada**, where historical exhibits and displays of contemporary art and crafts – costumes, embroidery, textiles, ceramics and wood carvings – trace the heritage of Canada's Ukrainian community. About 10 percent of Saskatchewan's population are of Ukrainian origin. A close neighbour of the Ukrainian Museum – at 950 Spadina

A canoeist paddles between the arches of one of Saskatoon's seven bridges.

160

Crescent – is the **Mendel Art Gallery and Conservatory** in which the work of local and nationally known artists is shown.

University of Saskatchewan

University Bridge crosses the river to reach the 1,062ha (2,550-acre) campus of the University of Saskatchewan, a handsome collection of stone buildings in English collegiate Gothic style. Here, there is a plethora of cultural and historical attractions which may be visited on a guided tour or on an individual basis. They include the **Museum of Antiquities**, featuring a collection of full-scale replicas of ancient Greek and Roman sculptures, the **Museum of Natural Sciences**, with sections on biology and geology, the **Little Stone Schoolhouse**, Saskatoon's first centre of learning, built in 1887, the **Kenderdine Gallery**, with exhibits of contemporary and historical art, and the **Gordon Snelgrove Art Gallery** which features works by students and faculty from the Art Department and local artists.

A major attraction at the university is the **John G Diefenbaker Centre**, which features the life and times of the former Prime Minister of Canada. Touring exhibits celebrate the political, historical and cultural heritage of Canada and its people. There are reconstructions of the Privy Council Chamber and the office used by Diefenbaker during his time in Ottawa.

Boomtown 1910

Saskatoon's branch of the Western Development Museum – Boomtown 1910 – is located in the Saskatoon Prairieland Exhibition Grounds on Lorne Avenue South. In addition to the reconstruction of an early 20th-century prairie town street, with wooden sidewalks and horse-drawn carriages and wagons, there are galleries featuring massive agricultural machinery and vintage cars. Boomtown 1910 also has a museum store and a café serving the wholesome fare of yesteryear.

Excursions from Saskatoon

Wanuskewin Heritage Park

Archaeological sites older than the Great Pyramids of Egypt have been uncovered at Wanuskewin Heritage Park, situated 5km (3 miles) north of Saskatoon, on Highway 11.

Opened in the summer of 1992, the 100ha (240-acre) park is both a working research centre and a living memorial to the Plains Indians, for whom it is said to have considerable spiritual significance. 'Wanuskewin' means 'seeking peace of mind' in the Cree language.

Indians have gathered and hunted at Wanuskewin for at least 6,000 years, according to the evidence provided by items uncovered from the lowest levels of archaeological digs on 19 separate prehistoric sites. As many as 115 levels containing materials from different periods have been identified.

Visitors can watch digs in progress and discuss finds with the scientists. They can also learn about the site and its importance to the Indians through indoor exhibits and video displays and on a series of hiking trails along which they can squat in a tipi as they listen to a traditional storyteller.

Native Americans from four tribes still live on reserves surrounding the park, where many of them work, acting as guides and performing dances and other ceremonies.

Wanuskewin's visitor centre, a glass and wood building symbolizing the four seasons, the four cardinal points of the compass and four stages of human life, contains two theatres, an art gallery, a craft shop and a restaurant where the menu includes buffalo stew, buffalo burgers – and french fries.

Batoche National Historic Park

About 90km (55 miles) northeast of Saskatoon is Batoche National Historic Park, site of the last battle fought on Canadian soil and the place where a small but distinct group of people fought for the right to maintain their way of life – and lost in the face of an overwhelming force.

The Métis, a mixed-race people resulting from the intermarriage of French-Canadian *voyageurs* and Cree and Salteaux women, originally settled in the Red River area of Manitoba where they thrived on buffalo hunting, trading and providing freight services for the Hudson's Bay Company. But dwindling buffalo herds and the pressures of advancing white settlement caused them to look elsewhere for a home. They decided to establish a settlement along the South Saskatchewan River, spanning the Carlton Trail, a major trade route. A ferry was built across the river, and by 1885 there was a community of about 500 people.

Like other settlers in the Northwest, the Métis were unhappy with the Ottawa government's policy of railway development and protective tariffs which prevented them from buying cheaper American agricultural equipment. The Métis also had difficulties in obtaining legal land titles and grants. In 1884 Louis Riel was appointed their leader, and as petitions to Ottawa were ignored discontentment turned to anger. At Duck Lake, just north of Batoche, police officers were killed in a skirmish. Riel formed a provisional government and appointed Gabriel Dumont commander-in-chief. Ottawa at last responded – by despatching troops under Major General Sir Frederick Middleton to quell the rebellion.

It was an uneven struggle – a government force of 800 against some 300 Métis and Indians. But the rebels fought well, shooting from trenches and using guerilla tactics. When Middleton sent some of his troops into battle by steamship, the Métis strung a cable across the river and crippled the vessel by bringing down its smokestack. But the odds were against them. On 4 May 1885 – the fourth and final day of the battle – Middleton was using a nine-pounder Gatling Gun and the rebels were firing nails and stones from their rifles.

As the battle ended, Riel and Dumont escaped. Riel later gave himself up, only to be tried for treason and hanged at Regina. Dumont fled to the United States where he joined Buffalo Bill Cody's Wild West Show as a sharpshooter. Pardoned, he returned to Batoche and died in 1906.

Today, an extensive **walking trail** enables visitors to retrace the progress of the battle. There are trenches used by both sides, an old farmhouse, the remains of Batoche village, and a church and rectory. A cemetery contains the mass grave of Métis who died in the battle and that of Gabriel Dumont. The visitor centre has displays giving the background to the rebellion and an exhibition of artefacts. An audiovisual programme tells the story of the Métis settlement along the South Saskatchewan River.

Batoche National Historic Park is signposted from Highway 11 north of Saskatoon.

The Battlefords

Facing each other across the North Saskatchewan River, North Battleford and Battleford are 137km (86 miles) northwest of Saskatoon along Highway 16, the Yellowhead Highway.

Battleford was the capital of the Northwest Territories until 1882. The original **Government House** is one of a number of historical buildings prized in the town. **Fort Battleford National Historic Park** is a real Northwest Mounted Police post, established in 1876. Inside the stockade are five original buildings, four of them furnished with period pieces. The old barracks house has an interpretive centre with costumed guides and exhibits relating to the history of the NWMP.

Neighbouring North Battleford is the junior of the two communities, in terms of age at least. It was founded in 1905 when Canadian National Railways decided to build its line on the north side of the river. The city's major attraction is the **Western Development Museum**, depicting a Saskatchewan village of 1925. Its unpaved street has a boarded sidewalk threading past a number of authentic buildings, including a barbershop, bank and drugstore. There are also pioneer homes, churches and an old railway station.

Also in North Battleford is the **Alan Sapp Gallery**, devoted entirely to the work of the prominent Cree artist.

MANITOBA

The Keystone Province

Manitoba gets its name from the Cree word 'Manitou' – the Great Spirit. The Indians believed the strange echoing sounds sometimes heard on the shores of Lake Manitoba were the voice of the Great Spirit. More prosaically, Manitoba is known today as the Keystone Province. It lies plumb in the centre of Canada and also at the very heart of North America: halfway between the Atlantic and Pacific Oceans, and halfway between the Arctic Ocean and the Gulf of Mexico. To the fanciful it might even look like a keystone, with a kink to the northeast where it interlinks with the Northwest Territories, Ontario and Hudson Bay.

Winnipeg, the capital city, is 3,190km (1,982 miles) from Halifax, Nova Scotia, in the east, and 2,292km (1,424 miles) from Vancouver, British Columbia, in the west. Manitoba's immediate neighbours are the Northwest Territories to the north and the American states of North Dakota and Minnesota to the south. The provinces of Saskatchewan and Ontario lie to the west and east respectively. Its central location leads many visitors to believe that Manitoba is landlocked, but in fact the province has 645km (400 miles) of coastline. It's not the kind of coastline that calls

*F*lax makes a splash of colour in Manitoba's fertile farmland.

for deck chairs, beach umbrellas and sun lotion, however, since it lies along the bleak, sub-Arctic shores on the western side of Hudson Bay.

Canada's fifth largest province, covering an area of 650,000sq km (251,000sq miles), Manitoba includes the eastern end of the great prairies. In the south the terrain is mostly very flat, but elsewhere there are rolling hills and valleys, forests and parklands. The rugged countryside of the Precambrian Shield is a rocky composite of rivers, lakes and swamps. The highest point in the province is the 831m (2,726ft) **Baldy Mountain**, in Duck Mountain Provincial Park.

Manitoba slopes in a gradual decline from the south and west to the northeast, and all its waters drain into Hudson Bay. Three rivers – the Churchill, Hayes and

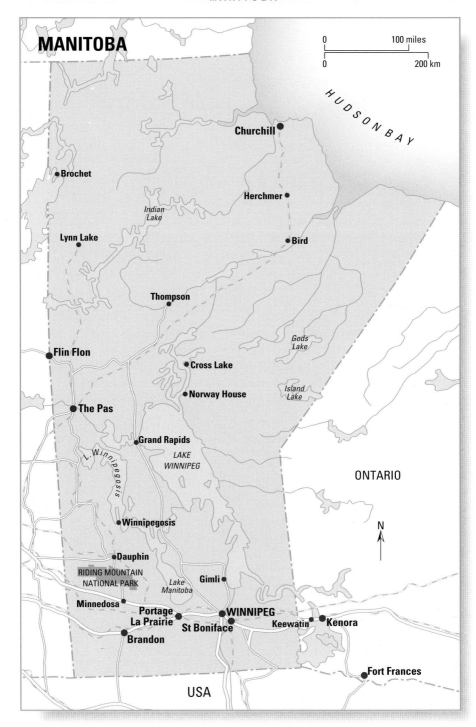

MANITOBA

0 — 100 miles
0 — 200 km

HUDSON BAY

Churchill

Brochet

Herchmer

Indian Lake

Lynn Lake

Bird

Thompson

Gods Lake

Flin Flon

Cross Lake

Island Lake

Norway House

The Pas

Grand Rapids

LAKE WINNIPEG

L. Winnipegosis

ONTARIO

Winnipegosis

N

Dauphin

RIDING MOUNTAIN NATIONAL PARK

Lake Manitoba

Gimli

Minnedosa

Portage La Prairie

WINNIPEG

Kenora

St Boniface

Keewatin

Brandon

Fort Frances

USA

Nelson – flow directly into the bay. The Red, Saskatchewan and Winnipeg Rivers flow into Lake Winnipeg. Another major waterway, the Assiniboine, joins the Red River at Winnipeg. About 100,000 lakes cover some 15 percent of Manitoba's total area, mostly in the north. The three largest lakes – Winnipeg, Manitoba and Winnipegosis – are in the south, survivors from the Ice Age when almost the whole of the province lay hidden beneath a vast glacial lake.

Flora and Fauna

A rich variety of vegetation covers the province, ranging from the prairie grasslands of the south – now mostly cultivated – to the lichens and sedges of the tundra. Between the two extremes are meadows, oak and aspen groves, evergreen forests and marshland plants. **Riding Mountain National Park** alone has some 500 different species of plantlife.

The province is also home to more than 350 species of wildlife – amphibians and reptiles, birds and mammals. In the south, rabbits and rodents are the prey of predators such as the lynx and bobcat. Frogs and salamanders thrive in the wetlands. Birds are abundant everywhere because so many migrant flight paths converge. Beaver, muskrat, deer, elk, moose, wolves and black bear are found in Shield country, and so many polar bears are found along the shores of Hudson Bay that the isolated city of Churchill calls itself the polar bear capital of the world. The waters of Manitoba teem with lake trout, pickerel, pike, whitefish and many other species, and the richest variety of freshwater fish in North America is said to be found in the province's three largest lakes. In the northeast beluga whales and four species of seal exist in Hudson Bay.

A freight train trundles across the Manitoba prairie after harvest time.

The Making of Manitoba

As the Ice Age ended, between 10,000 and 15,000 years ago, leaving behind vast expanses of water and grassland, people began to move into the area now known as Manitoba. Little is known about them, but they almost certainly existed as hunters, living off the great plains bison and possibly the mammoth.

By the time the first Europeans arrived in the 17th century the climate and the terrain had changed. A number of native tribes had settled in different parts of the region, each with a lifestyle based on local resources. In the south the **Assiniboine** depended for food and clothing on the huge herds of buffalo. To the east, the **Salteaux** hunted, fished and harvested the wild rice which is still found in Manitoba's marshlands. Farther north, the **Cree** supplemented their hunting and fishing by gathering berries, nuts and other plants. In the barren north, the **Chipewyans** lived off the caribou. A simple but effective trading system was in operation between the tribes.

The First Europeans

Manitoba's first Europeans arrived in 1612, led by Captain Thomas Button, a British explorer who landed in Hudson Bay while seeking a route to the Far East. Forced to winter in the bay, he mapped the western shore and its rivers and called the area New Wales. Some 70 years later the Hudson's Bay Company opened **York Factory**, a fortified warehouse on a spit of land between the mouths of the rivers Hayes and Nelson. Furs were brought here by canoe from places far to the west and stored to await shipment to England. For more than 150 years it was the busiest fur-trading post in Western Canada, declining in importance with the spread of the railways and finally closing down in 1957. It is now a National Historic Site.

French fur traders, who had been active for decades in Eastern Canada, also moved into the region and began pushing westwards. The explorer Pierre Gaultier de La Vérendrye reached Lake Winnipeg in the 1730s and built forts on the Red and Assiniboine Rivers, opening the way for more of his countrymen. Many French

---

Snakes Alive!

Every spring a phenomenon of nature that causes some people to shudder at the mere thought of it brings sightseers out in droves to the tiny community of Narcisse, 130km (81 miles) north of Winnipeg.

Perhaps it's the crowd instinct that draws them to witness the annual mating of red-sided garter snakes, which are also pretty gregarious, for they pour out of their rocky winter dens in late April or early May to engage in what can only be described as an orgy that can last up to three weeks.

The snakes don't simply pair off – hundreds of them form frenzied, writhing carpets. With tens of thousands gathered there, it's said that in the spring there are more snakes concentrated at Narcisse than anywhere else in the world.

Then just as suddenly the snakes lose the urge to merge and vanish into the surrounding marshes.

For people who care to watch such carryings-on, there are trails and viewing platforms around the den sites at the Narcisse Wildlife Management Area, on Highway 17 6km (3 3/4 miles) north of the town. When the red-sided garter snakes aren't stealing the show there's a chance to see white-tailed deer, moose and elk, and birdwatchers can observe the rather more respectable behaviour of sharp-tailed and ruffed grouse, great horned owls and scores of songbirds.

Wind power was an important source of energy to Mennonite settlers at Steinbach, Manitoba.

and English fur traders took Indian women as wives, and in time their descendants came to be known as **Métis**. In 1812 a group of Scottish crofters led by Thomas Douglas, the Earl of Selkirk, became the first European farmers to settle along the Red and Assiniboine Rivers.

The Population Expands

By 1871, one year after Manitoba became a province of the Dominion of Canada, the population had crept up to 25,000. Just 20 years later it exceeded 150,000. Many of the newcomers were from neighbouring Ontario, where all the best land had already been settled, but others came from Britain and Western Europe. Two significant groups were German-speaking Mennonites who had fled from religious persecution and Icelanders forced to emigrate as a result of natural disasters. In 1911 the population totalled 460,000, but there was still plenty of room for more. And they came. Large numbers from the Ukraine, Poland and Russia, and Jews from throughout central and eastern Europe, arrived before the start of World War I. Since the end of World War II Manitoba has welcomed immigrants from all parts of the world, especially refugees from Europe, Asia and Latin America.

Manitoba Today

In spite of all this immigration, this huge province still houses not much more than a million people – and more than half of those live in Winnipeg. In fact, 75 percent of Manitobans live in a city or town – which may not be saying much. Manitoba's second largest city, Brandon, has a population of just over 40,000, and the same number of people is distributed between the province's other three cities –

Flin Flon, Portage la Prairie and Thompson. Bearing these figures in mind, you realize that the population density of 1.65 people per sq km (4.27 per sq mile) is a gross underestimation of the space available for people in most of the province.

The Economy

Commerce in Manitoba began with the fur trade, but as settlers moved in agriculture took the lead. With some 8 million hectares (19 million acres) of land being farmed, agriculture is still important, but the largest sectors of the province's economy today are manufacturing and the service industries which between them provide about 238,000 jobs. As elsewhere in Canada, it is the service industries which have shown the greatest growth, employing more than a third of Manitoba's work force by the early 1990s. Among the leading manufacturing activities in the province are food processing, transportation equipment, printing and publishing, clothing and textiles and machinery and metal production.

Natural resources are also important to the economy, especially minerals, energy and forestry products. Nickel, the leading metal, comes from the Thompson region in northern Manitoba. Next comes copper, mined mainly around Flin Flon on the Manitoba–Saskatchewan border. Other important metals mined in the province are cobalt, gold, lead, selenium, tantalum, tellurium and zinc.

More than 90 percent of the province's electrical energy is produced by water power, generated mostly on the Nelson River system in the north, although there are major hydro systems on the Saskatchewan and Winnipeg Rivers. Excess power is exported to neighbouring provinces and the United States. Most of

Manitoba's petroleum and natural gas comes from the southwest, with production valued in recent years between $100 million and $200 million. Forestry plays a small but significant role, producing about $500 million worth a year of lumber, pulp and paper products.

Manitoba's Regions

Manitoba's diverse landscape was carved by ice and water. During the last Ice Age the province lay under a sheet of ice nearly 2km (1 mile) thick. When the ice retreated, mighty roaring rivers of meltwater were created, and these in turn led to the formation of a vast freshwater sea, Lake Agassiz, which was larger than the present-day Great Lakes put together. At that time, the great plains of Manitoba were the bed of the lake; the hills to the south and east of Brandon overlooked a huge river delta, and the Riding Mountain and Duck Mountain escarpment was a lakeshore. Lake Agassiz dried out some 8,000 years ago, leaving behind a thick deposit of silt – the fertile soil of today's prairies – as well as lakes Manitoba, Winnipeg and Winnipegosis.

The **Northern Region** covers two-thirds of the province north of the 53rd parallel, and is a rugged terrain with thousands of lakes, streams and marshes. Forests of spruce and jack pine give way to a huge treeless tundra in the far north and along Hudson Bay.

The **Parkland Region**, west of lakes Winnipegosis and Manitoba, is upland country dotted with lakes and covered with a mixture of deciduous and evergreen forests. Riding Mountain National Park and Duck Mountain Provincial Park both lie within the Parkland Region.

Rolling prairie punctuated by wooded hills characterizes the landscape of the **Western Region**, extending eastward from the Saskatchewan border to a line roughly corresponding to Highway 34 and south to the border with the United States.

The **Interlake Region**, extending northwards from Winnipeg to Grand Rapids, between Manitoba's two largest lake systems, is a broad, flat area of fertile marshes and beaches, with farmland in the south and mixed forests in the north.

Embracing the southwestern shores of Lake Manitoba and the city of Portage la Prairie, and extending west to Winnipeg and south to the North Dakota and Minnesota state lines, **Central Region** is how many people visualize the province: vast skies, far horizons, rich farmland, and prairie, prairie, prairie, which in the southwest is interspersed with hills and valleys, aspen bluffs and small areas of marshland.

The **Eastern Region**, extending to the border with Ontario, is everybody's idea of Canada: the craggy terrain of the Precambrian Shield, with brooding pine forests, wild rivers and still, reflective lakes. Many of Manitoba's provincial parks and forests are found in this untamed but beautiful region.

Parks and Wilderness

Manitoba has about a dozen major parks, including the renowned **Riding Mountain National Park**. There is also a wide range of minor provincial parks, wildlife management areas and sanctuaries, and historic sites. Many offer a wilderness experience, but there are also lots of opportunities for such family activities as swimming, hiking, horse-riding, canoeing, sailing and boating. Camping facilities are legion.

Riding Mountain National Park

Riding Mountain National Park is about 255km (160 miles) northwest of Winnipeg, more than 3 hours' drive at a legal speed. But it's a trip well worth taking, and there are hotels, motels, cottages and campsites – as well as restaurants, shops and a cinema built of logs – at the resort town of **Wasagaming**, just outside the park's southern entrance. There are campgrounds and picnic areas within the park. To get there from Winnipeg, you take the TransCanada Highway west, then Highways 16 west from Portage la Prairie and 10 north from Minnedosa.

Standing some 460m (1,500ft) above the surrounding terrain, the area was named by fur traders who switched from canoes to horses here as they travelled west. It was declared a national park in 1933 and now attracts about three-quarters of a million visitors a year. The park is a crossroads of habitats covering some 3,000sq km (1,150 sq miles) of boreal forest, aspen parkland, deciduous forest, open grassland and meadows. Its range of flora and fauna is one of the richest and most varied in Manitoba.

The province's largest population of elk lives in the park, and many of them can be seen at dusk and dawn as they feed along roadways and in grassland areas. Moose, also numerous, are frequently seen at the roadside and in wetlands during the summer. Coyotes, beaver, white-tailed deer and foxes are also commonly sighted. Patient wildlife watchers may be lucky enough to glimpse a cougar, mule deer, otters or a pine marten, and it is possible to sight the shy wolves and equally secretive black bears that inhabit the park. A herd of bison may be seen more readily in a 530ha (1,313-acre) enclosure of pasture and woodland near **Lake Audy**.

Birdwatchers will have the time of their life in Riding Mountain National Park. Bald eagles soar over a number of lakes, especially Moon Lake, Whirlpool Lake and Lake Audy, and there are pileated, black-backed and northern three-toed woodpeckers, ospreys, sharp-tailed and spruce grouse and many species of song birds. The great grey owl may be seen at dusk throughout the year. Grey Owl, the controversial conservationist of the 1930s, lived in the park for a time before moving to Saskatchewan. His cabin still stands at **Beaver Lodge Lake**, north of Clear Lake, and is accessible by hiking, mountain bike or ski trail.

The park has about 400km (250 miles) of trails which can be covered on foot, horseback or mountain bike. The network includes day-use and overnight trails, and detailed guides and maps are available at the park office and **Visitor Centre**, both at Wasagaming (tel. 848-2811). The Visitor Centre has displays, and a selection of literature and audiovisual presentations, plus programmes for children and adults.

Duck Mountain Provincial Park

North of Riding Mountain National Park is **Duck Mountain Provincial Park**, an extensive area of woodland, prairie and marsh, where the northernmost aspen and birches meet briefly and mingle with coniferous boreal forest. Duck Mountain is part of the Manitoba Escarpment and is rich in wildlife – song birds galore, black bears, white-tailed deer, moose, lynx, coyotes and wolves. It is also one of the best places in Manitoba to see elk. And hear them, especially in September when the bulls make their distinctive, haunting bugling sound. Some people make a hobby of calling for elk by imitating the noise, and commercially made elk calls

The Man Who Charms Birds

Dan Weedon charms the birds out of the trees to make sure his clients see what they came to see. Dan and his wife, South African-born Thuraya, run Riding Mountain Nature Tours from the town of Erickson, just a few kilometres south of the national park, and have been organizing birdwatching tours and wildlife safaris for small groups since 1985.

Before launching their business, Dan served a useful apprenticeship for ten years as the Park Naturalist in Riding Mountain. But he realized on going it alone that to satisfy the needs of a paying clientele he needed sharper skills than he had acquired with the Canadian National Parks Service.

'You need a thorough knowledge of habitats, of course,' Dan says, 'but it isn't enough to know where to find a particular bird. There isn't time on a tour to wait around for it to show up. So I had to learn how to mimic bird calls, so that if we were looking for a Scarlet Tanager, say, I could get it to come up close.'

Sometimes an encounter in the wild can be a bit too close. In the autumn, Dan and Thuraya run polar bear safaris in the Churchill area on the shores of Hudson Bay.

'Polar bears can be very dangerous,' says Dan, 'and on this occasion there had been a tremendous snowfall which meant the bears could climb snowbanks and get closer to our base. One bear figured out where the entrance was and tried to break in. I felt like a seal in its hiding hole as the bear was smashing the door with these incredibly powerful karate chops. There was just a thin piece of plywood between me and the bear.'

On another occasion Dan was charged by a black bear. 'I ran like a chicken, which they say you should never do. But I did the right thing in just getting out of his personal space so that when he got to where he thought I was, I'd already gone. I don't know if he chased me – I didn't look back.'

In general, though, wildlife viewing is completely safe. 'The biggest fear in the wilderness is of falling and hurting yourself. Wild animals – even polar bears – are afraid of humans most of the time.'

Thuraya's job is to look after the inner wildlife watcher, and her gourmet picnics are legendary, with bread, cakes, pastries and preserves all home-made.

'Food always pacifies the crew, especially if the weather is sour,' says Dan. 'But it's important on safari to eat well at all times. If the weather is good and the wildlife co-operative then good food is a bonus.'

The couple live in a lovely, remote location barely a kilometre (half a mile) from the park boundary. Their home overlooks a small lake, marshes and woodland. A pair of binoculars lies permanently on a table beside a huge picture window at the rear of the house, and when they are not leading a tour the Weedons keep an eye on the birds and beasts that visit their own backyard.

---

can be bought from sports goods stores. But it can be a dangerous skill – especially in the hunting season!

Located in the park's southeast corner is **Baldy Mountain**, Manitoba's highest point. Here you can climb an observation tower to gaze out over the surrounding forest of spruce and aspen.

Duck Mountain is criss-crossed with hiking trails. Many are the unmarked leftovers from the days when logging was carried out in the area, but there are half a dozen designated trails which link up with the two provincial highways that cross the park. The most accessible of these, close to the Duck Mountain Forest centre at the junction of Highways 366 and 367, is the **General Ecology Trail**, consisting of two loops. One loop is a 2.2km (1.37-mile) circuit through some of Manitoba's oldest jack pine forest; the other winds through the forest for 2.5km (1½ miles), crossing the Valley River twice on wooden bridges and offering spectacular views of the area from a three-storey viewing tower.

The park has a number of lakes and streams brimming with trout, splake, muskellunge, walleye, northern pike and perch. The lakes are so clear that the bottom is visible at 9–12m (30–40ft).

Cabins and campsites are available in the park, and there is horseback riding, as well as boat rentals, canoeing and cycling. Duck Mountain Provincial Park can be reached from the town of **Dauphin**, just north of Riding Mountain Provincial Park, by travelling 50km (31 miles) west on Highway 5, then 35km (22 miles) north on Highway 366.

Two other provincial parks – **Clearwater Lake** and **Grass River** – are located north of Lake Winnipegosis, and both are reached by continuing north on Highway 10.

Clearwater Lake Provincial Park

Clearwater Lake Provincial Park is just a few kilometres north of **The Pas**, a town of 7,250 inhabitants. The lake from which the park takes its name is a spring-fed stretch of remarkably clear blue water. A hiking trail leads to a 15m (48ft) limestone cliff along the lake's southern shore in which there are a number of deep crevices known as the **Clearwater Caves**. These were formed more than 400 million years ago when Manitoba was covered by a warm, shallow sea. The self-guided **Cave Trail** winds through a forest of spruce, tamarack and jack pine and leads to a series of viewing platforms which look out over the lake.

Much of the park's remaining 595sq km (230sq miles) consist of coniferous forests with a wide variety of berries and wild flowers. There are facilities for fishing, swimming, boating, hiking, overnight lodging and camping.

Grass River Provincial Park

About 75km (47 miles) north of The Pas Highway 10 meets Highway 39 at the southwestern corner of Grass River Provincial Park, a wilderness of lakes and evergreen forest straddling Precambrian Shield rock. The park is home to a wide range of waterfowl as well as woodland caribou, deer, moose and other animals.

Wild and empty though it seems, the Grass River region has provided refuge and sustenance for travellers for more than 5,000 years. The first arrivals were refugees from drought on the great plains, and they thrived among its clear, cold lakes and fast-running rivers. Rock paintings made by these early people are to be found along some of its rivers and streams.

The Grass River system, connecting 150 lakes, provided a convenient route for European explorers and fur traders led by Cree guides. Samuel Hearne travelled this way in 1774 to establish the Hudson's Bay Company's first inland trading post at Cumberland House, across the border in Saskatchewan. Canoes are still a favoured mode of transport in the park, where a 190km (118-mile) canoe trail links 24 lakes. Experts say you need 8 days to cover the whole route, which requires basic wilderness skills and canoeing experience at intermediate level.

The town of **Cranberry Portage**, on Highway 10, is the park's nearest community. It offers accommodation, supplies, services and canoe rentals and can be reached by rail and air as well as by road. There are various campgrounds inside the park.

Whiteshell Provincial Park

Manitoba's southeastern corner is almost entirely given over to three provincial parks, each one flush against the Ontario border. The southernmost of these, Whiteshell Provincial Park, is one of the largest in the province with an area of 2,590sq km (1,000sq miles). It contains 200 lakes and a quarter of the province's fishing lodges, as well as picnic sites and campgrounds. Its lakes teem with northern pike, perch, smallmouth bass, walleye and lake trout.

Whiteshell can easily be reached from Winnipeg in 2 hours by car – a journey of 125km (78 miles) east along the Trans-Canada Highway reaches the resort town of **Falcon Lake**, which is actually within the park perimeter.

Considering its proximity to Winnipeg and the resort facilities of Falcon Lake – the town has a shopping centre, riding stables, miniature golf, a fine 18-hole golf course and the province's largest sailing club – it's not surprising that Whiteshell is the most popular provincial park in Manitoba. Lodge and hotel accommodation can be found in the southern and western sections of the park, along with fully serviced campgrounds, and two provincial roads – 307 and 309 – permit motorists to penetrate farther north and east. At the other end of the scale, a designated wilderness zone along the eastern boundary is limited to hikers and canoeists, while fly-in lodges present an op-

portunity to visit areas even more remote in the north.

About 12km (8 miles) north of Falcon Lake, on Provincial Road 301, is **West Hawk Lake**. Created by a meteor 150 million years ago, it is Manitoba's deepest lake, with a maximum depth of 111m (365ft), and is popular with scuba divers. Nearby, on Highway 44, is the **Lily Pond**, formed by glacial action and named after the profusion of fragrant water lilies that bloom on its surface from June to September. Many of the shallower lakes, slow-running rivers and marshes in the park yield an abundance of wild rice, harvested in August and early September by Indians in canoes.

Continuing west, Highway 44 leads to the community of **Rennie** (population 100), best known for the **Alf Hole Goose Sanctuary**, where hundreds of geese can be seen in September and October. Founded in 1939, when naturalist Alfred Hole nurtured four abandoned goslings, the sanctuary is on the Mississippi flyway migration route. The visitor centre includes displays, exhibits and an observation gallery overlooking a small lake. A self-guided trail circuits the lake.

Near **Betula Lake**, about 30km (19 miles) north of Rennie on Provincial Road 307, is a 3.6ha (9-acre) site containing a number of petroforms – stones laid out in the shapes of snakes, fish, turtles and birds. Lying on a barren shelf of granite bedrock beside the Whiteshell River, the petroforms are believed to have been created some 1,400 years ago by ancestors of the modern Ojibwa people. The largest outline, depicting a turtle, is an impressive 7.5m (25ft) long.

Further evidence of the lifestyle of the park's ancient dwellers is on show in the log-built **Whiteshell Natural History Museum** at Lake Nutimik. Weapons and tools fashioned from stone and shells are displayed, together with natural history exhibits and various minerals from the Canadian Shield.

Wildlife is abundant in Whiteshell Provincial Park. Black bears, red foxes, beavers, moose and white-tailed deer all make their home there, as do bald eagles, great grey owls, ruffed grouse, loons and pelicans. The park's wetland areas attract sandhill cranes, herons and a variety of waterfowl.

The park is a great draw for hikers, with 15 trails ranging from easy strolls of a couple of kilometres (a mile or so) to the challenging **Mantario Trail**, 66km (42 miles) of trekking through swamp and forest and traversing rock ridges. In some places hikers have to wade through waist-deep water, and in others the trail is likely to be almost overgrown. Those contemplating the trip will need to set aside at least 3 days, and it goes without saying that they need to know what they're doing – not to mention be fit.

Nopiming Provincial Park

If all that sounds like the true back of beyond, stand by to think again, for at the Winnipeg River, Whiteshell gives way to Nopiming Provincial Park – and in the Saulteaux language Nopiming means 'the *entrance* to the wilderness'. The Saulteaux Indians knew what they were talking about, for beyond the park's northern boundary the road loops back towards Winnipeg, as if retreating from the loneliness ahead, and a vast, pristine wilderness marches on for hundreds of kilometres to Hudson Bay.

Not that Nopiming itself is in any sense suburbia. People have made their home in the area for about 2,000 years, but there are many places where it is likely that hu-man feet have never stepped. Towering granite outcrops rise from below the surface of cool, clear lakes or thrust from the forest floor. There are forests of birch, jack pine, poplar and spruce and small, shallow lakes of wild rice. Black bear, white-tailed deer, moose and woodland caribou are frequently sighted. Less frequently seen are wolves and cougar, the largest of Manitoba's big cats. Bald and golden eagles also inhabit the park.

Nopiming can be traversed by car north to south along Provincial Road 314. In the extreme south, Provincial Road 315 heads east from the park entrance towards the Ontario border and there are provincial campgrounds at **Bird Lake**. In the north there are campgrounds at **Beresford Lake** and at **The Narrows** section of the Manigotagan River, near Quesnel Lake. A number of lakes within the park have privately operated fly-in fishing lodges. Excellent fishing and canoeing is to be found at **Bissett** (population 132), just outside the park's northern limit. A former gold-mining centre, Bissett is the last town before entering Atikaki Provincial Wilderness Park at **Wallace Lake** – and from here on the term 'wilderness experience' is used with feeling.

Atikaki Provincial Wilderness Park

There are no roads beyond Wallace Lake. A number of lodge operators provide air access from Winnipeg, an hour's flight from the park, but the best means of transport within the 404,700ha (1 million-acre) park is the canoe. The adventurous can paddle for hundreds of kilometres, aware that they are unlikely to meet anyone else for days on end.

Two spectacular waterways offering supreme whitewater challenges and the chance to travel through magnificent scenery are the **Bloodvein** and **Pigeon** Rivers. The Bloodvein, designated a Canadian Heritage River, rises in Ontario's Woodland Caribou Provincial Park and flows into Lake Winnipeg. The Manitoba section contains nearly 100 rapids and falls, putting a canoeist's skill to the severest of tests. In many places walls of rock rising 30m (100ft) above the water are inscribed with pictographs, the work of ancient native artists. The Pigeon river also empties into Lake Winnipeg and presents an opportunity for rigorous whitewater canoeing or rafting. It is now regarded as one of North America's best places for whitewater rafting. At one point the river passes through a canyon where waves can reach a height of 1.5m (5ft).

To the Saulteaux-Ojibwa people, who still live in a community at the mouth of the Bloodvein River, Atikaki means 'the country of the caribou', an apt name, for herds of the beasts are frequently seen in the park, which is also home to the bald eagle, often seen soaring magnificently on a wingspan of 2m (6ft).

Turtle Mountain Provincial Park

Manitoba's most southerly park is Turtle Mountain Provincial Park, 100km (62 miles) south of Brandon on Highway 10 and hard against the US border. This was the first dry land to appear in the province after the glacial period and it is the oldest inhabited area, where the early Assiniboine and Saulteaux people sought winter shelter among its slopes.

An island of deciduous forest, Turtle Mountain rises like a mirage from the surrounding prairie. More than 200 lakes and ponds provide a year-round home for beavers, muskrats, salamander and western painted turtles, and attract many species of duck as well as grebes, loons, herons and double-crested cormorants. A viewing tower enables moose to be observed as they feed along the shores of **Adam Lake**. The park has a number of hiking trails, ranging from 1.5km (1 mile) to about 15km (10 miles), and there are two campgrounds.

Motel and country inn accommodation can be found at the town of Boissevain, about 16km (10 miles) north of the park and noted for the Canadian Turtle Derby staged there each July. Adjoining the park is the International Peace Garden, which straddles the Manitoba–North Dakota border at a point midway between the Atlantic and Pacific oceans. Opened in 1932, it has acres of formal gardens which are traversed by well-groomed, wheelchair-accessible paths.

Spruce Woods Provincial Park

Spruce Woods Provincial Park, on Highway 5, some 20km (12 miles) south of **Carberry**, contains the ecological contradictions of a desert and a forest of white spruce normally found 200km (125 miles) farther north.

Known as Spirit Sands, the barren windswept hills are all that is left of a great river delta which dates from 11,000 years ago. The sands provide a habitat for the northern prairie skink, Manitoba's only lizard, the western hognose snake and the wolf spider.

Elsewhere, the park's varied habitats support white-tailed deer, elk, prairie song birds, ruffed grouse, raccoons and weasels. There are numerous trails for walking, cycling and horse-riding, and there are camping facilities.

Oak Hammock Marsh

One of the most exciting places to see

> **A Wildlife Valhalla**
>
> Hecla Provincial Park, strewn over a number of islands 140km (88 miles) north of Winnipeg, was once an independent Icelandic republic. Hecla Island was named after a volcano in Iceland which erupted in the 1870s, causing hundreds of fishermen and farmers to abandon their homes and emigrate to Canada.
>
> Many of the migrants settled along the western shores of Lake Winnipeg and on the island. In 1875 they founded the Republic of New Iceland, a colony which survived for six years before being swept up into the expanding province of Manitoba. Reminders of the republic's brief existence, including a Lutheran church, are to be found in the restored **Hecla Icelandic Fishing Village**, near Gull Harbour at the northern end of the island.
>
> Today, Hecla is a haven for wildlife, including moose, white-tailed deer and muskrats. Wolves are occasionally seen. In addition to geese, herons, loons, grebes, ducks and pelicans, there are osprey, bald eagles and great grey owls.
>
> A popular place for hiking, cross-country skiing and other leisure pursuits, Hecla offers a wide range of accommodation year-round. The park is reached by Highway 8 from Winnipeg. A causeway links the island to the mainland, and a ferry runs between Gull Harbour and Black Islands. Other islands may be reached by boat.

wildlife in Manitoba – and a great place for a family outing – is less than an hour's drive north of downtown Winnipeg. **Oak Hammock Marsh Wildlife Management Area** is 3,600ha (8,896 acres) of managed marshlands, grasslands and lure crops – the home of hundreds of wildlife species, including 280 kinds of birds and 25 types of mammals. In addition, more than a million migrating shorebirds, ducks and geese are attracted to the area each year.

The Oak Hammock Marsh Interpretive Centre, opened in May 1993, features observation decks (binoculars available), wetland exhibit halls, a theatre, classroom, gift shop and cafeteria. Other facilities include a nature craft shop, picnic sites, marsh boardwalks where you can take close-up peeps at birds, muskrats and other species, observation mounds and trails and several kilometres of hiking trails.

Jointly operated by the Manitoba Department of Natural Resources and Ducks Unlimited, a private, non-profit organization devoted to waterfowl and wildlife habitat conservation, Oak Hammock Marsh is reached from Winnipeg by following Highway 7 north to Highway 67, turning east for 8km (5 miles) to the Oak Hammock sign, where you turn north for another 4km (2^1/$_2$ miles) to reach the car park.

Winnipeg – The Crossroads City

Situated more or less in the centre of the Canada–United States land mass, Manitoba's capital city Winnipeg is a traveller's bullseye – a place that draws the eye, the heart, the wandering soul. All roads seem to meet here, and two major waterways – the Red River and the Assiniboine – converge to create a place where people have been meeting for more than 6,000 years, trading goods, exchanging news and performing ceremonial rites.

The Forks – that place where the rivers meet – brought Indians, explorers, fur traders and settlers together. Some of them moved on, but a good many stayed to create a settlement that soon became a city when the railway arrived in 1885, bringing more newcomers. By the start of World War I Winnipeg had become a metropolis, with cast-iron buildings and skyscrapers evidently aiming to make the city as tall as it was wide.

Those who came and stayed formed the basis of a bustling city of 650,000 people – more than half the province's population – representing some 40 ethnic groups. Today, the place where the Assiniboine and Red River trails met is a world-famous junction – Portage Avenue and Main Street, said to be one of the windiest intersections in civilization – and Winnipeg is a major centre of commerce, manufacturing industries and transportation. Cul-

M ore than a million migratory birds visit Oak Hammock Marsh Wildlife Management Area annually.

turally, it has an excellent reputation for ballet, music and drama.

Getting There
Winnipeg International Airport, served by Canada's two major carriers as well as other leading airlines, is conveniently placed 8km (5 miles) west of the city centre so transfers are cheap and easy. Complimentary shuttle services are provided by some hotels.

Getting Around
The city is covered by a wide network of bus services operated by **Winnipeg Transit** (tel. 983-5700), and free **DASH** (Downtown Area Shuttle) buses serve the downtown area on weekdays between 11am and 3pm. Special DASH bus stops are located on Broadway, Graham Avenue, King Street, Main Street and some other thoroughfares. Long-distance bus services are provided by **Greyhound** (tel. 786-8891) and **Grey Goose** (tel. 783-8840).

VIA Rail train services (tel. 949-7400) are operated from the CN Union Station on Main Street. Overlooking the Forks, the station was designed by Warren and Wetmore, architects of New York's Grand Central Station. Railway buffs will also be interested in the **Prairie Dog Central Steam Train** operated by Winnipeg's Vintage Locomotive Society. There's a 2¹/₂-hour, 58km (36-mile) excursion from Winnipeg to Grosse Isle and back every Sunday between June and the end of September. The trips run from St James CN Station at 1661 Portage Avenue (tel. 832-5259).

The vessels *Paddlewheel Princess*, *Paddlewheel Queen* and *River Rouge* operate **cruises** along the Red and Assiniboine Rivers from docks at the southwest end of the Provencher Bridge on the Red River (tel. 942-4500). Double-decker bus tours depart from the same area. Another waterborne service is the **Splash Dash Water Bus** (tel. 943-7752) which operates between the Forks, Osborne Street Bridge, the Manitoba Legislative Building, Taché Promenade and Alexander Dock.

Orientation

Winnipeg is a city on the skew, with its gridiron of streets twisted out of shape by the curves of the two rivers. This means that some major intersections form peculiar angles by North American standards of town planning. Nevertheless, it's relatively easy to find one's way around, and much of the downtown area is connected by overhead and underground walkways.

If you do need help, look out for a car with a yellow octagonal sign in its rear window proclaiming: 'Tourist – need help? Stop me.' There are 500 of these cars in the city, driven by volunteers ready to provide directions, information and a pack of event information, schedules and discount vouchers under the Visitor Information Program, efficiently organized by the Tourism Industry Association of Winnipeg.

Tourism Winnipeg has travel information centres at Winnipeg International Airport (tel. 774-0031) and on the second floor of the Winnipeg Convention Centre, 232-375 York Avenue (tel. 943-1970, or 1-800-665-0204 toll-free from anywhere in North America).

The Forks

The city's birthplace, formerly an area of warehouses and railway workshops, has been revitalized as a 23ha (56-acre) waterfront development with recreational, cultural, commercial and historical amenities located at the confluence of the Red and Assiniboine Rivers. There is a public market with shops and restaurants, and a landscaped riverside walk leads to the Legislative Building.

The Forks is a good place for visitors to get the feel of Winnipeg at play and also for first-timers to the province to decide what they are going to see and how they are going to organize their programme – a new attraction here is the **Explore Manitoba Travel Idea Centre** which offers tourist information through interpretive exhibits and displays. Information on special events and activities throughout the province is available year-round and travel counsellors are on hand to assist. Pre-visit information can be obtained from **Travel Manitoba**, Dept AB4, 7th Floor-155 Carlton Street, Winnipeg, MB R3C 3H8 (tel. 204-945-3777 ext. AB4, or 1-800-665-0040 ext. AB4 toll-free within North America; fax 204-945-2302).

The Forks **Historic Port** provides free

casual docking facilities for small craft, and sailboats, canoes, rowing boats and water cycles may be rented. The port also features an open air amphitheatre, a play and picnic area and a marina.

Manitoba's newest national park, the **Forks National Historic Site**, rests on 3.75ha (9 acres) on the west bank of the Red River and offers a scenic view across the water of **St Boniface**, Winnipeg's French Quarter. Interpretive programmes, special group tours, festivals and heritage entertainment are presented during the summer months and in February when Le Festival du Voyageur is staged.

The **Johnston Terminal**, a renovated four-storey warehouse, now houses a variety of shops and a large railway-theme restaurant. On the lower level is the Forks **Archeological Center** with laboratories, classrooms and displays complementing the Public Archaeology Programme in which members of the public work alongside professionals in the recovery, cleaning and cataloguing of artefacts in daily summer training sessions.

Another new attraction at the Forks is the **Manitoba Children's Museum** which has a wide range of hands-on galleries. These include 'The Tree and Me', designed for pre-school children, the 'Sun Gallery', which explores the science and environment of the sun, and 'Live Wire', a collection of high-tech exhibits. 'All Aboard' features a 1952 diesel locomotive with a 25m (80ft) passenger car, railroad station and a repair shed.

Downtown Area

The doyen of Winnipeg's lively shopping district is the huge **T Eaton Company** store which opened as a five-storey building on Portage Avenue in 1905. Later it was expanded to eight storeys, providing 8.75ha (21 acres) of floor space. Other shops quickly sprang up between Eaton's and Main Street. Today, a series of covered, air-conditioned skywalks enables shoppers to roam over much of the downtown area without setting foot outside.

Portage Place, a large indoor mall at 393 Portage Avenue, is also a major cultural and entertainment centre. The Manitoba Opera performs here at the Centennial Concert Hall. Here also is the Prairie Theatre Exchange, an intimate theatre with a reputation for staging unorthodox productions. The IMAX Theatre, also at Portage Place, features stunning films on a five-storey high screen. The prestigious Royal Winnipeg Ballet is housed in its own building at 380 Graham Avenue, one block south of Portage Place.

The triangular-shaped **Winnipeg Art Gallery**, at 300 Memorial Boulevard, houses 9,000 pieces of Inuit art, one of the most significant collections of its kind in the world, as well as important collections of Canadian and Manitoban art.

Those who are fascinated by the sight of Mammon at work will be in their element at the **Winnipeg Commodity Exchange**, founded in 1887 and Canada's oldest and largest futures market. From a fifth floor viewing gallery, visitors can watch frenzied deals being struck in agricultural products, gold, silver and interest rates. The gallery is open 9.30am-1.20pm Monday to Friday, and the exchange is at 360 Main Street, on the corner of Portage and Main.

On the south side of Broadway, at its junction with Main Street, a small park contains **Upper Fort Garry Gate**, all that is left of a fort built in 1836 by the Hudson's Bay Company. The fort served the fur trade until 1870 when it became the seat of government for the District of

Assiniboia. In 1885 the fort was demolished except for one gate.

The **Dalnavert/Macdonald House**, at 61 Carlton Street, is a fine example of a Victorian house built in the Queen Anne Revival style. Built in 1895, it was the home of Sir Hugh John Macdonald, the only son of Canada's first Prime Minister and himself a Member of Parliament and Premier of Manitoba. There are conducted tours of the house, but telephone 943-2835 to check opening times.

The **Manitoba Legislative Building**, on the corner of Broadway and Osborne Street, is an imposing Beaux-Art Classical structure completed in 1919. The dome is topped by the Golden Boy, a 4m (13ft) statue weighing 5 tons and sheathed in 23.5 carat gold. Inside, a grand stone staircase is guarded by a pair of massive bronze bisons.

The Exchange District

Straddling Main Street north of its junction with Portage Avenue, the Exchange District was the heart of Winnipeg's commerce during the boom that lasted from 1880 to 1920. It gets its name from the fact that the Winnipeg Grain Exchange – now renamed as the Commodity Exchange – was originally located here.

A walk through the compact district reveals one of North America's finest collections of Victorian and Edwardian warehouses and other commercial buildings, many of them unchanged from the outside, although their interiors have been refurbished as offices, nightclubs, restaurants and shops.

The Exchange District is the city's cultural heart. Here, the **Manitoba Centennial Concert Hall**, at 555 Main Street, is the setting for performances by the Winnipeg Symphony Orchestra, the Royal Winnipeg Ballet, the Manitoba Opera and travelling shows of international calibre. The **Manitoba Theatre Centre**, 174 Market Avenue, is Canada's oldest English-language theatre, performing six plays a year and also operating the intimate MTC Warehouse Theatre, situated nearby at 140 Rupert Avenue.

The boards of **Pantages Playhouse Theatre**, at 180 Market Street, have been trodden by some of the most famous feet in vaudeville since the theatre was opened in 1914 by Alexander Pantages. Among the players have been Charlie Chaplin, Laurel and Hardy and Bob Hope, who is said to have played his first game of golf in Winnipeg.

North America's largest repository of Ukrainian historical and cultural artefacts is located in **Oseredok**, the Ukrainian Cultural and Educational Centre at 184 Alexander Avenue East. The centre contains a museum, library, art gallery and archives. The **Ukrainian Academy of Arts and Sciences Historical Museum** houses a collection of maps, medals, flags, photographs and memorabilia at 456 Main Street.

The district's crowning glory, however, is the **Manitoba Museum of Man and** **Nature**, at 190 Rupert Avenue, next door to the Centennial Concert Hall. One of Canada's top museums, it consists of seven galleries which explore mankind's relationship to the environment through realistic dioramas and such reconstructions as an Indian encampment, a primitive settler's hut and a street of shops from Victorian Winnipeg. The most popular exhibit, however, is almost certainly the full-size replica of the *Nonsuch*, a ketch that sailed in Hudson Bay in 1668 and returned with a cargo of furs – an enterprise that led to the founding of the Hudson's Bay Company.

Other museum attractions are the **Planetarium**, featuring original multimedia shows, and **Touch the Universe Science Gallery**, where science, technology, art and illusion are explored through entertaining hands-on exhibits.

Chinatown

A lavishly decorated Chinese gate providing a covered walkway across King Street, between James and Rupert Avenues, marks the heart of Winnipeg's Chinatown, founded in 1909. Chinatown covers eight blocks, and there are dozens of Chinese restaurants and shops.

The Winnipeg **Chinese Cultural Centre** is in the Dynasty Building, at 180 King Street – one end of the China Gate – and there is a beautiful Chinese garden where summertime entertainment is staged. The shiny green multi-roof of the Dynasty Building is a symbol of good luck. At the opposite end of the China Gate, the **Mandarin Building**, built in 1988, contains a replica of the famous Mural of the Nine Imperial Dragons, a statue of Guan Yin and a bronze Buddha.

Assiniboine Park

Winnipeg's major park, at the end of Wellington Crescent to the west of the downtown area, covers 159ha (393 acres) of wooded lawns, picnic sites, playgrounds and cricket fields. There are English and French gardens, a miniature railway, a conservatory and a Tudor-style refreshment pavilion.

The **Leo Mol Sculpture Garden** features the bronze sculptures of prominent people, female forms and wildlife by the Winnipeg artist Leo Mol. A collection of the artist's porcelains, small sculptures, drawings and paintings is housed in an adjoining gallery.

More than 1,200 animals can be found in the **Assiniboine Park Zoo**, including such endangered species as the Siberian tiger and Amur leopard, as well as many species indigenous to Canada. The **Kinsmen Discovery Centre** gives children an opportunity to explore a variety of habitats, from forest floor to desert.

A statue of Winnie the Bear, just inside the zoo's main entrance, commemorates the connection between Lieutenant Harry Colebourn and A A Milne's character, Winnie the Pooh. Lieutenant Colebourn bought a small black bear as a pet in White River, Ontario, when he was on his way to England in 1914. He named it Winnie after his home town, Winnipeg. Unable to keep the bear, he handed it to London Zoo, where it became something of a celebrity, attracting the attention of Milne and his son Christopher Robin among others.

Adjacent to the park, **Assiniboine Forest** is a 280ha (700-acre) nature preserve with rare wild flowers, a resident herd of deer and great flocks of waterfowl. The forest is open year-round and there are a number of nature trails. Within the preserve is the Living Prairie Museum, home to more than 200 species of native plants, where naturalists are available to answer questions. There are guided hikes during the summer.

Five minutes south of the park is the **Fort Whyte Centre for Family Adventure and Recreation**, 83ha (200 acres) of forest, lakes, marshes and self-guided trails which lead through seven wetland habitats. Floating boardwalks lead through the centre of the marshes, bringing visitors face-to-face with wildlife in its natural habitat. A number of fascinating exhibits offering more information are located in the visitor centre.

St Boniface

Located on the east side of the Red River, St Boniface is the largest French-speaking community west of Quebec Province and is known, not surprisingly, as Winnipeg's French Quarter. St Boniface was founded by Father Joseph Norbert Provencher, later Bishop Provencher, who established the first Roman Catholic mission in the West here in 1818. He built a church, school and a convent for a community of Grey Nuns. Today, the Gallic ambience of St Boniface is evident in its shops, cafés and restaurants, to say nothing of the speech you hear on the streets.

The focal point of Franco-Manitoban culture is the **Centre culturel franco-manitobain** at 340 boulevard Provencher, home of Le Cercle Molière, the oldest theatre group in the province, the dance troupe Danseurs de la Rivière Rouge, a French-language radio station, and Winnipeg's largest outdoor terrace, **Le Café Jardin**.

Le **Musée de Saint-Boniface**, 494 avenue Taché, is in the oldest building in

Winnipeg, built by Father Provencher between 1846 and 1851 for the Grey Nuns. It is also claimed to be the largest oak log structure in North America. The museum depicts the lives of the Métis people and French-Canadian settlers.

A dramatic stone facade, with a huge, empty, round window facing west across the Red River, is all that remains of the St Boniface **Basilica**, built in 1908 and destroyed by fire in 1968. The present cathedral, constructed in 1972, was incorporated into the ruins. The tomb of Louis Riel, the Métis leader who was hanged for treason in 1885 in Regina, Saskatchewan, is in the grounds.

Riel South

Visitors can take a glimpse into the life of the Riel family at the **Riel House National Historic Site** at 330 River Road. This was the home of Louis Riel's mother from 1880, and was occupied by the family until 1969, but the Métis leader himself never lived here. The building has been restored to its 1886 appearance.

One of only two branches of the **Royal Canadian Mint** – the other is in Ottawa – is at 520 Lagimodière Boulevard, and a glass-enclosed gallery enables visitors to view the minting of coins for Canada and countries around the world without being exposed to the temptation to help themselves. Guided tours are available from May to September.

A dramatic stone facade is all that remains of the original St Boniface Basilica.

The River Road

Main Street heads north of Winnipeg as Highway 9, following the west bank of the Red River to the town of **Lockport**. The route, known as the **River Road Heritage Parkway**, is lined with historic points, walkways and interpretive displays.

The **Captain Kennedy Tea House and Museum**, at the junction of the Parkway and St Andrew's Road, was built in 1866 by Captain William Kennedy, a Métis fur trader and Arctic explorer. Three rooms of the house are furnished in the style of the 1870s, and tea is served in a conservatory overlooking an English garden. Captain Kennedy and his English wife are buried in the grounds of St Andrew's-on-the-Red Anglican Church, the oldest stone church in Western Canada still used for public worship. Kneeling benches in the pews are covered with buffalo hide.

At Lockport you can cross to the river's east bank to call at the **Kenosewun Visitor Centre and Museum**. 'Kenosewun' is the Cree word meaning 'there are many fishes' and exhibits and an audiovisual presentation explain the archaeological significance of the Red River and its importance to native culture. Tourist information is available, and picnic sites and footpaths overlook the historic St Andrew's Lock and Dam, built in 1910 and still in use.

Selkirk

Highway 9 continues north to **Selkirk**, the major town in the Interlake region, with a population of around 10,000. It was established in 1882 and named after Thomas Douglas, 5th Earl of Selkirk, who brought hundreds of Scottish and Irish settlers to the Red River area. Every July the town is the setting for the **Manitoba**

Highland Gathering, a festival of Scottish dancing, pipe and drum competitions, sheep-shearing and herding, York boat races and a traditional *ceilidh*.

Selkirk's major attraction is **Lower Fort Garry**, built in 1830 by the Hudson's Bay Company governor George Simpson. A National Historic Site, it is the oldest stone fur-trading fort still intact in North America. Costumed guides bring the past to life, describing their daily tasks and recounting tales of adventurous journeys by York boat – the craft that took over from the canoe to ply the route to Hudson Bay and 'won the West'. Pelts of beaver, fox, raccoon and wolf hang in the fur loft. Other buildings also authentically recreate the days of the fur trade.

The **Marine Museum of Manitoba**, also located in Selkirk, is the home of six historic ships which once sailed on Lake Winnipeg, including the 1896 SS *Keenora*, Manitoba's oldest steamship, and of a lighthouse built in 1898.

Gimli

Highway 9 terminates about 60km (37 miles) north of Selkirk at Gimli (population 1,800), which has the largest Icelandic community outside Iceland. Each year in early August the town celebrates *Islendingadagurinn*, more easily enunciated as Icelandic Day, when descendants of those sturdy immigrants of the 1870s don traditional dress and hurl themselves into a festival of athletics, drama, poetry and music. Gimli **Historical Museum**, near the harbour, depicts the history of fishing on Lake Winnipeg and has a collection of pioneer artefacts and a reconstructed log cabin.

Canada's Arctic Seaport

Those who haven't seen the Arctic tundra may imagine a bleak landscape, featureless and colourless. In spring, however, the tundra is a thick, bouncy carpet of miniature blooms with red, orange, purple and yellow predominating as lichens, flowers and tiny shrubs burst into new life.

Manitoba has 650km (406 miles) of seacoast on Hudson Bay. At the mouth of the Hudson River, around **Churchill**, Canada's only Arctic seaport, there are patches of taiga, or sub-Arctic forest. Churchill's resident population is around 1,200. By late May people are swarming

A Viking statue commemorates the Icelandic origins of the people of Gimli.

into the little town from many parts of the globe, in camouflage clothing and bestrewn with binoculars, telescopes and cameras. They are eager to see some of the 200 migrating and breeding bird species, including the rare Ross's gull which has been returning to Churchill since the early 1980s. In June, with snow still piled high beside the town streets, the first of the summer whale-watchers arrive. Inflatable boats circle the icebergs in the Bay to locate belugas and seals for visitors to photograph.

October is a peak tourism month, when polar bears migrate from the Bay's shores in search of ice. Groups go out with professional naturalists in tundra buggies to see the majestic bears, which weigh up to 700kg (1,540lb) sauntering casually over the tundra.

For wildlife, human history and geology – and as a viewpoint for the Aurora Borealis – Churchill is a fascinating place to visit. It has an excellent Eskimo museum, a Visitor Reception Centre with exhibits on the fur trade and the Hudson's Bay Company posts, and nearby National Historic Sites at **Fort Prince of Wales, Sloops Cove** and **Cape Merry**. You can buy beautiful crafts, sculptures and carvings by Inuit and Indian artists.

Students from around the world attend courses in Arctic biology, botany and geology at the Northern Studies Centre. Grain from the prairies is loaded into ships during the short summer.

Regular scheduled weekday jet flights into Churchill from Winnipeg are operated by Canadian Airlines International and Calm Air. VIA Rail's 1,600km (1,000-mile) service from Winnipeg takes 2 nights and a day and enables you to experience one of North America's last great wilderness journeys in comfort.

ONTARIO

Water, Water Everywhere

The Iroquois Indians put their finger on it in the distant past. Their word, Ontario, translates as 'beautiful water', 'beautiful lake' or 'water beside high rocks'. Whichever way you look at it – whether your mind turns to Niagara Falls, the wide St Lawrence River with its Thousand Islands, Lakes Ontario, Huron and Erie, or the fact that one-sixth of the province's 916,700sq km (358,000sq miles) consists of lakes, rivers and canals – Ontario means an awful lot of water.

Ontario is probably the place that springs into the minds of most people when they think of Canada – not surprising when you consider that the province has captured the bulk of the country's most impressive statistics.

Although its massive area makes it only the second largest province – after Quebec – Ontario has the largest population with 10.1 million people, more than a third of Canada's total population. The greatest concentration of people is in Southern Ontario, where manufacturing industries and agriculture are located. Most of the natu-

There's a wealth of contrasting architectural styles in downtown Toronto.

ral resource industries are found in Northern Ontario.

The province borders the US states of New York, Michigan and Minnesota and its largest cities are Toronto, Ottawa, Hamilton, Kitchener, St Catherine's/Niagara, London, Windsor, Oshawa, Thunder Bay and Sudbury.

Rich in recreation facilities, Ontario has more than a quarter of a million lakes, where fishing, boating and swimming may be enjoyed, and more than 400 public and semi-private golf courses. There is plenty of room for campers and hikers in 261 provincial parks and 360 conservation areas, all accessible to the public.

The province is culturally active, with 95 professional theatre companies, 57 symphony orchestras and 16 professional dance troupes. There are about 250

ONTARIO

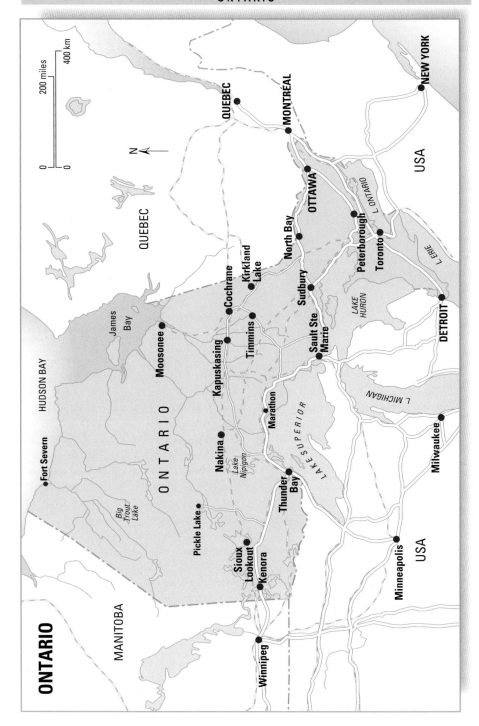

community theatres and close on 450 performing arts facilities. Toronto's theatre industry is the third largest in the English-speaking world, after London and New York. Ontario's world-famous **Stratford Festival** is renowned for its Shakespearean repertoire. The Shaw Festival, at Niagara-on-the-Lake, is devoted to producing the works of George Bernard Shaw and his contemporaries. In addition to theatre, there are 304 museums and 96 historic sites in the province.

Ontario is a multicultural society with people drawn from many different countries and cultures. Cold statistics which show that 78 percent of Ontarians speak English as their mother tongue, 5 percent French and 16.7 percent other languages hide their full polyglot extent. In fact, newspapers, radio and television programmes are altogether produced in more than 70 languages.

However, these Ontarians are an urban lot. Nearly 4 million of them – almost four in every ten – live in Greater Toronto. And some people will ask: Who can blame them?

Toronto – The Meeting Place

Perhaps Peter Ustinov was being no more than facetious when he described Toronto as 'a kind of New York operated by the Swiss'. But if he meant that here is a clean city where things work and you can walk the streets in safety, then anyone who knows the place well could only agree with him. Toronto is like New York. But it has excitement without fear. Its architecture is inspiring, rather than awesome. It has streets without squalor, commerce without coldness. Its sidewalks have room

for dawdlers, its cafés time for idlers. Here, the city tempo seems to adjust itself to your pace.

A Brief Background

In the language of the Huron Indians, Toronto meant 'a meeting place'. Before the white men came it was an important gathering point at the end of a shortcut between Lakes Ontario and Huron. Naturally protected, it became an important harbour, and in 1750 was established as a French fur-trading post. In 1793 it was colonized by the British who named it York.

The town was laid out in a grid pattern which remains to this day. The construction of Yonge Street, still the main drag, began in 1790. Built chiefly as a military road to replace the old canoe route to Lake Huron, it also served to open up the hinterland for settlement. Torontonians will say with a straight face that Yonge is the world's longest street, stretching from Queen's Quay, down by the harbour, to Rainy River near James Bay, 1,900km (1,190 miles) to the northwest.

During the War of 1812 an American force of 14 ships and 1,700 troops raided York, burned down the parliament building and ransacked the settlement. In retribution, the British invaded Washington and tried to burn down the President's residence. The building remained intact, but its scorched walls had to be whitewashed, thereby causing it to be renamed The White House.

York became Toronto when the city was incorporated in 1834, and by the time of Confederation in 1867 was the capital of Upper Canada. Over the years, Toronto's proximity to natural resources, agricultural land, cheap energy and the markets of the US heartland enabled it to prosper, and investment surged into the city with the opening of the St Lawrence Seaway in the 1950s.

Work on the Toronto Transit Commission's subway system also began in the 1950s, while the 1960s saw a huge expansion in the city's road network. The next decade saw the arrival of many businesses which had switched operations from Quebec, and this resulted in the development of Toronto's glistening downtown towers, many of them built within the past 20 years.

Toronto Today

Banking and financial services make up Toronto's largest industry – followed by tourism, manufacturing and communications – and it is the towers of Mammon that glow so seductively at sunset. From the lakeshore side of the city the nearness of the

skyscrapers gives the impression that Toronto is a high-rise, high-pressure powerhouse without a soul: a place without people. Walk just a few blocks north and you find that it's all a golden facade. Behind the glitz lies a vital low-rise city of streets in which people actually live; streets with frame-houses and brownstones, corner stores, delicatessens, laundromats and markets. Toronto is a city of neighbourhoods.

Getting There

By air: Toronto is served by two airports. Visitors from overseas, the United States and most major cities in Canada will arrive at the **Lester B Pearson International Airport**, about 30km (19 miles) northwest of the downtown area. With scheduled services provided by some 35 major airlines, Lester B used to be something of a nightmare, but the opening of its new Trillium Terminal and extensive refurbishment of the other two have improved things considerably. Travelling downtown by **taxi** can be a slow and expensive ride, especially at rush hour, but fortunately there is a cheaper, less frustrating alternative. Airport Express **coaches** travel every 20 minutes in each direction between the airport and half a dozen downtown hotels.

The small **Toronto Island Airport**, actually on an island at the foot of Bathurst Street and reached by special ferry, is used by Air Ontario with services between Ottawa, Montreal and London, Ontario. There is a shuttle bus service between the airport and the Royal York Hotel, opposite Union Station.

By rail: **VIA Rail** passenger services (tel. 366-8411) from across Canada and **Amtrak** trains (tel. 800-872-7245) from Chicago and New York City arrive at Union Station, on Front and Bay Streets. An underground walkway connects with the Royal York and other nearby hotels.

*T*oronto's night skyline is dominated by the slender CN Tower.

By bus: **Greyhound** (tel. 594-0338) and other long-distance buses arrive and depart from the bus terminal on Bay Street at Edward Street (nearest subway is Dundas).

Toronto's big city character is tempered by open spaces, like this by old City Hall.

Getting Around

Compared with many other big cities, Toronto is easy to navigate. Yonge Street is the key to the grid system, with cross streets numbered east and west of their junction with Yonge.

The city has a clean, safe and efficient public transport system operated by the **Toronto Transit Commission** (tel. 393-4636). The system consists of some 1,300km (818 miles) of subway, bus, trolley and streetcar routes.

The **subway** system, astonishingly clean and quiet, has two lines covering 60 stations. The Yonge/University/Spadina line is a giant U-shape, running south from Finch Avenue, down Yonge Street to Union Station, then turns north again along University and Spadina Avenues to Wilson Avenue. The Bloor/Danforth line runs along Bloor Street and Danforth Avenue from Kipling Avenue in the west to Main Street, then heads northeast to Kennedy Road. From Kennedy the Scarborough Rapid Transit line continues as an overhead rail extension to McCowan Road in Scarborough city centre. Subway trains run daily from 6am to 1.30am (from 9am on Sundays).

Buses, **trolleys** and **streetcars** fill in most of the gaps left by the subway, and many downtown routes, including those which run along King, Queen, Dundas and College Streets, operate 24 hours a day. Night buses are also available along Yonge and Bloor Streets.

The **Harbourfront Light Rail Transit** (LRT) provides a charmingly old-fashioned tram ride from Union Station to Queen's Quay, then west along the harbourfront to Spadina Avenue.

Ferry boats operated by the Metro Parks Department leave regularly from the foot of Bay Street, behind the Harbour Castle Westin Hotel, for the Toronto Islands: Centre, Ward's, Olympic and Hanlon's Point. It takes less than 10 minutes to reach the islands, a welcome escape, you may find, after a heavy bout of sidewalk pounding in the hot summer. There are 230ha (550 acres) of parkland, some good, clean beaches, an amusement park, a children's petting farm – and a splendid view of downtown Toronto with the CN Tower dominating the skyline. Cars are forbidden on the islands, which are interconnected by boardwalk, but you can give your feet a rest by renting a bicycle.

Using Public Transport

A single fare (exact cash or token) operates throughout the transit system and travellers can make considerable savings by purchasing five, ten or 50 tokens at a time. **A Day Pass**, costing less than the price of three one-off journeys, allows unlimited travel for one person on any one day, either after 9.30am weekdays or all day on Saturday. On Sundays and holidays the pass is good for up to two adults and four children.

Passengers can transfer between subway and surface systems, but must obtain a free transfer ticket first. It's best to take your transfer when you first board the bus or streetcar, or enter the subway station. A free **Ride Guide**, obtainable at subway stations, includes a useful map and lists major places of interest with details of how to reach them.

Guides and Tours

An easy way to find your way around is to join an Olde Towne Toronto **trolley tour** (tel. 368-6877), which passes more than 100 points of interest during a narrated 2-hour excursion. You can get off and on all day long at any of the 16 stops.

If you enjoy **walking**, you can join a Toronto Architecture tour (tel. 922-7606) to explore the art and architecture of the financial district.

Visitor Information

Information about the city can be obtained from the **Metropolitan Toronto Convention and Visitors Association**, Suite 590, 207 Queen's Quay West, Toronto, Ontario M5J 1A7 (tel. 203-2500). The association sets up visitor information centres throughout Toronto during the summer. The **Shell Info Centre**, accessible from the eastbound lanes of Highway 401 at Mississauga, west of Toronto, offers 24-hour year-round computerized information about events, attractions and accommodation.

On the Waterfront

The elevated **Gardiner Expressway** acts like a city wall, separating downtown Toronto from the shore of Lake Ontario. At one time this was a dingy, dismal waterfront area that could have served as the setting for one of those 1950s movies about dockland racketeers. But not any more.

Now, the **Harbourfront Centre** is a lively place with an ambience almost Mediterranean, and some of its old industrial buildings have been almost unrecognizably refurbished as centres for recreation, shopping and the arts. Expensive yachts bob jauntily in smart marinas. People saunter along the wide promenade

195

or sip drinks beneath the colourful umbrellas of terrace cafés.

The **Queen's Quay**, eight storeys of specialty shops, cafés, restaurants and home to the Premier Dance Theatre – with expensive office accommodation above – started out some 60 years ago as a grain terminal. It took a lot of imagination and $60 million to bring about the transformation. The **Power Plant** next door was once just that – a place that generated the wherewithal to fuel an ice-making factory. Now it provides the setting for exhibitions of design, paintings, photography and sculpture.

Concerts, live theatre, poetry readings and the like are staged in **York Quay Centre**. On 6 days a week (but never on Monday) Toronto's lively **Antiques Market** takes place on Maple Leaf Quay. The busiest day is Sunday when more than 200 dealers set up stall.

The CN Tower

Dominating the skyline from almost every angle, the CN Tower is the world's tallest free-standing structure with the tip of its communications aerial standing head, shoulders and chest above the rest of the city, at a staggering altitude of some 600m (1,815ft).

If you're fit, they say, you can walk down the tower's 2,570 steps in about 20 minutes. No one contemplates the thought of walking up – although it has been done by a stuntman on the *outside* – but by elevator you can reach the **observation deck**, about two-thirds of the way, in 58 seconds. The elevators take off like rockets, achieving an ascent of 6m (20ft) a second, about the same as a jet plane taking off. At peak times in the summer, however, it can take an hour just to get from

A frequent ferry service connects the city with the Toronto Islands.

It's difficult to keep the CN Tower out of any photograph of Toronto!

the turnstiles to the elevators, so it pays to get there early.

Not surprisingly, the CN Tower presents a stunning view of Toronto and the surrounding area. On a clear day you can see the spray rising from the Niagara Falls 100km (62 miles) to the south.

If your desire for far horizons has been heightened by a trip up the tower, you might like to call in on the **Tour of the Universe** at ground level. This is a simulated trip to Jupiter in the year 2019. Human guides and robots lead you through a laser inoculation centre, through interstellar passport control, past a 64-screen information wall and on to the 40-seater 'spaceship' that takes you on a convincingly real but all too short voyage across the solar system.

The tower's next-door neighbour is **Skydome**, the first stadium in the world to have a retractable roof. With the lid on, so to speak, it looks like a turtle in its shell – which was in fact the image that inspired the architect, Rod Robbie.

It takes 20 minutes – and costs $500 a time – to open or close the roof, and a 31-storey building could be accommodated under the dome. More practically, it is home to the Blue Jays baseball team and football's Argonauts.

Ontario Place

West of the Harbourfront Centre, Ontario Place is a 40ha (96-acre) amusement park on three man-made islands. In addition to a waterslide and vast wading pool for chil-

dren, cafés, pubs and open-air dance floors, it has an outdoor concert stage and **Cinesphere**, a six-storey, 800-seat geodesic dome in which stunning IMAX films are shown. The IMAX film system was developed in Ontario.

Home of the Blue Jays baseball team. Skydome has a retractable roof.

Ontario Place was created by the provincial government, which also owns and operates it. General admission is free, but there are varying fees for Cinesphere and for performances at the **Forum**, the outdoor concert stage.

Downtown Toronto

Standing on the map like a pivot at the base of the U-shaped Yonge/University/Spadina subway line, **Union Station** is both a landmark and a gateway to downtown Toronto. It is also a sightseeing attraction in its own right. Completed in 1924 and opened by the Prince of Wales 3 years later, it is the kind of station the ancient Greeks would have built if they had invented the train.

The hall is cavernous and its high ceiling is supported by 22 pillars, each 12.5m (40ft) high and weighing 75 tons. Light pours into the hall from high arched win-

dows. From the lower concourse a wide tunnel provides access to the Royal York Hotel, almost as handsome a building, and the start of Underground City on the other side of Front Street.

Financial District

Embraced by the arms of the subway line, Toronto's Financial District extends from Front Street to Queen Street. This is the zone of the golden towers. The **Royal Bank Plaza**, on the northwest corner of Bay and Front Streets, actually has real gold as an element in its construction materials – 70,820g (2,500 ounces) of the stuff embedded in its window panes to act as an insulator, reducing the cost of heating and cooling the building. Aesthetically, it has the effect of making the building glow wonderfully at daybreak and dusk.

One block to the east, on the corner of Front and Yonge Streets, is another architectural wonder: **BCE Place**, built in 1992. It has two towers and a stunning glass gallery of cathedral dimensions – so huge in fact that it encompasses and diminishes one of the city's older bank

198

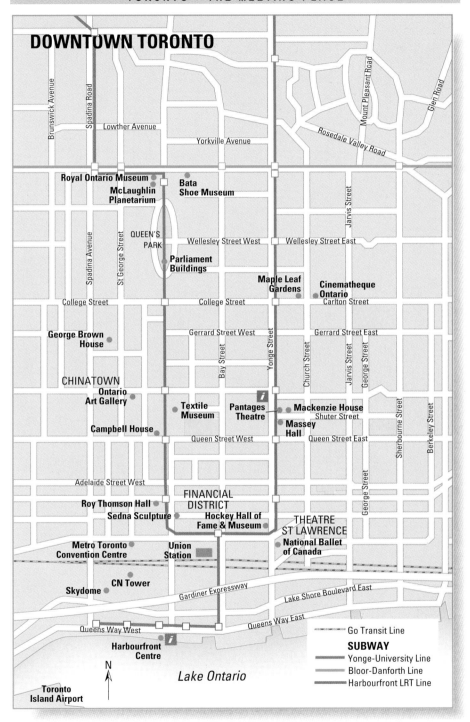

DOWNTOWN TORONTO

Brunswick Avenue

Spadina Road

Lowther Avenue

Yorkville Avenue

Mount Pleasant Road

Glen Road

Rosedale Valley Road

Royal Ontario Museum
McLaughlin Planetarium

Bata Shoe Museum

Jarvis Street

Spadina Avenue

St George Street

QUEEN'S PARK

Wellesley Street West

Wellesley Street East

Parliament Buildings

Maple Leaf Gardens

Cinematheque Ontario

College Street

College Street

Carlton Street

George Brown House

Gerrard Street West

Gerrard Street East

Bay Street

Yonge Street

Church Street

Jarvis Street

George Street

CHINATOWN
Ontario Art Gallery

Textile Museum

Pantages Theatre

Mackenzie House
Shuter Street

Massey Hall

Sherbourne Street

Berkeley Street

Campbell House

Queen Street West

Queen Street East

Adelaide Street West

FINANCIAL
DISTRICT

Roy Thomson Hall
Sedna Sculpture

Hockey Hall of Fame & Museum

THEATRE
ST LAWRENCE

George Street

National Ballet of Canada

Metro Toronto Convention Centre

Union Station

CN Tower

Skydome

Gardiner Expressway

Lake Shore Boulevard East

Queens Way West

Queens Way East

Harbourfront Centre

N

Lake Ontario

Toronto Island Airport

Go Transit Line

SUBWAY
Yonge-University Line
Bloor-Danforth Line
Harbourfront LRT Line

buildings. It also provides access to the **Hockey Hall of Fame**, a 5,000sq m (52,000sq ft) museum featuring what is said to be the world's most comprehensive collection of ice hockey artefacts, displays and memorabilia. The museum has exhibitions, theatres and high-tech areas where visitors can pit their skills against the automated cunning of computerized goalies and shooters.

Bay Street is Toronto's Wall Street. At **No. 232** – just beyond the junction with Wellington Street – is the building that housed the Toronto Stock Exchange for 46 years until 1983 when it moved to its present whizz-bang electronics location on King Street West. The old Art Deco building is a reflection of more relaxed days when high finance didn't take itself quite so seriously as it does now. Take a look at the slyly humorous frieze above the solid steel doors of the main entrance.

The present **Stock Exchange**, at 2 First Canadian Place, has a Visitors' Centre (admission free) with a large public gallery, a 140-seat auditorium and an audiovisual presentation. It's open Monday to Friday, 9.30am to 4pm, with guided tours at 2pm.

Despite the concrete canyons and architectural styles that run the whole gamut from wedding cake to cheesegrater, Toronto's Financial District is visitor-friendly, with tree-shaded corners and squares with fountains and sculpture where you can sit and be thankful that you're not working in one of those diamond-bright offices hanging in the sky.

Between Queen Street and Bloor Street, but still locked in those loving subway arms, Toronto becomes schizoid. On the one hand there is a city going about its everyday business – shopping, making decisions, eating, drinking. On the other, there is a city deep in thought – in museums, colleges and government.

The Workaday City

The **Eaton Centre**, which begins at Yonge and Queen and extends northwards to Dundas Street, marks the boundary between those who make money and those who spend it. And there are certainly plenty of opportunities in the Eaton Centre. It's more like a space city than a shopping mall: some 350 shops, restaurants – even a nine-floor department store and a complex of 17 cinemas – with lots of chrome and glass and a skein of sculpted

*A*n old bank building is encompassed by the new glass gallery in BCE Place.

geese flying in formation. Glass-sided elevators and the kind of escalators you might expect to find in heaven whisk shoppers from one level to the next.

Behind the Eaton Centre at the corner of Queen and Bay Streets is Toronto's **Old City Hall**. Opened in 1899, it has turrets, gargoyles – said to satirize Victorian politicians – and a huge stained-glass window. And it could not be in greater contrast to the **New City Hall**, just across the street in Nathan Phillips Square. Designed by the Finnish architect Viljo Revell and opened in 1965, it has become one of the city's most striking landmarks with its two curved towers and circular council chamber. Just inside the main entrance is *Metropolis*, a spectacular mural made from more than 100,000 nails. Nathan Phillips Square is downtown's largest public space, part of which is used as a skating rink in winter. On the square is Henry Moore's sculpture, *The Archer*.

The streets to the west and north of New City Hall mark the outer reaches of **Chinatown**, claimed as North America's largest with a population of around 100,000. It stretches west along Dundas Street, between Bay Street and Spadina Avenue which it straddles northwards from Queen Street to College Street. It's a very colourful and exciting area, full of bustle and chatter as shoppers haggle over strange fruit and vegetables and Chinese music pours from loudspeakers. Chinese writing abounds and red and gold are the predominant colours.

Just west of Spadina Avenue, off Dundas Street, is **Kensington Market**, Toronto's bargain basement. Here, terraces of old houses have been turned into shops so overstocked with garments for men and women that racks spill out into yards and even the street. Kensington is

*M*odern sculptures are a feature of Toronto. These runners are by the Eaton Centre.

probably the nearest thing you'll find to an Eastern bazaar in North America. It's certainly an ethnic hotchpotch rooted in the cobbled streets of Portugal, the Baltic States, Russia and Jewish communities throughout Europe. Dark shops with bare floorboards have barrel loads of herbs and spices, and the sidewalks are cluttered with shelves of brightly coloured produce from the Caribbean and Latin America.

The Thinking City

University Avenue and College Street provide the clues to a major preoccupation in this part of Toronto. Here are the city's higher educational, cultural and political institutions.

The gateway to this Academia is actually a few blocks south, at the corner of University Avenue and Queen Street. This

*T*oronto's colourful Chinatown is said to be the largest in North America.

is **Campbell House**, built in 1822 and one-time home of Sir William Campbell, the sixth chief justice of Upper Canada. The house is furnished in the style of the 18th and 19th centuries and costumed hostesses lead conducted tours.

The lower part of University Street is by no means the most interesting thoroughfare in the world, so it's best to hop on to a subway train to Queen's Park, where the near-Gothic pile of Ontario's **Parliament Buildings** broods amid a relaxing area of flowers and trees. There are free guided tours (tel. 965-4028) of the many corridors and halls hung with paintings and the chamber in which Members of the Provincial Parliament engage in verbal battle.

The 17 colleges and faculties of the University of Toronto are scattered be-tween College Street and Hoskin Avenue to the west of Queen's Park. The university traces its origin to 1827 when George IV granted a charter for the founding of a college administered by the Church of England. It became a non-denominational university controlled by the province in 1850. Guided walking tours of the campus and university buildings take place on summer weekdays (tel. 978-5000).

Other Attractions

A 5-minute walk north of Queen's Park brings you to the **Royal Ontario Museum**, North America's second largest after the Metropolitan Museum of Art in New York. It has a collection of more than 6 million items, with archaeology, art and science exhibits on show under one roof. There are dinosaur remains, Roman artefacts, musical instruments, and relics of Ancient Egypt. There is a Discovery Gallery for children and a Bat Cave in which visitors can go on an eerie walk through the reconstruction of a limestone tunnel in Jamaica.

Two other departments of the museum are the George R Gardiner Museum of Ceramic Art, on the opposite side of University Avenue, and the Sigmund Samuel Canadiana Collection, on the northwest of University Avenue and College Street.

Next door to the Royal Ontario is the **McLaughlin Planetarium**, which features 45-minute star shows and enables visitors to gain hands-on experience in the Astrocentre.

A short walk east along Bloor Street is **The Colonnade**, a complex of luxury apartments, smart offices and upscale shops. Here also is the Bata Shoe Museum Collection, in which the history of footwear is traced over a period of 4,000 years. The museum has boots, shoes and shoe-making tools from all parts of the world and footwear of the rich and famous is on show.

North of Bloor Street, Spadina Avenue leads to Toronto's castle, **Casa Loma**. The ultimate in self-indulgence, it was built before World War I by Sir Henry Pellatt, tycoon and soldier, at a cost of some $3 million. It has 98 rooms, turreted towers that ought to be overlooking the River Rhine, secret passageways, a Great Hall, carriage room and a breath-taking view of the city. A self-guided audio system enables visitors to wander through Casa Loma at their own pace.

The Outer Limits

Black Creek Pioneer Village on Murray Ross Parkway, Downsview, on the northwest extremity of Metropolitan Toronto, is a reconstructed mid-19th-century community, with more than 40 restored homes and shops. The village has a modern visitor centre, gift shop, exhibition gallery and restaurant, and if you like you can arrange to be married there.

A little further north, at 9580 Jane Street, is Paramount Canada's **Wonderland**, a 125ha (300-acre) theme park featuring about 150 attractions, including 50 rides, a water park, games and live shows all covered by a general admission charge.

A 30-minute drive to the east of downtown Toronto, the **Metro Toronto Zoo** is on Meadowvale Road, Scarborough, north of Highway 401. More than 4,000 animals live here in conditions as close as possible to their natural habitats. Exotic plantlife is enclosed in climate-controlled pavilions which enable visitors to experience different regions of the world without suffering the extremes of Canada's weather. The zoo is massive – they say it takes 4 days to see everything – so plan your visit carefully and wear sensible shoes.

Toronto Theatres

Toronto has more than 40 theatres, many of them refurbished to their old glory from the brink of dereliction. The most spectacular rescue was that of the **Royal Alexandra**, on King Street West.

Opened in 1907, with all the Edwardian grandeur of red velvet seats, gold brocade, chandeliers and ornate plasterwork, the Royal Alexandra had gone into decline and was scheduled for demolition in the 1960s when 'Honest Ed' Mirvish, a discount store tycoon, bought it, restored it and turned it into a profitable institution. 'Honest Ed' and his son David also built the 2,000-seat high-tech **Princess of Wales Theatre**, also on King Street West.

Another entrepreneur, Garth Drabinsky, spent $20 million restoring **Pantages Theatre**, built on Victoria Street in 1920 as a vaudeville and silent-film cinema. Resplendent in plush and gilt and seating an audience of more than 2,000, the Pantages re-opened in 1989.

The **Elgin** and **Winter Garden** complex, two theatres stacked one on top of the other on Yonge Street, underwent a $29 million restoration – the Elgin elegant in gold leaf and burgundy, the Winter Garden bedecked with shrubs and flowers – and has been designated as a historic site. Seating 3,500 people between them, the houses present programmes of theatre, music and dance from Canada and around the world.

Toronto's newest theatrical venue is the **North York Performing Arts Centre**, a complex of three theatres which opened on Yonge Street in the autumn of 1993. Its 1,850-seat Main Stage Theatre was soon filling night after night.

For those who like to eat in their seat, Toronto has about a dozen top-class **dinner theatres**.

Performing Arts in Toronto

Three other centres provide a wide range of performing arts. International superstars appear at the **O'Keefe Centre**, on Front Street East, which is also home to the National Ballet of Canada and the Canadian Opera Company. The Canadian Stage Company's home is the **St Lawrence Centre for the Arts**, also on Front Street East. Encompassing the Bluma Appel Theatre and the Jane Mallett Theatre, the centre presents a variety of theatre, music, dance and film.

A renovated ice house from the 1920s, the **du Maurier Theatre Centre** at Harbourfront Centre also stages a range of musical and theatrical events.

The **Roy Thomson Hall**, on Simcoe Street, is home to the Toronto Symphony and the Toronto Mendelssohn Choir. It also presents top international artists and performances of classical music, jazz, big bands and comedy.

Half-price tickets to a wide variety of shows are available on the day of performance only from **T O Tix**, located in a small round building just outside The Eaton Centre, near the corner of Yonge and Dundas Streets. Owned and operated by the Toronto Theatre Alliance, the bureau is open Tuesday to Saturday from noon to 7.30pm and Sunday 11am to 3pm. Tickets must be purchased in person, but you can find out what's available by phoning 596-8211.

Shopping

Toronto is a shopaholic's paradise. The best-known shopping area is the **Eaton Centre**, on the corner of Yonge and Dundas Streets. Here, on several galleria levels, there are more than 350 shops, large and small, as well as restaurants and a British-style pub. The centre, with access directly from both Dundas and Queen subway stations, is open Monday to Friday 10am to 9pm, Saturday 9.30am to 6pm, Sunday noon to 6pm.

For posh shopping – exotic jewellery, fine leather, expensive fashion labels and the like – head for the Yorkville Avenue/Bloor Street area. The chic streets running off Yorkville Avenue are filled with exclusive boutiques, while Bloor Street is a bit more down-to-earth, with stores like The Bay, Holt Renfrew, Tiffany...

At the other end of the scale, try Spadina Avenue (pronounced Spa-diner, by the way) between Wellington and College Streets. This is the area for budget clothing and factory and discount outlets, as well as inexpensive leather goods and luggage.

Between Spadina Avenue and Bathurst Street and Wellington and College, Kensington is the place for ethnic foodstuffs and exotic spices, as well as inexpensive clothing. Toronto's lively Chinatown adjoins Kensington.

Booklovers will certainly be seduced into entering **The World's Biggest Book Store**, at 20 Edward Street, a block north of the Eaton Centre. It has 27km (17 miles) of shelves and more than a million books. It is claimed – not surprisingly – that its 85 departments cover everything from abseiling to zoology.

And if the idea of subterranean shopping appeals, you can disappear into the **Underground City** – the vast network of caverns and tunnels that reaches from beneath the Royal York Hotel to the Eaton Centre. There's nothing special about the shops, but the convenience of their location becomes apparent on a raw winter's day when a snow-filled wind is howling along the streets. Summer or winter there's always something going on down there – a special promotion, maybe, or an art exhibition – and the talented buskers, actually licensed to perform, certainly jolly things along.

Eating Out

There was a time when eating in a hotel dining room was the peak of culinary experience in Toronto and most people's idea of a good meal was a steak that covered the plate. Now, Toronto is a city of bistros. Yorkville is probably the best-known area for dining out, and despite the chi-chi nature of its shops there's a good range of restaurants from the point of view of price as well as menu – everything, in fact, from potato skins in a Western-style saloon to the haughtiest of *haute cuisine*.

Ethnic cooking – which has always thrived among the neighbourhoods of this immigrant city – can now be found in one form or another in restaurants on almost every block south of Bloor Street. Cajun, Hungarian, Indonesian, Portuguese... It's all there, to say nothing of Chinese, Japanese, Mexican and, of course, Continental, especially French.

You can eat low – in Underground City – or high – in the Top of Toronto, in none other than the world's highest revolving restaurant two-thirds of the way up the 600m (1,815ft) CN Tower.

Bars and Clubs

Toronto has always been a great place for **jazz**. One of the oldest jazz venues is **George's Spaghetti House** (tel. 923-9887), on the corner of Dundas Street East and Sherbourne Street, where they've been playing traditional jazz for close on half a century. Another well-known spot is the **Bermuda Onion** (tel. 925-1470), on the second floor at 131 Bloor Street West.

Live traditional, modern and New Orleans jazz is on the menu with French and American cuisine at the **Montreal** (tel. 363-0179), 65 Sherbourne Street, while **The Saloon** (tel. 360-1818), 901 King Street West, offers live Country 'n' Western acts – some of them big names – and a huge dance floor.

BamBoo (tel. 593-5771) at 312 Queen Street West offers everything from rock to reggae with dishes from Thailand and the Caribbean. As with most clubs, there is a cover charge that varies according to what's on offer.

For those with quieter tastes, the city has a good selection of **piano bars**, especially in some of the more upmarket hotels. **Notes**, a bar/restaurant in the elegant Brownstone Hotel (tel. 924-7381), 15 Charles Street East, has a well-deserved reputation, while the **Aquarius Lounge** (tel. 967-5225), on the 51st floor of the ManuLife Centre at the corner of Bloor Street West and Bay Street, is so popular that sometimes you have to wait in line.

The CN Tower also contains the world's highest nightclub, **Sparkles**, on the same level as the revolving restaurant. The cover charge includes the elevator ride and the unrivalled night-time view of the city.

The Golden Horseshoe and Southwest Ontario

The area that sweeps southwest from Toronto, following the curve of Lake

Ontario's shoreline to the Niagara River, is known as the Golden Horseshoe. The 'horseshoe' comes from its shape and the 'golden' from the fact that this is Canada's most concentrated money-making area. Toronto accounts for a lot of it, of course, but the vineyards and farms that scratch rather more than a modest living from the region's rich soil also push the average up.

For tourists the region has **beaches** and **islands** on Lakes Ontario and Huron; it has culture and countryside, history and quaint communities. And it has one of the most spectacular – and most spectacularly exploited – attractions in the world.

Niagara Falls

Only the most world-weary cynic could come away from Niagara feeling less than impressed. You don't just see the falls. You hear them, feel them, fear them. The experience will etch three separate images into your memory.

From above the falls, the urgent rush of all that grey-green water – 155 million litres (34 million gallons) a minute – slid-ing inexorably to the curving lip of a 54m (176ft) cliff, is quite a sight. The falls themselves – a furious curtain of foam nearly 1km (half-a-mile) wide. And below the falls the swirling waters of the Niagara River trying to collect themselves once more into an orderly waterway.

The Niagara Falls are actually three giant cascades. The biggest and most spectacular – the **Horseshoe Falls** – is in Canada. The others – the American and Bridal Veil Falls – are in the United States. Only from the Canadian side can you get a view of all three at one time.

The first European to record seeing the falls was the Jesuit missionary Father Louis Hennepin who wrote about them in 1678. In the old days the Indians used to hurl their most beautiful maidens over the falls as a sacrifice. Today, the city of Niagara Falls describes itself as 'Honeymoon Capital of the World'. Some 12 million people are drawn to the falls each year, and some of them, as always, feel the need to experience the ultimate – going over the edge.

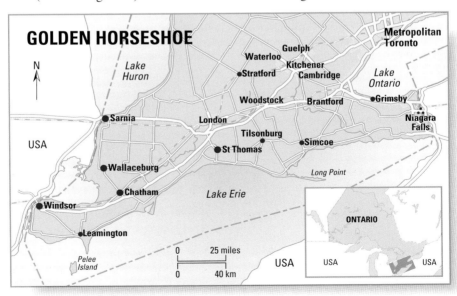

The first person to go over the Horseshoe Falls in a barrel was Annie Taylor, a 63-year-old teacher who survived the self-inflicted ordeal in 1901. Since then many others have attempted variations on the stunt – to say nothing of those who have tried walking tightropes across – but only another dozen have lived to tell the tale. Their stories are told in the Daredevil Hall of Fame in the **Niagara Falls Museum** next to the Rainbow Bridge. Nowadays, anyone caught trying to pull off any kind of stunt is liable to a fine of $10,000.

In spite of all the commercial enterprises that have attached themselves to Niagara, it costs nothing to stroll by and take in the view. It wasn't always the case. In the 19th century the area was a riot of fairgrounds and sideshows and if you wanted to view the falls you had to pay to peep through a hole in a fence.

By 1885 commercial exploitation had reached such a pitch that the Ontario government took over the area and created it as the first provincial park. Two years later the Niagara Parks Commission was formed and a greenbelt was gradually developed.

Now, the **Niagara Parkway** stretches from Fort Erie to Niagara-on-the-Lake, a 56km (34-mile) leisure drive with plenty of discreet car parks and picnic sites along the way. If you would rather walk, cycle or ski in winter, you could take the **Niagara River Recreation Trail**, which follows the same route.

The falls are a year-round attraction. In winter, spray turns into filigrees of ice as it settles on trees along the Parkway. The effect is enhanced by thousands of Christmas lights, moving light displays and fireworks during the **Festival of Lights**, a celebration that lasts from the end of November to the third week in February.

Organized Sightseeing

Thanks to modern commercialism, you can now view the falls from above, below and behind. One company offers **helicopter** rides, or you can get a good view from three towers – the Kodak Tower, the Minolta Tower and the Skylon Tower, which also has a revolving restaurant.

Probably the most popular sightseeing activity is to board one of the *Maid of the Mist* boats that take a 30-minute trip almost to the foot of the falls. It is an exciting voyage, noisy and full of drenching spray. Waterproof jacket rental is included in the cost of the ticket, but make sure you have a stout plastic bag for your camera.

Table Rock Scenic Tunnels enable you to walk almost to the middle of the falls where you can view the cascade – and feel the vibrations – from behind. Again, waterproofs are included in the admission charge.

Downstream, courageous souls can cross the Whirlpool Basin in a cable car which is known as the **Niagara Spanish Aero Car**, while others can experience **The Great Gorge Adventure**, taking an elevator ride to the bottom of the Niagara Gorge where a boardwalk follows the raging torrent.

If you would like to know what it feels like to plunge over the falls in a barrel try **Ride Niagara**, a computerized motion simulator.

Niagara-on-the-Lake

Originally named Newark, Niagara-on-the-Lake was the first capital of Upper Canada – from 1791 to 1796 – until the city of York (later Toronto) took over. It was virtually destroyed during the War of 1812, so most of the present town dates from the late 1800s. Nevertheless, it is a well-preserved place and aficionados say it is the prettiest town in Ontario. It is certainly a charming place, with a number of quaint old inns, roses round brass-knockered doors and a council ban on architectural or decorative features in a style later than Victorian. On Queen Street, the main thoroughfare, is the Niagara Pharmacy, a restored 1866 shop.

The **Niagara Historical Society Museum**, 43 Castlereagh Street, houses a collection of 20,000 items covering the region's history to the War of 1812. Opened in 1907, it is Ontario's oldest local history museum.

Fort George served as the British army headquarters on the Niagara Frontier and has been restored to its 1813 condition. There are daily demonstrations of drill, musketry, blacksmithing and other traditional skills. A National Historic Site, the fort is on the Niagara Parkway and is open from late May to early October.

Niagara-on-the-Lake has achieved an international reputation for its annual **Shaw Festival**, which runs from late April to early November. It is the world's only festival dedicated to the works of George Bernard Shaw and his contemporaries, and plays are performed in the Royal George Theatre, the Court House Theatre and the modern Festival Theatre.

Early settlers in Ontario soon realized that the climate in the Niagara Peninsula

is ideal for growing grapes for wine production. The province's first vineyard was established in 1873.

The Lake Erie Shore

Travelling south, the Niagara Parkway – or the Queen Elizabeth Way, if you are in a hurry – leads to Lake Erie and a shoreline that stretches westwards from the border with New York to the border with Michigan, a distance of about 400km (250 miles). It's an interesting route, full of variety, with beach resorts, fishing ports, provincial parks and echoes of the past.

Fort Erie

Fort Erie is linked with the city of Buffalo, New York, by the International Peace Bridge over the Niagara River. The two communities share a Friendship Festival, celebrating Canadian and American national holidays. But things were not always so chummy. Fort Erie was the last place in Canada to be occupied by American troops in the War of 1812.

Historic Fort Erie has been rebuilt after being destroyed at the end of the 1812 war. Originally built in 1764, it was destroyed twice – in 1779 and 1803 – during savage winter storms, but its present restoration is in the style of the early 19th century. It contains relics and equipment of the British and American armies and guides in period uniform show visitors around. There are demonstrations of drill and a cannon is fired.

T ourists have been taking exciting 'Maid of the Mist' voyages beneath Niagara Falls since 1846.

On the Wine Route

The pictogram of a bunch of grapes on road signs indicates that you are in Canada's major wine-growing region. About 15 wineries in the Niagara Peninsula produce 80 percent of Canada's wine grapes, and several of them are in the area around Niagara-on-the-Lake. Most offer tours and tastings.

For railroad buffs, the **Fort Erie Railroad Museum** on Central Avenue has memorabilia of the age of steam, including the steam locomotive, *Pride of Fort Erie*. And for sporty types there's the Fort Erie Race Track, said to be one of the most attractive in North America. It is also one of the oldest – founded in 1897 – but it has very modern amenities, including glass-enclosed dining terraces overlooking the two courses.

Port Colborne to Port Stanley

Port Colborne, about 30km (19 miles) west of Fort Erie, is at the southern end of the Welland Canal, a 40km (25-mile) waterway with eight locks that lift sea-going vessels more than 100m (326ft) from Lake Ontario to Lake Erie. Lock No. 8, one of the largest single locks in the world, can be viewed from Fountain View Park. Visitors can learn about the canal and Great Lakes shipping in the Port Colborne **Historical and Marine Museum**, a complex of seven buildings at 200 King Street.

Picturesque **Port Dover**, another 80km (50 miles) or so along the coast, makes the distinctive claim that it is the world's largest freshwater fishing port. A huge fleet of colourful fishing vessels brings in catches of bass, perch, pickerel, smelt and whitefish, large quantities of which end up steaming on plates in the town's restaurants.

Nature lovers will be keen to visit **Port Rowan**, an attractive agricultural and resort town on the edge of **Long Point Provincial Park**, a 32km (20-mile) peninsula that curves out into Lake Erie. The park is a prime birdwatching location, especially during migration.

About 3km (2 miles) north of Port Rowan, **Backus Heritage Conservation Area** is a complex of 20 restored pioneer buildings, including a homestead and an 1866 octagonal mill. The main attraction – and the one that gives its name to the complex – is the 'Backhouse Mill', built in 1798. There is also a 12km (8-mile) nature trail and facilities for both camping and fishing.

Port Stanley, south of the town of St Thomas, is a summer resort with a beach of fine sand. It's a good spot for boating, fishing and swimming. It's also the start of an immensely popular ride on a restored railway. The London and Port Stanley Railroad was built in 1856 with the intention of creating a major link between Canada and the United States. The traffic went elsewhere and the line became derelict. It was rescued by rail enthusiasts who restored some passenger cars and repaired the line – first to **Union**, a distance of about 8km (5 miles), then a further 16km (10 miles) to **St Thomas**. Now there are rail excursions year-round to Union and during the summer also to St Thomas.

Windsor and the Southern Tip

Right up against the US border, with Detroit, Michigan, as its next-door neighbour, Windsor was the centre of disputes between British, French and American interests from the arrival of the first missionaries in the 1640s to the end of the War of 1812. Its major activity, like that of Detroit, is the automotive industry and for many years the city had a rather drab image. Recently, however, there has been a big clean-up and the riverfront has become an attractive parkland area.

The **Art Gallery of Windsor**, at 445 Riverside Drive West, has three floors of galleries. There are permanent and touring exhibitions of contemporary and historic works from Canada and abroad. The **François Baby House**, 254 Pitt Street West, was built in 1811 by Colonel François Baby and used as headquarters of the invading American forces in 1812. It is now a museum of local history. **Willistead Manor**, Niagara Street and Kildare Road, was built in 1906 in the style of an English manor house in the Tudor-Jacobean period for Edward Chandler Walker, second son of Hiram Walker, founder of Walker's Distillery. The 6ha (15-acre) estate is now a city park and visitors may tour the house.

One of the oldest settlements in the area, **Amherstburg** is a quiet town at the mouth of the Detroit River, about 24km (15 miles) south of Windsor. Its eventful history is reflected in a number of historic sites and buildings. **Fort Malden National Historic Site** is a 4.5ha (11-acre) park with several stone buildings housing memorabilia of the Indians, British and Americans who controlled the area at different times. There are picnic tables and seats for those who like to watch the shipping. The fort is at 100 Laird Avenue, Amherstburg.

Another free attraction in the town is the **North American Black Historical Museum**, 227 King Street, which tells the story of the Underground Railway system that helped hundreds of slaves to escape to Canada between 1800 and 1860. Artefacts, photographs and art displays are on show in a log cabin and a church built in 1848.

Some interesting attractions are tucked away on the quiet byways east of Amherstburg. Just south of Essex, a former lumber town, is the **Southwestern Ontario Heritage Village** – a score of historic buildings on 22ha (54 acres) where volunteers in period costume show visitors how things were done in pioneer days.

Kingsville, Canada's most southerly town, is on the flight path of migrating Canada geese and other birds. Just north of the town, signposted off County Road 29, is **Jack Miner's Bird Sanctuary**, founded in 1904 by a hunter who became a conservationist. In his first year, Jack Miner gave protection to four geese; now some 50,000 winter here each year.

Some 8km (5 miles) west of Kingsville, on County Road 50, is the **John R Park Homestead**, one of Ontario's few examples of American Greek Revival architecture. The elegant 1842 home, now a museum of Upper Canada life in the 1850s, is surrounded by a pioneer village.

About 15km (10 miles) east of Kingsville, **Leamington**, a major canning centre amidst miles of farmland, calls itself the Tomato Capital of Canada. You can buy fresh tomatoes and other produce from stands at the roadside.

From Leamington, County Road 33 leads due south to **Point Pelee National Park**, the most southerly point on the Canadian mainland, on the same latitude as northern California. The 1,619ha (4,000-acre) park is a spit of sand, marsh, trees and grass jutting out into Lake Erie, with an interpretive centre, transit trains, nature trails, picnic grounds and a 1.6km (1-mile) boardwalk with observation tower. Bicycles and canoes can be rented.

South again – but this time by ferry boat from Kingsville or Leamington,

Pelee Island lies halfway between Ontario and the state of Ohio. It's the largest island in the lake, covering some 4,000ha (10,000 acres), and it has a permanent population of less than 300. For the past 60 years or so, the island's chief industry has been raising pheasants for hunters to shoot in the autumn, an activity initiated by the local council to reduce taxes. Pelee (pronounced pee-lee) Island has a number of small motels with simple facilities.

London

With a population of 300,000, London is the largest city in southwestern Ontario. Visitors can take tours on a big red double-decker bus or by passenger boat on – you guessed it – the Thames River. Known as the Forest City because of the 50,000 trees that shade its streets, it has 625ha (1,500 acres) of parks, mostly along the riverside, and houses the main campus of the University of Western Ontario. It is a quiet but very successful manufacturing, distribution and financial centre.

Storyland, a children's theme park owned and operated by London's Public Utility Commission, is in Springbank Park beside the Thames. It has a castle and zoo and young visitors can meet and play with a number of their favourite storybook characters.

London also has a **Children's Museum** at 21 Wharncliffe Road South. Its hands-on galleries feature caves, dinosaurs, the Inuit people and space.

A reconstructed native longhouse standing on its original site is a striking feature of the **London Museum of Archeology**, where archaeologists are still working to uncover further evidence of the Attawandaron people who lived here some 500 years ago. The museum contains some 40,000 artefacts and artists' impressions of the way the native people lived. It is located off Wonderland Road North, just south of Highway 22.

Six hoop-shaped glass buildings are joined together at the Forks of the Thames to make up the architecturally striking **London Regional Art and Historical Museum**. Opened in 1980, it offers changing exhibits of regional, national and international works as well as historical exhibits.

The **Fanshaw Pioneer Village**, east of the city off Clarke Road, recalls Ontario's rural origins in a complex of 22 restored buildings with costumed interpreters. There are craft demonstrations and special events are staged on some weekends.

About 30km (20 miles) west on Highway 2, just beyond Delaware, **Ska-Nah-Doht** is a recreation of a prehistoric Iroquoian Indian village with longhouses and a pallisade. Displays, audiovisual presentations and special events complement the authentic structures.

Two Cities in One

About 45km (28 miles) east of Stratford, the cities of **Kitchener** and **Waterloo** have merged so closely that the word 'and' has been replaced by a hyphen. Kitchener-Waterloo, K-W in popular parlance, is an entity with two universities, many parks and a heritage that springs from Mennonite settlers who moved from Pennsylvania at the beginning of the 19th century.

With their own roots in Germany and Switzerland, the Mennonites came in search of religious freedom and good land. Thanks to the local Indians, from whom they purchased thousands of hectares, they found both. The joy they must have felt is echoed each year in **Oktoberfest**, a celebration that draws 600,000 people to

North America's largest feast of sausages, sauerkraut, beer and oompah-pah music. It lasts 9 days and the eating and drinking takes place in 20 festival halls.

Talking of drinking, the **Seagram Museum**, at 57 Erb Street West, Waterloo, is dedicated – not unnaturally – to the distiller's craft, past and present. It is located in the original Seagram distillery barrel warehouse with liquor store and restaurant attached.

The Kitchener half of K-W emphasizes its European origins in a grand and famous **Farmers' Market**, established in 1869 and now housed spaciously in Market Square. It is held on Saturday mornings year-round, and on Wednesday mornings between mid-May and mid-October. Waterloo also has a picturesque market staged year-round on Saturday mornings and on Wednesday mornings between June and early October.

The boyhood home of William Lyon Mackenzie King, tenth prime minister of Canada for close on 22 of the years between 1821 and 1848, has been preserved as the **Woodside National Historic Park** at 528 Wellington Street North, Kitchener. It has been restored and furnished to reflect the time when the King family lived here.

Rural life in the early 1800s is encapsulated at **Doon Heritage Crossroads**, a restored pioneer village on 24ha (60 acres) on Homer-Watson Boulevard, a few kilometres southwest of Kitchener, off Highway 401. Guides wear period costume to guide visitors around the village of 23 buildings, including a museum, church, school, store, railway station and a collection of both Mennonite and Scottish artefacts.

Just north of the twin cities, the villages of **St Jacob's** and **Elmira** are real Mennonite and Hutterite communities. The people who live here resist modern technology, but produce wonderful craft items and live well off the land. There are many craft stands and antique shops in the area.

Stratford On... tario

In the beginning the only thing Stratford had in common with William Shakespeare's birthplace in the English Midlands was the name of its river – and that had been bestowed by the Canada Company which had organized settlement in the region. The town was first known as Little Thames (on Avon?), but in 1831 the settlers decided to change the name.

For decades the town thrived on the railways that intersected there, but when the steam went out of rail travel in the early 1950s it was good old Will who came to the rescue.

In 1953 Sir Alec Guinness played *Richard III* in a marquee – and the **Stratford Festival** was born. By 1957 the festival had a permanent home in a theatre with more than 2,000 seats, none more than 20m (65ft) from the stage. Now there are three theatres and performances include musical events as well as works by Shakespeare.

And Stratford, Ontario, flourishes with its gentle River Avon, swans and greensward. To say nothing of the 400,000 visitors who customarily fill its hotels, restaurants and shops from May to mid-November each year.

Cottage Country

Three highways – the multi-lane 400 and the less frenzied 11 and 27 – strike north from Toronto to head for **Muskoka**, otherwise known as Cottage Country, and on Friday afternoons, in summer especially, all three will be busy with city-dwellers desperate to get away from it all for the weekend.

Muskoka is one of Ontario's longest-established resort areas – 3,770sq km (1,473sq miles) of lakeland with mixed woods and evergreen forests hiding a playground of cottages, marinas, inns and trails for hikers and skiers. In the early 1800s the area was unknown, except to wandering bands of Ojibwa hunters. But in the 1860s determined young hikers from Toronto – setting out first by train, then by steamer and finally by rowboat and on foot – discovered the picturesque countryside that surrounded Lakes Muskoka, Joseph and Rosseau.

Word spread, and by the 1890s – thanks to the establishment of rail and steamship services – the area was attracting wealthy holidaymakers from the United States and Britain as well as people from Toronto.

Orillia

From the south the gateway to Muskoka is Orillia, a pleasant year-round vacation centre on the narrows between lakes Simcoe and Couchiching. A focal point of aboriginal life long before the explorer Champlain passed this way in 1615 – his statue is in a lakeside park – Orillia is a major link in the Trent-Severn Waterway system and has an attractive waterfront. Its chief claim to fame is as the 'little town'

Cheerful red barns dot the rural landscape in Ontario's productive farmland.

of Mariposa in Stephen Leacock's *Sunshine Sketches of a Little Town*. The Canadian humourist's summer home is now the **Stephen Leacock Memorial Home Museum**, located off Highway 12B at the eastern end of the city.

Gravenhurst

About 40km (25 miles) to the north, on Highway 11, is Gravenhurst, the first town in Muskoka proper. It stands on a narrow neck of land between Lake Muskoka and the smaller Gull Lake. Gravenhurst is an attractive town with a population of around 10,000, a Main Street of shops, boutiques and restaurants and an Opera House built in 1901.

The town's pride and joy is RMS *Segwun*, said to be the oldest fully operational steamship in North America. She was built in Scotland in 1887 and assembled in Gravenhurst to carry mail, freight and passengers to the communities surrounding the Muskoka lakes. Restored to her

MUSKOKA REGION

Ravenscliffe
Lake Vernor
Parry Sound • Haines Lake
Huntsville
• Aspdin
• Hayes Corner
• Rosseau   Skeleton Lake
Mary Lake
• Gordon Bay
• Ullswater   • Utterson   N ↑
• Dee Bank
Lake Joseph
Lake Rosseau
• Woods Bay   Mactier
• Port Carling
• Glen Orchard   • Macaulay
• Moose Point   North Bay
• Bracebridge
East Bay
• Bala   • Muskoka Falls
Potters • • Sahanatien   • Torrance   Muskoka Lake
Landing   • Muskoka Beach
Georgian Bay
Giants Tomb Island   Big Shute   • Southwood   • Gravenhurst
Severn River   Houseys Rapids
• Sawlog Bay   • Bayview Park   Severn Falls
• Silver Birch Beach   Severn Sound   0   10 miles   • Hamlet   • Coopers Falls
• Midland   0   16 km   • Washago

Victorian elegance, *Segwun* now takes up to 99 passengers on cruises ranging from 90 minutes to 2 days in a season that runs from June to October. The history of the vessel and of steamship travel in the past is told in the **RMS Segwun Heritage Centre** on Town Wharf, Bay Street.

Gravenhurst's other major attraction is the **Bethune Memorial House**, at 235 John Street North. Administered by the Canada Parks Service and restored to 1890, the old frame house was the birthplace of a Canadian hero better known in China than in his home country. Dr Norman Bethune spent years in China working as a field surgeon and medical tutor.

Bracebridge

Another 11km (7 miles) north and Highway 11 reaches Bracebridge, a busy town of 12,300 people with a long Main Street climbing from a spectacular waterfall on the Muskoka River. In 1894 the town became the first in the province to produce its own hydroelectric power, and the present power station at the foot of the roaring cascade is the oldest in continuous use in Canada.

Bracebridge likes to regard itself as the summer home of Santa Claus. This is because **Santa's Village**, a 20ha (50-acre) theme park is located 4km (2¹/₂ miles) west of the town on the Muskoka River.

There are rides, animals, a picnic area and, of course, Santa himself. Adjoining the village is **Mister Rudolph's Funland**, a family entertainment centre with go-karts, mini-golf, baseball batting cages and an activity centre. Admission to Funland is free, but you pay as you play.

Huntsville

Huntsville (population 15,000) is the largest and most northerly town in the Muskoka. It was founded as a logging town in the 1800s by a Captain George Hunt. Because of its distance from Toronto its development as a leisure destination was delayed, but today it is the liveliest and commercially most active town in the region, with year-round activities and a popular Festival of the Arts staged in July.

Muskoka, Ontario's Cottage Country, is a popular holiday area and weekend retreat for Toronto people.

The **Muskoka Pioneer Village** on Brunel Road, Huntsville, gives visitors a taste of life in a crossroads community between 1860 and 1910. There are 18 early homesteads on 23ha (55 acres), and costumed interpreters – all volunteers – demonstrate candlemaking, drying herbs and plants, spinning, weaving, blacksmithing and other pioneer crafts. Visitors even get the chance to dine in a Victorian restaurant.

Huronia

The area fringing Georgian Bay to the southwest of Muskoka is known as Huronia, Ontario's most historic area. Close to where the town of **Midland** now stands, a group of French Jesuit priests set out to convert the Huron Indians to Christianity and in 1639 built the province's first European settlement – the mission of **Saint-Marie Among the Hurons**.

The Indians taught the Jesuits how to survive the wilderness and its cruel climate and the settlers built a farm, school and hospital. Then the Iroquois declared war on the Huron nation and the Jesuits were caught up in a terribly savage conflict. In 1649 six of the priests were captured by the Iroquois and tortured to death. Shocked and scared the surviving missionaries and their Huron converts burned Saint-Marie to the ground and fled.

Saint-Marie Among the Hurons has now been reconstructed as an award-winning living museum with 22 reproduced structures, including a wigwam and a tribal longhouse. Costumed guides go about their 17th-century tasks as they answer visitors' questions. The village is overlooked by the twin towers of the Martyr's Shrine, dedicated to the six priests who were canonized by the Roman Catholic church in 1930.

Well signposted, Saint-Marie Among the Hurons is on Highway 12, 5km (3 miles) east of Midland.

Adjoining the village, the **Wye Marsh Wildlife Center** offers an insight into the ecology of the Georgian Bay marshlands through guided nature walks and canoe excursions.

Hundreds of artefacts unearthed in archaeological digs, together with drawings, photographs, models of early shipping and displays of native and pioneer lifestyles, are exhibited in the **Huronia Museum and Gallery of Historic Huronia** in Little Lake Park, Midland. Behind the museum building is the **Huron Indian Village**, a life-size reconstruction of a 16th-century native village. A single admission charge covers both the museum and village.

The neighbouring town of **Penetanguishene** (pronounced pen-ettang-wisheen, but everyone finds it easier to say 'Penetang') is an attractive old port with tree-shaded streets and a bicultural heritage, thanks to the French voyageurs who settled around the British naval and military bases which were established here after the War of 1812.

The port offers another opportunity to witness life in the past. This time, costumed interpreters in the **Historic Naval and Military Establishment** on Church Street act out the lives of 19th-century soldiers and sailors. Twelve reconstructed buildings contain furnishings of the period 1817-56, and three replica 19th-century schooners are moored at the wharf. For a fee, visitors can take a cruise on one of the schooners and join in the rope-hauling if they wish.

School children learn about 17th-century life at Ste Marie Among the Hurons.

Rather more conventional cruises aboard modern vessels set off from the town wharfs of both Midland and Penetanguishene for sightseeing among the 30,000 Islands area of Georgian Bay.

Midwestern Ontario

Driving through snow flurries during the last week in April on Highway 11 near Huntsville may lead you to believe that this is true northern travel. But the fact is that the north hasn't even begun yet. Non-city Ontarians generally agree that the south ends at **North Bay** on Lake Nippissing, another 130km (82 miles) along Highway 11. Beyond North Bay the communities gradually thin out until the wilderness takes over totally, sweeping relentlessly on to Hudson Bay.

North Bay

With a population of around 55,000, North Bay is a busy, year-round tourism city popular with anglers, hunters and railway buffs – lines of the Canadian National, Canadian Pacific and Ontario Northland Railways all converge here. In the winter the city is a centre for downhill and cross-country skiers.

North Bay has all the usual biggish city attractions, plus the unique **Dionne Quints Museum**, the homestead in which the Dionne Quintuplets were born on 28 May 1934. The five girls were the first identical quintuplets ever known to survive. The museum is at Seymour Street on the North Bay Bypass, next to the North Bay regional tourist information centre, and it contains the bed in which the girls were born, baby clothes, photographs and advertisements in which the babies were featured.

There are two roads out of North Bay. Highway 11 – the world's longest Main Street, remember – continues northwards, while Highway 17, which began its journey in Ottawa, 365km (228 miles) away, peels off to the west. Both roads will meet again at **Nipigon** on the northernmost point of Lake Superior.

The Southern Route

Highway 17, known as the Southern Route, follows a more populous route as it skirts Lakes Huron and Superior. The first sizeable community it meets is **Sudbury**, with a population of 93,000.

Sudbury

Poor old Sudbury – like many a long-established industrial city, it is still trying to live down the grubby image of its past. 'Ho, ho,' say the scoffers, 'this was where American astronauts were brought for training on the kind of terrain they would encounter on the moon.' But the joke is on the rest of the world because Sudbury's strange landscape is thought to have been caused by a meteorite which came down about 2 billion years ago, bringing a vast wealth of gold, silver, platinum, cobalt, copper and nickel.

To underline the economic importance of these rich ores – and of nickel in particular – Sudbury has erected a 9m high (30ft) Canadian 5 cent piece at the western entrance to the city – not a bad way to say shucks to the rest of the world.

And as for grubbiness, Sudbury has done a lot to burnish up its image and the place now has 30 lakes, some 2,500ha (6,000 acres) of protected woodland, clean, well-lit streets and a smart downtown. Among its tourist attractions is the **Big Nickel Mine**, near that giant coin on Highway 17. Here, visitors don hard hats, coveralls and boots to see mining techniques demonstrated underground. A **Path of Discovery Tour**, which leaves the Big Nickel Mine several times a day in summer, takes visitors on a bus trip of Sudbury's mining sites, including the place where it all began in 1884 when a railway worker unearthed copper and nickel ores.

Sudbury's major attraction, however, is **Science North**, a hands-on museum devoted to physics and geology. In two snowflake-shaped buildings visitors can lie on a bed of nails, watch a 3D film in a pitch-black cave, experience the Arctic and much, much more.

Manitoulin Island

At **Espanola**, about 70km (44 miles) west of Sudbury, Highway 6 strikes south for 63km (40 miles), crossing a swing bridge to reach the world's largest freshwater island. This is Manitoulin Island, 160km (100 miles) long and varying in width from 3km (2 miles) to 64km (40 miles).

With crystal-clear lakes, rivers, meadows and rolling countryside, as well as forests and rugged, granite-strewn areas, the island is ideal for outdoor pursuits. It has a good selection of hotels, motels, cottages, cabins and tent and trailer campgrounds.

The first community reached from the mainland, **Little Current** is also the island's largest with a population of just over 1,500. It was founded in the 1860s and soon became an important port with an economy based largely on lumber. The swing bridge originally carried rail traffic and remained open, except when a train neared, so that shipping could pass unimpeded. Now, it opens on summer days once an hour for about 15 minutes to let vessels through – and most of those are leisure craft.

In a wooded park in the village of Sheguiandah, 18km (11 miles) south of **Little Current, the Little Current-Howland Centennial Museum** displays pioneer and aboriginal artefacts in a number of log houses and two large buildings.

The large peninsula at the eastern end of Manitoulin Island is **Wikwemikong Unceded Indian Reserve** – the only one of its kind in Canada. It remains unceded because the Anishnabec people refused to sign a treaty and hand over their ancestral lands in 1862. The reserve covers about 770sq km (300sq miles) and is home to some 2,500 people of Odawa, Ojibwa and Potawotami descent. Each August the Wikwemikong **Pow Wow** attracts drummers, dancers and singers from all parts of North America.

Sault Ste Marie

Sault Ste Marie gazes across the St Mary's River at its namesake in the American state of Michigan. The two cities are connected by the International Bridge and both owe their origin – and their name – to French missionaries who established a settlement here in 1669, long before the boundary was drawn. The Canadian city – and the American one, too – is known simply as 'The Soo', which at least tells you how to pronounce the first word. 'Sault' is the French word for rapids.

The rapids in the narrow neck of the river between Lakes Huron and Superior have now been bypassed by the **Soo Lock**, the final lift for ocean-going ships travelling to the Upper Great Lakes by way of the St Lawrence Seaway. There are boat tours through the lock during summer months.

Sault Ste Marie is also the starting point for the **Agawa Canyon Train Tour**, one of two adventurous rail trips in Northern

219

Ontario. The Algoma Central Railway (tel. 705/254-4331) runs the scenic tour as a sideline to its main business of serving the iron mines at Hearst on Highway 11. Passengers travel in old-fashioned comfort as the train trundles through the wilderness to Agawa Canyon, some 20km (12 miles) long with cliffs up to 250m (800ft) high. The train runs year-round, but during summer months it stops in the canyon for a couple of hours so that passengers can enjoy a picnic and take a look around.

The **Ermatinger Stone House**, 831 Queen Street East, Sault Ste Marie, is the oldest house in northern Ontario. Constructed in stone in 1814, it is an elegant two-storey home in Georgian style. It was built for Charles Oakes Ermatinger, an eminent fur trader whose wife, Charlotte, was the daughter of Katawebeda, a chief of the Ojibwas. Costumed guides show visitors over the house, which has been fully restored. Demonstrations of pioneer cuisine are given in the kitchen.

North Along Lake Superior

About 120km (75 miles) north of The Soo, Highway 17 enters **Lake Superior Provincial Park** and stays within its bounds for 90km (56 miles). The park is a ruggedly beautiful wilderness area covering nearly 1,500sq km (580sq miles). It has camping facilities, hiking trails, picnic sites and beaches. **Agawa Rock**, a 23m (75ft) cliff towering above Lake Superior, bears carved pictographs which form the basis for Longfellow's saga of Hiawatha.

A massive steel goose, 9m (28ft) tall with a wingspan of 6m (19ft) heralds your arrival at the town of **Wawa**, an Ojibwa word meaning 'wild goose'. The log cabin standing next to the monument is the local tourist information office.

Another statue, this time of Winnie the Pooh, is to be found at **White River,** 90km (56 miles) further along the highway. This was the place where Lieutenant Harry Colebourne of Winnipeg bought the small black bear that was to inspire the stories of A A Milne. White River is also known as the coldest place in Canada.

Thunder Bay

Thunder Bay (population 114,000) is Canada's western terminus for the ocean-going ships that ply the St Lawrence Seaway. The country's third largest port, it is also the largest grain-handling port in the world.

With nine shopping malls and dozens of restaurants, Thunder Bay is a lively city, with the largest population of Finns outside Finland. More than 40 other nationalities are also represented.

The city's chief tourist attraction is **Old Fort William**, time-warped to 1815 when it was the headquarters of the Northwest Company. In its early days it was a wild and weird place, especially during the summer when more than a thousand company agents, Native people, trappers, explorers and adventurers gathered to trade pelts and furs in return for alcohol and blankets.

Scenes from those riotous days – drunks being hauled off to the cells, *voyageurs* cutting loose, agents and trappers trading – are re-enacted ad lib by an enthusiastic cast. With 42 historic buildings standing in 52ha (125 acres), Old Fort William is said to be the largest reconstruction of its kind in North America. The fort is south of Broadway Avenue and can be reached by car, city bus or the cruise ship *Welcome*, which also takes a trip around the harbour and nearby islands.

Amethyst, Ontario's official gemstone, is mined in the area east of Thunder Bay. Five of the mines – all signposted from Highway 11/17 – are open to the public and visitors are invited to pick their own stones in an open pit or buy them more conventionally across a counter.

The Northern Route

Highway 11, which started out as Yonge Street back in Toronto, slogs on from North Bay, passing through widely dispersed communities, many of which owe their existence to mining.

There are places like **Cobalt**, where the world's richest silver deposit was discovered in 1903 when a blacksmith threw his hammer at a fox, missed and chipped a rock. Or **Kirkland Lake**, a modern town built literally on gold-bearing rock and producing more than a fifth of Canada's gold. And **Timmins**, Canada's largest city in terms of area, once the largest gold producer in the western hemisphere and now boasting the world's richest silver-zinc mine.

Timmins

Timmins (population 48,000) is on Highway 101, about 60km (38 miles) west of its intersection with Highway 11 at Matheson. Here, you can join a guided **gold mine tour** 60m (200ft) below ground at the Giant Yellowknife Mines Hollinger site. Tours of other mines and plants in the area are available. Check with the Chamber of Commerce travel information office at 76 McIntyre Road, Schumacher. The **Porcupine Outdoor Mining Museum** is in the grounds of the Timmins Museum and National Exhibition Centre at 70 Legion Drive, South Porcupine. It features a collection of mining machinery, as well as trolley and steam locomotives. The indoor museum and exhibition gallery feature changing exhibits drawn from the community and from institutions across Canada. One gallery displays minerals from around the world.

The Polar Bear Express

From Timmins you can fly to **Moosonee** on James Bay, the lower part of Hudson Bay, but most people plump for the Polar Bear Express from **Cochrane**. This is one of the great railway journeys of the world, a trip of 300km (187 miles) across the wildest of wilderness. Three highways that set off bravely enough in the direction of James Bay peter out after 80km (50 miles) or so, and if you can't stand air travel or trains then your only other option is to go by canoe.

The Polar Bear Express – run by the Ontario Northland Railway – makes the round-trip every day of the week, except Friday, from late June to Labour Day. It leaves Cochrane at 8.30am, gets to Moosonee by 1pm, then leaves at 5.15pm to return to Cochrane by 9.20pm. Meals and snacks are served on the train which even has a piano car.

Moosonee (population 1,360) is very much an end-of-the-line place. The chief attraction downtown is the **James Bay Educational Centre** where visitors can buy the products of Indian craft-making.

A popular excursion from Moosonee is the 15-minute trip by freighter canoe to **Moose Factory Island**, site of the original Hudson's Bay Company post which was established in 1673. Several early 19th-century buildings remain, and there is a blacksmith's shop built in the 1850s. A museum is devoted to the fur trade and early development in the area. St Thomas Church, built in 1860, has moosehide altar cloths, silk embroidery on white deerhide and prayer books in the Cree language.

Reservations are strongly recommended for the Polar Bear Express – and for accommodation if you plan to stay overnight at Moosonee or Moose Factory Island. Contact Ontario Northland, tel. (705) 472-4500.

Algonquin Provincial Park

Ontario's oldest and best-known provincial park – and one of the largest in Canada – the Algonquin covers 7,600sq km (2,970sq miles) of wilderness – an area of beautiful lakes, bogs and rivers, forests, cliffs and beaches. And it all lies within a comfortable 4-hour drive of either Ottawa or Toronto.

The park was opened in 1893, and to mark its centennial a splendid new visitor centre was opened just off Highway 60 at the 43km (27-mile) mark (distances are

Algonquin Provincial Park has many campgrounds accessible by canoe or vehicle.

measured from the park's West Gate). The centre has a large audiovisual theatre, a book store, a restaurant seating 150 and lifelike exhibits illustrating the park's major habitats and tracing man's involvement with the area from aboriginal times to today. At the back of the centre a wide viewing deck overlooks a magnificent panorama of park landscape.

There are only two ways to explore the Algonquin's vast interior – by canoe or on foot. More than 1,500km (about 1,000 miles) of routes are available for canoeists of all grades. Hikers can choose from the Highland or Western Uplands, the park's two famous rugged backpacking trails with loops ranging from 19 to 71km (12 to 44 miles) in length.

If you don't have your own gear you can rent it from outfitting services within and around the park. Most outfitters will organize a total package, if required – food, equipment and supplies. Guided 1-day and overnight canoe trips are also available.

Visitors seeking a less demanding stay can enjoy camping, swimming, fishing, hiking, picnicking and learning about nature with the comfort of modern amenities along the 56km (35-mile) stretch of Highway 60 that cuts through the park's southwest corner. There are eight organized campgrounds along the Parkway Corridor. Three lodges – Arowhon Pines, Bartlett Lodge and Killarney Lodge – are inside the park boundaries, and there are many other lodges and resorts outside.

Experts claim the Algonquin offers the best moose-viewing opportunities in North America, especially in May and June when the animals are attracted to the highway by the slightly salty water left in roadside ditches. White-tailed deer, beaver and black bear also make their home in the park, as well as timber wolves, more often heard than seen, especially in August when park staff lead public wolf howlings to encourage the animals to respond to human calls. More than 250 bird species have been recorded.

Strung along Highway 60 are 16 interpretive trails of varying lengths and exploring different aspects of the Algonquin environment. Illustrated guide books are available at each site to help visitors get the most out of their hike. Just inside the East Gate the Algonquin Logging Museum tells the tale of timber.

The park is open year-round, with each season offering something special. In winter there are more than 80km (50 miles) of cross-country ski trails, and snowshoeing opportunities are unlimited. Spring brings what is claimed to be the best trout fishing in Ontario, and summer brings something for everyone. Autumn brings brilliance.

Information on the park can be obtained from The Superintendent, Algonquin

*T*he Algonquin is said to offer the best moose-viewing in North America.

Provincial Park, PO Box 219, Whitney, Ontario K0J 2M0; tel. (705) 633-5572. For campground reservations (essential at peak times) tel. (705) 633-5538/5725.

Ottawa and the National Capital Region

Canada's capital city is an accident of history. The capitals of other countries were chosen because they were great ports, on important trade routes, or were well placed strategically or politically. **Ottawa**, a rowdy little stopover for lumber raftsmen, happened to be the right place at the right time when a new capital was being sought for Upper and Lower Canada.

A Brief Background

There are many older settlements in Canada. This place, at the confluence of three rivers, was no more than a landmark of limestone cliffs to the English and French explorers, the missionaries and fur traders who passed by on their way to the western wilderness from the early 1600s. No one saw any reason to spend more than a night or two there – let alone establish a settlement – until the winter of 1800 when Philemon Wright, an Empire Loyalist from Massachusetts, arrived with five other families.

Wright had travelled up the Outaouais River – named after a tribe of Algonquin Indians – the previous year and had recognized the lumber trade opportunities in an area of dense forest and ample water power. The settlement of Wright's Town, later to be called Hull, sprang up on the north shore and soon became a centre for assembling rafts of white pine logs which were sailed downstream to Montreal for shipment to England.

The War of 1812 made the British only too aware of the vulnerability of the St Lawrence River as a supply route from Montreal to its naval dockyard at Kingston at the eastern end of Lake Ontario. The Ottawa and Rideau Rivers were seen as a much safer alternative, enabling British shipping to put a lot more distance between themselves and American forts as they crept from lake to lake on their way from Montreal to Kingston.

In 1826 the task of building a 200km (125-mile) canal was given to Colonel John By of the Royal Engineers. With a force of thousands of Irish and French Canadian labourers, the daunting job of pushing a canal route through rough bush, swamps and rocky wilderness was completed in 6 years.

Many of the military and civil personnel involved in the project were lured to stay by land grants. A new settlement – Bytown – developed on the south shore of the river and grew rapidly. In 1855 it was granted city status and changed its name to Ottawa, the anglicized version of Outaouais. Two years later Queen Victoria named it permanent capital of the Province of Canada, chosen largely because it was felt that its distance from the US border made it safe from attack. The Americans wryly agreed – as one newspaper commented, 'Invaders would be lost in the woods trying to find it.'

Orientation

You'd have no trouble finding the place today. From most approaches, the city offers a glittering welcome on the horizon – buildings of high-rise mirrors, flaunting each other's reflections, wink flirtatiously across the surrounding countryside. But this big city come-on is an illusion: Ottawa isn't all that big. Its high-rise core – mostly international hotels and corporate palaces – is concentrated over an area of not much more than three blocks and is only one aspect of the city's character.

Cross the street in one direction from all that glass and glitz and you're on **Parliament Hill**, dominated by the green-roofed, brownstoned neo-Gothic extravagance of Canada's seat of government and flanked by stolid Edwardian edifices housing branches of the civil service. Cross in another direction and you step into a homey world of tree-lined streets, two-storey frame-houses and people who like to stop for a chat on the sidewalk.

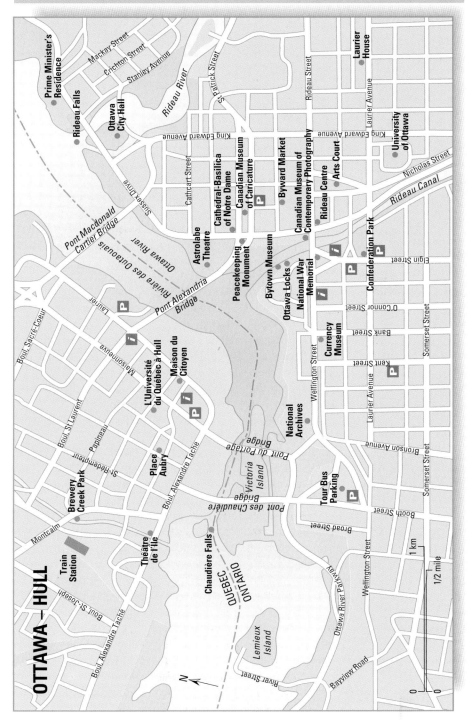

OTTAWA–HULL

Prime Minister's Residence

Mackay Street
Crichton Street
Stanley Avenue
Rideau Falls
Rideau River
St-Patrick Street
Laurier House
Rideau Street
Laurier Avenue

Ottawa City Hall
King Edward Avenue
University of Ottawa
King Edward Avenue
Nicholas Street

Cathcart Street
Cathedral-Basilica of Notre Dame
Canadian Museum of Caricature
Byward Market
Canadian Museum of Contemporary Photography
Arts Court
Rideau Canal

Sussex Drive
Pont Macdonald Cartier Bridge
Ottawa River
Rivière des Outaouais
Astrolabe Theatre
Peacekeeping Monument
Bytown Museum
Ottawa Locks
National War Memorial
Rideau Centre
Confederation Park
Elgin Street

Pont Alexandria Bridge

Laurier

Boul. Sacré-Coeur
Maisonneuve
L'Université du Québec à Hull
Maison du Citoyen
Wellington Street
Currency Museum
O'Connor Street
Bank Street
Somerset Street
Kent Street

Boul. St-Laurent
Papineau
St-Rédempteur
Place Aubry
National Archives
Laurier Avenue

Brewery Creek Park
Boul. Alexandre Taché
Pont du Portage Bridge
Victoria Island
Pont des Chaudière Bridge
Tour Bus Parking
Bronson Avenue

Montcalm
Train Station
Théâtre de l'Île
Chaudière Falls
QUÉBEC
ONTARIO
Broad Street
Booth Street
Wellington Street
Somerset Street

Boul. St-Joseph
Boul. Alexandre Taché
Lemieux Island
River Street
Bayview Road
Ottawa River Parkway
Wellington Street

1 km
0
1/2 mile
0

N

Most of Ottawa's attractions can be visited in a tour on foot, but a good introduction to the city is to take the shuttle bus that runs around Confederation Boulevard, a circular route embracing the heart of the Capital Region on both the Ontario and Quebec sides of the Ottawa River. Two places to call for information are the **National Capital Commission's information centre** at 14 Metcalfe Street (tel. 239-5000), and the **Ottawa Tourism and Convention Authority**, which has a visitor information centre in the National Arts Centre at 65 Elgin Street (tel. 237-5158).

Parliament Hill

Britons and anyone else who knows London will feel instantly at home on Parliament Hill, one of Ottawa's most popular tourist attractions. There's a definite Westminster ambience about the buildings, with their Big Ben-like **Peace Tower**, and in summer months there are even bearskin-hatted Redcoats performing the ceremony of Changing the Guard.

A lot happens to entertain visitors on the Hill – and it's all free. There are carillon concerts, tours of **Centre Block**, where the Senate and the House of Commons work in splendid chambers, and of **East Block**, where four historic rooms have been re-created. A popular tourist activity when parliament is in session is to watch the Prime Minister and members of the Cabinet ducking and diving at Question Time, but there may be a long line for the public gallery. There are **walking tours** of the grounds. The Noonday Gun – a cannon from the Crimean War – is fired daily, and in the summer a sound-and-light show displays Canada's history. Strollers will find a spectacular view of the river from a path behind the Hill.

Changing the Guard, which takes place on the lawn in front of the Peace Tower, is performed by members of two of Canada's most historic regiments – the Governor-General's Foot Guards, who wear red plumes in their hats, and the Canadian Grenadier Guards, who wear white plumes.

During the summer visitors should head for the **Infotent**, a large white marquee between the Centre Block and East Block, where they can pick up information and make same-day reservations for any of the tours. At other times of the year tours leave from the **Rotunda** of the Centre Block and only large groups need to make reservations.

Centretown

Ottawa's core, a mixed area of shops, office towers, restaurants and streets of restored Victorian homes, is bounded by Wellington Street to the north, the Queensway – Highway 417 – to the south, the Rideau Canal to the east and Bronson Avenue to the west.

Confederation Square, dominated by the massive arch of the National War Memorial, is at the northwest corner of Centretown and is a good place from which to get your bearings. More of a triangle than a square, it stands at the junction of Elgin, Sparks and Wellington Streets – the city's oldest thoroughfares – and is within walking distance of most of the major attractions.

The large brown hexagonal building at the southeast corner of the square, actually on Elgin Street, is the **National Arts Centre**. Completed in 1969, this is a major national venue for the performing arts, with three stages, an elegant dining room and a canalside terrace which is a popular meeting place in the summer. To the east of the NAC, the large colonnaded building that would look more at home in ancient Greece is Ottawa's old railroad station, built in 1912 and now the **Government Conference Centre**. It is not open to the public.

Opposite the conference centre, right beside the Rideau Canal, is the **Chateau Laurier Hotel**, an eccentric array of spires and towers more suited to glass coaches and bewigged footmen than stretched limos and delegates from across the street.

Parliament Hill is separated from the Chateau Laurier by the **Ottawa Locks**, a flight of eight locks that lifts the Rideau Canal 24m (nearly 80ft) from the Ottawa River and marks the canal's northern entrance. Standing beside the locks is the **Commissariat**, Ottawa's oldest building. This was Colonel By's headquarters when the canal was being built. Today, it contains the Bytown Museum.

Running south from Confederation Square, Elgin Street is a boulevard of up-market shops and restaurants. At the northeast corner of the intersection between Elgin Street and Laurier Avenue is **Confederation Park**, the setting of Ottawa's major festivals throughout the year. On Laurier, just east of the intersection, is the **Cartier Square Drill Hall,** built in 1882 for the Governor-General's Foot Guards, one of the two regiments that form the Ceremonial Guard on Parliament Hill.

Further south Elgin reaches Somerset Street and the start of the area known as **Somerset Village**, an interesting shopping district. Westwards, between Elgin and Bank Streets, Somerset is lined with Victorian-style gaslamps and restored 19th-century homes, as well as boutiques, restaurants and outdoor cafés. Continuing west, Somerset passes through Ottawa's **Chinatown**, close to the Bronson Avenue junction.

*P*arliament Hill is one of the most popular attractions in the nation's capital.

On the west side of Confederation Square is the **Sparks Street Pedestrian Mall**, the first of its kind in Canada when cars were banished in 1967. It's an interesting street which manages to be both busy and restful – full of boutiques, bookstores, bars and cafés, but with plenty of odd nooks and crannies and street furniture on which to loll on summer days. Bank Street, which Sparks crosses three blocks from Elgin, is Ottawa's most workaday shopping street, with lots of independent grocery stores, delicatessens and bargain outlets.

Sparks Street ends grandly on a promontory overlooking the Ottawa River. This last block is dominated by the Anglican **Christ Church Cathedral**, completed in 1873. Just below the cathedral is the **Garden of the Provinces**, where the union of Canada's provinces and territories is commemorated in sculptures, emblems and fountains.

Opposite the Garden of the Provinces, at 395 Wellington Street, is the building

housing the **National Library** and the **National Archives**, and just east of that is the **Supreme Court of Canada**, the nation's highest court of appeal.

Byward Market and Sussex Drive

East of Confederation Square, Wellington Street becomes Rideau Street and Ottawa assumes two different identities – one a bit brash, the other very upscale.

The **Byward Market** area is the original working heart of Ottawa. This was where the community of Irish and French-Canadian labourers set up their homes – and taverns – when work started on the Rideau Canal. It was a rough and ready place then, and it still seems to carry

The Chateau Laurier, Ottawa's most imposing hotel, dominates Confederation Square.

something of the tipsy navvie's swagger. It's an area of narrow, busy streets, lively taverns – though not as lively as they were when the canal was being dug, perhaps – bistros, wine bars, pubs and clubs. There's a colourful farmers' market, where maple syrup is a specialty, which Ottawans have been using since 1840.

Across Rideau Street from the Byward Market is the **Rideau Centre**, a modern shopping complex of more than 200 establishments under one roof.

Sussex Drive is almost as old as the Byward Market area, but its development has been rather different. In the beginning it was the city's commercial centre, a concentration of stores and hotels. Some of its older buildings have been preserved and at its southern end the drive is still commercial – though here it's commerce of the gold card kind. As it follows the Ottawa River and swings to the east, Sussex Drive becomes the diplomatic sector of the capital. **No. 24** is the official residence of the Prime Minister, and at No. 1 is **Rideau Hall**, home of the Governor-General of Canada. The Prime Minister's house is not open to the public, but there are conducted tours of the grounds of Rideau Hall – tel. (613) 998-7113.

Beyond Rideau Hall, Sussex Drive becomes the Rockcliffe Parkway which leads to the Canadian Police College, where horses and riders of the Royal Canadian Mounted Police Musical Ride practise regularly. Visitors are welcome to watch – tel. (613) 993-3751 for the timetable.

Hull and Gatineau Park

Hull, in the Province of Quebec, is part of the National Capital Region, though its Gallic ambience – evident the moment you cross the river – might lead you to

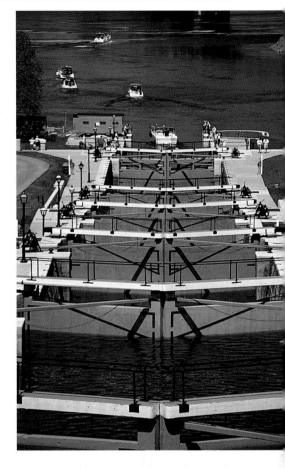

A flight of eight locks masks the northern entrance to the Rideau Canal.

think you have entered a totally different country. The language here is French and there is a French accent in the architecture, the culture and the cuisine.

Follow Taché Boulevard (Highway 148) west from Hull to reach **Gatineau Park**, which is signposted from the boulevard. Barely a 20-minute drive from downtown Ottawa, the park is owned by

229

the federal government and covers more than 36,000ha (88,000 acres) of hiking and cycling trails, swimming, picnic sites and superb winter cross-country ski trails. Within the park is **Kingsmere**, the country estate of William Mackenzie King, Canada's tenth Prime Minister. Mackenzie King was an eccentric man and the estate is festooned with follies.

Tulips from Amsterdam

Mid-May is the time for Ottawa's **Tulip Festival**, when millions of tulips bloom in massed ranks all over the city. The flowers are an annual gift from Queen Juliana of the Netherlands who, with members of her family, found refuge in Ottawa during World War II.

The festival has come to mark the end of winter – Ottawa holds the title of Coldest Capital City in the Western Hemisphere – and the city lets its hair down with firework displays, a regatta on the thawed-out canal, a marathon and lots of fun and games.

Museums and Galleries

The National Capital Region houses some of Canada's finest collections and treasures – and they seem to be growing all the time. Since the late 1980s three museums – the Canadian Museum of Civilization, the National Gallery of Canada and the National Aviation Museum – have moved into spectacular new premises, and more recently two new museums have opened: the Canadian Museum of Caricature and the Canadian Museum of Contemporary Photography. Free admission to most museums is on Thursday evenings.

The world's most comprehensive collection of Canadian art and galleries of European, American and Asian works are on show at the **National Gallery of Canada** at 380 Sussex Drive. The **Canadian War Museum** at 330 Sussex Drive

unveils the nation's military history through dioramas, extensive displays of badges and medals and an art gallery. Guided tours are available. Nearby, at 136 St Patrick Street, is the recently opened **Canadian Museum of Caricature**, in which you'll find more than 20,000 cartoons are exhibited.

In Hull, the stunningly curved **Canadian Museum of Civilization**, at 100 Laurier Street, traces Canada's history from prehistoric times. There are longhouses, totem poles and life-size reconstructions of historic events, as well as a hands-on children's section and CINEPLUS with mammoth-screen films in IMAX and OMNIMAX formats.

The Bank of Canada building on the corner of Bank and Wellington Streets houses the **Currency Museum**, which has the world's most complete collection of Canadian banknotes and coins as well as cash and other trade tokens – beads, shells, bracelets – from all over the world.

Down by the Rideau Canal Locks, near the Chateau Laurier Hotel, is the **Canadian Museum of Contemporary Photography**, with a collection of more than 158,000 images well displayed in specially lit galleries.

Housed in a castle-like building at the corner of Metcalfe and McLeod Streets, the **Canadian Museum of Nature** outlines the evolution of the earth, with a particular focus on the wildlife, plants and minerals of Canada. There is a special Discovery Den for children.

A 10-minute drive from downtown at 1867 St Laurent Boulevard, off Highway 417 East, the **National Museum of Science and Technology**, the largest of its kind in Canada, has displays covering transportation, communications, agriculture, industrial technology, space and other disciplines. There are demonstrations and hands-on exhibits, as well as a picnic area and gift shop.

The **National Aviation Museum** is on Aviation Parkway, off Rockcliffe Parkway, where visitors can picnic in the grounds if they wish (there's also a café). The museum has the nation's best collection of unique and vintage aircraft, and there are special programmes for families and children.

Southeastern Ontario

Wedged between the Province of Quebec and New York State, Ontario's southeastern corner is rich in history. The St Lawrence is a mighty river but a flimsy barrier nevertheless when determined forces are in contest, as was realized during the War of 1812. Today the two countries are linked by bridges, and the neighbourliness is such that you are as likely to travel on an American boat as a Canadian one if you take a trip among the Thousand Islands, and the people in this part of New York State regard Toronto's Lester B Pearson Airport as their international gateway.

Upper Canada Village

Pioneer life is lived to the full at Upper Canada Village, the ultimate living museum where more than 150 staff plant, sow, reap and mow as they would have done nearly 150 years ago – to say nothing of milling flour, baking bread, making cheese and weaving fabrics. They even use oxen to draw their ploughs, and visitors can take a trip in a horse-drawn barge.

The village is about an hour's drive south of Ottawa, 11km (7 miles) east of **Morrisburg** on Highway 2. It takes up about 30ha (70 acres) of the 833ha (2,000-acre) **Crysler Farm Battlefield Memorial Park**, site of a decisive defeat for the Americans in 1813.

The Rideau Canal

Built with war in mind but never used in anger, the Rideau Canal is probably the world's oldest leisure waterway. After its completion in 1832, the canal served for a time as a commercial route, carrying freight to remote communities. But completion of the St Lawrence Canal and the coming of the railways in the 1850s reduced trade to a trickle. Tourism came to the rescue in the shape of luxury steamboats which began carrying passengers along the Rideau over the next half century.

Today, the log rafts, barges and steamers have been totally replaced by pleasure craft and the once remote lock stations can be reached easily by road.

The Rideau is a beautiful waterway, winding from lake to lake, the mellowed stonework of the locks standing at portages used by Indians for centuries before the white man saw its potential for shifting munitions. It travels a distance of 200km (125 miles), climbing 84m (275ft) to pass over the dense rocks of the Canadian Shield, then drops 49m (160ft) to Kingston on Lake Ontario. There are 47 locks, 24 dams and 29km (18 miles) of artificial channels.

The canal is maintained by the Canadian Parks Service, whose staff work all but three of the locks by hand. The Rideau's story is told in a number of museums along its course, the newest of which is the Rideau Canal Museum at 34 Beckwith Street South, Smiths Falls.

Alongside the canal are hiking and cycling trails, overnight mooring facilities, picnic sites and campgrounds. And in winter the 8km (5 miles) stretch between Hartwells and Ottawa Locks becomes the world's longest skating rink, along which some Ottawa commuters glide to work.

Each of the 35 buildings – houses, churches, taverns, workshops and a school – is the real thing, dating from the 1780s to 1867 and rescued when its original site was submerged during construction of the St Lawrence Seaway in the 1950s. The oldest building is the residence of John Graves Simcoe, first Lieutenant-Governor of Canada.

Prescott

About 30km (19 miles) west of Morrisburg, Prescott is a port whose involvement with shipping dates from the early 19th century. Today, its harbour is filled with pleasure craft and visitors are attracted to the fine heritage buildings in its main street. The town is connected with Ogdensburg, New York, by the International Bridge.

Prescott's major attraction is **Fort Wellington**, holding a commanding position on the St Lawrence. The fort (admission free) was built in 1838-9 to replace an earlier post from the War of 1812. Its barracks, armoury, guardhouse and officers' quarters have been restored to the style of 1846. Each July soldiers from Canadian, French and American regiments take part in a historic and colourful military pageant.

Brockville and the Thousand Islands

Continuing west, Highway 2 reaches the elegant city of Brockville, founded in 1784 and one of the first Loyalist settlements in Upper Canada. Among its many old buildings is the **County Court House and Jail**, built in 1842 and still serving its original function. For three months each summer – and right through the winter – the city's major buildings are outlined by more than 20,000 twinkling white lights.

Brockville marks the eastern gateway to the **Thousand Islands**, an attractive boating and resort area that continues along the St Lawrence for about 50km (31 miles) as far as **Gananoque** (pronounced Gan-ann-Ockway).

T he Rideau Falls – the Rideau River and Canal have played an important role in Canadian History.

*B*uildings *at Upper Canada Village were rescued during construction of the St Lawrence Seaway.*

The islands – no one seems to know exactly how many there are – range in size from small rocks to pieces of land large enough to carry attractive summer homes and the whimsical indulgences of eccentric millionaires. One of these, **Boldt Castle**, was built in the 1890s for the wife of a man who even had the island reshaped as a heart. Unfortunately, the wife died and the castle remains unfinished. It can be visited by trip boats from Gananoque and Kingston.

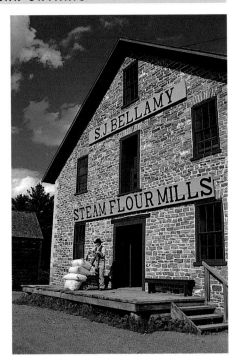

Kingston

The capital of Canada for three years from 1841, Kingston is an imposingly handsome city graced with a plethora of restored 19th-century buildings of mellowed limestone. The most striking of these is the **City Hall**, designed as a national legislature but never used as such because the capital was moved to Montreal soon after construction started. There are guided tours of the building daily except Sunday during summer months.

A Brief Background

Strategically placed where the waters of Lake Ontario drain into the St Lawrence River, Kingston started as an Indian village, then became a French stronghold when Governor Frontenac built a wooden stockade to protect a fur-trading post in 1673. It remained in French hands until 1758 when it was captured by the British. Under the British it became an important garrison, port and commercial centre. After the American Revolution it was colonized by Loyalists who named it Kingston to honour the monarch, George III.

The War of 1812 left the British aware of Kingston's vulnerability. Nervous over the prospect of further conflict, in 1832 they began work on a massive stone fortification equipped with 37 guns and manned by 500 troops. But **Old Fort Henry** has never echoed to a shot fired in anger and is now a major tourist attraction with a force of uniformed students who perform infantry drills and show visitors around.

Around Kingston

Kingston's importance as a port is illustrated in the **Marine Museum of the Great Lakes**, 55 Ontario Street. The museum covers the history of Great Lakes shipping from 1678, and among its exhibits – though covered by a separate admission charge – is the 3,000-tonne ice-breaker *Alexander Henry*. Nearby, at 23 Ontario Street, is the **Pump House Steam Museum**, a restored Victorian municipal water-pumping station housing what is believed to be the world's largest collection of steam-powered engines and models. Visitors can purchase a ticket giving access to both museums and the ice-breaker.

Bellevue House, 35 Centre Street, is a former home of Canada's first Prime Minister, Sir John A MacDonald. Now a National Historic Site, it was built around 1840 by Charles Hales, an entrepreneur who had made a fortune in real estate. Sir John rented the house and because of its wonderful view over the St Lawrence named it Bellevue. Because of its extravagant architecture, reminiscent of the decorated tea caddies of the time, neighbours called it the Pekoe Pagoda. Admission to the house is free.

Sports fans probably know that Kingston was the birthplace of organized ice hockey – the first league game was played here in 1885. The game's development is traced through equipment, photographs and memorabilia at the **International Hockey Hall of Fame** on York and Alfred Streets.

During the summer visitors can take a 16km (10-mile) **tour** of Kingston on a trackless train. The tours leave regularly from Confederation Park, which is opposite City Hall.

Quinte's Isle

Some 50km (30 miles) west of Kingston is Prince Edward County, a popular vacation peninsula better known as Quinte's Isle. The area has 800km (500 miles) of shoreline and lots of white sandy beaches, especially in **Sandbanks Beach Provincial Park**.

Quinte's Isle is reached from Kingston by Highway 33. A free 10-minute ferry crosses from just west of Adolphustown to Glenora. The area has a rich history. The first settlers were United Empire Loyalists who arrived here in 1784, dubbing the place where they landed – on the shores of Adolphus Reach – the Plymouth Rock of Ontario. Echoes of the Loyalist past are to be found in old churches and graveyards, Georgian-style houses and small local museums.

The hub of Prince Edward County is **Picton**, a genteel town which is home to 4,500 people and has a natural deepwater harbour. The 6ha (15-acre) **Macaulay Heritage Park** contains St Magdalen Church, built around 1825 and now housing the county museum, and Macaulay House, restored to the period of the mid-19th century.

Trenton, western gateway to the scenic Loyalist Parkway, leading to Quinte's Isle, is very much a city based on water. Standing on the Bay of Quinte, it offers excellent sailing, fishing and swimming. It is also the starting point of the Trent-Severn Canal, a waterway system through which craft can navigate 386km (240 miles) and 44 locks to reach Georgian Bay on Lake Huron.

Heritage Highway

West of Trenton, Highway 2 becomes part of the Heritage Highway, a historic route linking Toronto and Ottawa. This stretch, following the shore in a more leisurely manner than the tearaway Macdonald-Cartier Freeway (Highway 401), introduces travellers to an old and gentle Ontario where white frame and red brick houses built in Georgian times slumber at the wayside.

The homesickness some of the pioneers

must have felt from time to time is reflected in the Old World names of communities through which the Heritage Highway passes: Brighton, Gosport, Wicklow and Cobourg.

Cobourg

With its maple-lined streets, steepled churches and 19th-century houses, Cobourg has two claims to fame. It is the birthplace of the actress Marie Dressler – her home is now an 1830s-style restaurant – and site of the very grand **Victoria Hall**, built when the community thought it might become the provincial capital and opened in 1860 by the Prince of Wales, later King Edward VII. The hall houses an art gallery, concert hall and a provincial courtroom modelled after one in London's Old Bailey (admission free, guided tours in the summer).

K ingston's Old Fort Henry has never heard a shot fired in anger.

Peterborough

From **Port Hope**, a pretty lakeside town noted for its rainbow trout fishing, Highway 28 heads north towards Peterborough, a lively city of 68,000 people and the major link in the Trent-Severn Canal. Other pluses for the city are Trent University and the **Centennial Fountain**, gushing to a height of 77m (250ft) to become Canada's highest.

But the city's trademark, so to speak, is the hydraulic lift lock – the world's largest. Like a giant elevator, it lifts or lowers pleasure craft, and the water they float in, 20m (65ft) from one stretch of canal to another in less than 10 minutes. It has provided entertainment for bystanders since its opening in 1904. Now, you can take a cruise through the locking system and along the canal, and there is also a visitors' centre, where slides and films tell the story of the lock and show how it works. The lock is closed from mid-October to mid-May but the visitor centre stays open, though it's best to telephone (705) 745-8389 to check times first.

235

La Belle Province

With over 1.5 million sq km (nearly 600,000sq miles) of land – more than twice the size of Texas – three-quarters of which is undeveloped forest, taiga and tundra, Quebec stretches north above the Canadian Shield. Most of its people live near the St Lawrence River, which flows for 1,000km (600 miles) through the south of the province. More than a million lakes hold 16 percent of the world's fresh water.

Canada's largest province, Quebec has a population of 6.5 million, 83 percent of whom are French-speaking descendants of French people who settled there in the 16th century. French is the first language. English is the language of 12 percent of the people. Another 35 languages are spoken in the province – mostly Italian, Greek, Chinese and.native Indian and Inuit. Road signs and street and shop signs are in French.

French explorer Jacques Cartier discovered the Gaspé Peninsula in 1534, claiming the land for France. More than

*M*ontmorency Falls,
*near Quebec City, are as high as
a 30-storey building.*

two centuries later, Quebec fell to the British in 1759, although the influence of the French and the Roman Catholic Church continued to dominate. Many Québécois feel they should be independent of Canada; whether the province will opt to go it alone remains, at the time of writing, to be seen. Whatever its future, it is an interesting area for tourism, with scenic beauty, strong cultural and historic appeal, superb cuisine, sophisticated city nightlife and a whole range of sporting and recreational activities.

Tourism Options
Quebec has a wide choice of tourism, from a city-based stay in Quebec City or Montreal or a gentle drive in the Gaspé Peninsula to arguably the most diverse choice of adventure tourism in Canada.

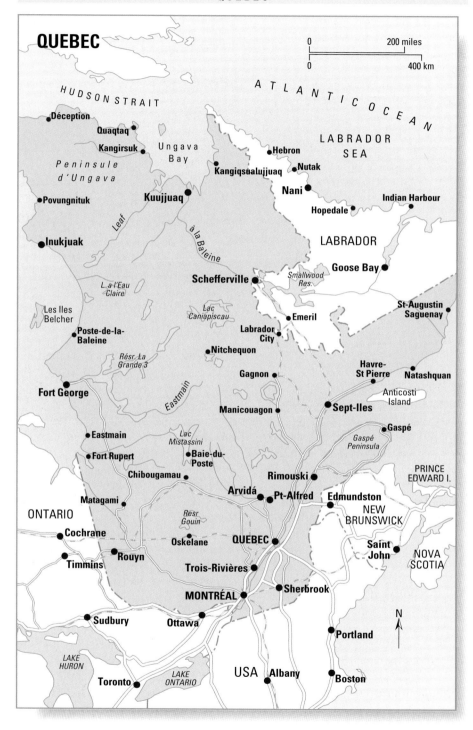

QUEBEC

0   200 miles

0   400 km

HUDSON STRAIT

ATLANTIC OCEAN

Déception

Quaqtaq

Kangirsuk

Ungava Bay

Hebron

LABRADOR SEA

Peninsule d'Ungava

Kangiqsualujjuaq

Nutak

Povungnituk

Kuujjuaq

Nani

Indian Harbour

Hopedale

Leaf

à la Baleine

Inukjuak

LABRADOR

L. a l'Eau Claire

Schefferville

Smallwood Res.

Goose Bay

Les Iles Belcher

Lac Caniapiscau

Emeril

St-Augustin Saguenay

Poste-de-la-Baleine

Labrador City

Nitchequon

Havre-St Pierre

Natashquan

Résr. La Grande 3

Gagnon

Fort George

Eastmain

Manicouagon

Sept-Iles

Anticosti Island

Eastmain

Gaspé

Lac Mistassini

Baie-du-Poste

Gaspé Peninsula

Fort Rupert

Chibougamau

Rimouski

PRINCE EDWARD I.

Arvidá

Pt-Alfred

Edmundston

Matagami

ONTARIO

Resr Gouin

NEW BRUNSWICK

Cochrane

Oskelane

QUEBEC

Saint John

NOVA SCOTIA

Timmins

Rouyn

Trois-Rivières

MONTRÉAL

Sherbrook

Sudbury

Ottawa

Portland

N

LAKE HURON

Toronto

LAKE ONTARIO

USA

Albany

Boston

And, of course, the winter scene is big here. You can join a snowmobiling trek, sample the Inuit lifestyle or travel by dogsled in the far north. In summer you can go on camping and canoeing expeditions with native Indians, join a horseback trek through maple woods and the Appalachian Mountains or take a safari by bush plane, float plane and ski plane.

'Sugaring-off' parties are held in spring in Quebec, Canada's leading producer of maple syrup. Maple-seasoned ham, pancakes and syrup-based desserts are served at family get-togethers and commercial sugar houses.

The vast province of Quebec is divided into 19 tourism regions. In addition to Montreal and greater Quebec, we describe three of the most popular and most easily accessible – the Laurentians, the Gaspé Peninsula and the Magdalen Islands.

Getting to Quebec

Most visitors to Quebec start their holiday in Montreal, the province's biggest city.

By air: Montreal has two airports, **Mirabel** and **Dorval**, with more than 50 airlines making 3,000 regular weekly flights. Flights from North American locations go into Dorval, which is 25km (15 miles) from downtown Montreal. Many international flights arrive at Mirabel, which is 53km (37 miles) from the city. Airport buses run between both airports and downtown Montreal.

Quebec City International Airport, nearly 20km (12 miles) from the city centre, is served 6 days a week by direct flights from New York (Newark). Most US airlines fly into Toronto or Montreal, connecting with Air Canada's Air Alliance and Canadian Airlines international services. Maple Leaf buses operate between the airport and downtown Quebec City.

The province's **regional airports** are served by Inter-Canadian, Air Nova, Air Alliance and, in the far north, Air Inuit.

By rail: VIA Rail's service links Montreal and Quebec City with Ottawa and Toronto. The rail journey from Montreal to Quebec City takes under 3 hours.

By road: The TransCanada Highway and the New York State Thruway are just two of the major highways into Quebec. An extensive network of highways (called autoroutes) links with major routes from Ontario, the Atlantic Provinces and with the US Interstate system. The **bus** service between Montreal and Quebec City takes about 3 hours.

By ferry: Ferries offer a seasonal or year-round service on the St Lawrence River and other major rivers, and a ferry sails between Prince Edward Island and the Magdalen Islands (Iles de la Madeleine), in the Gulf of St Lawrence.

Accommodation

Self-catering cabins and chalets in national parks, and self-catering cottages and gites are available, as well as campsites, fishing lodges, youth hostels and bed and breakfast enterprises. There are hotels of all grades, from budget properties to splendid 5-star edifices like Canadian Pacific's Frontenac Hotel in Quebec City. American-style summer camps, with dormitory accommodation or tents, are run for children from five to 17 years.

Climate

Quebec has four clearly defined seasons. Average temperature in July is between

15°C (59°F) and 26°C (79°F) in Montreal. In January the temperature in Montreal is from -15°C (5°F) to -6°C (21°F). Quebec City temperatures are generally slightly lower. Spring and autumn are cool. You can expect snow from December, if not earlier, to March.

Visitor Information

More than 200 tourist information offices are dotted about Quebec. A tourist guide for each of the 19 regions is published. Further information from **Tourism Quebec**, PO Box 20000, Quebec, G1K 7X2. From Canada and the United States tel. 1-800 363-7777; from outside North America tel. (514) 873-2015.

Montreal

Montreal is a cosmopolitan two-tier city of smart squares, museums, churches, gleaming skyscrapers and Chinese and Latin Quarters above ground, and a subterranean city stretching for about 30km (20 miles) below. Hundreds of homes and offices, more than 1,700 boutiques, department stores, cinemas, theatres, restaurants, seven major hotels and a Metro station handy wherever you go, are beneath the streets of the outside world. If they want to, people can live, work, eat, be entertained and ignore the weather indefinitely without emerging into the open air.

Guides and Tours

One of the most pleasant ways to get to know Montreal and its history is from the St Lawrence River. A glass-enclosed *bateau mouche* departs from Jacques-Cartier Pier four times a day for 90-minute scenic trips with bilingual guides, and again in the evening for a 3-hour dinner

cruise, between May and October. Alternatively, you can take a guided **cruise** aboard a replica New Orleans-style steamboat or on a double-deck trip boat with several departures daily.

As much for thrills as for sightseeing, shoot the Lachine Rapids by **jet boat**. The 2-hourly departures from May to September are from the de l'Horloge Pier at the foot of rue Berri. **Rafting** trips are also available between May and October, either through the towering waves of the main channel of the Lachine Rapids (be prepared for a thorough soaking) or the tamer family 'River Discovery' trip. Another exciting option is the **Amphie-Bus**, in which you can have a guided tour by river and road of Old Montreal and the Old Port. The Amphie-Bus operates from May to October.

Moored at the Jacques-Cartier Pier is a replica of a 17th-century French warship, the magnificent three-master *Le Pélican*. Captain Pierre Le Moyne d'Ibèreville and his crew from the past tell you of their exploits in a voyage from Newfoundland to the Mississippi and reminisce about the Battle of Hudson Bay.

The Montreal/Langueil and Montreal/Islands **ferry** at Jacques-Cartier Pier enables pedestrians and cyclists to cross the St Lawrence River between Old Port and Parc-des-Iles. The ferry runs from mid-May to mid-October. Private **yachts** accommodating up to 12 people can be chartered, and there are cruises to Quebec City, Ottawa, Thousand Islands and Upper Canada Village.

Sightseeing tours around Montreal and the surrounding area are run by a number of companies. The old-style **Murray Hill Trolley Bus** enables you to take unlimited daily round trips on one ticket in summer, seeing the sights of Montreal, getting off and reboarding when you like. Minimum duration is 3 hours. The season is from late June to early October. During the rest of the year a non-stop 3-hour trolley bus tour is available twice a day.

Old Montreal

As well as 'up there' and 'down there' zones, Montreal has a 'back then' region. Old Montreal has cobbled streets and architecture from three centuries – 17th to 19th. The only 20th-century influence has been the restoration of the buildings and a 2km (1-mile) waterfront area – the **Old Port** (Vieux-Port) – with a sensitivity that has earned international awards for redevelopment.

Montreal originated along the shores of the St Lawrence River. Its population has grown to 3 million. Since the inauguration of the new and improved facilities at the Old Port in 1992, visitors have been flocking in to make Old Montreal the city's major recreation and tourism attraction – horse and carriage tours are an appropriate way to see it.

Montreal was originally founded by Paul de Chomedey, Sieur de Maisonneuve, and other colonists in 1642. It was a fur-trading post known as Ville-Marie. The province known as Nouvelle France (New France) fell into the hands of the British and surrendered to Great Britain in 1763. Stone walls surrounded the city until 1801, when they were demolished by Royal Assent, enabling expansion to take place. Montreal was incorporated as a city in 1832.

Old Montreal, which began as a missionary colony, had become very down-at-heel by the 1960s. The Viger Commission was set up to supervise the restoration of the historic area and to promote and protect it. By the time the 350th anniversary came round in 1992, the citizens had an Old Town and Old Port they could be proud of – a place for which tourists make a bee-line.

It's difficult to imagine now that the revamped Champ-de-Mars, a military parade ground until the 1920s and later a public market, degenerated into a car park.

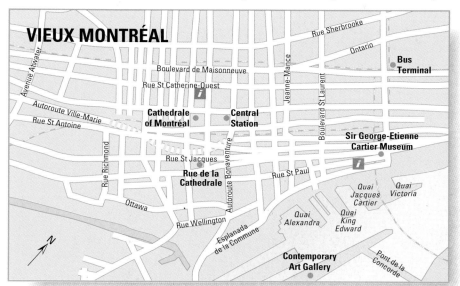

Archaeologists uncovered fortifications from the 1700s there and restored a section to bring alive a conception of Montreal in its walled city days. Cobblestones were revealed as asphalt was torn up, and a 'new Old Montreal' greets the world.

Street entertainment, music, artists painting street scenes and waterscapes, the clip-clopping of horses' hooves and calèche wheels on the cobblestones, food and drink served outdoors in bistro and café frontages and courtyards, a flea market, flower sellers, pastry shops – all contribute to a relaxed 'Gay Paree' style of life. There's always something going on.

Where to Start

Before exploring the Old Town's grand old buildings and sights, it's a good idea to spend some time in the new **Museum of Archeology and History** (Pointe-à-

Tugboats are a reminder that inland Montreal is a busy port.

Callière) overlooking the river at Place Royale, where a multimedia show, archaeological finds and many artefacts cover 600 years of history, from the Amerindian period to modern times. The **History Centre of Montreal** (Centre d'Histoire de Montréal) in Place d'Youville in the Old Town is housed in a former fire station. It outlines the city's history from 1642 through World War II to recent times.

Along Rue Notre-Dame

In rue Notre-Dame Ouest (west), one of the oldest buildings in Old Montreal is the **Sulpician Seminary**, completed in 1685. **Château Ramezay** (Château de Ramezay), in rue Notre-Dame Est (east), was built in 1705 for the Governor of Montreal, Claude de Ramezay. During the winter of 1775 it served as headquarters for the American revolutionary forces who occupied the city, attempting to persuade citizens to join the revolution. The château houses a museum detailing Montreal's and the province's history.

Pierre de Calvet, a Huguenot from

The towers of the Notre Dame Basilica in Old Montreal are known as Temperance and Perseverance.

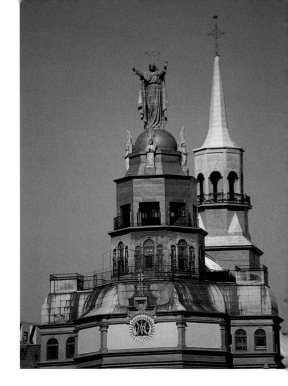

France, was jailed for helping the Americans during this time. He had meetings with George Washington's envoy, Benjamin Franklin, in 1775-6. He lived at 401 rue Bonsecours, a fieldstone house with a sharply sloping roof built in 1770, and now known as the **Pierre du Calvet House**. It houses a café and pastry shop, and is considered a fine example of French-influenced 18th-century architecture. Incidentally, a number of the bed and breakfast homes in Old Montreal date from the 16th and 17th centuries.

Notre-Dame Basilica is an impressive structure built in the 1820s. It has two towers, Temperance and Perseverance, the latter containing a huge bell known as 'Le Gros Bourdon'. Note the ancient wood carvings and paintings around the great altar. At the back of the basilica are the Sacred Heart Chapel and a museum, which houses religious artefacts and gifts from Louis XV of France.

Built in Second Empire style in the 1870s, imposing **City Hall** offers free guided tours of its interior from May to October (weekdays only).

Other Attractions in Old Montreal

The **Bank of Montreal**, founded in 1817, is Canada's oldest financial institution. In 1847 the bank's head office was moved to the present building in rue Saint-Jacques, which for a long time was Canada's Wall Street. The **Royal Bank** situated nearby and 23 storeys high, was the tallest building in the British Empire when it was erected in 1928.

When Paul de Chomedey and his fellow Frenchmen arrived in what was to become Montreal, their idea was to convert the native American Indians to Christianity. With missionary zeal they built churches, one of the earliest being **Notre-Dame-de-Bonsecours**, completed in 1657. It was a wooden chapel erected in what is now rue Saint-Paul Est. Behind the project was Marguerite Bourgeoys, the city's first teacher, who pressed hard for a place of worship. Because of fires it was rebuilt in stone in 1773. From its rafters neat little replicas of ships are suspended, offered to the Virgin Mary over the years by sailors praying for a safe voyage.

Like Old Montreal, the **Old Port** area was rejuvenated in time for the 350th anniversary celebrations. The waterfront is a delightful promenading area for residents and visitors with its parkland and wharves, exhibitions and musicians. At the **IMAX Theater** movies can be seen on a screen seven storeys high.

One of Old Montreal's busiest places in summer is **place Jacques-Cartier**, an enchanting square whose cobbled streets and ancient buildings evoke the atmosphere of a bygone age. There has been a public market here since 1804, with Nelson's Column presiding over events since 1809.

A splendid building in the neo-Classi-

*F*ormerly housing
Montreal's City Hall and market,
Bonsecours Market is now an
exhibition hall.

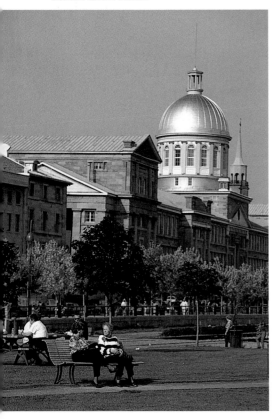

cal style, **Bonsecours Market** (Marché Bonsecours) in rue Saint-Paul Est was constructed nearly 150 years ago to house Montreal's city hall and public market. The market continued until 1963. After restoration in 1964, the building became home to city government offices, while further work in 1992 turned the building into a grand exhibition hall.

Mont-Royal Park

When Jacques Cartier sailed up the St Lawrence River in 1535 to the island of Montreal, where it converges with the Ottawa River, he climbed what is known locally as 'The Mountain' and declared it 'Mont Royal'. (There are in fact three peaks, the highest being 232m/754ft.)

Mont-Royal Park (Parc Mont-Royal) was designed by American landscape architect Frederick Law Olmsted, who was responsible for Central Park in New York. It has been open to the public since 1876. Two **lookouts** provide views of the city and river and, on clear days, across to the Appalachian Mountains. A cross 30m (100ft) high, illuminated at night, was erected on top of Mont Royal in 1924. The park has a network of **trails** and **cycle paths**.

St Joseph's Oratory

This magnificent shrine, built by Montreal's Catholics to honour St Joseph, patron saint of Canada, was completed in 1966. With its great dome, this impressive Italian Renaissance-style basilica is a city landmark. At 862ft (284m), the shrine is also the highest point in Montreal. Pilgrims flock here, many climbing the middle set of steps on their knees.

Olympic Park – 'Big O'

One of Montreal's magnificent 'must-see'

Mont-Royal Park has two look-outs providing views of the city and river.

modernistic wonders is the 'Big O'. That's what they affectionately call the 1976 Olympic Stadium at Olympic Park in avenue Pierre-de-Coubertin. There's a fantastic view from the **observation deck** of its gracefully inclined 190m (618ft) tower: it's claimed you can see for 80km (50 miles) on a clear day. Montreal's baseball team, the Expos, is based at the Olympic Stadium, which accommodates 55,000 spectators.

For a rare experience of four ecosystems from the Americas, spend some time in the **Montreal Biodome**, next door to the Big O in the former Olympic velodrome. Under the huge transparent roof you can explore tropical rainforest, polar regions, the Laurentian forest and marine life of the St Lawrence.

Botanical Garden

Chinese and Japanese gardens are among some 30 themed gardens on display at Montreal's extensive Botanical Garden (Jardin Botanique) in rue Sherbrooke Est, next door to the Olympic sports complex. More than 26,000 varieties of plants from around the world grow here, including a fine bonsai collection. As well as the gardens, there are nearly a dozen interconnected exhibition greenhouses.

Founded in 1931 and open year-round, Montreal's Botanical Garden can be toured in comfort aboard guided *balades* – trains with rubber wheels.

The Botanical Garden is also home to the **Insectarium**, a fascinating place and a favourite with children. Some of the creepy, crawly occupants, like butterflies, moths and some of the beetles, are beautiful, while all are intriguing as each species' indispensable place in life is described. Incidentally, you can buy tickets which give you joint access to the Biodome, the Botanical Garden and the Insectarium. There's also a free shuttle service which runs between these three attractions and the Olympic Stadium.

Dow Planetarium

Astronomical shows projected on a 20m (75ft) diameter dome at the Dow Plane-

Each year millions visit St Joseph's Oratory, which marks the highest point in Montreal.

tarium reveal the answers to some of the questions about the universe you may have asked yourself. Shows at the 385-seat Planetarium, which is in rue Saint-Jacques Ouest, change according to the season.

Parc-des-Iles

The Expo '67 World's Fair was set up on a site in the man-made Parc-des-Iles in the St Lawrence River, specially constructed for the purpose. It can be reached by Metro to Ile-Ste-Hélène station on St Helen's Island.

Today the French Pavilion houses the new Montreal **Casino**, which offers roulette, blackjack, baccarat and other games at 86 gaming tables. The Casino exudes elegance, and its clients are expected to do the same.

Near the Expo site is **La Ronde**, an amusement park *par excellence*, with more than 30 rides, including a larger-

than-life line in roller coasters. There are special rides for children, and in July and August there's an international fireworks competition. The entertainment includes nine pyro-musical displays.

On the island's north shore is Alexander Calder's splendid sculpture *Man*, created especially for the 1967 World's Fair. The **Floral Park** on Notre-Dame Island has thousands of roses and other blossoms from around the world.

Montreal Museums

Montreal has over 30 museums; 1-day or 3-day passes (individual or family) provide unrestricted access to 17 top museums and galleries.

The **Museum of Discovery** at the Old Fort (Vieux Fort), St Helen's Island, traces the exploration of the New World. Ancient maps, scientific and navigational instruments and firearms are displayed. In summer military manoeuvres are performed by men in 18th-century uniform.

The Montreal **Museum of Fine Arts** (Musée des Beaux Arts) in rue Sherbrooke Ouest hosts major temporary exhibitions and has a highly esteemed permanent exhibition. Founded in 1860, the museum is Montreal's oldest.

The **Museum of Contemporary Art** (Musée d'Art Contemporain) in the Place des Arts complex has a substantial permanent exhibition in every medium. There are eight large galleries featuring local, national and international artists.

The **McCord Museum of Canadian**

Fête des Neiges

Faced with long, hard winters, Canadians take a positive attitude and enjoy the snow, with skiing and skating, snowmobiling, snowshoeing and ice-fishing. In early February Montreal's 17-day **Fête des Neiges** starts. It takes place on St Helen's and Notre-Dame Islands and in the Old Port. The activities include canoe racing among the ice floes in the St Lawrence River, cross-country skiing, dogsled races, ice-sculpture contests and the building of a giant snow castle.

History, in rue Sherbrooke Ouest, houses a rather eclectic collection of paintings, furniture and costumes from the 18th to the 20th centuries. There is also a photographic record of Canadian life from the mid-19th century to the 1930s.

Also in rue Sherbrooke Ouest is the **Redpath Museum**, otherwise known as the Dinosaur Museum. Part of McGill University, it has a collection of dinosaurs and other extinct creatures, fossils and a number of Egyptian antiquities.

Canada's only museum devoted to architecture is the **Canadian Centre for Architecture** (Centre Canadien d'Architecture), founded in 1979. It moved to its present home in Shaughnessy House, rue Baile, in 1989. It functions as a study centre as well as a museum, and houses thousands of internationally important drawings, books and documents as well as displays of materials.

Montrealers have a reputation for their sense of fun, as witnessed by the 11-day bilingual festival of humour, 'Just for Laughs', held here in late July. In 1993 the **International Museum of Humor** opened in a former brewery – on April Fool's Day, of course. It is dedicated to 'the conservation and diffusion of humour in all its forms, from all periods of history and from all parts of the world'. The museum, in boulevard St-Laurent, has a hall of fame and a school of humour, as well as a cabaret theatre.

The **Canadian Railway Museum** in rue Saint-Pierre, open from early May to mid-October, features railway, tramway and steam locomotive equipment. Tram rides are available daily and train rides on Sundays and holidays. Silent movies, classic films, animations and old posters and equipment can be seen at the **Museum of Cinema** (Musée du Cinéma) at boulevard de Maisonneuve Est.

Spectator Sports

Montreal **Forum** is a major sports and recreational centre. It is the place where crowds cheer their home team, the Montréal Canadiens, in National Hockey League matches. The season is from October to mid-June. The Forum seats 16,500 people and is the venue for ice-skating shows, rock concerts, musicals, tennis, boxing and wrestling promotions.

Baseball fans can watch the Montreal Expos in action at the Olympic Stadium from April to September. **Horse-racing** – both riding and driving events – take place at the Blue Bonnet Racetrack in boulevard Décarie.

Two annual racing events dominate the scene on two different days in June. One is the amazing **Tour de l'Ile de Montréal**, an event which up to 45,000 amateur cyclists have pedalled into the Guinness Book of Records by making it the race with the most participants. The other is the **Molson Grand Prix de Canada**, held on Notre-Dame Island's Gilles Villeneuve racetrack. A third major event takes place in September – the famous **Montreal Marathon** which attracts more than 8,000 runners.

On the Cultural Scene

Festivals

Montreal's **International Jazz Festival** takes place on 11 days in the first half of July and is one of North America's most important jazz events. More than 350 concerts are presented at outdoor and indoor venues. Later in the summer there's the **World Film Festival**.

Performing Arts

The widely renowned **Montreal Symphony Orchestra**, under conductor Charles Dutoit, plays at the Salle Wilfred-Pelletier at the Place des Arts. The orchestra also undertakes international tours. The **Metropolitan Orchestra of Montreal** plays classical music, introducing new young musicians.

Four productions a year are staged at the **Opéra de Montréal,** Place des Arts. In this bicultural city the audience benefits from the projection of the script in French and English onto a screen above the stage.

Classical and modern **ballet** is performed by Les Grands Ballets Canadiens. Its production of *The Nutcracker Suite* in December is an eagerly awaited occasion.

For over 25 years **Les Sortilèges** have been presenting the folklore and folk-dances of Quebec in an entertaining format. They can be seen in a variety of venues throughout the city.

Theatre and Film

Most of Montreal's dozen or so theatrical companies' productions are in French. Contemporary and classical plays are staged by the **Théâtre du Nouveau Monde**. Plays and variety shows are presented at **Théâtre Olympia** in rue Sainte-Catherine Est. **Théâtre Aujourd'hui**, in rue Saint-Denis, stages French-language plays only by Quebec writers. Open-air concerts are put on from mid-June to the end of August by **Théâtre de Verdure** in Lafontaine Park.

Théâtre Biscuit, in rue Saint-Paul Ouest, is Montreal's only permanent puppet theatre. Only group bookings are taken for weekdays, but families and individuals can attend on Saturdays and Sundays.

Some theatres are in unusual settings. **Théâtre de Quat'Sous**, which encourages young Quebec talent, is located in a converted synagogue, while **Théâtre de la Poudrière** performances take place in a gunpowder magazine built in 1822 with walls 3m (10ft) thick.

English-speaking productions are staged by the **Centaur Theatre** in the former Stock Exchange building located in Old Montreal.

The **National Film Board-Montreal**, in rue Saint-Denis, at the corner of the boulevard de Maisonneuve, combines a movie theatre, a video theatre and a number of CineScope stations through which individuals can call up films of their choice. More than half a century of Canadian life is stored on film at the NFB.

Sugaring-Off

Sugaring-off parties are held in March and April, when people flock to the sugar shacks to enjoy the delights of maple syrup. At Rigaud, about 45km (28 miles) west of downtown Montreal, is the **Sucrerie de la Montagne**, a large maple grove visited by thousands at sugaring-off time.

Here visitors learn how the sap is evaporated over furnaces to convert it into syrup and sugar. Hot syrup is poured onto clean snow to produce an unusual delicacy, 'taffy on snow'. For further information about sugar shack parties, call the Association des Restaurateurs de Cabane à Sucre du Québec, tel. (514) 953-0673.

> ### The Story of Fur
> Wearing furs may not be regarded as politically correct in some parts of the world, but where the temperature swoops far below zero sheer pragmatism dictates that the fur trade is an important part of the economy. Montreal's prosperity was based on the fur trade for two centuries, and an exhibition, 'The Fur Trade in Lachine National Historic Site', traces its development. The exhibition, accessible by Metro, is in a stone warehouse built for the Hudson's Bay Company in 1803.
>
> Montreal's Fur District is in the region of rues de Bleury and Sainte-Catherine and boulevard de Maisonneuve. About 85 percent of Canada's fur coats are made here in small workshops by craftspeople using traditional methods.

A City for Shopping

Whether you're looking for *haute couture*, bone china, original art work or practically anything else, Montreal provides plenty of choice. It has spacious department stores, malls and specialist boutiques on two levels. The underground city alone has more than 1,600 shops. Above ground, **Eaton's** opened in 1925 and **The Bay** has been in business since the 1880s. The history of **Ogilvy's** goes back further. A Scottish merchant opened the store in 1866. It now houses several smart boutiques, and its Scots origins are marked by a bagpiper who plays Highland music outside.

These three stores are in rue Sainte-Catherine, which is the city's main shopping artery. The downtown area also embraces fashionable streets Sherbrooke and Maisonneuve. There are large malls in and around the city.

Around Montreal

Lachine Canal

The 14km (9-mile) Lachine Canal, built to bypass the Lachine Rapids, was in operation from 1825 until 1970. It provided a gateway for navigation to the Great Lakes before the St Lawrence Seaway supplied this facility in 1959.

Now run by Parks Canada, the canal banks have become a linear park, developed as a cycle path which is used as a cross-country ski trail in winter. The path is well lit and can be used by walkers and joggers as well as cyclists from sunrise to midnight.

The Lachine Canal **Interpretive Centre**, at Monk Pavilion on the corner of 7th Avenue and boulevard Saint-Joseph, Lachine, has an exhibition illustrating the canal's history. The centre is open daily (except Monday morning) between mid-May and early September.

Laval

Just to the west of Montreal, on the same archipelago, Laval is the province's second largest city, with nearly 285,000 people. Laval has a new **Cosmodome**, with a space science learning centre incorporating Canada's first space museum as part of a new tourism and educational complex. There's a bonus for young people from 10 to 14 years. They can sample simulated life in outer space, attending a 5-day astronaut training course.

Quebec City

With its venerable ramparts high above the St Lawrence River, Quebec City, the provincial capital, is the only walled city in North America outside Mexico. Its old quarter was declared a World Heritage treasure by UNESCO in 1985. Yet despite the wealth of carefully restored buildings from the 17th and 18th centuries, and the star-shaped citadel, city walls and gates, it is a late 19th-century building which probably makes the greatest impact of all on visitors to the city.

This is the **Château Frontenac**, owned by Canadian Pacific Hotels and Resorts. The huge Victorian pile, with its gables and turrets and green copper roofs, was built in 1893 on top of Cape Diamond (Cap Diamant) high above the river. Over a 5-year period the hotel underwent a major facelift which was completed in time for its centenary. It now has more than 600 guestrooms. Britain's wartime Prime Minister Winston Churchill and US President Franklin Roosevelt attended conferences here with Canadian Prime Minister Mackenzie King in 1943 and 1944.

Orientation

To get your bearings historically and geographically, watch the **Quebec Experience** at the Multimedia Theatre at 6 rue de Trésor (second floor) in the Latin Quarter. The non-stop 3D shows with hologram characters, lasers and other special effects run daily from 9am to 10pm, telling of the city's development as the cradle of French civilizations in North America, its hard times in the past and the good times in store for visitors in the present.

For an overview of the city have a meal at Loews Le Concorde's **Astral** Restaurant at place Montcalm. It revolves gently 183m (600ft) above the river, giving you a panoramic tour without your ever having to leave your seat.

Quebec is fairly compact. Most of its historical aspects are close enough to-

gether to explore on foot, but bear in mind that it isn't Canada's flattest city. There are **organized tours**: walking tours, bicycle tours, tours by horse and calèche, horse-drawn trolley bus tours and boat tours. For further information contact the **Greater Quebec Tourism Office** at 60 rue d'Auteuil, Quebec, G1R 4C4, tel. (418) 692-2471.

Battlefield Park

A wide boardwalk at Dufferin Terrace (Terrasse Dufferin), beside the Château Frontenac, 110m (360ft) above the river, provides a wonderful view of the St Lawrence, the town of Lévis on the far bank and the Laurentian Mountains. The boardwalk leads to the Governors' Promenade (Promenade des Gouverneurs) which gives access to Battlefield Park (Parc des Champs de Bataille), the site of the 1759 battle between the French and English.

The park, created in 1908, encompasses the **Plains of Abraham**, named after Abraham Martin, to whom a concession was made in 1635. Battlefield Park is a pleasant place to stroll or picnic on a sunny day. It offers gardens and woodland, and has commemorative plaques, monuments and artillery artefacts relating to the war. A **monument** marks the spot where Britain's General James Wolfe died in the battle, having succeeded in capturing Quebec.

Near the battlefield is the **Quebec Museum** (Musée du Québec), which contains works of art from the early years of European influence in North America to modern paintings and sculptures. It is open daily all year except Mondays. On Wednesdays admission is free.

Battlefield Park has a new **Interpretation Centre** where the latest technology

The Chateau Frontenac Hotel, towering above Quebec City, has more than 600 guestrooms.

VIEUX-QUEBEC

Théâtre Capitole
Parc-de-L'Artillerie
D'Auteuil
Rue Saint-Jean
Théâtre de la Bordée
Salle de l'Institut
Palais Montcalm
Chapelle des Jésuites
Rue Dauphine
St Andrews Presbyterian Church
Musée des Ursulines
Fortifications of Québec
Rue Saint-Louis
Sanctuaire Notre-Dame-du-Sacré-Coeur
Cavalier du Moulin
Rue Mont-Carmel
Château Frontenac
Anglican Cathedral of the Holy Trinity
Promenades du Vieux-Québec
Urban Life Interpretation Centre
Avenue Chauveau
Rue Cook
Avenue Dufferin
Centre Catherine-de-Saint-Augustin
Rue Sainte-Paul
Musée Bon-Pasteur
Rue Hébert
Rue de L'Université
Musée du Séminaire de Quebec
Rue Sainte-Famille
Rue Sainte-Anne
Musée historique de cire
Côte-de-la-Montagne
Rue Sainte-Ursule
Rue Sainte-Pierre
Terrasse Dufferin

0   100 m
0   110 yrds

is used to the full. Specific aspects of the park and the Plains of Abraham are highlighted by a themed exhibit.

Quebec's extensive defence system includes three Martello towers built by the British between 1808 and 1811 as resistance against naval artillery. Two of the towers overlook the Plains of Abraham (the other is in rue Lavigueur overlooking the valley of the St Charles River). Guided **bus tours** of the park include the towers, the Interpretation Centre, gardens and light-hearted theatrical animations of some historic aspects.

Upper Town

Like Montreal, Quebec City is built on two levels, but both parts of Quebec are in the open air. The Lower Town is beside the St Lawrence River, while the Upper Town is high above it. From Dufferin Terrace you can descend via 'breakneck

stairs' (*L'escalier cassecou*) to the Lower Town. Actually it's not that perilous for the sure-footed, though the prospect of climbing back up may be daunting. Fortunately, for a fee, you can use the **funicular** from (or to) the station at Maison Louis-Jolliet. More than two dozen staircases cut into the rock link the Upper and Lower Towns at various points.

Although Jacques Cartier set foot on Quebec's shore in 1534, it was the explorer Samuel de Champlain who founded a community there after he landed in 1608. His statue in bronze, by Paul Chèvre, is at the approach to Dufferin Terrace. It was unveiled in 1898.

The Citadel

The Citadel (Citadelle), on top of Cape Diamond, was built in the shape of a star. Construction work began in 1820 and went on for more than 30 years. The

252

Royal 22nd Regiment has been based at the Citadel for over 70 years, maintaining the tradition of beating the retreat and changing of the guard in summer. The latter ceremony takes place at 10am daily from mid-June to early September, while the former can be seen on Tuesdays, Thursdays, Saturdays and Sundays following the last guided tour at 6pm, in July and August. Neither ceremony takes place if it's raining.

Guided **tours** of the Citadel are available from mid-March to the end of October (booked groups only in winter). The Citadel's 25 buildings include the Cape Diamond redoubt of 1693, the Governor-General's residence and five heavily fortified bastions. Firearms, uniforms, insignia and other items from the 17th century onwards can be seen at the regimental **museum**, located in a former powderhouse. The Regiment's continued presence at the Citadel makes it North America's largest fortified group of buildings still occupied by troops.

Other City Defences

From 1690 until the Treaty of Utrecht in 1713, the French built batteries and redoubts in Quebec City's Upper Town. Building work resumed after the British captured Louisbourg on Cape Breton Island, Nova Scotia, in 1745. In later times a major part of the western area of the city was fortified.

An Upper Town **rampart** was built encircling the old city in the early 19th century. A walk along the wall of 5km (3 miles) can be taken between rue St-Louis and côte du Palais. The walls and gates might have been demolished but for the intervention of Lord Dufferin, who was Governor-General of Canada from 1872 to 1878. Later, St Louis Gate, Kent Gate and St Jean Gate were rebuilt, and Prescott Gate was rebuilt as recently as the 1980s. The gates bear interpretive panels.

Near the St Louis Gate is a former powder magazine which has been converted into a Visitor Reception Centre for the Fortifications of Quebec, which form a National Historic Site. In addition to the Citadel, the city's defence system has two other National Historic Sites – Fort No. 1 and Artillery Park.

Admission is free to **Fort No. 1** National Historic Site, built in the late 1860s, complete with vaults, ditches and underground passages. It was constructed at Lévis on the south shore as a defence against American attack.

Another National Historic Site, **Artillery Park**, at rue d'Auteuil, is where French-built defence structures fulfilled their purpose for more than 250 years. A cartridge factory which was set up on the site in 1879 provided the Canadian Army with ammunition until 1964. The park's interpretive centre is in a former iron foundry. On display is a detailed model of Quebec as it was in 1898. The Dauphine redoubt and the officers' mess – the latter now a heritage initiation centre for children – can also be visited.

Admission is free to two other parts of the city's defence system.

The **Royal Battery**, at the corner of rues St-Pierre and Sous-le-Fort, dates from the early 18th century, being rebuilt in 1970. It was used to defend Quebec in the siege of 1759. Cannon fire is demonstrated daily from late June to early September.

Formerly the site of a 17th-century windmill, the **Cavalier du Moulin** fortifications at Mont-Carmel are now a landscaped park with paths and gardens.

Parliament Building

Quebec's Parliament Building on Parliament Hill is an impressive sight. From 1791 Quebec City was the capital of Lower Canada. After the 1840 Act of Union it had two spells in the mid-19th century as national capital, becoming capital of Quebec province with Confederation in 1867.

By the time work began on the imposing French Renaissance-style Parliament Building in 1877, the city had outgrown its walls, and a site outside them, along the long thoroughfare called Grande-Allée, was chosen. The building's four wings form a quadrangle 100m (330ft) square, and if you take the guided tour you'll appreciate why it took 7 years to complete the construction work. The tour includes the National Assembly Chamber and the Legislative Council Chamber. No tours take place during most of June. Admission is free.

Other Upper Town Highlights

Among places of note in the Upper Town is rue Sainte-Anne, with its bistros and cafés, street entertainment and musicians. A tourist office at 12 rue Sainte-Anne provides information on all the province's 19 tourism regions. A neighbouring building houses the **Musée du Fort**, where a model of the city as it was in 1750 is the focus of a sound and light show. Quebec's six sieges, including the Battle of the Plains of Abraham and the American invasion, are enacted. Close by, the **Wax Museum** (Musée de Cire) has a collection of 80 figures who influenced Quebec's and North America's history.

The **Seminary Museum** (Musée du Séminaire), in rue de l'Université, is one of the city's foremost museums, with collections and works of art covering three centuries. As well as paintings, scientific items and rare books, it has works in gold and silver, a major coin collection – and an Egyptian mummy.

The heavily ornamented **Basilica of Notre-Dame**, in rue Buard, contains a wealth of stained glass and craftsmanship in other media from more than three centuries. A new and enlightening feature for visitors is the basilica's multimedia 3D cultural and historic screen presentation illustrating a period of Quebec's history and its people. Tickets for the show, which is presented simultaneously in French and English, can be bought at the door.

Built in the style of London's Church of St Martin in the Fields in Trafalgar Square, the **Holy Trinity** Anglican Cathedral, built around 1804 in rue des Jardins, has pews made of English oak from the Royal Windsor Forest. Holy Trinity, which underwent major renovation work in 1992, is the first Anglican cathedral built outside Britain.

In the early days of European settlement in Quebec, educational establishments were set up in the 1630s by Jesuit priests and Augustine and Ursuline nuns. The **Ursuline Museum** (Musée des Ursulines) in the rue Donnacona sketches the Ursuline heritage under the French regime between 1639, when the nuns founded a girls' school, and 1759. Engravings and embroidery carried out by the nuns from the 17th to 19th centuries are exhibited. The museum is open from early January to late November. The 1902 **chapel**, open from May to October, contains an altar screen, pulpit and other work sculpted by Pierre-Noël Lavasseur from 1726 to 1736.

In the Convent of Augustine Sisters in rue Charlevoix is the **Augustine Museum** (Musée des Augustines). It has a collection of furniture, silverware, embroidery and paintings from the days when these nuns set up the country's first hospital. Medical instruments from the 17th century can also be seen.

Lower Town

Place Royale

Place Royale is the fast-beating heart of the Lower Town. Samuel de Champlain began to establish the first permanent settlement in New France here, at the foot of Cape Diamond, in 1608. Wealthy merchants built opulent homes, but as time went on Britain and France had constant skirmishes and many residents moved to the safer territory of the Upper Town. When the British defeated the French in 1759, Place Royale resumed its role as an economic and business centre, flourishing for years until it began to lose its lustre. Decline set in firmly in the early 20th century, and by the 1950s Place Royale was virtually moribund. Today, revitalized, its gracious old houses proudly restored, it buzzes with activity once more.

The story of Place Royale unfolds at two locations. 'Place Royale, 400 Years of History' is an exhibition at 25 rue Saint-Pierre tracing the major historical events there and in the Lower Town generally. 'Place Royale, Center of Trade in New France' is at 3A Place Royale. This exhibition and multimedia show demonstrates the practice of trade with the fur, shipping and other interests under the French regime.

Ancient and Modern

Quartier de Petit Champlain, one of the oldest parts of Quebec City, has been the subject of major award-winning restoration work in recent years. It now has the air of a charming old riverside village, with narrow streets, jugglers and musi-cians. Rue de Petit Champlain, beneath the cliff on which the Upper Town sits, is the city's most ancient street. It has boutiques and cafés, and craft shops with Inuit carvings and local artists' work.

Walk eastward to **Explore**, a new sound and light show illustrating the discoveries of the Native Indians and the exploration of the New World in general, and Quebec in particular, by European adventurers. A little farther on is the **Museum of Civilization** (Musée de la Civilisation), where ten or more exhibitions – four of them permanent – are staged at the same time. There is a tremendous amount to see, including a 250-year-old boat excavated from the museum site.

The **Old Port** of Quebec, a National Historic Site, is nearby in rue St-André. Here the development of the port and its links with the lumber trade and shipbuilding are explained through exhibitions and audiovisual presentations. The port is around the area where the waters of the St Charles River meet those of the St Lawrence. A lock goes into the Louise Basin, where there are hundreds of boat moorings. Between the river and the Customs Building stands the **Agora** amphitheatre, seating 5,800 for concerts and other entertainment.

On the Water

Ferry operators claim that if you haven't seen Quebec from the ferry, you haven't really seen Quebec. Well, they would, wouldn't they? But it is indeed a splendid sight, with the waterfront properties beneath the old buildings of the Upper Town, and the Château Frontenac lording it over the whole scene. The ferry carries up to 700 passengers and 55 vehicles, and takes about 10 minutes to cross to Lévis. It operates year-round, departing from each shore every 30 minutes from 7.30am and every hour in the evenings.

Louis-Jolliet, who discovered the Mississippi River, had a house built in Quebec in 1683 and lived there until his death in 1700. The lower station of the funicular is located there, and boat tours aboard the motor vessel named after him leave from Chouinard Pier in Place Royale three times a day between May and mid-October. Tours last from 1 to 3 hours. Tickets can be bought from kiosks on the pier and at Dufferin Terrace, or from major hotels. More extensive river cruises, including island visits, are operated by Beau Temps, Mauvais Temps (Rain or Shine) from Pier 19 at the Old Port.

*S*treet cafés are as popular in Quebec City as they are in Paris.

Excursions from Quebec City

West of the city in Sainte-Foy, Quebec **Aquarium**, in avenue des Hôtels, displays 259 species of fish, reptiles, an insect collection and five seal species. The seals entertain twice daily all year. The botanical gardens at Sainte-Foy have 2,500 American, European and Asian plant species and a new water garden. The gardens are open between late April and the end of October.

Montmorency Falls

A 15-minute drive east of Quebec City takes you to one of the province's most exciting attractions – the **Montmorency Falls Park**. The falls, of course, have impressed with their might and height since the year dot. At 83m (270ft) they are one and a half times as high as Niagara Falls and equivalent to a 30-storey building. The surrounding provincial park opened in 1993, giving visitors the chance to ride beside the falls in a cable car. You can also take a helicopter trip above them.

The falls are lit up at night. A walkway leads to the falls and a footbridge crosses them. Lookouts provide panoramic views. There are souvenir shops and restaurants, and a visitor centre where you can explore the military history and the geology of the site. This is where General Wolfe and his men camped when the first 1759 battle against the Marquis of Montcalm's troops was fought at the foot of the falls.

In winter vapour from the falls freezes, forming an ever-growing cone of ice for people to climb.

Further Afield
About 50km (30 miles) east of Quebec the Canadian Wildlife Service runs **Cap**

Tourmenté wildlife area on the north shore of the St Lawrence River at Saint-Joachim, Côte de Beaupré. During the migration season 300,000 snow geese spend time there, and 250 other bird species have been recorded.

For a glimpse into North American Indian life of the past and present, go north of the city to the **Huron Ancestral Village** at Wendake. You'll see a traditional home and a workshop selling beautiful hand-made snowshoes, canoes, paddles and other crafts. You can also sample Native Indian cuisine at the Atichiendo restaurant.

Follow Route 175 about 40km (25 miles) north of Quebec City for **Jacques-Cartier Park** at Charlesbourg. It has guided nature tours on foot or by canoe. Activities include fishing (May to early September), hiking, rock climbing, mountain biking, mini-rafting, canoeing and kayaking. Equipment can be hired.

Ile d'Orléans

Quebec's largest officially classified historic district, the Ile d'Orléans is worth spending half a day exploring. The island (population 7,000) is reached via the Pont d'Ile. **Chemin Royal** takes you to most of the places of interest, including the Saint-Laurent shipyard, in operation from 1908 to 1967, and an arts and crafts centre, also at Saint-Laurent, where you can choose from a wide variety of ornaments, clothing, jewellery and practical items. At weekends in July and August artists and craftspeople demonstrate their skills.

The island is Quebec City's market garden area, and stalls piled with fresh farm

*O*utdoor art exhibitions enhance the bohemian ambience of Quebec City.

A Tale of Two Bridges

Side by side, crossing the St Lawrence River west of Quebec City, two bridges each have their own claim to fame.

Between its two main pillars **Pont de Québec** has a span 549m (1,800ft) long, and is considered the world's longest cantilever bridge.

Twice during its construction, in 1907 and 1916, it collapsed, sending many workers to their deaths. Civil engineering organizations in Canada and the United States have proclaimed the bridge an international historic monument of civil engineering. It has carried railway traffic since 1917 and road traffic since 1929.

The **Pierre Laporte Bridge** beside it was built in a short 4 years, and motor traffic has used it since 1970. The two cables to which its floor is attached are made up of more than 12,500 steel wires – enough, it is said, to stretch three-quarters of the way round the world if they were laid end to end.

---

and garden produce are a feature of the island in summer – a good excuse for mainland Québécois to make frequent trips.

Sport

Skiing is, of course, a major sporting activity. World-class resorts such as Mont Sainte-Anne and Stoneham offer a range of popular winter sporting activities in addition to skiing.

Ice hockey enthusiasts can watch the Québec Nordiques in action at the Quebec Coliseum, parc de l'Exposition. The season runs from mid-September to April. In the same park **harness-racing** takes place

---

Howling with Wolves

Now for something completely different – a moonlight wolf howl. You can do it (with a guide) in Jacques-Cartier Park in July and from January to April.

'Wolves' Nocturnal Call' sessions, held three times a week, start with a lecture and slide show. Then you go out into the forest between 8pm and midnight and listen and howl, learning to imitate the eerie cries.

The same company, Observation Safaris, runs moose safaris, too. It is based at 9530 rue de la Faune, Charlesbourg (Quebec) G1G 5H9, tel. (418) 848-5099.

---

at the hippodrome, which has been a popular racecourse since 1916. Evening and weekend meetings take place according to the time of year.

Entertainment

Like Montreal, the Quebec region has a splendid new gambling facility, the **Casino de Charlevoix**, housed in the 317-room Manoir Richelieu resort property 300m (900ft) above the St Lawrence River. It offers blackjack, roulette and baccarat at 15 tables, and slot machines. The usual dress code is imposed.

Another new night spot, though for groups only, is **Le Cabaret de Champlain** in Quebec City. Diners are escorted to their table in an establishment typical of 17th-century Quebec, and costumed waiters serve food native to the New World. The entertainment presented at different times encompasses sound and light shows, singing, storytelling, theatrical productions and interactive games.

The downtown area has a number of **theatres**. Variety shows, rock concerts and classical and contemporary **music** performances take place at the Agora. In summer much of the city's entertainment moves into the open air.

Shopping

The shopper has a choice of modern malls or boutiques, craftshops and antique shops amid historic buildings in narrow streets and squares of Old Quebec. Quartier Petit Champlain claims to be the oldest shopping area in North America. More than 50 stores offering a wide range of goods can be found in rue Petit Champlain, boulevard Champlain and adjacent streets.

For a choice of shops in a compact area, try the multi-level **Place Québec** which adjoins the Hilton International Hotel. Inuit art can be found at galleries and stores at **Les Promenades du Vieux Québec** at rue de Trésor.

A 15-minute drive west of the city, along Grande-Allée with its restaurants and open-air dining terraces, is **Sainte-Foy**. Here you can browse in some of the 350 stores of **Place Laurier**.

For bargain shopping, visit **Sainte-Anne-de-Beaupré** about 35km (20 miles) eastward along the shore of the St Lawrence River, where there's a designer outlet factory centre. Two dozen manufacturers' stores offer men's, women's and children's fashions, shoes, accessories, jewellery, houseware, kitchen goods and other items priced at between 30 percent and 70 percent lower than usual retail prices. The centre, which is open 7 days a week, is close to the famous Basilica at Beaupré which attracts 1,500,000 pilgrims and visitors yearly.

Elsewhere in Quebec

The Laurentians

In a province rich in skiing facilities, the Laurentians attract thousands of winter sports enthusiasts, being within 60km (37 miles) north of Montreal. The Laurentians,

part of the Canadian Shield, are ancient, rocky and while not particularly high, provide excellent downhill skiing and cross-country trails. The highest peak is **Mont Tremblant**, at 986m (3,150ft).

The region stretches from the Ottawa River to the Saguenay River. Much of it is rugged wilderness. **Mont Tremblant Provincial Park** alone covers 1,500sq km (580sq miles).

Tourism is a year-round business in the Laurentians. Mont Tremblant Park opened in 1894, when people seeking a summer break, to enjoy the scenery and some fishing, began to arrive by train. It wasn't until the 1900s that winter sports developed and a whole new recreational scene opened up. Ski lodges, resort hotels, slopeside condos, inns and other types of accommodation are available in the small towns along the route.

The Mont Tremblant Ski Resort is currently being further developed as a winter sports destination, with an investment of more than $400 million spread over a 5-year period. The winter season is from the beginning of November to the end of May, thanks to the largest snow-making plant in Canada. Some 33 new ski trails make a total of nearly 60 runs, served by a number of new high-speed quad chair lifts. New facilities include a mountain-top restaurant, and a slopeside village with more than 100 ski-in, ski-out condos.

There are 19 ski centres within a 50km (30-mile) radius in the Laurentians. Of more than 325 trails, more than 80 are illuminated for night skiing.

Snowmobiling has long been a popular sport in the region. The first club was formed at Sainte-Agathe-des-Monts, where the winter festival lasts from mid-December to mid-March. The region has more than 2,000km (1,250 miles) of

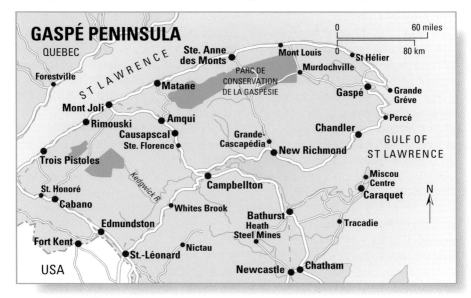

GASPÉ PENINSULA

QUEBEC

Forestville

Mont Joli
Rimouski
Causapscal
Ste. Florence

Trois Pistoles

St. Honoré
Cabano

Edmundston

Fort Kent
St.-Léonard

USA

ST LAWRENCE

Matane

Amqui

Redgwick R.

Whites Brook

Nictau

Ste. Anne
des Monts

PARC DE
CONSERVATION
DE LA GASPÉSIE

Grande-
Cascapédia

Campbellton

Bathurst
Heath
Steel Mines

Newcastle

Mont Louis

Murdochville

Chandler

New Richmond

Chatham

St Hélier

Gaspé

Percé

Grande
Gréve

GULF OF
ST LAWRENCE

Miscou
Centre
Caraquet

Tracadie

0   60 miles

0
80 km

N

snowmobile trails, and there are numerous frozen lakes to add to the thrills.

The Gaspé Peninsula

This beautiful away-from-it-all region is ideal for motor touring, but its great parks warrant abandoning the car for a bicycle or hiking boots for a while. The peninsula has the wide St Lawrence River to the north, Chaleur Bay and New Brunswick to the south, and the Gulf of St Lawrence to the east. Most of the people live in fishing villages around the circumference of the region, which has farms and green fields, tall, steep mountains, salmon rivers, high cliffs and small silvery beaches. The densely wooded **Chic-Choc Mountains**, part of the Appalachians, reach up to 1,268m (4,160ft).

The **Métane Wildlife Reserve** has one of Quebec's largest moose populations. Moose, wood caribou and Virginia deer live in the **Gaspésie Park**. Visitors can take a guided climb up the highest peak,

Mont Jacques-Cartier.

Percé, right on the nose of the peninsula, is a highly popular little resort town where visitors are welcomed with typical Gaspésie warmth and hospitality. Probably Percé's most photographed feature is a dramatic-looking rock implanted in the sea, with an archway at one end. At low tide you can walk across to it.

In summer frequent boat trips go to nearby **Bonaventure Island** to see a vast colony of gannets.

The Magdalen Islands

Set about 288km (180 miles) off the Gaspé Peninsula, though reached by ferry from the much nearer Prince Edward Island, the Magdalen Islands (Iles de la Madeleine) are becoming increasingly popular as a holiday spot. The string of about a dozen small islands in the Gulf of St Lawrence form a crescent shape and extend about 112km (70 miles) from tip to tip. The ferry trip from PEI, operating from April to January, takes about 5 hours. A weekly ferry goes between Montreal and the islands. There are daily flights from Quebec and Montreal.

The climate is the mildest in Quebec province, and summer sea temperatures are pleasantly warm. Other attractions are the seafood and strawberries, beaches, watersports, riding, golf, tennis, hiking, biking and birdwatching.

*R*ugged Gaspé *Peninsula attracts hikers, cyclists, birdwatchers and others with outdoor interests.*

Where Nature Goes to Excess

Famous for natural wonders like the phenomenally high tides and the Reversing Falls at the mouth of the Saint John River, New Brunswick features increasingly on Canada's tourism map. Four Scenic drives covering much of the province and some Discovery Byways have been introduced to direct tourists to places of beauty and interest.

With a strong Acadian heritage, New Brunswick is Canada's only officially bilingual province, with notices and signposts appearing in English and French. It is bordered by Quebec to the north and the US state of Maine to the west. Nova Scotia is across the Bay of Fundy to the south, and to the east, Prince Edward Island is a short ferry ride away over the Northumberland Strait.

The capital, **Fredericton**, is inland on the Saint John River. It is small enough to walk around. Its Beaverbrook Art Gallery

*T*he world's highest tides have sculpted the curious flowerpot rocks of Hopewell Cape in the Bay of Fundy.

contains North American and European masterpieces. A riverside walkway provides a worthwhile view of two dozen heritage buildings.

Saint John, larger than the capital, is a busy port and Canada's oldest city, incorporated in 1785. Two years earlier, Loyalist refugees had arrived in a fleet of sailing ships, having been thrown out of their homes by triumphant rebels in the War of Independence. A re-enactment of the landing takes place annually in a 5-day Loyalist City Festival.

New Brunswick has two **national parks**, Fundy and, in the northeast, Kouchibouguac. Both are coastal, but are different in character. In addition there are four major **provincial parks** and several smaller ones. Many of the parks have camping facilities.

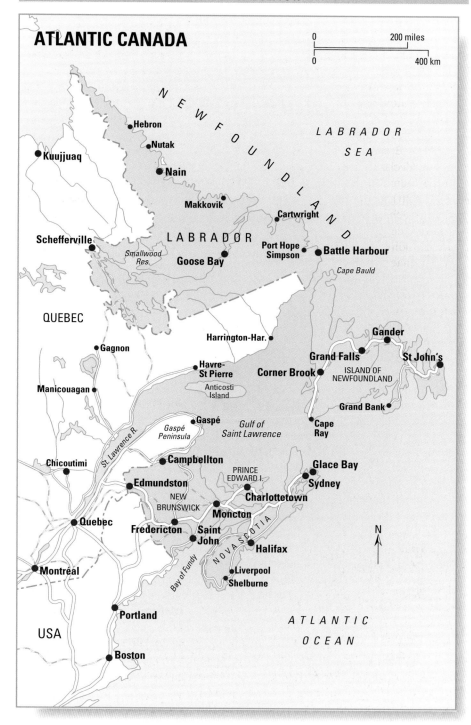

ATLANTIC CANADA

0 — 200 miles
0 — 400 km

Hebron
Nutak
Kuujjuaq
Nain
Makkovik
Cartwright
Scheffervile
LABRADOR
Port Hope
Simpson
Battle Harbour
Smallwood
Res.
Goose Bay
Cape Bauld

N E W F O U N D L A N D

LABRADOR
SEA

QUEBEC

Gagnon
Harrington-Har.
Gander
Havre-
St Pierre
Grand Falls
St John's
Corner Brook
ISLAND OF
NEWFOUNDLAND
Manicouagan
Anticosti
Island
Grand Bank
Gaspé
Gaspé
Peninsula
Gulf of
Saint Lawrence
Cape
Ray

Chicoutimi
Campbellton
Glace Bay
PRINCE
EDWARD I.
Sydney
Edmundston
Charlottetown
NEW
BRUNSWICK
Moncton
Quebec
Fredericton
Saint
John
Halifax
Montréal
Liverpool
Shelburne

St. Lawrence R.

Bay of Fundy

NOVA SCOTIA

N

Portland

USA

Boston

ATLANTIC
OCEAN

264

As you tour around New Brunswick you will become familiar with the name Irving. Irving Oil is a major employer in the Saint John area, with a number of sea-based industries. The refinery company has filling stations and restaurants around the province.

Covered bridges are a picturesque feature of New Brunswick. Although their number has declined, there are still several dozen, including the world's longest at 391m (1,282ft).

Whale-watchers in the Bay of Fundy have a chance of seeing more whale species, including the rare right whale and the huge finback, than at any other location. More than 20 species have been recorded here. The most frequently seen varietiesare finback, minke, humpback, right, Atlantic white-sided dolphin and harbour porpoise.

A number of islands dot the water off New Brunswick. In the Bay of Fundy are the lovely islands of **Campobello**, **Deer**

Lobster traps on Deer Island, one of several lovely islands in the Bay of Fundy.

and **Grand Manan**. A free ferry goes to Deer Island from Letete near St George. As well as attracting whale-watchers, Grand Manan is a great place for bird-watchers, with up to 275 species recorded annually, including the piping plover and the puffin. Nearby Machias has a bird sanctuary.

Campobello Island is where former president Franklin D Roosevelt had his summer home, a 38-room mansion with immaculate grounds which are open year-round. The house, open daily from late May to mid-October, is in Roosevelt International Park. Campobello is connected to Lubec, Maine, USA, by a bridge. The International Park is jointly administered by Canada and the United States.

Getting There

New Brunswick has good **road** access from Quebec and Maine. Marine Atlantic **ferries** cross from Nova Scotia and Prince Edward Island. Major New Brunswick cities are served by Canada's **VIA Rail**.

By air: Air Canada, with its Maritimes partner Air Nova, operates flights into Saint John, Moncton, Fredericton, Bathurst and Saint-Leonard. Canadian International Airlines serves Saint John,

Moncton, Fredericton, Charlo and Chatham through its Maritimes partner Air Atlantic. Northwest Airlines and its European connection KLM serve Saint John, Moncton and Fredericton.

Accommodation

You can camp, stay in a fishing lodge, a seashore cabin, an inn or on a farm. There are hotels, motels, resorts, condominiums, bungalows and self-catering properties. The bed and breakfast concept is fairly recent in the province, but by 1994 there were more than 50 members in the New Brunswick Bed and Breakfast Association and the list is growing. These are well-appointed establishments where the owners are your hospitable hosts, sharing their local knowledge. Breakfast time is like a party as you compare notes with fellow guests, possibly from other countries.

Sports

The vast majority of New Brunswick's population of under 750,000 live in only 15 percent of the province. Most of the other 85 percent is thickly forested wilderness criss-crossed by rivers, so **hunting** and **fishing** are major sporting activities.

Hunters go after white-tailed deer of an average weight of 80kg (175lb), though each year there are specimens of 122kg (270lb) recorded. Black bear is another quarry. The province has a healthy black bear population. Some outfitters specialize in bow-and-arrow hunting, for which there is a separate season. Game birds include woodcock and ruffed grouse, while black duck is the most popular waterfowl species.

Trout and smallmouth bass as well as the Atlantic salmon attract anglers to New Brunswick. Licences are obtainable from outfitters. Anyone planning to hunt or fish

should be equipped with the *Aim and Angle* guide which lists outfitters and locations. It is available from the Department of Economic Development and Tourism, PO Box 6000, Fredericton, NB, E3B 5H1, tel. (506) 453-8757, or, within North America, toll-free 1-800 561-0123. Other outdoors activities include mountain biking, hiking, scuba diving, canoeing, kayaking, sailing and windsurfing. Contact the same Fredericton office above for the useful New Brunswick *Outdoor Adventures* guide.

Scenic Drives

Visitors with time to explore the province fully couldn't do better than follow the scenic drives and some of the Discovery Byways, as these cover virtually all the main places of interest and visual appeal.

There are four scenic drives, each with its own symbol: **River Valley Scenic Drive** between the fertile Saint John River Valley and the Quebec border; the **Fundy Coastal Drive**; the **Acadian Coastal Drive** from Aulac to Campbellton; and the **Miramichi River Route** which runs between Chatham and Fredericton, right through renowned Atlantic salmon fishing country.

The scenic drives follow major highways. Discovery Byways go through less travelled roads off the scenic drives. Details are available from the Visitors Information Centre, City Hall, Queen Street, PO Box 130, Fredericton E3B 4Y7, tel. (506) 452-9500.

The Reversing Falls Rapids are caused by seawater pounding into the Saint John River.

River Valley Scenic Drive

Saint John

The oldest incorporated city in Canada was the place where explorer Samuel de Champlain landed in 1604 on St John the Baptist Day. The first settlement was founded in 1631. The city itself was incorporated in 1785 by American Loyalist refugees turned out of their homes in 1783 in the War of Independence. A large boulder marks the place where they landed, and a 5km (3-mile) Loyalist Trail can be followed through the city. It goes by the old Loyalist Burial ground where gravestones of 1784 mark the last resting place of some who didn't survive their first winter in New Brunswick.

Anyone revisiting Saint John after a gap of several years will find that the **Market Square** and **Dockside** area have been upgraded from the down-at-heel to the chic and gentrified. Galleries, shops and restaurants have replaced delapidated warehouses, and King Street, the main thoroughfare, has brick sidewalks and the gentle air of an earlier age.

No market addict should miss the **Old City Market**, a spacious indoor enclave vibrant with colourful goods of all sorts and general good humour and friendliness. From King Street the 120-year-old market is reached through Germain Street.

The city is built on steep hills at the mouth of the Saint John River. The best way to explore it is on foot, even though the calf muscles may be challenged. Challenge them further by walking to the hills of **Rockwood Park** for a view of the bay, the Saint John River – the largest river in the Maritime provinces – and the famous Reversing Falls Rapids. Twice daily the force of the water pounding into the Bay of Fundy causes the river to flow backwards. You can see this phenomenon, too, from a bridge high above the falls.

If you go only a few minutes from the downtown area, harbour seals and many bird species can be observed at **Irving Nature Park**.

On the way north to Fredericton, leave

***B**rilliant vermillion –*
just one shade in the multicolour
show presented in the fall.

the River Valley Scenic Drive at **Gage-town** and take a ferry trip across the river to **Lower Jemseg** for a look at small communities in a pretty region of pick-your-own fruit farms, waterside inns and summer festivals.

Fredericton

Small for a provincial capital, but elegant, with tree-lined streets and a military background, Fredericton is finely positioned on the wide Saint John River. Its 5km (3-mile) riverside walkway provides a view of some fine heritage architecture. The

Loyalist Days

Although the Loyalists landed in early May 1783, an annual re-enactment – the 5-day Loyalist Days programme – takes place at the harbour in late July, when the weather is more reliable and more visitors are in town to join in the fun. The Mayor and many of the citizens wear 18th-century costume, the Union flag flies proudly and the celebrations include a street parade and fireworks.

downtown area and Odell Park can be toured by horse and carriage. River trips are also available.

Most of the sightseeing centres on Queen Street and its environs. **City Hall** is at the corner of Queen Street and York Street. In its council chamber two large tapestries, the meticulously stitched work of two local artists, illustrate historical events covering more than 200 years. **Christ Church Cathedral** has been standing grandly between Queen Street and Brunswick Street for more than 140 years. Inside is a smaller version of Big Ben, the famous Westminster clock in London, England, for which it was the prototype.

Much of Queen Street is occupied by the **Military Compound**. The soldiers' barracks here are open to the public in summer. Visitors can also watch the daily Changing of the Guard at 11 o'clock on summer mornings in Officers Square.

The **Provincial Legislative Assembly** building at the corner of Queen Street and Saint John Street contains a set of coloured prints by Audubon, the ornithologist and naturalist, dating back to 1834. Locked away in the library – you have to put in a request to see it – is a rare copy of the Domesday Book, a vast tome recording England's first census compiled in the 11th century.

The **York-Sunbury Historical Society Museum** is in the old British Officers' Quarters in Queen Street. Here the history of the area is traced from the days long before European settlement through the establishment of the French military community in the 1690s, the arrival of the British who ousted them and the Loyalists remaining loyal to the King who settled in the 1780s, to modern times.

Perched irreverently on the staircase of

Beaverbrook Art Gallery

The world-renowned Beaverbrook Art Gallery is a splendid waterside building. The gallery was donated by newspaper magnate Lord Beaverbrook (formerly Max Aitken), one of New Brunswick's most famous sons, who spent much of his life wielding power in Britain. He died in 1964. The gallery contains the works of many prominent Canadian and British painters, and displays the huge surrealist masterpiece of Salvador Dali, *Santiago el Grande*. A window in the main gallery provides an inspiring view of the Saint John River.

this august museum is a stuffed giant frog, discovered in a local lake. It grew to an amazing 19kg (42lb).

On the other side of the street are the **National Exhibition Centre** and, above it, the popular **New Brunswick Sports Hall of Fame**.

Fredericton can boast the oldest provincial university in Canada – it was founded in 1785 – and the first astronomical observatory, built in 1851.

Adjoining the Beaverbrook Art Gallery is the **Playhouse**, donated by the Beaverbrook and Dunn Foundation, where professional performances are presented. Shows take place daily at noon at the outdoor summer theatre in Officers Square. If you are shopping for gifts or mementoes of the province, look at woven goods and ornaments and jewellery in pewter in the city's craft shops.

About 24km (15 miles) west of Fredericton is the beautiful **Mactaquac Provincial Park**, with its beaches and bass fishing. Some 6km (4 miles) farther on is **Woolastook Provincial Park** and Wildlife Park.

Kings Landing Historical Settlement

One of New Brunswick's top ten attractions is this re-creation of village life between 1790 and 1870. About 100 people in costume go about rural life as it was in the province in the 19th century. More than 60 restored buildings are on the site.

Summer visitors can help churn butter and spin flax, or chat to the blacksmith, the sawmill workers, the schoolteacher and children and the man running the ox cart.

From here, the scenic drive goes west along the TransCanada Highway to **Woodstock**, a small town of nearly 5,000

Kings Landing Historical Settlement: a presentation of village life up to two centuries ago.

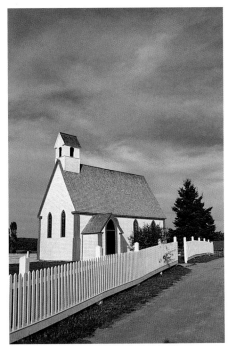

people. Its Old Courthouse, sensitively restored, was built in 1833. From Woodstock the route goes north, still following the Saint John River, crossing it at **Hartland** by what is claimed to be the world's longest covered bridge at 291m (1,282ft).

Salmon Country

Anglers may want to try to land an Atlantic salmon or some bass from the Tobique River (note that it is a rule of the Department of Natural Resources and Energy that you hire a qualified guide if you are salmon fishing). Turn off the Trans-Canada Highway near **Perth-Andover**. The route is one of the Discovery Byways recommended to tourists and passes through beautiful, wild country. There are guiding camps where everything is provided for you – meals, accommodation, canoes, even cooking one of your

salmon or preserving your catch in dry ice for you to take away.

You are now in an area where French is the more prevalent language. Stop at **Grand Falls**, by the international border with Maine, for a sight of the power manifested as the Saint John River drops violently over a cliff and pounds through a 1.5km (1-mile) narrow gorge before returning to its wider mode. The force of the water has punched deep round holes in the rock bed. You can see the whole fascinating show from the Gorge Walk.

From Grand Falls you can take Highway 108 to **New Denmark**, North America's largest Danish colony.

Back on the Saint John River Route, you can either drive on to Edmundston or switch off Highway 17 at Saint-Leonard for a Discovery Byway tour to **Mount Carleton Provincial Park**. At Saint-

Covered Bridges

New Brunswick still has about 70 covered bridges. They are also known as kissing bridges, because lovers in horse-drawn buggies welcomed the darkness and comparative privacy which they provided.

The province's oldest covered bridge, Nelson Hollow, near Doaktown on the Miramichi River, was built in 1870 and restored by the local historical society some 20 years ago.

Apart from spanning a divide, what is the purpose of the covered bridge? There are two main reasons for these attractive, barn-like structures. One is that an uncovered 19th-century wooden bridge was likely to rot after 20 Canadian winters. The other is that horses found it difficult to keep a hoof-hold and slid about on them in icy or snowy conditions, and also tended to shy or bolt if alarmed by the rushing water they were crossing.

Quentin take Highway 180 to the park. The Appalachian Trail passes through it. The tour takes about 2¹/₂ hours and goes through deep, wild forests. Mount Carleton, with a height of 820m (2,665ft), has hiking trails which provide spectacular views around one of the world's oldest geological regions.

To experience another Discovery By-way, stay on Highway 17 at Saint-Quentin and continue north to the **Kedgwick** area, where you can drive up a mountainside, see a heritage Lumber Camp, canoe on the Restigouche River and visit a handicraft centre at Saint-Jean-Baptist-de-Restigouche – all in one go.

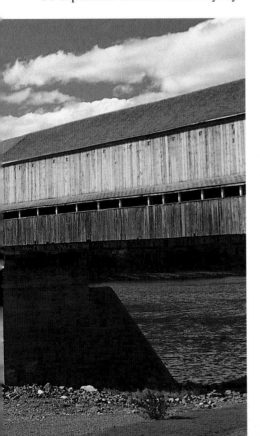

Madawaska County and Edmundston

It's a short drive on to Campbellton from Kedgwick, so if you want to switch routes and explore the province's north and east coasts along the Acadian Coastal Drive (see p.275), now is the time. Those sticking to the Saint John River Route are now in Madawaska County. If you see or hear it referred to as La République de Madawaska, this is why: Madawaska occupies a region which juts into Quebec province and the US state of Maine like a pointing finger. In the early 19th century both neighbours wanted it for themselves. Quebec was soon knocked out of the running by the throw of a dice, but the local

*T*he world's largest covered bridge crosses the Saint John River at Hartland, New Brunswick.

people fought the Americans for years to hang on to it, finally triumphing in 1842. At last they knew for certain which country they lived in, and dubbed the county: 'The Republic of Madawaska'.

Edmundston, Madawaska's main city, is the scene of New Brunswick's biggest French-style festival in late July, the **Foire Brayonne**. The 5-day celebration includes

*A*n observation deck faces a view of the mile-long Grand Falls.

western and rock music by international performers, entertainment on a grand scale and much merry-making. In winter most of the people of Edmundston and district take to their skis.

The **Madawaska Historical Museum** and the **Gallerie Colline** are both in Herbert Boulevard. The city has an 18-hole golf course established more than 90 years ago which is regarded as one of the best in the Maritime provinces.

Follow the TransCanada Highway 8m (5 miles) north of Edmundston tolook at the only botanical gardens in Atlantic Canada, at **Saint-Jacques**. More than 50,000 plants are on show in eight gardens and two arboreta.

Fundy Coastal Drive

This tour ensures that you see all the extraordinary natural wonders for which New Brunswick is famous – the world's highest tides, the Reversing Falls and Magnetic Hill – and many other sights. Starting at **St Stephen** in the province's southwest at the mouth of the St Croix River, the drive is about 350km (225 miles). Home of Ganong chocolates, the town has an annual chocolate festival in the first week in August, with a candy hunt, sinful desserts and a 'choctail' hour.

Travel east for the seaside resort of **St Andrews**, an attractive little town with well-preserved 18th- and 19th-century buildings and an active fishing community. Many people return to this holiday spot

*F*all foliage colours decorate the banks of the Saint John River.

Dulse and Fiddlehead

As you travel around New Brunswick you may come across two possibly unfamiliar food items – dulse and fiddleheads. Dulse is a type of seaweed, very beneficial to health. Local people look for it at low tide in the Bay of Fundy. The fiddlehead is a delicacy that grows on the floor of pine forests in the early spring. It is the unopened frond of a particular type of fern, the ostrich fern. The tender shoots are harvested and appear on gourmet menus.

summer after summer. Neighbouring **St George** and **Letete** are departure points for the peaceful Fundy Bay Islands (see p.48). The largest and most distant island, **Grand Manan**, a 2-hour sail from the fishing port of Black's Harbour, has motel, guest house and bed and breakfast accommodation.

The Coastal Drive continues through pretty villages and small fishing ports to Saint John. For beaches, stop at **St Martins**, east of Saint John, which has several.

This former shipbuilding centre has cliffs, caves, covered bridges and lighthouses which get the cameras clicking. The Quaco Museum outlines the history of shipbuilding in St Martins. Turn inland for another area which is a photographer's delight – the network of waterways north of Saint John off Highway 1 along the Kingston Peninsula. Visit **Rothesay** with its mansions – and jail – then snap a few take pictures of the old church, rectory and school at **Kingston**.

Rejoin the Fundy Coastal Drive to **Sussex**, where the tourist information centre has a brochure on the 17 local covered bridges. The Agricultural Museum of New Brunswick is in downtown Sussex. A farmers' market is held on Friday mornings between May and October.

Fundy National Park

Just east of Sussex, turn off Highway 2 to Highway 11, which goes through **Fundy National Park**. Although it has its share

of wild and rocky forested scenery, with rugged hiking trails, it also has such civilized amenities as tennis courts, golf course, heated saltwater swimming pool, bowling green, good fishing and good dining. Boats, horses and chalets can be hired, and there's a campground for tents and trailers. The park has about 15km (9 miles) of coastline. The former shipbuilding town of **Alma**, in a corner of the park, has an interpretive centre tracing its shipbuilding and seaport heyday. Today the little town offers facilities for people using the park.

World's Highest Tides

Hopewell Cape, at the mouth of the Petitcodiac River, is where everyone flocks to see that great twice-daily show, the world's highest tides, and the flowerpot rocks. At high tide you just see green vegetation surrounded by water. At low tide, when between 9m (30ft) and 14.8m (48ft) of seawater has receded – that's equal to the height of a four-storey building – you can walk on the ocean bed and see the rocks sculpted into curious flowerpot shapes by the swirling water. Rockhounds and beachcombers scour the Fundy Bay shoreline at low tide.

It has been calculated that each incoming tide involves 100 billion tons of water pouring into the Bay of Fundy approximately every 12^1/$_2$ hours, and that this almost equals the 24-hour flow of every river in the world.

At low tide the beach and mud stretch far into the distance. Then the tide turns. It rises up to 0.3m (1ft) in seven minutes and to 12m (39ft) in less than 6^1/$_2$ hours.

Acadian Territory

Nature has something else up its sleeve in **Moncton** – the tidal bore that zooms up the Petitcodiac River as a result of the Fundy tides. Because of some silting in the harbour, the twice-a-day tidal wave has dwindled in recent years, except at high spring tides, but it's still impressive. The wave varies from a few centimetres to nearly 0.5m (2ft). You hear its approach before you see it. You can watch it from Main Street, where a notice announces the timings.

Moncton is tagged the Gateway to Acadia, with a neat balance of English and French. The **Acadian Museum** at the University of Moncton, open year-round daily except Mondays, traces three centuries of local history. A noted cultural centre, Moncton has a number of art galleries, including the University of Moncton gallery on the campus in the Clement Cormier Building, and the Moncton City Hall Gallery. The Capitol Theatre in the downtown area has been renovated. The city's **Champlain Place**, a large shopping complex all on one level, draws people from a wide area. Formerly an important railway town, Moncton displays a steam locomotive in **Centennial Park**.

Acadian culture is celebrated with a variety of festivals and fairs. In 1994 Moncton hosted the World Acadian Congress. The area has five 18-hole golf courses. The new **Crystal Palace and Science Centre** claims to be the only indoor amusement complex in Atlantic Canada.

The Fundy Coastal Drive continues to the attractive town of **Sackville**, about 55km (35 miles) southeast of Moncton. If you're planning to experience the Acadian Coastal Drive, it would be a good idea to call at the **Acadian Odyssey National Historic Site** at Saint-Joseph de Memramcook on your way to Sackville. This will provide you with an insight into the Acadians' arduous past. Sackville is the home of Mount Allsion University. In West Main Street an out-of-the-ordinary shop, Sackville Harness Shop, is run by the only manufacturers of handmade horse collars in North America.

Those interested in nature study have two good reasons to visit the Sackville area. One is the bird sanctuary at **Sackville Waterfowl Park**, which offers good viewing from a boardwalk, while the other is the popular Tintamarre National Wildlife Area.

Aulac, near the border with Nova Scotia, marks the end of the drive. This is where the final battle of the war between the French and the English took place, and Fort Beauséjour National Historic Site is worth a visit. It's off Exit 550A on the TransCanada Highway.

Acadian Coastal Drive

For wonderful beaches and warm water to swim in, the Acadian Coast along the Northumberland Strait and the Gulf of St Lawrence is supreme. Those who live there say the beaches are the best in Canada and the water among the warmest north of Virginia (some even say Florida). At **Parlee Beach**, Shediac, and farther north at **Kelly's Beach**, July and August sea temperatures are between 19°C (66°F) and 24°C (75°F).

New Brunswick has the highest concentration of Acadians in the world – more than a quarter of a million – and most of them live in this eastern and northern region.

From Aulac drive through Port Elgin to **Shediac**, which the locals call 'lobster capital of the world' (Canada is rich in lobster capitals). Shediac supports its claim with a 6-day Lobster Festival in early July. It is

followed by a Jazz and Blues Festival. Parlee Beach – about 3km (2 miles) of sparkling sand – is at Shediac. All along the coast you'll come across beautiful beaches and friendly Acadian communities. This is an area of wharves, dunes, lighthouses and seafood. At **Bouctouche** you can call at Le Pays de la Sagouine in Acadia Street to see a re-creation of an Acadian village that never really existed – except in the work of award-winning local author Antonine Maillet.

Leave the Acadian Drive at **Chatham** and follow Highway 117 along the coast to visit Kouchibouguac National Park on a Discovery Byway trip.

Kouchibouguac National Park

This is 384sq km (150sq miles) of beaches, lagoons, dunes, inland bogs, saltmarshes, rivers and woodland. Its wildlife ranges from clams (dig them yourself) to moose. The wide variety of birds include osprey and the endangered piping plover. Tern Island is an important nesting place for terns. You can cross the fragile sand dunes and grass by boardwalk, from which you may see the protected nests of piping plover in the dunes.

There are cycling trails which double as cross-country ski trails in winter. Bicycles, boats, canoes and fishing equipment can be hired, and there are extensive camping facilities. On hot days in high summer Kelly's Beach gets crowded, but there are quieter beaches close by.

North to the Acadian Peninsula

Near Bartibog Bridge is the **MacDonald Farm Historic Site** on Highway 11, 30km (18 miles) north of Newcastle. It depicts the Scottish heritage of the region through the life of Alexander MacDonald, a Scots immigrant who arrived in 1784.

Baroque Music

Lamèque is the venue of the annual International Baroque Music Festival in July. Musicians and composers travel from many parts of the world for the 3-day celebration which pays tribute to the Jesuit priests who brough Baroque to the area on their missions.

Small town museums in the north of the region trace more than 200 years of Acadian culture following the arrival of the French seeking refuge after 1755.

To visit **Miscou Island** on the Acadian Peninsula – it has superb beaches and a wooden lighthouse – leave the Acadian Coastal Drive at Pokemouche and take Highway 113 for Shippagan. This is a Discovery Byway enabling you to see peat bogs, a multicoloured church on Lamèque Island and possibly much wildlife. An added fascination of Miscou Island is hearing the local people speaking a dialect of French which disappeared long ago in France. While in Shippagan call at the Aquarium and Marine Centre, which has many species of Atlantic marine life and a seal pool.

It is worth hopping on and off the Acadian Coastal Drive for some Discovery Byway sightseeing in this northern area. Keep an eye open at **Pokeshaw** for Highways 135 and 325. Also watch for Highway 303 at **Anse-Bleue** and Highway 145 at **Caraquet**. You will find yourself in attractive villages and countryside.

The **Acadian Historical Village** is at Caraquet. In the costumes of the time, people grind flour, spin, weave and cobble shoes. They grow corn on land reclaimed from the sea and drained by a system of dykes. A dinner theatre performance is presented with music (and lobster). It is 1755, the year of the Acadians' expulsion by the British, and a story of struggle and survival unfolds. The Acadian Village is open from early June to late September, with a series of special events, such as sheep shearing,

a traditional 19th-century christening or a wheelwright's demonstration occasionally taking place.

Caraquet is a pretty fishing port with good seafood restaurants. **Grande-Anse** has the only Popes Museum and Art Gallery in North America, where impressive papal exhibits can be seen.

Bathurst and Around Chaleur Bay

Bathurst, at the mouth of the Nepisiguit River, is a resort for summer relaxation. Its 18-hole golf course, owned by a local family, is leased to its members. The annual rent: a bushel of oysters from Chaleur Bay (Baie de Chaleur). The Gowan Brae Golf and Country Club's course overlooks the harbour.

The Royal Canadian War Museum is in the Legion Hall at Bathurst. About 5km (3 miles) north of the town is Youghall Beach Park. Wildlife can be seen in the extensive **Daly Point Reserve**, a mixed habitat of saltmarsh, upland, meadow and forest. The Tetagouche Falls are also near Bathurst. In Atlas Park, at **Pointe Verte**, a clear lake created from an old quarry is set in solid rock. It is more than 30m (100ft) deep and its visibility of up to 20m (75ft) endears it to scuba divers.

Campbellton is set at the western end of Chaleur Bay in the shadow of Sugarloaf, the 305m (1,000ft) mass of volcanic rock that provides a hiking trail and exhilarating downhill skiing. The Restigouche River provides sport for canoeists, kayakers and anglers. The seaport is the commercial centre of the Acadian region. It caters for the sports fisherman; there's a week-long annual Salmon Festival in the first week of July. The local youth hostel is situated in a waterfront lighthouse. Art works are exhibited at the Restigouche Gallery, where art courses and workshops are held.

Miramichi River Route

This tour is only 180km (111 miles). It departs from Chatham, at the mouth of the Miramichi River, to Fredericton. Along the way it passes through wild country and the heartland of New Brunswick's celebrated Atlantic salmon water.

The rich and famous, not to mention royalty, respond to the challenge of Miramichi's 'king of the game fish', staying in camps and lodges and exchanging tall stories by the camp fire. Parts of the river system are accessible only by water, and some anglers take guided canoe trips between lodges. Every summer specimens up to 18kg (40lb) are caught. Non-residents fly fishing for salmon are required to hire a guide. This is not required for those fishing for bass in the province, though it is advised.

Many of the people in the Miramichi region are descended from Scottish, Irish and English settlers. A Celtic Cross at **Loggieville**, close to Chatham in Miramichi Bay, marks the site of a former hospital and quarantine centre and honours the thousands of Irish people who landed there. A 4-day Irish Festival is held annually on the river at **Chatham** in mid-July. The Miramichi Natural History Museum is in Wellington Street and there's a genealogical centre in Howard Street.

Newcastle, where Lord Beaverbrook spent his childhood and where he is buried, holds a major 6-day Folksong Festival in early August. At the end of the month a Highland Gathering lasts for 3 days. Newcastle Shipbuilding Park is at Ritchie Wharf in the downtown area. River cruises are available in summer.

Leave the Miramichi Route at Newcastle for a Discovery Byway drive to the **Red Bank Reserve**. Highway 430 takes you to Red Bank and the province's oldest village, **Metepenagiag**, where archaeological digs have revealed 3,000 years of Native American life, followed by Acadian, Loyalist and Scottish habitation. Unearthed artefacts are displayed at Red Bank Federal School.

The Miramichi Atlantic Salmon Museum is at Main Street, **Doaktown**. You get a clear view of the salmon in an aquarium, and if you're there at feeding time you'll appreciate just how voracious these salmon are. The museum displays a fine collection of salmon flies. Some of the celebrities who have fished the Miramichi River are acknowledged in the Hall of Fame. The Doak Historic Site gives an interesting glimpse of 19th-century rural life in the area.

Nearby, at **McNamee**, you can cross the river by a slightly wobbly suspension footbridge – not for the faint-hearted – which provides a splendid view.

Next stop is Boiestown, geographically in the middle of New Brunswick. The Woodmen's Museum pinpoints the history and importance of lumberjacking in the province and the lives led by the hardworking lumbermen. Boiestown has one of those old-style country stores that stocks just about everything – McCloskey's.

After **Boiestown** the highway moves away from the Miramichi River and accompanies the Nashwaak River for the last leg of the drive into Fredericton.

Small Is Beautiful

Prince Edward Island is the country's smallest province, and the place where the Dominion of Canada was born in 1867. The capital, Charlottetown, is the island's only city, though there are dozens of small towns and villages set along the rugged coasts and in the pastoral interior of this predominately rural province.

To visit Prince Edward Island in summer is like finding yourself in a child's picture book. Dazzling white houses stand among emerald lawns. Glossy dairy cattle graze in manicured meadows. From early June great swathes of wild lupins colour roadside verges purple, pink, yellow and white. A clear blue sea laps at dozens of beaches. Top quality potatoes, exported to many countries, grow in the fertile soil, richly red with iron oxide. Most of the island's roads are paved, but

*P*retty fishing villages dot the Prince Edward Island coast, and the catches are readily available.

about 1,920km (1,200 miles) of them – maybe for old time's sake, maybe because they look good – are compacted red clay.

Roughly the shape of a banana, Prince Edward Island (PEI) is separated from Nova Scotia and New Brunswick by the **Northumberland Strait**. It is about 270km (170 miles) from tip to tip, with **Charlottetown** roughly in the middle.

With 126,000 people, PEI is Canada's most densely populated province. Some are descended from the Acadians who were there before Great Britain assumed control in 1763, and Scottish and Irish cultures are celebrated at summer festivals. The Micmac Indians lived on the island for hundreds of years prior to being usurped by Europeans. Their traditional craft skills have been passed down the generations, and their work can now be seen at **Lennox Island** and other outlets. The Micmac people today represent about 0.4 percent of PEI's population.

Prince Edward Island is an island of lobster suppers, lighthouses, friendly faces and welcoming restaurants. Much of the accommodation is in people's homes, giving a high standard of comfort and cuisine and the chance to meet Islanders as well as other visitors.

Anne of Green Gables is much in evidence. The heroine of Lucy Maud Montgomery's classic story, published in 1908, lives on, attracting thousands of visitors. They go to **Cavendish**, where the novel was set, to the cemetery where the author

While fishermen follow their centuries-old industry, charters are available for visiting anglers.

was buried in 1942, and to the Confederation Centre in Charlottetown, where original manuscripts are exhibited.

Getting There

By ferry: The island is connected to New Brunswick and Nova Scotia by car ferry services which run frequently every day in summer. Marine Atlantic operates the 45-minute New Brunswick service into **Borden**, and Northumberland Ferries run the 75-minute Nova Scotia service into **Wood Islands**. Neither company takes reservations – or your money on the way out. You pay for the round trip only when you leave. Work is in progress constructing a bridge between PEI and the mainland. Completion is expected by 1997.

By air: Flights into **Charlottetown Airport**, with connections between major cities in eastern Canada and the United States, are operated by Air Canada and

Canadian Airlines International. The flight from Halifax, Nova Scotia, to PEI takes 25 minutes.

Sport and Leisure on PEI

Seal-watching

Seal-watching trips are available from the eastern shore, and usually include a look at a blue mussel nursery at sea. Thousands of baby Harp seals are born within a 24-hour period at the end of February, and tours to the ice floes of the Gulf of St Lawrence are run in March to see the fluffy white babies.

House Parties

Visitors can get to know each other and the Islanders at house parties. They take place on four evenings a week from July to September at country inns and community halls. For a few dollars you join in traditional musical entertainment, dancing and humour led by a group of musicians and get a taste of local fish and farm products. Details of dates and locations are available at Visitor Information Centres dotted about the island.

Special-interest Holidays

Some accommodations specialize in a particular activity or special-interest package. These include golf, cycling, ocean kayaking, Anne of Green Gables, romance and honeymoons, Acadian culture, lighthouses, nature appreciation, painting and photography. You can study garden-to-table organic herbs while staying at the **Doctor's Inn** at Tyne Valley, or try the potter's art at the **Stanley Bridge Country Resort** at Kensington. You can attend a chocolate-making workshop (and sam-ple the results) at Victoria, or learn to play the fiddle at Cavendish.

Organized Tours

There are island **bus** tours, **harbour** tours and **lobstering** trips – which require your rising before the sun and getting afloat to observe the technique of setting the traps and reaping the harvest before enjoying your lobster for supper at a country inn.

Outdoor Pursuits

All the usual **watersports** are available, such as sailing, surfboarding and scuba diving. Summers are pleasantly warm and sunny, but seldom hot – temperatures rarely exceed 20–23°C (about 73°F) – making **hiking** and **cycling** popular pursuits. PEI has lost its railway in recent years but the **Rails to Trails** policy has resulted in new off-road walking and cycling options along a growing network of trails. Hikers also have numerous beach and woodland marked trails to follow.

Golf is as popular a recreation as it is elsewhere in the world, and Prince Edward Island is proud of the beauty and challenge presented by its affordable courses. Some offer special off-season and evening rates. Newest course is at **Crowbush Cove** in the east, described as 'a punishing Scottish-style masterpiece'. Another new one is the nine-hole **Clyde River**, 15 minutes out of Charlottetown.

Deep-sea fishing for cod and mackerel, with the chance of halibut, can be arranged, and **river fishing** for trout and salmon, with guide services if required, is also available. **Fly fishing** equipment can be hired. Brook trout are the most likely catch. Rainbow trout are caught in some rivers and lakes.

Charlottetown has **harness-racing** year-round, with at least 125 race dates. In winter there is sometimes **ice racing** on the North River Causeway when weather permits. It's an exciting sport with pari-mutuel betting.

Also in winter there's downhill and cross-country **skiing** in provincial parks; some of the golf courses double as ski trails, and **snowshoeing** and **tobogganing** are enjoyed. The abandoned railway routes that cyclists and hikers follow from May to the end of October are used by **snowmobilers** in winter.

Around the Island

For tourism purposes PEI is divided into six regions. They are called North by Northwest, Ship to Shore, Anne's Land, Charlotte's Shore, Bays and Dunes and Hills and Harbours. The capital is in Charlotte's Shore. There are three scenic drives, identified by symbols on signposts. The **Lady Slipper Drive**, named after the province's floral emblem, is a 288km (180-mile) drive in the west of the island.

The **Blue Heron Drive**, which includes PEI National Park along the north shore, is a 190km (114-mile) tour of the central area. The **King's Byway Drive** is the longest, taking you 375km (225 miles) around the coastline of Kings County.

Charlottetown

Small and compact, with immaculate old buildings and a newly developed waterfront at Peake's Wharf, PEI's capital, in the Charlotte's Shore region, is named after the consort of King George III. The **Charlottetown Festival** runs from late June to September. Its main feature is an 'Anne of Green Gables' musical, a popular entertainment for 30 years. It takes place in the Festival Theatre at the **Confederation Centre** of the Arts, in Grafton Street.

The Centre incorporates three other theatres, art galleries and a museum. It was built in 1964 to mark the 100th anniversary of the conference in Charlottetown of delegates from British North American colonies which led, in 1867, to the

founding of the Dominion of Canada. As it happened, Prince Edward Island demonstrated its independent streak and waited six years before joining, becoming the seventh province to do so.

Next to the Confederation Centre is **Province House**, at the corner of Richmond and Great George Streets. This is considered the actual birthplace of Canada, where the 1864 conference was held. Much of it, including the Confederation Chamber, has been restored to its 1860s appearance. An audio presentation outlines the building's history. In the Provincial Legislative Chamber in Province House the table and chairs used by the 1864 delegation can be seen.

The Anglican **Church of St Paul**, dating from in 1747, is the island's oldest Protestant church. The Roman Catholic **Basilica of St Dunstan** is one of the biggest in Canada.

Charlottetown is noted for its good small **restaurants** and excellent food. Lobsters, oysters, mussels and clams are likely to appear on the menu. Craft shops selling high quality art works and textiles made by islanders are found all over PEI. Pottery, hand-knit sweaters, etched glass, woodcarvings, decoy ducks and geese, jewellery, porcelain dolls, exquisite quilts and intricate Indian beadwork and other items are on sale. Samples of many different crafts can be seen at the **Island Craft Shop** in Richmond Street, Charlottetown, which is the headquarters of the PEI Crafts Council. The Confederation Court Mall in the downtown area has nearly 100 shops and services spread over three floors.

Peake's Wharf provides a pleasant waterfront stroll with its boardwalks, restaurants, craft shops and boat trips.

South of Charlottetown, at the mouth of the harbour, is **Fort Amhurst/Port-La-Joye National Historic Site**, marking both the first French settlement on PEI and the British fort which followed. All that remains are earthworks, but the grounds and shoreline attract picnickers and people out for a stroll. The site, which has an interpretive centre, provides a wonderful view of Charlottetown and the harbour.

On the south coast, east of the Borden Ferry terminal, the village of **Victoria** delights visitors with its craft shops, boutiques, galleries, tearooms and restaurants, its little harbour and its turn-of-the-century look. There's a lot of activity here in the height of summer, including concerts and repertory theatre at the Victoria Playhouse.

Just north of Charlottetown, at **West Royalty**, you'll find the Precious Memories Royal Doulton Museum. It has more than 700 fine china limited editions, and a shop where you can find bargains.

North by Northwest

Having visited the capital region, let's now explore the rest of Prince Edward Island from west to east. The Lady Slipper scenic drive takes you round the coast of this fishing and farming area, past four lighthouses. At one of these, **West Point**, in use since 1875, in the southwest of the region, you can climb to the top and admire the view of the sea and extensive quiet, sandy beaches. This now fully automated lighthouse is the only functioning one in Canada which provides accommodation for visitors. It incorporates an inn with nine guestrooms..

White farmhouses set in bright green fields give P.E.I. a picture-book quality.

Drive inland among the blueberry farms and potato fields. At **O'Leary**, on Highway 142, is another of Canada's one-and-onlys – a Potato Museum, newly built to demonstrate the importance of the not-so-humble potato to the island economy. Disease-free seed potatoes are exported to many countries from PEI. On the museum site (open from June to September) are a community museum, a Little Red schoolhouse and a heritage chapel. Potato snacks – what else? – are served.

North Cape, as far north as you can go in North by Northwest, has magnificent red rock reefs, a lighthouse and the Atlantic Wind test site which, apart from its laboratories, is open to the public in July and August. A video presentation in the Visitor Centre explains how state-of-the-art wind turbines operate. A very short drive southwards takes you to **Norway**, where you can pause for a moment to look at the Elephant Rock. It is clearly recognizable as a great red elephant with its trunk adrift in the sea.

To see the rural meadow and woodland landscape from a different perspective, take a 20-minute ride on the Prince Edward Island **miniature railway** at Kildare on Highway 12. The train, which goes through a tunnel and over a trestle bridge, runs from June to early September, and later in good weather. Another place that children enjoy is the **Mill River Fun Park**, which is at Woodstock on Highway 2. It has an on-shore pirate ship, bumper boats and water slides.

Ship to Shore

This region offers much summer activity, with a programme of festivals, a variety of regular attractions and a number of major sports events, including the International World Senior Softball Championships. It is a noted ice hockey training centre. Year-round harness-racing also takes place here. The **Lobster Carnival** in July is followed by the Tyne Valley **Oyster Festival** in early August, when oyster-shucking championships are held. Hydroplane events take place at the harbour.

The Lady Slipper Scenic Drive takes you around Ship to Shore country. Many holiday activities centre on **Summerside**, PEI's second largest town and a former shipbuilding community in the good old days of sail.

In the early part of the 20th century the commercial breeding of silver foxes, originated from wild stock, was initiated on

---

Irish Moss

If there's a severe storm overnight while you're in the northwest of the region, stand by for a lot of activity on the shoreline the following day, when the ocean delivers a harvest of seaweed on to the beaches and local families rush out to collect it.

The seaweed is Irish Moss, which was first appreciated as a cash crop at Carageen, County Waterford in Ireland. It has unusual properties – emulsifying is one – which make it a valuable ingredient in food manufacture and in other products.

Fronds of Irish Moss can be gathered from the beach after a storm. To collect more which is uprooted from the sea bed by the turbulence, trawling nets are harnessed to horses and ponies, which are ridden into the water. Investigation into the full potential of the product is taking place at an interpretive centre in a former fishing vessel at Miminegash, on Highway 14, open from late June to late September. It is fascinating to see the number of everyday items in which Irish Moss plays an important part.

PEI. Fortunes were made and opulent houses built, which today are still referred to as 'fox houses'. At its peak, in the 1920s, the industry represented 17 percent of the island's economic base, but by the 1940s, for various reasons, the fox fur trade declined. The International Fox Hall of Fame and Museum is at Summerside, open from June to September.

Scottish immigration to Prince Edward Island is depicted at the **College of Piping** in Summerside. From early June to late August visitors can attend demonstrations of bagpiping, drumming, Highland dancing, step dancing and fiddle playing. Concerts are given on Thursday evenings.

The **Eptek National Exhibition Centre**, with history and fine arts exhibits from throughout Canada, and the PEI Sports Hall of Fame, honouring the island's foremost sports personalities, are among Summerside's both various waterfront buildings.

Some of the special-interest activities and places encountered in North by Northwest and Ship to Shore regions are introduced at the **Lady Slipper Visitor Information Centre** on the eastern outskirts of Summerside.

Native Indian artefacts and paintings can be seen at **Lennox Island** on Highway 163 off Highway 12, where more than 50 Micmac families live. They are descendants of the first Christianized Native people in Canada. Visiting is from Monday to Friday in July and August, but the gift shop, offering masks, ceremonial headdresses, stone carvings, beadwork belts and ornamentation, basketware and silver jewellery, is open all year.

At **Misconche** on Highway 2 west of Summerside, the local Acadian culture and heritage are preserved in a museum presenting Acadian history from 1720 to

A succulent supper. One of the island's most popular products is plentiful - and cheap.

modern times. Audiovisual presentations are given. Attached to the museum is a documentation centre where people can carry out genealogical research. From Misconche follow Lady Slipper Drive west to **Mont-Carmel** in the Evangeline region, where the Acadian culture flourishes. The **Cultural Pioneer Village** recreates an Acadian settlement of the 1820s, with church, village store and blacksmith's shop, and murals illustrating the history.

Port Hill is a popular stop on the scenic drive. Green Park Shipbuilding Museum is here. It was the 1865 home of a ship-building magnate, and the site of his shipyard. Shipbuilding was PEI's major industry in the 1800s. The museum opens daily except Mondays from mid-June to early September.

For sheer novelty value, take a look at the little chapel, house and tavern at **Cap-Egmont**, just west of Mont-Carmel. They were built in the 1970s by a retired fisherman, recycling 25,000 bottles of varied shapes and sizes.

Anne's Land

Anne of Green Gables has made such an impact on tourism in Prince Edward Island that one has to remind oneself that she was the figment of Lucy Maud Montgomery's fertile imagination and not a real person at all. Nevertheless, she has a tremendous following – the Japanese in particular adore her – and she has made a vast contribution to the PEI economy.

Touring the central north shore on the Blue Heron Scenic Drive, Anne fans will probably head for **Cavendish** for a start, where **Green Gables House** in **Prince Edward Island National Park** is managed by the Canadian Parks Service. The house is furnished in late 19th-century style and staffed by people with the details of Anne's adventures at their fingertips. The house belonged to elderly relatives of Anne's creator. In the grounds visitors can

*T*he Anne of Green Gables house attracts a stream of visitors all summer.

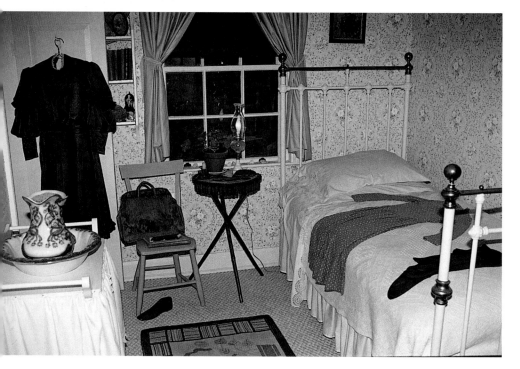

wander in some of the places mentioned in the book – Balsam Hollow, Haunted Woods, Lovers Lane. Green Gables House is open daily from late May to late October. Off-season tours are available by request – tel. (902) 894-4246.

The site of the farmhouse where the author was brought up by her maternal grandparents, the Macneills, can also be seen at Cavendish. *Anne of Green Gables* was written there. Lucy Maud Montgomery lived there from 1876 to 1911. Nothing remains except the cellar, surrounded by gardens, but members of the Macneill family still occupy the farm.

A little to the west on the Blue Heron Drive is **New London**, where the author was born in 1874 in a little house overlooking the harbour. Although she left here at the age of 21 months, her wedding dress and some personal books containing stories and poems are on display.

A short drive northwards brings you to **French River**. On Highway 263 is Anne's **House of Dreams**, where fictional Anne and her newly wed fictional husband lived. Nearby is **Park Corner**, home of the author's grandfather and still lived in by members of the family. The **Anne of Green Gables Museum** is at Silver Bush, Park Corner, where Lucy Maud Montgomery often visited her aunt and uncle and from where she was married in 1911.

The Cavendish area offers assorted activities and attractions for summer visitors. Prince Edward Island National Park stretches 40km (25 miles) from Cavendish eastward. There are beaches – some with lifeguards – sand dunes where marram grass helps prevent erosion, red cliffs, salt marshes, ponds and woodland. There are hiking, cycling, camping, picnicking, swimming, tennis and golf facilities. Bird-watchers find much to interest them along the shore. An entrance fee is charged in July and August.

Cavendish has two **golf** courses, the 18-hole Green Gables and the challenging nine-hole Forest Hills course.

Cranberry Village, Cavendish, is the home of Ripley's Believe It or Not Museum, with curiosities and extraordinary exhibits displayed in nine galleries. Anne of Green Gables is here, painted on a grain of rice.

Family Activities in and around Cavendish

There is plenty of family fun and entertainment in the Cavendish area. The **Royal Atlantic Wax Museum** displays famous personalities from many walks of life, including British royalty. The **Enchanted Castle** presents a children's musical show and animated scenes from more than a dozen fairy tales. **King Tut's Tomb and Treasures** is a full-size replica of the multi-chambered Tomb of Tutankhamen with computerized effects and displays of replica valuables found in the tomb. At **Grandpa's Antique Photo Studio** you can choose a costume and dress up for a sepia photograph as a character from the past.

Rainbow Valley is a large amusement park with three lakes dotted with islands, several types of boats, some exciting rides, water slides, animated shows and all sorts of displays and entertainments.

A science theme park, the **Great Island Adventure Park**, is at Stanley Bridge, 4km (2 1/2 miles) west of Cavendish on Highway 6. There are guided tours of a walk-in replica of the space shuttle *Columbia*, two floors of hands-on science attractions, a dinosaur museum, a children's village, a maze and the Adventure Forest. Mini-golf, swimming, boating and a Coca-Cola memorabilia museum keep the youngsters happily occupied.

PEI Marine Aquarium is about 2km (1¹/₄ miles) west of the Adventure Park. A fully functional model of an oyster bed illustrates the cultivation of the shellfish. Numerous native fish and seals can be seen, and there are hundreds of species of preserved birds and butterflies.

Santa's Woods at North Rustico, east of Cavendish on Highway 6, provides the experience of a Christmas atmosphere from mid-June to early September. The Christmas theme park offers more than 50 activities – from petting small animals and trampolining to Christmas shopping – and Christmas music from many countries is played.

Also at North Rustico, the popular **Fisherman's Wharf** is famous for its lobster suppers. Whatever you choose – lobster, scallops, steak, ham – you can have unlimited steamed mussels as well. And there's an 18m (60ft) salad bar.

Brackley Beach Entertainment Centre, along the Blue Heron Drive, has a playground, bumper boats, 18-hole minigolf, water slides and beachside boardwalk for strolling and shopping, and a drive-in cinema. **Broccoli Beach Lighthouse** at Brackley has a five-storey observation tower open to the public. It has a photographic display of PEI lighthouses, a display of birds seen on the island and a gift shop for souvenirs.

Located inland in the west of Anne's Land is **Kensington** where, on Highway 2 at Summerside Road, **Ye Olde Manor House** presents scenes picked out in thousands of points of coloured light. A staircase leads down to Tudor-style streets and new features are constantly being added. North of Kensington on Highway 234 is **Burlington Amusement Park**, with a go-

kart track, bumper boats and cars, a roller coaster and trampolines. Also on Highway 234 is **Woodleigh**, a 14ha (33-acre) country garden containing large-scale replicas of noted British buildings. York Minster, the Tower of London and Dunvegan Castle were erected by a PEI man inspired by an interest in British architecture and his Scottish ancestral home. People go to Woodleigh, too, for the new **Historical Research Centre** there. Family name histories and coats of arms from around the world can be researched.

Housed in a former Presbyterian church on the extreme western section of the Blue Heron Drive at Malpeque is the **Keir Memorial Museum**. It depicts life in the district from the times of the Micmac people through the Acadian occupation and up to the 19th-century settlement of the British.

For a fine display of dahlias of many varieties and of numerous other flowers, call at **Malpeque Gardens**. It also – inevitably – has its own Anne of Green Gables section.

Bays and Dunes

PEI's northeast region is quiet and uncommercial. It has lovely beaches and few people on them. The scenic drive, marked by a crown, is called **King's Byway**, this region being in Kings County. (The island's other two counties are Queens, which is in the centre, and Prince, in the west.)

The newest **golf** course on the island, opened in 1993, is at **Crowbush Cove Provincial Park** at Lakeside, amid water and sand dunes. The region has trails to follow on horseback, on foot or by bicycle. PEI's Rails to Trails project provides recreational trails along the cause where the railway track used to be.

Sailing trips by schooner are available from the village of **Cardigan** on the King's Byway Drive. A box lunch is supplied by a local lobster restaurant. For a really scenic cruise along the southeast coast to **Basin Head**, go aboard the vessel Souris Light at the Harbour Wharf at **Souris**. With fewer than 2,000 people, Souris is the region's main town, and a busy fishing port. **Basin Head Fisheries Museum** gives a comprehensive picture of the lives of local fishermen. Methods of catching different fish species and the equipment used are illustrated. On the site are fish sheds, a display of small craft and a 1930s cannery.

At **Elmira**, 16km (10 miles) east of Souris, is the Railway Museum, detailing the history of the railway, its stations and its telegraph equipment which is still in working order. This was the eastern terminus of a railway system linking Prince Edward Island with the rest of North America. Many photographs and documents are displayed.

East Point Lighthouse, at PEI's eastern tip, is open for tours in July and August. It has been moved twice since it was built in 1867.

Deep-sea fishing and tuna fishing charters are both available from several parts of the region.

Hills and Harbours

This is a place for those who want a quiet, relaxing holiday with some gentle motoring, discovering beautiful vistas, visiting art galleries, choosing unique gifts in craft shops, sampling the famous Island blue mussels, going by boat to watch seals and birds and generally taking life at an leisurely pace.

Designated scenic heritage roads and unpaved back roads pass through woodland and beside streams. For those with energy to spare, there are guided scuba-diving jaunts, deep-sea and sport fishing, kayaking along rivers and coastline, trail riding, golf courses and a driving range.

Part of the King's Byway follows Highway 1, the TransCanada Highway. If you branch off it westward on Highway 209, along a narrow spit of land, you will come to **Point Prim Lighthouse**. Built in 1845, the 18m (60ft) tower is the oldest on Prince Edward Island, and the only round brick lighthouse in Canada. Tours are available in July and August.

Northeast of Point Prim, signposted from Highway 1, is **Orwell Corner Historic Village**, open from late June to early September. This agricultural crossroads village, settled in the 1800s, became redundant with 20th-century technology and has been resurrected as a showcase for PEI's farming heritage. Church, school, smithy, community hall, farmhouse and farm buildings are all there. Fiddle music and step dancing draw crowds on Wednesday evenings in summer and early autumn at the weekly *ceilidh*.

The Wood Islands Ferry terminal is in the central south of the region. North and east of here are two provincial parks. Follow the King's Byway through Murray Harbour to **Kings Castle Provincial Park** and **Gladstone** on Highway 348 just east of Murray River. There is a beach here with showers, changing rooms and barbecue facilities, and the park offers children's play equipment and statues of storybook characters.

Highway 4 leads to Milltown Cross and Buffaloland Provincial Park, where a boardwalk takes you to a wooden deck overlooking a 41ha (100-acre) enclosure in which herds of buffalo and whitetail deer roam.

Canada's Ocean Playground

By the time you've crossed Canada from west to east, you think you've seen all the superlative scenery there is to see. Rivers, Rockies, forests, lakes, shorelines and sunsets… Then you get to Cape Breton in Nova Scotia, drive along a twisting highland road and vista after dramatic vista presents itself – blue Atlantic bays, pale, narrow beaches, steep headlands of massed greenery. Car registration plates proclaim Nova Scotia to be Canada's Ocean Playground.

Nova Scotia is an ideal summer destination for couples in all age groups who enjoy touring through forested countryside and historic communities, where many of the frame houses are set beside their own lake, and where welcoming people seize any excuse for a fete or festival.

Halifax, the capital, is a city which pleases everyone. Big ships berth in the natural harbour, the schooner *Bluenose II* provides tours under full sail, old waterfront warehouses have been given new life and on Citadel Hill the noonday gun is fired daily.

*F*lamboyant fall *colours reflected in the waters of a Nova Scotia lake.*

Nova Scotia is 560km (350 miles) long, and nowhere is more than 56km (33 miles) from the sea. More than one-third of the 900,000 population live in the Halifax metropolitan area. Represented in the population are Micmac Indians, Scots, French, Scandinavians, English, Irish, Germans, Swiss, Africans, Dutch and Lebanese people.

North America's first permanent European settlement, apart from a few Spanish in Florida, was established by the French in Port Royal, Nova Scotia, in 1605. In 1710 Park Royal fell to the British, who changed the name to Annapolis Royal, now a lush farming area.

They say more Gaelic is spoken in parts of Nova Scotia than in Scotland – Gaelic is one of the subjects taught at the Gaelic College in Cape Breton.

As in some of the other smaller provinces of Canada, tourism professionals have devised scenic drives enabling visitors to cover Nova Scotia in bite-sized pieces. There are seven major Scenic Travelways, including the capital area, which introduce you to many aspects of the province's life and heritage. You may prefer to see most of Halifax-Dartmouth on foot or by public transport.

Getting There

By air: Canadian Airlines International has daily flights into Halifax from a number of Canadian cities with worldwide connections. Scheduled connections within Atlantic Canada are provided by CAI's affiliated partner Air Atlantic. Air Canada flies from England and Scotland to Halifax, and has daily flights from New York, Boston, Toronto, Montreal and St John's, Newfoundland. Its partner, Air

Nova, operates scheduled services within Atlantic Canada. KLM Royal Dutch Airlines has three flights a week into Halifax from Amsterdam, with connections to Amsterdam from the UK and other parts of Europe. Car rentals are available at Halifax International Airport and at Sydney and Yarmouth Airports, Nova Scotia.

By sea ferry: Nova Scotia has Marine Atlantic sea ferries twice daily year-round between North Sydney and Port aux Basques, Newfoundland, with more frequent services in summer. Marine Atlantic also runs daily year-round services between Saint John, New Brunswick and Digby, Nova Scotia. Daily services between Caribou, Nova Scotia and Wood Islands, Prince Edward Island, are operated from 1 May to 20 December. Ferries between Yarmouth, Nova Scotia and Bar Harbor, Maine, sail daily in summer – oth-

erwise thrice-weekly – and daily between Yarmouth and Portland, Maine, from early May to late October.

By train: VIA Rail has a trans-continental rail service in Nova Scotia.

By road: Highways from all parts of the United States and Canada join the Trans-Canada Highway from New Brunswick into Nova Scotia.

Getting Around

Buses stopping at points between Halifax and Yarmouth are operated by two companies, **Acadian Lines** and **Mackenzie Bus Lines**. **Metro Transit** serves the Halifax-Dartmouth area. Its **Access-a-Bus** service is wheelchair accessible. A number of other bus companies operate in different parts of the province, and there are at least a dozen tour companies which ar-

range sightseeing excursions within and beyond Nova Scotia.

Accommodation

For information about accommodation in Nova Scotia, and to make reservations, there are toll free numbers for Canada and the continental US. Within Canada tel 1-800 565-0000. From the United States tel 1-800 341-6096. For written inquiries the address is Nova Scotia Tourism and Culture, Box 130, Halifax, Nova Scotia, B3J 2M7, Canada.

The province has all the types of accommodation found elsewhere in Canada, from campgrounds and hostels to farm and country homes and resorts – and one more option which is unique: a malt whisky distillery complex which also includes an inn.

Sports and Leisure Activities

Boats can be chartered for birdwatching, whale-watching, scuba diving among wrecks – of which there are more than 3,000 – general sightseeing and for fishing off Nova Scotia's 7,459km (4,625 miles) of coastline.

Fishing is for mako, blue and porbeagle sharks, giant bluefin tuna or for your supper of striped bass or mackerel. Freshwater fishing might catch you salmon, trout, bass or shad.

Sea kayaking, canoeing in Kejimkujic National Park along routes used by Micmac Indians over many centuries, sailing, windsurfing, fossil hunting and rock-hounding, landscape painting and

*T*he dory, a traditional small boat designed for off-shore fishing, is still in use.

photography tuition, rock climbing, hiking, cycling, hot air ballooning, golfing, lawn bowling, learning to skydive – the opportunities are widespread. The downhill skiing season is from mid-December to early April. Snowmobiling is another winter option.

A private yacht moored on the waterfront in Halifax Harbour.

Halifax-Dartmouth

The twin cities sit on opposite sides of **Halifax Harbour**, which, at 16km (10 miles) long is the world's second largest and deepest natural harbour, surpassed only by Sydney's in Australia. The harbour, crossed by the A Murray-Mackay Bridge and the Angus MacDonald Bridge – both toll bridges – opens out into **Bedford Basin** at its northwestern end. Bedford Basin served as an assembly point for North Atlantic ship convoys in World War II. Today it is an area for yachting and pleasure boating.

With eight major parks, Halifax is known as the City of Trees. A passenger ferry service operates from the downtown area across the harbour to downtown Dartmouth, which has 23 lakes and is therefore dubbed City of Lakes. Halifax is Canada's most historic city of British origin. It was founded in 1749 to establish Britain's strength in the North Atlantic. Dartmouth was founded in 1750.

Halifax

Halifax has the sophisticated hotels one would expect in a capital, some friendly inns and a growing bed and breakfast facility. There are good shopping malls. Street entertainers and rickshaws powered by energetic young people add to the atmosphere. A wide choice of restaurants and eateries offer seafood, steaks and other filling fare. Nightlife centres on and around Argyll Street.

Bedford, at the head of Bedford Basin, a fast-growing community in a lovely setting, has a number of new hotels and other accommodations. Atlantic Playland is at Bedford Basin, at Lucasville Road off Highway 213. It opens from April to early November.

Shoppers crowd around a produce stall at Brewery Market, near the restored Halifax Waterfront.

Around Halifax Harbour

Daytime and evening **harbour tours** and **boat trips** are available. The famous schooner *Bluenose II*, pictured on the Canadian dime, attends festivals around the Nova Scotia coast, but is in Halifax for two-hour public sailings three times a day except Mondays in July and August. It departs from Privateers Wharf, Historic Properties. Cruises with the *Harbour Queen*, a New Orleans-style riverboat, leave from Cable Wharf between mid-May and late October. Dinner party cruises are an option on this boat. You see large ships and container vessels from many parts of the world, and some of the important buildings of Halifax and Dartmouth, on these harbour cruises. The *Haligonian III* provides two-hour cruises with an informed commentary through the harbour and the North West Arm, where homes built for millionaires can be seen.

The waterfront at Halifax is an attractive place to stroll in, with its museums, street entertainers and its interesting mix of timber or stone buildings up to 200 years old and modern structures. The **Historic Properties** are three blocks of Canada's oldest surviving waterfront warehouses, sensitively restored as offices, restaurants, pubs and shops. Nearby is the **Brewery Market**, a great meeting place for Haligonians, as Halifax people are called. It has art and craft shops and boutiques and fashion stores selling woollens and tartans.

Citadel Hill

The leading historical attraction in Halifax, said to be the most visited historic site in Canada, is the **Citadel**, on a hill overlooking the city and harbour. It is the fourth fortification on the site. Construction of the star-shaped citadel, with its

Big Bang
Halifax Harbour was the scene of the world's largest non-nuclear explosion caused by man. It happened during World War I, in December, 1917, when a munitions ship, the *Mont Blanc*, blew up after a collision with another vessel, causing 2,000 deaths, countless injuries and smashing windows up to 80km (50 miles) away.

295

ramparts, vaulted rooms and musketry gallery, began in 1828 and was completed 28 years later. There's a lot to see, and in June, July and August there's plenty of action, too, with kilted Highlanders, the naval Brigade and the Royal Artillery presented in 19th-century uniforms, demonstrations of pipes and drums, sentry duty changeovers, drilling and signalling and, of course, the firing of the Noonday Gun. Before you do the tour, allow 50 minutes to see the 'Tides of History' video, which provides an historical insight into Halifax and its defences.

A Highland piper performs at the Citadel, the leading historical attraction in Halifax.

On Citadel Hill is the **Old Town Clock**, presented to the city in 1803 by Prince Edward, who spent some years in Halifax. It has different peals for the hour, half-hour and quarter-hour.

The **Army Museum**, housed in the Cavalier Building at the Citadel, is a separate attraction, with British and Nova Scotian military uniforms, medals and firearms displayed. Also much concerned with the defence of Halifax was **York Redoubt**, a National Historic Site just outside the city on Highway 253 off Purcells Cove Road. The fortification dates back to 1793, when war broke out between Britain and revolutionary France, and it continued to play a part in defences through World Wars I and II. It is open between June and early September.

Province House, in Hollis Street in the heart of Halifax, is where the Nova Scotia Government sits. It is open year-round, with free admission. Charles Dickens, the English writer, described it in 1842 as 'like looking at Westminster through the wrong end of the telescope.' Opposite Province House is the **Art Gallery of Nova Scotia**, a lovely heritage home for nearly 3,000 works in the permanent collection. The gallery is open all year. On Tuesdays admission is free. Some fine handicrafts are available in the gift shop, and paintings by Nova Scotia artists can be purchased in the Art Sales gallery.

Parks and Gardens
At the south end of the city are extensive coastal and forest paths in the 75ha (186-

T he Old Town Clock - a gift from Prince Edward to Halifax in 1803.

acre) **Point Pleasant Park**, which is on a 999-year lease from the British Government, for which a shilling (about 10 cents) a year is paid. Fortress ruins and a 1797 Martello tower are found in the park. Another park, known as **The Dingle**, is the Sir Sandford Fleming Park in Dingle Road on the North West Arm. Sir Sandford, who donated it, was the creator of Standard Time Zones. The **Public Gardens**, cultivated since 1753, provide a pleasant retreat in South Park Street. Originally private, they have a much-photographed bandstand opened in 1867, the year the province joined the Confederation of Canada. Sunday afternoon concerts are given in summer. The gardens are open from spring to late autumn.

A Good Day's Work
Take a look at the little chapel of Our Lady of Sorrows at South Park and Morris Streets. On 30 August 1843 there was an empty site. The following evening the chapel stood there, completed in a day. More than 1,800 people were involved in its construction.

Museums
Eleven thousand years of human settlement are revealed in archaeological exhibits at the **Nova Scotia Museum of Natural History** in Summer Street. Its seven galleries cover botanical, geological, marine, bird, insect and reptile topics.

The **Maritime Museum of the Atlantic**, open year-round, is at Lower Water Street. It recalls the great days of sail, when shipbuilding was a major industry in Nova Scotia. Shipwrecks and sea rescues, small wooden craft, the age of steam and Canada's first hydrographic vessel are represented. Moored outside the museum is HMCS *Sackville*, a World War II convoy escort corvette, restored in tribute to the

courage of the Canadian sailors who served in the war. Next to the *Sackville* is an interpretive centre, open only in summer, where a multimedia presentation is narrated by a World War II veteran of the Battle of the Atlantic.

Dartmouth
The scenic ferry trip across the harbour to Dartmouth is good value at 85 cents one way. A boardwalk at Dartmouth's waterfront provides views of the two long bridges which span the harbour, and the McNabs and Georges Islands.

Canada's leading marine research centre, the **Bedford Institute of Oceanography**, open all year on weekdays, is at the Dartmouth end of the Mackay Bridge. A self-guided tour takes 45 minutes. Admission is free.

Dartmouth has 23 lakes within its city boundaries. The Micmac Indians used them as part of a canoe route to the Bay of Fundy. In the 19th century the Shubenacadie Canal was developed, connecting Halifax Harbour with the Shubenacadie River system. The canal soon fell into disuse, but recent archaeological digs have unearthed artefacts now exhibited in the **Fairbanks Interpretive Centre** at Waverley Road. Visitors can operate a 9m (30ft) working model of a lock. Two key sections of the canal have been restored, and the **Shubenacadie Canal Interpretive Centre** in Alderney Drive shows how the canal was built and operated. Displays explain the working of turbine waterwheels and locks. Both centres open from early June to early September, all day on weekdays, afternoons only at weekends. Admission is free.

Westphal, Dartmouth, is the core of the oldest black community in the metropolitan area. The **Black Cultural Centre for**

Nova Scotia, in Cherrybrook Road, presents black people's history and culture in the province from the 1600s.

Festivals and Events

Summer festivals are a great feature of Halifax. Regulars include the Nova Scotia International Tattoo, Canada Day celebrations and the Moosehead Grand Prix, all in early July, the 7-day **Atlantic Jazz Festival** in mid-July, and – also in July – the Metro Scottish Festival. The first weekend in August sees Natal Day celebrations in Halifax and Dartmouth, with fireworks and street parades among the activities. One of the favourites, the Buskers International Street Performers Festival, is also in August, and a lot of people make a regular date with the Summer Market of the Nova Scotia Designer Craft Council in August.

Dartmouth is the meeting point for competitors from across North America during the first half of July for the 3-day, foot-tapping Maritime Old Time Fiddling Contest and Jamboree.

Nova Scotia Travelways

Each trail has its own symbol identified on signposts and on the Scenic Travelways Map which is available from more than 70 visitor information centres throughout the province. They follow slower-paced trunk and collector roads rather than the rapid transit highways.

The Evangeline Trail

This 320km (200-mile) route between Yarmouth on the west coast and Halifax goes through the lovely **Annapolis Valley**, a fruit-growing region of fertile red soil with a blossom festival in late May celebrated from Windsor to Digby. There are side trips to little fishing communities on the Bay of Fundy. The towns and villages along the way are small: the biggest are **Kentsville** (population 5,500) and **Yarmouth** (population 7,800).

Our route is from east to west, leaving Halifax by Highway 101. History buffs will find Nova Scotia's last surviving blockhouse at the 1750 Fort Edward, a National Historic Site at **Windsor**. Two historic house museums here can be visited in summer, Haliburton House and Shand House. **Grand Pre National Historic Site** is located at the Acadian village in which Longfellow's epic poem *Evangeline* is set. **Wolfville** is a pleasant university town with Victorian houses, an art gallery and a museum. For one of the best views of the Annapolis Valley and Minas Basin, turn right on to Highway 358 at **Greenwich** to the lookout. Off Highway 101 (Exit 16) at Aylesford, **Oaklawn Farm Zoo** has the largest number of cats and primates in the Atlantic Provinces among its many animal and bird species.

Works of noted painters Ken Tolmie and Ted Colyer can be seen in an 1806 house, the Gallery at Saratoga, on Highway 201 at Carleton Corner, Bridgetown. From Highway 1 in the centre of Bridgetown, drive about 10km (6 miles) to the Bay of Fundy to explore the trails and waterfalls of Hampton, Young's Cove, Parker's Cove and Delaps Cove. A 3km (2-mile) wilderness trail at Delaps Cove leads to a 13m (43ft) waterfall.

Annapolis Royal

Back on the Evangeline Trail, Annapolis Royal has a prototype installation at the

Annapolis River Causeway generating hydroelectric power from the Bay of Fundy tides. The Tidal Power Project can be viewed from mid-May to mid-October, with free admission.

Kejimkujic National Park

Before Annapolis Royal, take a diversion from the Evangeline Trail and turn left for Highway 8 for Kejimkujic National Park. The park, with its own scenic drive, is a great recreational area of boreal forest, lakes and waterways – canoes can be rented – hiking and cycling trails, back country camping, fishing, swimming and cross-country skiing. There's a chance of seeing rare Blandings turtles, white-tailed deer, porcupines, beavers, frogs, loons and owls. The drive of about 115km (71 miles) provides a link between Annapolis Royal and Liverpool, on the south shore.

Fort Anne National Historic Site at St George's Street is Canada's oldest, the original fort having been built by the French in about 1643, and British officers' quarters and gunpowder magazine dating back to the early 18th century. Neighbouring Port Royal's National Historic Site is a reconstruction of the 1605 Habitation, a French fur-trading post. A few minutes west of Annapolis Royal is **Upper Clements Park**, an amusement centre with rides, including a flume, pedal boats, a roller coaster, carousel and other attractions. Native Nova Scotia animals are at Upper Clements Wildlife Park across the road.

Digby

The ferry to Saint John, New Brunswick, goes from Digby, which claims to have the world's largest scallop fleet. About 1.5km (1 mile) from the ferry terminal is **Fundy Summer Park**, with water-

slides, a pool and mini-golf. A thin spit of land called **Digby Neck** continues westward on Highway 217. Along here is a much-photographed tall pillar of rock, balanced precariously with part of its base on land and part hanging over the sea. Just beyond the end of the Neck is **Brier Island**, a prime place for whale-watching and birdwatching trips. Seabirds from Antarctica are sometimes seen.

Return to the Evangeline Trail and join Highway 1 to **Church Point**, where St Mary's Church, the largest, tallest wooden church in North America, serves a population of 500. Built in the early 20th century, it is 58m (195ft) long and 41m (135ft) wide, with a 56m (185ft) spire which sways so perilously in the sea wind that it has been stuffed with 40 tons of rock to act as ballast.

The ferries to Bar Harbor and Portland, Maine, leave from **Yarmouth**. Yarmouth County Museum has collections of nautical paintings, furniture, glass, china, toys, costumes, musical instruments and genealogical material on local families.

Lighthouse Route

You are now positioned to start the Lighthouse Route along the coast to Halifax. This is a region of watersports, commercial fishing, boatbuilding and a seafaring history. Anyone researching family trees will find helpful genealogy records in small museums. **Tusket**, on the outskirts of Yarmouth on Highway 3, has the oldest standing courthouse in Canada, built in 1805. From early June to the end of August, guided tours are available. As well as the courtroom you see the judges' chambers, grand jury room, cell block and jailer's quarters.

Follow Highway 3 south to **Shag Harbour**, where a former church built in 1856 houses the Chapel Hill Museum, open from mid-June to mid-September. Domestic and community life is depicted, and the belfry is used as an observation tower. Out to sea, with binoculars, you can see offshore islands. After dark the lights of five lighthouses are visible, but the museum closes at 5pm.

The Lighthouse Route continues south to a collector highway, number 330, to **Cape Sable Island**, after which a very stable and shallow-draught boat is named. It was designed here in 1907. The standard Cape Islander is 11.5m (38ft) long and nearly one-third that in beam. It is used mainly for lobstering. Cross the causeway to the island's **Archelaus Smith Museum** which portrays local history, fishing techniques and equipment including the Cape Sable Island boat, shipwrecks and genealogical records of the fishing community in pre-Loyalist days.

The Old Meeting House at **Barrington**, on Highway 3, dates back to 1765, and is the oldest nonconformist place of worship in Canada. Wool processing from fleece to hand-spinning can be seen at Barrington Wool Mill.

Trails can be followed on horseback and canoe trips are available on the Clyde River north of **Port Clyd**e.

Shelburne

In 1783, 30 ships from New York City arrived at Shelburne, then a wilderness area, and some 3,000 United Empire Loyalists disembarked. Others followed, and over the years the population grew to 10,000 (it has now dwindled to about 2,250). Shelburne's Loyalist heritage story is told in the **County Museum** in Dock Street, along with the town's shipbuilding and fire-fighting interests. The **Genealogical Research Centre** has extensive material

*S*helburne, a settlement of 18th-century United Empire Royalists, is on the Lighthouse Route.

and family files. **Ross-Thomson House**, built around 1784, is part of the museum complex. It has been refurbished with pre-1820 furniture and stock and is Nova Scotia's only surviving 18th-century store. Now a museum, it is open daily from early June to mid-October. The town once had seven companies building dories for the fishing fraternity. The **Dory Shop**, like Ross-Thomson House, maintained as one of Nova Scotia Museum's 25 properties around the province, is a three-storey factory which produced dories for 90 years, closing in 1970.

Liverpool

There are opportunities for wildlife viewing between Shelburne and Liverpool, including a region known as the Seaside Adjunct of the Kejimkujic National Park. The Kejimkujik Scenic Drive (see p.300) ends (or begins) at Liverpool. The **Queens County Museum** reflects its turbulent past and features genealogical data for the county. Liverpool was the home of privateers who roamed the seas and raided American ships during the war of 1812. Themed events, costumed parades and displays are held at the annual 4-day Privateer Days event at the beginning of July.

From Liverpool you can follow Highway 8 north to Kejimkujik National Park, stopping to see the blacksmith working in the 1903 forge (Monday to Friday, June to August) and the Heritage House Museum at **Caledonia**. It has items relating to life in the 1880s and the North Queens Gold Rush. Craft demonstrations are given. The village has a trout hatchery open to visitors, with an interpretive centre.

The Lighthouse Route leaves Highway 103 for Highway 331 at Exit 17 near **Mill Village**, and passes through a string of scenic seaside villages with walking, swimming, beachcombing and clam digging possibilities. The **Fort Pointe Museum** at LaHave is in a former lighthouse keeper's home and is the site of the first landing in 1632 of the Acadians under Isaac de Razilly.

At Riverport is the 81ha (200-acre) **Ovens Natural Park** – this one isn't a National Park – where in summer, weather permitting, you can take a guided tour by inflatable boat into caves or 'ovens'. The park, which has a small museum, is the site of Nova Scotia's 1861 Gold Rush. You go down concrete steps in the cliff face to the caves. People pan for gold on the pebble beach. The park has self-catering cottages and a campground.

Bridgewater

Bridgewater is a major town of 7,250 people and has a range of visitor services. The annual South Shore Exhibition and International Ox Pull draws crowds in late July. The **Desbrisay Museum**, set in a spacious park, traces the natural history, early settlement and industrial development of Lunenburg County from the early 1700s. About 6km (4 miles) northeast of Bridgewater at **Newcombville** is the Indian Crafts Museum, which is open in July and August.

Lunenburg

Lunenburg (population 2,800) is Nova Scotia's major fishing port and a popular tourism spot. The **Old Town** area is a National Heritage District, with distinctive architecture. The town was settled by Germans and Swiss in 1753, and German was spoken there well into the 19th century. In the last week of August the Nova Scotia Fisheries Exhibition and Fishermen's Reunion takes place, complete with 4 days of dory races, lobster trap making, scallop shucking, music and celebrations. Later on the 4-day Oktoberfest celebrates the German heritage.

The **Fisheries Museum of the Atlantic**, on the Lunenburg waterfront, tells the story of Canada's Atlantic fishermen, their boats and equipment and the fish they caught. There are three floors of exhibits, and visitors can board a schooner and a trawler. In addition there are 90-minute tours of the harbour and its approaches four times a day between mid-June and mid-September on the traditional schooner *Timberwind*.

The Lighthouse Route continues through **Mahone Bay**, which has the Settlers Museum and holds a 5-day Wooden Boat Festival at the end of July, including a boat-building contest. Just up the coast is **Chester**, settled by New Englanders in 1760 and a popular resort with many summer homes. Professional performances are given at Chester Playhouse in July and August. Chester is also the scene of the biggest regatta in the Atlantic provinces in mid-August.

Some way off inland, but worth a diversion if you have the time, is **New Ross**, on Highway 12. Join it from Highway

Bluenose II, Nova Scotia's ambassador schooner, moored at Lunenburg, her home port.

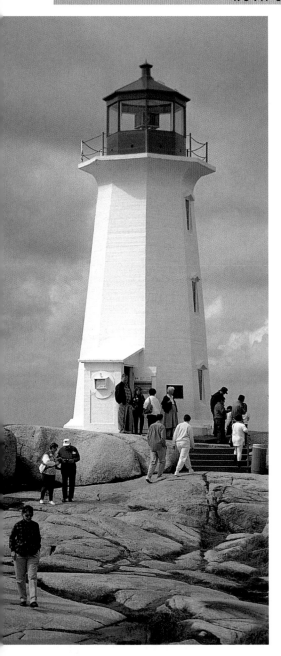

*P*eggy's Cove
Lighthouse is possibly the most photographed in the world.

103, Exit 12, after leaving Mahone Bay. The **Ross Farm Museum** is a farm worked 19th-century style. Daily demonstrations are given of agricultural methods of a past age, and you can see barrels made in the cooperage. Oxen pull the wagon and there are other old breeds of farm animals.

The final lighthouse on the Lighthouse Route is at **Peggy's Cove**. It is no longer operating, but is arguably the most photographed lighthouse in the world. Coachloads and carloads of people arrive daily in summer from Halifax and elsewhere to see the small but archetypal picturesque fishing village (population 120). The lighthouse, with a tiny Post Office in its ground floor, is set among great rounded boulders often slapped by the wild sea. Peggy's Cove has a 30m (100ft) sculpture showing fishermen, their wives and children, with a guardian angel. It was carved in the granite rocks outside his home by William deGarthe, as a permanent memorial to Canadian fishermen.

The Glooscap Trail
According to Micmac legend, the Bay of Fundy tides were created by Glooscap and the Great Spirit long ago, hence the name of this trail around the Fundy shore covering a total of 365km (228 miles) between Amherst and Windsor. You can search the beach for semi-precious stones, look for fossils millions of years old, go down a coal mine and experience river rafting – backwards!

The trail begins at the gateway to New Brunswick, where the Missaguash River forms the border with Nova Scotia. Highway 2 leads to **Amherst**, where settlers from Yorkshire, in the north of England, arrived in the 1780s. Four Fathers of the Confederation were born in the area. The

Bluenose

The famous schooner *Bluenose*, built at Lunenburg in 1921, was undefeated champion of the North Atlantic fishing fleet and winner of international schooner races. It even won its way on to the Canadian dime. Lunenburg is the home port of *Bluenose II*, a replica of the original. It was launched in 1963 and is a grand sight around the coast or in Halifax Harbour.

home of one of them, Senator RB Dickey, is the Cumberland County Museum.

Blueberries are a major crop in the fertile land around Amherst. **Springhill**, at the junction of Highways 2 and 142, is worth a visit southeast of the trail for its Miners Museum, off Highway 2 at Black River Road. The museum commemorates a coalmine that had more than its share of disaster – 125 miners killed in 1891, a rock fall killing 39 in 1956 and 75 men trapped 3km (2 miles) underground in 1958 – 19 of them were rescued alive after being buried for a week or more. Retired miners are your guides on the surface and 274m (nearly 900ft) below. A statue in the town pays tribute to the miners involved in the disasters.

South of Amherst at Upper Nappan, the trail leaves Highway 2 and joins Highway 302, then turns right on Highway 242 at Maccan to **Joggins**. This is a fascinating place where you can see trees and plants which have become fossilized in cliffs, and are more than 100 million years old. Although this is a protected site, you are allowed to take away small fossils which can be carried by hand. From June to September Joggins Fossil Centre offers two-hour tours of the fossil cliffs with guides who can indicate fossilized trees, ferns, insects and amphibians. There's only one tour a day, so it's wise to pre-book: tel. (902) 251-2727.

If you're interested in Joggins, visiting the new Fundy Geological Museum at **Parrsboro** is imperative. Poised above the Bay of Fundy's high tides, eroding cliffs reveal wonderful fossils which contribute to this important collection. Specimens of

The tiny village of Peggy's Cove, near Halifax, attracts thousands of visitors every summer.

amethyst, agate, jasper and onyx are among stones displayed. Parrsboro Rock and Mineral Shop and Museum, run by collector Eldon George for nearly 50 years, has displays of fossilized footprints of dinosaurs and other creatures.

From July to September the Ship's Company Theatre presents evening performances of plays, mainly by new Maritimes writers, aboard the *MV Kipawo*. The vessel was a passenger ferry used in the Minas Basin and Newfoundland waters from 1926 to 1976. The dramatic effect of the high tides can be seen at Parrsboro, where the harbour empties completely, and farther into the Minas Basin at **Economy**, where red sand is left bare at low tide for 1.5km (1 mile).

Bible Hill, at the approach to **Truro**, has harness racing on Sunday afternoons and Thursday evenings all year. More than 50 bird species, including game birds, peacocks, tropical birds, finches and doves, can be seen at Acres of the Golden Pheasant. Truro's **Victoria Park** at Brunswick Street has a children's playground, a baseball field and tennis courts within its 400ha (1,000 acres). It also has hiking trails and two waterfalls. Getting to the top of a deep gorge in the park involves climbing 200 steps up Jacob's Ladder. **Shubenacadie Provincial Wildlife Park**, 5km (3 miles) south of Highway 102, Exit 11, is 20ha (50 acres) of woodland containing native animals and birds and some imported ones. The deer are remarkably tame.

The Glooscap Trail continues along the Minas Basin shore to Windsor (see p.299).

Marine Drive

This trail takes you from Dartmouth to the Canso Causeway on the eastern shore – about 400km (250 miles). Along the way you'll encounter picturesque fishing communities, scenic beach parks, forests and a village from the 1860s brought to life. There's not as much active sightseeing here as on some trails, but you'll have plenty of opportunities to relax on a beach.

From Dartmouth join Highway 7 to **Musquodoboit Harbour**. Musquodoboit Railway Museum is in the former CNR Station built in 1918. You can board an old caboose and other rolling stock and follow the story of Nova Scotian railways. Middle Musquodoboit offers the Musquodoboit Valley Forest Nursery and Education Complex, which is acclaimed as one of Canada's finest forest awareness centres. Here you'll find trails, demonstrations, a study area and an arboretum of young native trees.

Back at the coast, **Martinique Beach**, 5km (3 miles) long, is the most extensive in the province, It is a Provincial Park with picnic facilities and supervised swimming. Other first-class beach parks in the area are at **Clam Harbour** and **Spry Bay**.

Follow Highway 7 for Jeddore Oyster Pond. The Fisherman's Life Museum il-

---

Tidal Bore

Set on the main line of the Canadian National Railway, between Montreal and Halifax, Truro is known as the hub of Nova Scotia. The Salmon River runs through Truro. The tidal bore which rolls along against the current can be seen from several points, including Tidal Bore Road. It can be up to 1.5m (nearly 5ft) high. To find out tide times telephone **Call a Tide** on 426-5494.

It is on the Shubenacadie River that you can go rafting backwards, or up-river, as the Fundy tidal bore pushes upstream. Two local companies operate trips between mid-May and mid-October. Expect a truly exhilarating (and wet) experience.

lustrates the life of an inshore fisherman and his family at the turn of the century. In August, Clam Harbour Beach Sand Sculpting Contest draws crowds.

Look out to sea at **Ship Harbour** and you'll see thousands of white buoys. These mark North America's biggest cultivated mussel farm. The Department of Aquaculture Demonstration Centre has a small interpretive centre. Along the coast you will encounter small communities whose people have earned their living from the sea for generations. From Spry Harbour a local road goes northwest to **Moose River Gold Mines**, where a mine site and museum mark the area's gold-mining heritage and the story of a famous 1936 rescue unfolds. At **Tangier**, south of Spry Harbour, nearly 30,000 ounces were mined between 1860 and 1890. Today the coastline around Tangier is popular for sea kayaking. From north of **Sheet Harbour**, where the lumbering industry has long been established, a local road leads to **Liscomb Game Sanctuary**, where native wildlife lives in a vast wilderness area, and people can camp, canoe, fish and watch birds. It's used for snowmobiling, too.

Sherbrooke Village

Originating as a fur-trading post in the 1650s, Sherbrooke developed as a lumbering and shipbuilding town. Gold was discovered, and for two frenetic decades in the 1860s and 1870s, hordes moved in hoping to become millionaires. The route to Sherbrooke was known as the Gold Coast in those heady days. Now Sherbrooke is best known for its restored 19th-century village. It is very much alive and in working order, with people busy at the water-powered sawmill, the smithy and the wood turner's shop. A horse-drawn wagon goes by, and the tea room provides welcome refreshments.

With the decline of shipbuilding, Sherbrooke's fortunes nosedived until, in the early 1970s, the Nova Scotia Museum's restoration project revived the village. More than two dozen buildings on their original sites include an emporium, a craft shop, a doctor's office and an opulent home. The 1858 courthouse is still used for court sessions, the general store has been renovated and services are held at the Anglican and Presbyterian churches. Visitors can put on 19th-century costume and pose for a portrait at the photographer's studio, where 19th-century techniques are demonstrated.

For many the most impressive aspect of Sherbrooke Village is the sawmill, fed by five lakes, typical of mills operating on streams and rivers throughout Nova Scotia more than a century ago. It is believed to be the only one of its kind in the province today capable of full production by water power. Sherbrooke Village is open daily from June to mid-October.

Grassy Island

Another of the eastern shore's beach parks is at **Tor Bay**, on the road to Canso. A newly developed National Historic Site is accessed from Canso – Grassy Island, 1km (about half a mile) off the coast. The Grassy Island Interpretive Centre is on a wharf in Canso. A daily boat takes visitors to the island, the site of a number of ruins where a small community from New England once flourished. An interpretive trail links the sites. The **Whitman House Museum**, once the home of a wealthy merchant, has a traditional Widow's Walk.

Humpback and finback whales are sometimes sighted from the Marine Drive in the narrows north of **Chedabucto Bay**. The drive ends at **Canso Causeway**.

Sunrise Trail

This 316km (162-mile) route explores the shore along the Northumberland Strait between Amherst and the Canso Causeway. The western end is one of the world's great blueberry-producing areas. Bays, beaches, saltmarsh, pastoral and arable country are featured in a region settled by Scottish Highlanders more than two centuries ago. The skirl of the pipes is heard as their heritage is celebrated at various centres in summer.

Amherst (see p.304) is the first town in Nova Scotia at the isthmus which connects the province to the rest of Canada. Follow Highway 366 to **Tidnish**. There are several good beach parks as you follow the trail to **Port Howe**, and almost every village has its lobster pound where you can choose your supper. **Pugwash** is a pleasant place to swim in the sea – the water is the warmest in the province – laze on beaches of fine sand, play golf or take a trip on a converted lobster boat. The Gathering of the Clans and Fishermen's Regatta is a great day of celebration at the beginning of July.

The Sunrise Trail goes along Gulf Shore Road from Pugwash to **Wallace** and **Malagash**, where you can tour Jost Vineyard – one of only two in the province. At the farming and fishing community of **Tatamagouche** is the Sunrise Trail Museum in Main Street, outlining history and lifestyles of the area from the times when Micmac Indians were the only residents to the early 20th century. Some 19km (6 miles) southeast of Tatamagouche, off Highway 311 on Highway 256, the **Balmoral Grist Mill**, built in 1874, is on a deep gorge on Matheson Brook. Grain is ground into flour by water power – morning and afternoon demonstrations are given – and a unique

Scottish oat-drying kiln can be seen.

Another use of power from a past age is demonstrated at a Denmark museum on Highway 326. **Sutherland Steam Mill** is a restored woodworking mill where sleighs, carriages and other smaller items were made with the aid of a steam boiler between 1894 and 1958. The museum opens daily from June to mid-October, and occasionally the steam boilers are fired up to drive the machinery. Both this and Balmoral Grist Mill are run by Nova Scotia Museum.

Pictou

A shipload of Scottish Highlanders – 33 families and 25 bachelors – landed on 15 September 1773 at Pictou, dubbed 'Birthplace of New Scotland'. Their ship was the *Hector*, and the passengers were the first of many Scottish immigrants. A 5-day celebration of Scottish heritage and culture is held, not in September but in August while the tourist season is in full swing. The **Hector Heritage Quay** is on Pictou's waterfront, where a newly built full-scale replica of the three-masted ship proudly stands. In the interpretive centre at the Quay you can experience the rolling motion the immigrants endured on board. A carpenter's shop, blacksmith's and gift shop are at the site, open daily from July to October. The **Hector National Exhibit Centre** in Old Haliburton Road has exhibits relating to the early Scottish immigrants, with much archive material.

Pictou **Lobster Carnival** is a 4-day celebration begun, more than 60 years ago, during the first half of July. It includes a seaside parade, boat racing, fishermen's competitions and lobster suppers. The town's de Coste Entertainment Centre has drama, ballet, music, comedy and other shows year-round. The Burning Bush

Centre Museum records two centuries of Presbyterian history, and has records of early settlers. Pictou's Olde Foundry Art Centre encompasses antique dealers with an auction barn and the Ship to Shore complex of arts and crafts outlets. Potters, sculptors, weavers and other artists can be seen at work at the site. A display of paintings, a working blacksmith's shop of 1855 and a museum of shipbuilding artefacts can be visited.

New Glasgow and Stellarton

With nearly 10,000 people, New Glasgow is the largest community on the Sunrise Trail. Its **Nova Scotia Museum of Industry**, opened in 1994, exhibits industrial machinery from throughout the province. *The Samson*, dating from 1838, was the first locomotive in British North America, working at the Albion Mines at **Stellarton**, just south of New Glasgow. Coal was discovered in 1798 in Stellarton. Canada's coal mining was pioneered here, and continued until quite recently. You'll know you're in Stellarton when you see the fire hydrants smiling. Faces have been painted on about 60 of them.

Antigonish

The Sunrise Trail skirts the north shore and drops south at **Cape George** to Antigonish, another major town. Antigonish put itself firmly on the map by hosting the Antigonish **Highland Games**, a 3-day event in mid-July, with Highland dancing, piping, caber-tossing, concerts and a tattoo. They've been doing it every year since 1861. The town also has a theatre festival through July and August at the Bauer Theatre on the campus of the St Francis Xavier University. Students from more than 80 countries study community development programmes at the univer-

sity. The Heritage Association of Antigonish displays pioneer artefacts and local records in the former CNR station in East Main Street.

The Sunrise Trail ends at the Canso Causeway – gateway to popular Cape Breton Island.

Cape Breton Island

Allow at least a week if you're planning to tour Cape Breton Island at a leisurely pace. The island, where John Cabot is believed to have landed in 1497, divides neatly into three chunks, one of which is the glorious **Cabot Trail** in the northern highlands, which we will keep for a final treat. It can be approached from the **Ceilidh Trail**, most of which hugs the west coast, or from **Baddeck**, on the Bras d'Or Lakes. Two further trails are suggested by the Nova Scotia tourism authority, although we shall regard them as one entity. The **Fleur de Lis Trail** signposting was not complete at the time of writing, and although we shall make visits along its route, we will not follow it precisely. The **Marconi Trail** is short – 70km (44 miles) – and follows a coastal route from Louisbourg to Glace Bay.

Thirty different cultures are represented in Cape Breton Island. Arts and crafts can be bought, from the bright, beaded tapestries and basketware of the Micmac people to Acadian hooked rugs.

Southeast: St Peter's to Glace Bay

Our tour begins in the island's southeastern region. **Port Hastings** is where you find yourself when you've crossed Canso Causeway (opened 1955). From there drive east to **Port Hawksbury**, an indus-

New Harris Forks

trial town, and follow Highway 104 to **St Peter's**, where a canal enables small boats to enter the **Bras d'Or Lakes** from the Atlantic Ocean. This is an inland sea – a 1,165sq km (450-sq mile) saltwater lake which is one of the world's great sailing waters. It freezes over in winter.

St Peter's Canal, open from May to October, was built in the mid-19th century. Overlooking it is the **Nicolas Denys Museum**, named after the Frenchman who set up a fort at St Peter's in 1650, and containing items emphasizing the contribution made by Denys to local history. For centuries the native Micmacs have lived around the Bras d'Or Lakes. One of their reserves, **Escasoni**, is the largest in Nova Scotia. At **Chapel Island Reserve**, near St Peter's, a spiritual and cultural event for the Micmac nation attracts thousands at the end of July.

Bras d'Or Lakes Scenic Drive

This scenic drive provides a circular tour which can be accessed from several points. It's a noted route for seeing bald eagles. From St Peter's you could do the complete 960km (600-mile) circuit, or use part of it as a scenic route to **Sydney**, the province's third largest town. The lake is surrounded by hills, and small communi-

Mist shrouds the Cape Breton Island end of the Canso Causeway.

ties are dotted around the shores. One of them, **Iona**, is the 7ha (17-acre) site of the **Nova Scotia Highland Village Museum**, presenting the Scottish heritage in nearly a dozen historic buildings, tracing the settlement of Highlanders 200 years ago. The buildings include a Hebridean croft house, a forge and a school house. On the first Saturday in August, Highland Village Day is celebrated here.

From Big Bras d'Or birdwatching boat trips, with an expert on board, go daily to the islands of **Hertford** and **Ciboux**, nesting grounds of the Atlantic puffin. At **Big Pond**, on Highway 4 on the East Bay of the lake, there are daily guided Bald Eagle Tours in summer, and woodland and shoreline nature walks. A little farther east, at **Ben Eoin**, is a mountain trail with a lookout over the lake.

Sydney has been a major steel and coal-mining centre for many years. Coal mining has been the basis of the economy in much of Metropolitan Cape Breton – North Sydney, Sydney Mines, Dominion,

New Waterford, Reserve Mines, Glace Bay and Louisbourg. Three-quarters of Cape Breton's population live here – 28,000 of them in Sydney. Artefacts in Sydney's Roman Catholic **St Patrick's Church Museum**, built in Pioneer Gothic style in 1828, depict the history of the city and Cape Breton. Sydney has an international airport, from where there are daily flights serving major Canadian and American cities.

The **Marconi National Historic Site** at Table Head, Glace Bay, on Highway 255, documents the sending of messages across the Atlantic by electromagnetic waves. It has a model of the radio station by which Marconi sent the first message in 1902.

Retired miners guide you through the **Ocean Deeps Colliery** at the Miners Museum at Glace Bay. On Tuesday evenings a programme of mining songs sung by 'Men of the Deeps' is very popular.

Louisbourg

South of Glace Bay on Highway 22, Louisbourg is a fishing village which is home to the Atlantic Statiquarium Marine Museum. Opened in 1976, it exhibits recovered sunken treasure, model ships, fishing gear and a saltwater aquarium of fish and sea creatures. The Sydney and Louisbourg Railway Museum tells the history of the local railway system in a restored 1895 station. An old caboose, baggage car and coach are on site.

Fortress of Louisbourg

The famous Fortress of Louisbourg Historic Site brings hordes of people to the area from June to September, when costumed actors and reconstructions place you firmly in 1744. (In May and October there are free tours to some of the buildings, but no animators.) This is an authentic reconstruction of a 250-year-old town with a living, working community. It is the biggest historic reconstruction in North America, covering a total area of 50sq km (20sq miles). Started in 1961, it never stops growing. Among some 50 buildings are taverns, a chapel, prison and the magnificent **King's Bastion**, complete with officers' quarters and a 10-room suite for the governor.

Ceilidh Trail

This 107km (67-mile) drive starts at Port Hastings. Highway 19 goes north, mainly by the coast, where you will find good supervised swimming at **Court House Beach** in Port Hood. Colindale Road, which is unpaved, leads to more beaches. Through rolling hills and farmland you reach **Mabou**, where Gaelic is taught in the school. Mabou Gaelic and Historic Society Museum, The Bridge, is a centre for crafts and local music and poetry as well as historical and genealogical records.

Near Mabou, at **Glenville**, is Glenora Distillery, which can be toured. This is reputedly North America's only distiller of single malt whisky. The local population of about 45 is augmented by visitors staying at the distillery's inn. The nine guestrooms, restaurant, lounge and shop are around a courtyard through which a stream runs.

The largest town on the Ceilidh Trail is **Inverness** (population 1,950), a fishing port and home of Inverness Miners Museum, housed in the 1901 CNR station, which relates mining history in the area. It has a craft shop. An 1840s farmhouse on Highway 395, the MacDonald House Museum, occupies a good site overlooking Lake Ainslie. Old farm machinery, carpentry tools, a loom, spinning wheel and other items are exhibited.

*A*lexander Graham Bell
and his wife spent their summers
in Baddeck for many years.

Cabot Trail

The Italian navigator John Cabot is believed to have sighted Cape Breton Island in June, 1497, while exploring North America on behalf of the English Crown. Hailed as one of the most beautiful drives on the continent, and even in the world, the Cabot Trail is 296km (185 miles) long, and goes through **Cape Breton Highlands National Park**. In places you can stand at a clifftop viewpoint and see the sea more than 300m (1,000ft) below. You can join the Cabot Trail at **Margaree Harbour** at the northern end of the Ceilidh Trail, if that is your point of ar-

rival. Many poeople make straight for the Cabot Trail from the Canso Causeway via the TransCanada Highway (Highway 105), joining it at Baddeck on the shore of the Bras d'Or Lakes. Our tour follows the trail clockwise from here.

Baddeck

Baddeck, an international yachting centre with a week-long regatta in early August, is a delightful place to spend a night or two. Small in itself – its population is about 1,100 – it has world class resort accommodation offering such activities as boating tours, canoeing, mountain biking, tennis, gymnasium workouts and 90-minute lake trips by schooner. From mid-May to the end of October, daily 8-hour guided bus tours of the Ceilidh Trail leave from Baddeck.

Baddeck is where Scots-born inventor and humanitarian Alexander Graham Bell spent his summers for 37 years, until his death in 1922 at the age of 75. The **Alexander Graham Bell National Historic Site** at Baddeck commemorates his work in the fields of medicine, genetics, aeronautics and marine engineering as well as the telephone. There is a great deal to see, including the hydrofoil boat which was built under Bell's supervision.

From Fish to Folk Art

The Margaree River is one of the world's great salmon rivers, and the Margaree Anglers Association operates the **Margaree Salmon Museum** in a former schoolhouse. Cape Breton arts and crafts are displayed and spinning and weaving demonstrations given at the **Museum of Cape Breton Heritage**. Both these enterprises are located at North East Margaree. A little farther north, four-hour boat trips to **Margaree Islands** wildlife preserve depart from Margaree Harbour at 9am and 2pm.

Cheticamp is an Acadian fishing village by the Gulf of St Lawrence at the western entrance to Cape Breton Highlands National Park. The **Acadian Museum** at Cheticamp has a craft shop with locally made hooked rugs. Acadian-style food is served. In **Les Trois Pignons** is the Dr Elizabeth LeFort Gallery and Museum, containing historical and cultural artefacts but especially noted for its collection of Dr LeFort's works. Known as Canada's 'Artist in Wool', she has crafted more than 300 tapestries, some of which are in the Vatican, the White House and Buckingham Palace.

Cape Breton Highlands National Park

Hiking trails in the National Park, which opened in 1936, range from short strolls to treks with overnight camping. Call at Cheticamp Visitor Information Centre – or **Ingonish** if you're using that entrance – for details of facilities and points of interest. Incredible views can be seen from lookoffs. Animals in the park include black bear, bobcat, lynx, mink, beaver, moose and white-tailed deer. Golden eagles and bald eagles also live there.

Near Pleasant Bay is the **Lone Shieling**, a replica of a crofter's cottage. It was built in 1942 in tribute to Scottish settlers. One of the park's highest waterfalls is **Beulach Ban Falls,** where silvery water drops 3km (nearly 2 miles) near Big Intervale. Whale-watching boat trips go from several points along and near the trail – Cheticamp, Capstick, Cape North and Ingonish.

The northernmost part of the Cabot Trail is **Cape North**, a village near **Cabot's Landing Provincial Park**. Spectacular seascapes and landscapes reveal themselves round each hairpin bend as you drive along the park's western edge. **Ingonish** has a beach and is the home of the renowned Keltic Lodge resort. **Cape Smokey**, a 366m (1,200ft) headland above the Atlantic Ocean, provides great views.

The Gaelic College

North America's only Gaelic educational institution is the Gaelic College of Celtic Arts and Crafts at South Gut St Anns. All summer young people attend classes to nurture Scottish culture and heritage – the Gaelic language, Scottish dancing, music and singing, the weaving of tartans, even the making of musical instruments. Some say there is more Gaelic spoken in Nova Scotia than in Scotland.

For the descendants of Scottish settlers and their friends, the big event of the summer is the 4-day **Nova Scotia Gaelic Mod**, an annual celebration since the late 1930s. The gathering takes place during the first half of August, with competitive events, solo piping, pipe band performances, drums, and highland dancing. Demonstrations may cover sheepshearing, spinning the wool, dyeing and weaving it.

Within the college, and open to the public from June to mid-October, is the **Great Hall of the Clans**, where the history and culture of the Scots and their development over the centuries are depicted, including the Great Migration from the Highlands from the early 18th century. Displays with figures in national dress represent the 12 clans who first settled in the area. In July and August the Great Hall of the Clans is open daily, with *ceilidhs* performed each day. In June and from September to mid-October it is open from Monday to Friday.

Between September and June educational programmes are held in Scottish music, language and culture. There are hiking, biking and cross-country skiing trails on the property.

NEWFOUNDLAND AND LABRADOR

Land the Vikings Found

Where in Canada has a Viking settlement of 1,000 years ago been discovered? Where do people speak with the soft accents of Ireland and England's southwest? Where are there such quaintly named places as Blow Me Down Provincial Park, Heart's Delight and Come By Chance? And where do the dogs have webbed feet?

The web-footed dogs are Newfoundlands, which gives you all the other answers: Newfoundland and Labrador, the province whose capital, St John's, is the most easterly in North America. The province has about 570,000 people in a land mass of 72,586sq km (28,354sq miles).

A Viking settlement dating back to about ad1000 was discovered at L'Anse aux Meadows in Newfoundland's northern peninsula by a Norwegian archaeological team in 1960. John Cabot sighted Cape Bonavista on the Avalon Peninsula in June, 1497, and claimed the land for England. The French and English were

An iceberg off the coast of Newfoundland dwarfs a fishing boat.

subsequently to fight over it for years, but in 1763 the Treaty of Paris gave Newfoundland to Great Britain. **St John's** was built on the sheltered harbour and is one of North America's oldest cities. The province is the latest to join the Dominion of Canada, retaining its independence until 1949.

The earliest known inhabitants of Newfoundland and Labrador were Maritime Archaic Indians, whose burial ground at L'Anse-Amour, Labrador, dates back to 7,500 years ago.

It was John Cabot – the Italian explorer Giovanni Caboto – who showed the way for the expansion of European culture into North America, and celebrations marking the 500th anniversary of Cabot's visit will be attended by people from many parts of the world in late June, 1997.

315

Newfoundland and Labrador lives largely off the sea. It has 17,000km (10,625 miles) of deeply indented coastline. Immigrants from several European countries arrived to harvest the cod and Newfoundland became a fishing outpost of Europe. The province's dense forests provide lumber for the great paper mills of Corner Brook and Grand Falls, which supply much of the world's newsprint. Mining is another industry which has contributed to the economy.

In recent years more people have been getting to know Newfoundland for its skiing. It is also known for the number of whale species to be found around its shores, including pilot whales and killer whales, and for its birds – particularly seabirds. There are puffins, piping plovers, black guillemots, storm petrels and black-legged kittiwakes. At the Cape **St Mary Seabird Sanctuary**, thousands of gannets jostle for a place on Bird Rock, which looms out of the sea. Whale-watching and birdwatching are only two of the many activities available. Another is **iceberg watching**. Icebergs the size of skyscrapers, some with spires and other sculpted adornments, drift by in early summer, eventually to melt in more southerly waters.

Labrador is separated from the island of Newfoundland by the Strait of Belle Isle.

Getting There
By air: **St John's International Airport** is served by Air Canada, Canadian International Airlines, with their associated carriers, and other airlines. Flights within the province are provided by Air Atlantic, Air Nova, Air Alliance, Provincial Airlines, Labrador Airways and Canada 3000. The flight to St John's from London, England, is about 5 hours, from Toronto and Boston about 3 hours, and from Goose Bay, Labrador, 2 hours. The airport is situated 10km (6 miles) from the city. **Taxis** run from the airport into St John's.

By ferry: A Marine Atlantic car ferry service operates daily all year between **Port aux Basques**, Newfoundland and North Sydney, Nova Scotia. The crossing takes 5 hours in summer and longer in other seasons. From mid-June until the end of September, a twice-weekly ferry service runs between **Argentia**, Newfoundland and North Sydney, Nova Scotia, taking about 14 hours. Twice weekly from mid-June to early September, a ferry service operates between **Lewisporte**, Newfoundland and **Goose Bay**, Labrador. Direct sailings take about 35 hours. Those calling at **Cartwright**, Labrador, take about 38 hours.

By rail: The **Quebec**, **North Shore and Labrador Railroad** has a passenger service between Sept-Iles, Quebec and Western Labrador.

By long-distance bus: Long-distance bus (coach) services provides links within the province.

Accommodation
Hospitality homes are an option in the province. Some are open only in summer, others are year-round. They are in houses with one, two or more guestrooms – you'll probably have to share a bathroom. A hearty breakfast may be complimentary, possibly with home-made bread. You eat with the family. Newfoundland people are extremely hospitable, friendly and welcoming, with a gift for recounting stories, some of them 'tall' ones. Because of this, as well as the

home cooking, hospitality homes have become an increasingly popular form of accommodation.

Alternative accommodation includes housekeeping cabins and cottages, bed and breakfast accommodation, inns, motels and hotels – St John's has three- and four-star hotels. **Campgrounds** are usually in attractive park locations. Camping facilities in Labrador are less abundant than in the south. Most trailer parks with hook-ups open from late May to late September, though some extend the season a little at either end, and some do not open until mid-June. One or two offer free space for senior citizens. Primitive campgrounds in national parks may be free, but advance registration at a Visitor Centre or the warden's office is required.

Climate

July and August temperatures range from 11°C (52°F) to around 20°C (68°F) in St John's, with only slight variations in other parts, bearing in mind that any given day can vary in areas where the weather is affected by mountains or the sea. Summer temperatures can reach 30°C (90°F), even in southern, western and central Labrador. Winter temperatures can drop to -8°C (-47°F) in St John's and -25°C (-80°F) in Goose Bay.

St John's

Weatherboarded houses painted in different colours and modern office blocks make an interesting mix along the waterfront in St John's in the province's **Avalon Peninsula**. Much of the city was wiped out by a fire in 1892. It has changed little since being rebuilt, with narrow streets. **Water Street**, situated by the exception-ally sheltered harbour, escaped the fire and is considered one of North America's oldest commercial streets, dating from the 16th century.

Signal Hill provides a good view of the city. This National Historic Site was originally where flags were hoisted to signal the approach of ships so that merchants could prepare for them. The final battle of the Seven Years War took place between English and French forces at Signal Hill. In 1901 Marconi received the first transatlantic wireless signal. The **Cabot Tower**, built in 1897 to commemorate the 400th anniversary of Cabot's voyage, has exhibits and a gift shop. From mid-July to mid-August a military tattoo is held.

The **Colonial Building** in Military Road, built of white limestone brought

A scientist visits a gannet colony on Baccalieu Island, north of Conception Bay.

from Cork, Ireland, housed the Government of Newfoundland from 1850 to 1960, when the 12-storey Confederation Building East Block opened in Prince Philip Drive. The Legislative Assembly meets here. In 1985 the six-storey West Block opened, housing provincial government offices.

Guided tours of the **Basilica Cathedral of St John the Baptist** in Military Road are available all year. Built in the shape of a Latin cross, and consecrated in 1855, it has twin towers 42m (138ft) high, and is noted for its stained glass by Irish, English and French artists. The Anglican Cathedral of St John the Baptist at Church Hill is considered a prime example of ecclesiastical Gothic architecture. The original building was destroyed in the 1892 fire, and the present construction was completed in 1905.

Commissariat House in King's Bridge Road is a fine Georgian house. It was built

*T*he Basilica of St John the Baptist towers over Newfoundland's capital city.

Visitor Information

For further information, contact the **Department of Tourism and Culture**, Box 8730, St John's NF A1B 4K2; tel (709) 729-2830. More than two dozen Visitor Information Centres dotted around the province are open daily in summer.

---

between 1818 and 1821 as a residence and office for the Assistant Commissioner General of the British garrison. It has been restored to the 1830 period – and therefore has no electricity. Costumed guides show visitors around daily during the summer.

Some 9,000 years of the province's history unfold at the **Newfoundland Museum** in Duckworth Street. The museum outlines the cultures of six Native groups – the Maritime Archaic, Dorset, Beothuck, Micmac, Montagnais/Naskapi and Labrador Inuit – as well as the lives and traditions of European settlers. The St John's area also has museums on pharmacy, nursing and police work.

The **Murray Premises** at the waterfront in Harbour Drive has speciality shops, boutiques, craft shops, pubs, restaurants and offices in a restored 1845 fishing and trading warehouse. Close by the

memorial to Newfoundland's war dead in Water Street, a **plaque** marks the area where Sir Humphrey Gilbert planted the Royal Standard of Queen Elizabeth in 1583, thereby claiming 'the new found land' for Britain.

St John's has a population approaching 100,000, and **Pippy Park**, at the north end of the city, is one of the extensive recreational areas enjoyed by residents and visitors alike. It has cross-country ski trails, hiking trails, a fitness trail, playgrounds, picnic areas and a trailer park. There are two public golf courses – 18-hole and 9-hole.

The memorial **University Botanical Garden** is at Mount Scio Road, Pippy Park. It has rock gardens, wildlife gardens, a heather collection, alpine house and a display of plants grown in the province before 1940. Trails outside the formal gardens lead through different terrains where 26 butterfly species, more than 250 native plant species and 126 bird species have been identified.

The **Newfoundland Freshwater Resource Centre** – the Fluvarium – is in Pippy Park. Brook trout, brown trout and Arctic char can be seen on guided walking tours in July and August. The Fluvarium is one of the few attractions in hilly St John's that is wheelchair accessible.

Guides in Royal Artillery uniform of the period staff the **Quidi Vidi Battery**, a fortification erected by the French during their capture of St John's in 1762. It was shortly to be reconstructed by the British, who occupied it for 90 years. The battery has been restored to its 1812 state and is open daily in summer. **Cape Spear National Historic Site**, 11km (6½ miles) south of St John's, is the easternmost part of North America. Its wooden lighthouse guided sailors from 1836 to 1955. The

beacon has been moved to a new tower and the lighthouse restored to the 1840 period and refurnished as a lightkeeper's home. With its visitor centre and gift shop it is open daily between mid-June and early September. The grounds, which provide spectacular coastal views, are open all year.

A rowing regatta, claimed to be the oldest continuing sporting event in North America, is held on the first Wednesday in August. The first was held in 1826. The **Royal St John's Regatta** is held on Quidi Vidi Lake, with six oarsmen to a fixed-seat boat rowing a 2.6km (2-mile) course.

Newfoundland and Labrador **Folk Festival** takes place at St John's in the first weekend in August, attracting performers from throughout the province.

Several skippers run **boat tours** of St John's Harbour and Cape Spear under sail. Others go to seabird-watching locations.

Original Newfoundland plays are staged in the 200-seat theatre at the **Resource Centre for the Arts** in Victoria Street. Modern and classical programmes are also held, and an art gallery is maintained at the premises.

Excursions from St John's

Several small coastal communities, or outports, are within an easy drive **northeast** of St John's – Petty Harbour, Logy Bay, Torbay, Pouch Cove. Take Highway 30 from the capital and turn on to **Marine Drive**. The **Ocean Science Centre** is at Logy Bay. Oceanic research is carried out at the centre, which is a division of the Memorial University of Newfoundland. Guided tours lasting an hour start every half-hour from late June to early September. You see harbour seals and native species of fish, crustaceans, sea anemones and other marine creatures.

Marine Drive takes you through places like **Middle Cove** and **Outer Cove**, which provide great **sea views**, particularly if a cathedral-sized iceberg happens to be floating south in spring or early summer. They may be centuries old, breaking off Arctic glaciers and drifting south to melt in waters warmed by the Gulf stream southeast of Newfoundland. **Pouch** (pronounced Pooch) **Cove** is one of the earliest settlements, documented at least from 1611. **Torbay** was probably named by immigrants from Devonshire, in southwest England, where there's a town of the same name.

The Web-footed Dog

As well as having webbed feet, the Newfoundland dog, a gentle giant, has two fur coats to keep out the cold when he rescues someone from the icy water. The dogs have proved themselves time and time again to be instinctive life-savers, looking after sailors and fishermen for hundreds of years. They are believed to be descended from the North American black wolf, crossed with great bear dogs brought over by the Vikings, and tamed by the indigenous people.

To visit **Bell Island** in Conception Bay, take Highway 40 out of St John's and drive to Portugal Cove. From there a 20-minute ferry ride gets you to Bell Island. Once a small farming community, the island became a prosperous hive of activity when iron mining began there in 1896. It continued until a gradual phasing out in the 1960s. Bell Island was the first casualty of enemy action in Newfoundland waters in 1942, when a German submarine sank two ships being loaded with iron ore. A monument pays tribute to the sailors who died and the islanders who rescued the survivors. In **Wabana** internal and external murals can be seen at the Community College and other buildings. They are local art students under the direction of artist John Littlejohn.

Highway 10 from St John's leads to **Witless Bay Ecological Reserve**, through dairy cattle country farmed by the descendants of Irish settlers. From **Bay Bulls** you can get a tour boat to see three rocky islands where seabirds nest by the thousand. It is estimated that more than three-quarters of a million Leach's storm petrels nest on Gull Island and Great Island and

A sculpted iceberg glides past the harbour lighthouse at St John's, Newfoundland.

74,000 murres nest on Green Island. Thousands of Atlantic puffins dig burrows in the steep sides of the islands, to protect their chicks from marauding gulls. Whales are often seen by the shore in late spring and summer, feeding on tiny fish called capelin. More than a dozen species of whale are recorded in the ocean around Newfoundland. Those most frequently seen are minkes and huge humpbacks.

La Manche Provincial Park is worth a stop for its wildlife, marshland flowers, remains of an abandoned settlement and La Manche River, popular with canoeists and photographers. A herd of 5,500 caribou lives in the **Avalon Wilderness Reserve**. A permit to visit the park is obtainable from the La Manche park office.

The public can see an archaeological site at **Ferryland**, west of the Avalon Reserve, where teams have been working since 1993 in an area which was settled from the early 1600s until it was destroyed by the Dutch in 1763. Some of the finds are on display. Northwest of the Avalon Reserve is the **Salmonier Nature Park**, a wilderness reserve with a large enclosed exhibit area where visitors can get a close-in look at about 30 animal and bird species

native to Newfoundland and Labrador. They include owls, otters, beavers, lynx, moose, caribou and foxes.

In the south of the Avalon region is **Cape St Mary's Ecological Reserve**, a seabird sanctuary. It is signposted from Highway 100 and is along a 16km (10-mile) road. Walk from the lighthouse to the point overlooking Bird Rock. You have to see it to believe that so many gannets each with a wing span of 2m (6ft 6in) could find a foothold, let alone nest there. Thousands of kittiwakes and murres rear their young at the sanctuary.

Placentia, on Highway 100, was called Plaisance when it was the French capital of Newfoundland in the early 1600s. It has an extensive beach. **Castle Hill National Historic Park** has the ruins of a fortification which was very active when the French and British were constantly at loggerheads. Appropriately the interpretive centre at the site is in the form of a bunker built into the hillside. North of Placentia, off Ship Harbour in 1941, US President Franklin D Roosevelt and British Prime Minister Winston Churchill had a meeting at sea which led to the drawing up of the Atlantic Charter. A monument marks the meeting.

Travellers driving north on Highway 80 go through **Heart's Delight** and **Heart's Desire** to **Heart's Content** and the cable relay station, now a provincial historic site, where the first successful transatlantic cable was landed in 1866. Guides in period costume show visitors around.

17th-century Wreck
The wreck of a British ship, HMS Sapphire, lies in deep water at Bay Bulls. It was sunk in action against the French in 1696. During the 1970s it was excavated by Newfoundland Marine Archeological Society.

Western Newfoundland

Port aux Basques
The ferry terminal for North Sydney,

The Newfie Bullet

They still talk about the Newfie Bullet. For more than 70 years it carried passengers along nearly 880km (550 miles) of narrow gauge track from St John's to Port aux Basques, going north into Newfoundland's wilderness interior. A steam locomotive pulled the first train in 1898. Diesel engines powered the last one in 1969.

With wry Newfoundland humour, it was nicknamed the Bullet because of its slow speed: the story goes that you could get off a front coach, pick enough blueberries for a small pie and climb back on to a rear coach.

Building the railway involved long and arduous labour in the days before mechanization. When it was finished it was subject to flooding in places, moose on the line, deep snowdrifts which halted the Newfie Bullet for more than a fortnight in 1941, and high winds that caused havoc. These were no ordinary high winds. At Table Mountain, north of Stephenville, a curious geological situation has the effect of transmitting wind gusts of more than 160kph (100mph) which have blown railway freight trucks into the Gulf of St Lawrence.

Eventually a man named Lauchie MacDougall, who lived by the railway in the valley below Table Mountain, was appointed to the post of human wind gauge. He was under contract to decide whether the wind was strong enough to endanger the train. If the gusts were too high, the Bullet was anchored by chains – sometimes being held up for 2 or 3 days until the gale abated. MacDougall sniffed the wind for years, until his death in 1965.

Nova Scotia, is in Newfoundland's **southwest** corner at Port aux Basques. The accent is on nautical matters at the community museum. A rare 17th-century astrolabe and other antique navigation aids, a century-old diving suit and artefacts from the ferryboat SS *Caribou* are displayed. The *Caribou* was torpedoed in World War II with the loss of 133 lives. The **Long Range Mountains**, thickly wooded and stretching along the western side of Newfoundland, are part of the Appalachian escarpment.

Corner Brook

Corner Brook, the province's second city, is about a 3-hour drive from Port aux Basques, at the mouth of the Humber River. The TransCanada Highway connects the two towns. Corner Brook has a population of about 23,000. Its paper mill is one of the largest in the world.

Corner Brook is a convenient base for exploring the west. The town has an **Arts and Culture Centre** with a 400-seat the-

atre and an art gallery. The work of Newfoundland artists is highlighted at the **Franklyn Gallery** in West Street. The public library is within the impressive 10-storey **Government Centre**, which has on its ground floor the glass fountain featured at the Czechoslovakian Pavilion at Expo '67 in Montreal. **Margaret Bowater Park** is in the centre of Corner Brook. It has a grandstand, children's play area and an outdoor swimming pool.

At the former Humbermouth Station, the Railway Society of Newfoundland has a narrow gauge passenger train with steam locomotive, a good train with diesel engine and other equipment on view from mid-June to mid-September. There are mountains on three sides of the town. **Blow Me Down Cross-Country Skiing** operates from mid-December to early May. On a site at **Curling**, with a view of Corner Brook and the Bay of Islands, there is a monument to Captain James Cook, the British explorer, who surveyed the west coast.

In February Corner Brook's famous **Winter Carnival** is centred on Marble Mountain, and in July the annual **Hangashore Folk Festival**'s traditional music and fun attracts people from all over the province. Boat tours go from Corner Brook along the Humber River and into the Bay of Islands.

Southeast of Corner Brook, in the St George's Bay area, is **Stephenville**, where the month-long **Festival of Arts** takes place in July and early August.

North of Corner Brook

Follow the TransCanada Highway north to **Deer Lake**, where the Humber Valley Heritage Museum offers a look at local life in the early 1920s. North of Deer Lake is **Cormack**, which has Funland Resort, a summer attraction with heated swimming pool, water slides, playground, mini-golf, games arcade and trailer park. A little farther north is Granny Tucker's, an old-time general store with goods displayed from as long ago as the early 18th century, to the 1900s. It has a craft shop and tea room.

Near Deer Lake fork left off the Trans-Canada Highway on to Highway 430 to **Wiltondale Pioneer Village**, a reconstruction of an early 20th-century community, with a house, barn, school, church and general store. A tea shop and gift shop are also on site. Wiltondale is near the southern edge of **Gros Morne National Park** at Rocky Harbour. This was designated a World Heritage Site in 1988 for its geological qualities, its mountains, gorges and fiords. Hikers find a range of trails, some of them challenging. Among other activities are camping, nature study, boating, snowshoeing and cross-country skiing. The park covers 1,943sq km (760sq miles). Within the park is the **Fun Park**, open from late May to early September. It has boating at Rocky Harbour Pond, a go-kart track, mini-golf, tube riding, swimming, canoeing, bumper boats, aqua bikes, water skiing and a 'moonwalk' for children. Riding stables at Rocky Harbour offer rides from half an hour to overnight trips.

As you leave Gros Morne National Park northwards on Highway 430, call at the **Arches Provincial Park** to see a natural triple archway in the rock, the effect of the tides over thousands of years. Halfway along the Great Northern Peninsula of Newfoundland is **Port au Choix National Historic Site**. In 1968 three burial grounds containing nearly 100 human skeletons were discovered. Known as the Red Paint People because of the red ochre lining of their graves, carbon dating revealed the remains to be between 3,200 and 4,300 years old; they were identified as Maritime Archaic Indians who inhabited the Newfoundland and Labrador coasts up to 9,000 years ago. Some of the remains, and relics buried with them, are exhibited at the park's interpretive centre.

An inflatable boat takes a group of iceberg watchers for a close-up view.

The Northern Peninsula

From **St Barbe** a car ferry service runs across the Strait of Belle Isle to Blanc Sablon in Quebec between May and December. Blanc Sablon is just over the border with Labrador. In late spring and early summer the mighty icebergs from the High Arctic and Greenland cruise southward down the Gulf of St Lawrence.

L'Anse aux Meadows National Historic Site

The first European settlement in North America was established about 1,000 years ago by the Vikings, in the north of the Northern Peninsula of the island of Newfoundland. L'Anse aux Meadows National Historic Site is believed to be where Leif Eiriksson founded a colony following the discovery of the region when Bjami Herjolfsson was blown off course during a voyage from Iceland to Greenland in 986. Around ad1000, Eiriksson and a team of 35 searched for the lands, believed to be Newfoundland and Southern and Northern Labrador, which Herjolfsson had spotted, and found what they called 'Vinland'. The Viking site at L'Anse aux Meadows was discovered in 1960 by a Norwegian team, and work continued into the 1970s. Designated a UNESCO World Heritage Site in 1978, the site has the remains of two cooking pits and several buildings – four workshops, three dwellings and a smithy. Reconstructed sod houses illustrate the type of dwelling of the period. The interpretation centre displays some artefacts found at the site.

St Anthony

About 42km (26 miles) south of the Viking site is St Anthony, where a craft centre raises money for the Grenfell Mission. The Mission was founded by Dr Wilfred Grenfell in 1892, to provide medical services for the isolated populations of the Northern Peninsula.

Central and Eastern Newfoundland

The large **central** region of Newfoundland is virtually wilderness, with scattered communities, provincial parks, hiking trails, good fishing and hunting and coastal settlements like **Harbour Breton** which are accessible only by boat. Some of the roads are partially paved. There is much natural beauty, with dense forests where loggers earn their living.

Archaeological sites provide evidence of the lives of the Beothucks – the now-extinct aboriginal tribe – in the area. The Beothucks travelled the river systems to the coast to fish and hunt in summer, returning to live by rivers and lakes in winter. The **Baie Verte Peninsula** has many worked-out mines which produced copper, lead, zinc, asbestos, some gold and silver, and other minerals. Some mine sites can be visited, and the Miners' Museum in Baie Verte town has displays of the different minerals found in the region and mining artefacts from the mid-19th century.

One of the main towns in the central region is **Grand Falls** (population 9,130), where a major supplier of newsprint is based. The Mary March Regional Museum at St Catherine Street depicts the 5,000-year history of the Beothucks, who survived until the early 19th century.

Gander

Gander (population 10,200) is well

known for its international airport, which began as a transatlantic base set up by the British Air Ministry in the early 1930s and has operated as an airport since 1938. The camouflaged wartime Lockheed Hudson bomber mounted outside the terminal commemorates the pilots of the Atlantic ferry who crossed the Atlantic many times during World War II. A plaque records the bomber's first flight from Gander to Aldergrove, Northern Ireland, and finishes: 'Better be not at all than not be noble'. Historic aircraft and a water bomber (used to fight forest fires) can be seen at the Hudson Bomber Memorial Voodoo at Elizabeth Drive, Gander.

Cape Bonavista

The **eastern** region is set between Cape Bonavista and the Burin Peninsula, with **Trinity** and other communities along its coastline and a network of provincial parks, and **Terra Nova National Park** occupying much of the northern sector at its northwestern edge. Its eastern neighbour, connected by a neck of land at **Chance Cove**, is the Avalon region. Bonavista Bay has tuna, swordfish and giant squid as well as cod, and the town of Bonavista is a centuries-old fishing centre. The lighthouse at Cape Bonavista has been restored to the 1870 period, having first guided shipping in 1845. Costumed guides show visitors around.

Terra Nova National Park

Terra Nova National Park, overlooking Bonavista Bay, protects some 400sq km (156sq miles) of rugged, deeply indented coastline and sheltered bays. Activities include camping, nature study, cross-country skiing, mountain biking and boating. There's an 18-hole golf course at **Twin Rivers**, the southern entrance to the park.

Tea Dolls

You can find handicrafts in Labrador rarely seen in other parts of the province. An Innu needlewoman, Angela Andrew, who went to school at Happy Valley, was taught to make tea dolls by her mother. She developed her own type of doll – woman dolls, mother and papoose dolls, Innu hunter dolls – smoke-tanning caribou skin in the traditional way for some of the clothing. The dolls have become collectors' items. They are stuffed with tea leaves from the local store. Traditionally, this meant that when Innu families were on the move, even tiny children carried something useful.

The Visitor Reception Centre here has interpretive exhibits and an audiovisual presentation about the park's flora and fauna, trails and facilities. At the western entrance at **Eastport Park**, the Splash 'n' Putt Resort has mini-golf, bumper boats, water slide, go-karts and heated pools.

Trinity

North America's first Court of Justice was established at Trinity in 1615. The Trinity Loop Attraction at Trinity Bay has a miniature train, bumper boats, water trikes, pedal boats, kayaks and mini-golf. The town has a railway museum and the **Trinity Interpretive Centre**, where the town's establishment and development from the 17th century is traced. A shoe-making shop, cooperage and commercial fishing, sealing and sailing exhibits can be seen at Trinity Community Museum, open from mid-June to mid-September. .

The region offers a choice of boat trips, from harbour tours in Bonavista Bay to 2-hour 'Iceberg Alley' tours between Bonavista Bay and Trinity Bay. *The Adventure I*, based at Southport, Trinity Bay, takes up to 12 passengers to see humpback whales and to look at the puffin colony at

Duck Island. They also go beachcombing at Great Heart's Ease.

Grand Bank

Grand Bank, on the Burin Peninsula, at the edge of some of the world's richest fishing grounds, takes a great pride in its history, having been first settled in 1650. In a building resembling the sails of a schooner is the Southern Newfoundland **Seamen's Museum**, with interesting displays and models of boats. Soccer is a passion in the Burin Peninsula, which has a **Soccer Hall of Fame** at Grand Bank. National championship teams have been spawned in places like St Lawrence and Grand Bank. Boys and girls play, graduating to the senior team.

Labrador

Labrador is for the traveller rather than the tourist. This region of mainland lakes and mountains extends a long way north to **Ungava Bay**. The vast interior is one of the world's last great wildernesses. People who make the journey speak of the extraordinary beauty of the **Torngats**, where glacial action, erosion and geological upheavals over many thousands of years have produced a weird and wonderful landscape.

In an area of nearly 300,000sq km (117,000sq miles), the resident population is only 29,000. Aborigine people lived in Labrador 9,000 years ago, when it was on the edge of retreating glaciers. Today there are Innu and Inuit people and descendants of European settlers who have arrived since the 16th century. An archaeological dig at **L'Anse-Amour** in the southeast of Labrador uncovered a burial ground of the Maritime Archaic Indians. It is now a Site of National Historic Significance. A mound of rocks here is the earliest-known funeral monument in the new world. It marks the grave of a child who lived about 7,500 years ago. Buried with the body were a walrus tusk, a harpoon head and a bone whistle.

Between 1550 and 1600, a score of whaling ships from France's Basque country and Spain sailed to **Red Bay**, on Labrador's southeast coast, to hunt right whales and bow head whales. A visitor centre opened recently by the community of Red Bay interprets the early industrial complex revealed by archaeological research and the setting up of a whaling station more than 400 years ago.

At Happy Valley/Goose Bay the **Labrador Heritage Museum**, open in summer, displays native animal skins – beaver and silver and red fox – and a trappers' tilt – the form of shelter used in the wilderness. In the same area is the Snow Goose Mountain Ski Club, with five trails of varying degrees of difficulty.

A Moravian Mission was set up at **Nain**, in northern Labrador, in 1771. A collection in Piulimatsivik-Nain Museum reflects the history of the Mission. There are also implements and artefacts giving an insight into daily life in the north. Piulimatsivik, incidentally, is a Inuktitut word meaning 'place where we keep old things'. The museum is open only by appointment – tel. (709) 922-2842. Even farther north, at **Hebron** on the shore of Kangershutsoak Bay, the Moravian Mission built a church and mission house in 1830. It is said to be the oldest wooden building in Eastern Canada. It stands at the water's edge in a bleak, windswept terrain, and was finally abandoned in 1959. In 1970 it was designated a National Historic Site.

Canadian international teams train at the

Labrador's lakes and rivers teem with large salmon, char and a variety of other fish.

Menihek Nordic Ski Club in **Labrador City**, in western Labrador, an iron ore-mining area. In recent years a road has been built to link Happy Valley/Goose Bay with Labrador City. The road goes through **Churchill Falls**, a modern town which grew up around the 300m (975ft) falls on the Churchill River. It is the site of one of the world's largest hydroelectric generating stations.

Organized Trips in Labrador

The ferry-operating company Marine Atlantic has a working vessel, the *Northern Ranger*, which plies the Labrador coast from Lewisporte, on the island of New-foundland, right up to Nain, taking in a total of more than 40 ports of call. Trips of 5, 8 and 15 days are available for passengers.

A number of operators offer adventure packages in Labrador. Sport fishing and hunting, canoeing, wildlife watching, natural history tours, camping by horseback, hiking and biking are among the options.

Day **cruises** operate from Happy Valley/Goose Bay along the Churchill River and from Cartwright into Sandwich Bay and Gannet Island. The birds here include many puffins but not a gannet to be seen. The island was named after a 19th-century ship which sank nearby.

The Far North

Many people claim that their idea of a holiday is a back-to-nature experience, away from the crowds, in a place with stunning scenery. So how does the wilderness country of Canada's northern territories appeal? Between them the Yukon and Northwest Territories have a population well below 100,000 and a land mass equal to half that of the continental United States. The Northwest Territories alone takes up about one-third of Canada. It adjoins six provinces to the south, and is the size of India.

Mountain wilderness country, deep canyons, sculpted icebergs as big as high-rise office blocks, the summer tundra of miniature bright flowers, taiga and boreal forests and whitewater rivers will supply enough wonderment to last a lifetime in your memory.

Huge herds of bison, elk and caribou flourish. There are lynx, Dall sheep, Arctic and red fox, wolves, mountain goats, black bears and grizzly bears, polar bears and musk oxen. The birdlife includes whooping cranes, white pelicans and great horned owls. Anglers glory in the Arctic char and other species which they haul out of the rivers. The people of the far north greet visitors with genuine delight and a warm handshake. Visitors to this area are fascinated by the ancient aboriginal cultures they encounter.

Getting There

By air: Whitehorse, Yukon and Yellowknife in the Northwest Territories are served by Air Canada and Canadian Airlines International in conjunction with their respective connectors, Air BC and NWT Air. A number of airlines operate both scheduled and charter flights within the territories themselves.

A warden on patrol in Ellesmere National Park Reserve, Northwest Territories.

By sea: Many visitors reach the Yukon by cruise ship along the Inside Passage, landing at Ketchikan, Alaska, or from

Bellingham, Washington, on an Alaskan Marine Highway car ferry, or from Vancouver to Prince Rupert, British Columbia, by BC Ferries.

By bus: Greyhound Lines has bus services from Edmonton, Alberta, to Hay River on the southern shore of the Great Slave Lake, NWT, and from Edmonton and Vancouver to Whitehorse, Yukon.

Accommodation

The usual range of accommodation is found in the major centres, including bed and breakfast. Motels and inns are usually great distances apart on northern highways and not all guestrooms have private facilities. It is possible occasionally that you may be asked to share a room.

Tourist Information

Visitor Information Centres are open from mid-May to mid-September. For more information about the Yukon and Northwest Territories, contact **Tourism Yukon**, PO Box 2703, Whitehorse, Yukon, Canada, Y1A 2C6, tel. (403) 667-5340, fax (403) 667-2634; **Tourism Marketing Division**, Department of Economic Development and Tourism, Government of the Northwest Territories, Box 1320, Yellowknife, NWT, Canada X1A 2L9, tel. (403) 873-7200 or toll-free from Canada and the United States 1-800 661-0788, fax (403) 873-0294.

When to Go

Unless you're a real hardliner prepared to challenge nature at her harshest – and there are plenty of people who get tremendous enjoyment and a fantastic view of the Northern Lights out of that – the time to go is between **June** and **early September**. They have a T-shirt joke in the Northwest Territories depicting the four seasons as

June, July, August and Winter. Winters are long, and the almost round-the-clock daylight of midsummer is counteracted by the dark days of midwinter. Tourism figures, however, are increasing winter and summer; the Dempster Highway has opened up more of the region and attracts greater numbers of venturesome vacationers every year. The Yukon's tourism figures are enhanced by the thousands who go there primarily for their fascination with the Klondike gold rush days, centred on Dawson City, and find much else to their liking.

Mounties

Many people will have photographs of hunky officers of the Royal Canadian Mounted Police, following their celebrations of 100 years in the Yukon, with a series of their world-famous musical rides during July, 1995. Back in 1894 two officers assessed the region for police requirements and decided 22 would be sufficient in such a sparsely populated area. The 22 took up their duties in 1895. Soon afterwards the police requirement soared as gold prospectors stampeded in.

Peoples of the Far North

Nine official languages, including English, are spoken in the far north, where land claims are being settled throughout the region. Visitors can hear the languages and experience the aboriginal cultures of the small communities of the **Dene**, or native, people. The Dene have lived in the Western Arctic for many centuries. Their ancestors crossed the Bering land bridge from Asia at the end of the last Ice Age.

Ancestors of the **Slavey Indians**, who live near the Nahanni River today, are

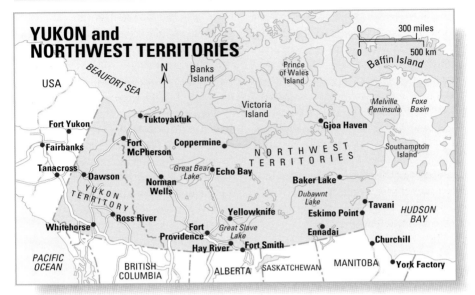

YUKON and NORTHWEST TERRITORIES

0 — 300 miles
0 — 500 km

N

USA
BEAUFORT SEA
Banks Island
Prince of Wales Island
Baffin Island
Melville Peninsula
Foxe Basin
Victoria Island
Fort Yukon
Tuktoyaktuk
Gjoa Haven
Fairbanks
Fort McPherson
Coppermine
NORTHWEST TERRITORIES
Southampton Island
Tanacross
Dawson
Great Bear Lake
Echo Bay
Baker Lake
YUKON TERRITORY
Norman Wells
Dubawnt Lake
Tavani
HUDSON BAY
Ross River
Yellowknife
Eskimo Point
Whitehorse
Fort Providence
Great Slave Lake
Ennadai
Hay River
Fort Smith
Churchill
PACIFIC OCEAN
BRITISH COLUMBIA
ALBERTA
SASKATCHEWAN
MANITOBA
York Factory

believed to have been in Canada's north for about 5,000 years. The **Métis** are descended from Dene and Europeans. The **Inuvialuit** live around the Mackenzie Delta. The **Inuit**, who were formerly known as Eskimos, live north of the tree line. They are descended from a people called the Thule, who arrived in the central and eastern Arctic about 1,000 years ago. The **Europeans** are the descendants of prospectors, traders and Evangelists – mainly English, Scots, Irish and French, who penetrated into the north in comparatively recent times.

Altogether it seems to make for a good mix of the modern and the traditional, though times inevitably are changing. A Dene family in a modern house may have a teepee outside, probably used for drying fish or processing moosehide. It is not unknown for a polar bear pelt to be seen hanging on the guy wire of a satellite dish.

The Dene and Inuit peoples have a foot in each camp, traditional and modern. Many work in business, industry and administration. Others live off the land and water. Their traditional skills and artistic talent are exercised and greatly valued. Many of the hunting and sport-fishing guides employed by outfitters are Native people, whose knowledge of habitats, game stalking and the preparation of trophy catches is invaluable. Visiting big game hunters depend on them.

Native people are proud to share their culture and traditions with fascinated visitors, and are keen to ensure that their languages remain a living part of that culture. The **Yukon Festival of Storytelling**, an annual 3-day event at Whitehorse in late June, was initiated by the First Nations people. A resurgence of interest in their languages has been noted in recent years, and these languages are in the curriculum of a number of schools. Yukon College has a Native Language Centre. The Yukon First Nations people host the **Native Arts** festival, **Native Folklore** and **Indian Days** annual events.

Through packaged tours, visitors can get an insight into the lives of Native people, taking part in a drum dance, seeing moose skin being prepared for making clothes and footwear, eating caribou stew and bannock, listening to ancient Inuit tales. Native culture is demonstrated through museums, Visitor Information Centres, archaeological sites and traditional camps. Their arts and crafts can be found in galleries and shops. Birch bark baskets patterned with porcupine quills, masks and ornaments carved from wood, whalebone and antler, soapstone sculptures, Inuit prints, jewellery, beaded moccasins, mukluks and moosehair tufting are all of a high standard.

Making the Most of Your Trip

Don't expect quite the degree of tourism infrastructure found in so many parts of the world which have been transformed – and perhaps lost their character and individuality – by the influx of holidaymak-

ers. Daily life in Canada's far north is by no means primitive, but because of its geography and low population level many of the roads are unpaved, and special preparations are needed for touring along lonely gravel and dust roads.

Independent and Adventure Travel

If you're travelling independently in this vast northern area, you will need to select a particular region to explore, unless you have your own plane or can afford several charter flights. The distance between the Alberta border and the North Pole is greater than that between London and Athens.

The Northwest Territories has eight tourism zones: Arctic Coast; Baffin; Big River, in the central south; Keewatin, on Hudson Bay's west coast; Nahanni-Ram, in the southwest; Northern Frontier Country, extending north to the barrenlands from Great Slave Lake; Sahtu,

which includes the northern ranges of the Mackenzie Mountains and Great Bear Lake (the eighth largest lake in the world); and Western Arctic, including the Mackenzie Delta. You will find history, First Nations culture, crafts and, wildlife, not to mention magnificent landscapes in all of these areas.

It is suggested that before setting off into the wilderness, you should contact the nearest detachment of the Royal Canadian Mounted Police to tell them your expected date of return – not forgetting to inform them when you get back. That applies also to hikers, trekkers and canoeists. Many areas visited by tourists are so remote that the only means of access is by light aircraft which are available for charter. They are fitted with wheels, floats or skis, depending on your destination.

The Yukon and the Northwest Territories are highly conscious of the fragility of their Arctic and sub-Arctic environment, and a policy of 'no trace' camping is followed. Minimum-impact travel techniques practised by adventure tourism companies such as Whitehorse-based **Arctix Edge** include recommending the wearing of shallow-tread hiking boots, to avoid the effects of trampling and compaction of soil. The company runs guided expeditions involving rafting, ski-mountaineering and dogsledding.

Outdoor Pursuits

Outdoor adventure is the major appeal of the far north. A new and growing sport is

An Inuit warden welcomes tourists arriving at Tanquary Fiord in Ellesmere National Park Reserve.

wild river touring, for ace canoeists. They hurl themselves through the canyons and violent rapids of the South Nahanni River which flows through the wilderness of Nahanni National Park Reserve in the Northwest Territories. Outfitters provide Nahanni River adventures for all grades of canoeists. All the equipment for a 12- to 21-day camping trip is provided except your sleeping bag and roll-up mattress. If you prefer, you can go by **raft** instead of canoe and let someone else do the paddling. Take along some insect repellent. As in much of Canada, once the sun has some warmth in it, vicious mosquitoes take to the warpath.

For a truly Arctic experience you can take a few days' break in April and see the countryside by **dogsled**. The sleds are pulled by teams of hardy Canadian Eskimo dogs. Also available are **polar bear-viewing** expeditions, **trophy fishing**, **hiking** on Baffin Island, **nature study** in the High Arctic and watching the summer migration of thousands of caribou in the barrenlands – these are just a few of the many options.

Organized Tours

The packaged tour is probably the best introduction to the Yukon and the Northwest Territories. Tours are planned to ensure that you get a range of rare experiences. You can, for instance, take a two-centre Arctic Circle holiday with a Northwest Territories company called **Touch the Arctic Adventure Tours**. You have 3 days in the capital, Yellowknife, cruising the Great Slave Lake and visiting the Cameron Falls among other sightseeing. Then you fly over the Arctic Circle to Inuvik. The package includes a trip on the Mackenzie River, a tour of an Inuit village and its craft shops, a typical northern meal

333

in an Inuit home and the chance to dip your toe in the Arctic Ocean.

Many other operators offer packaged tours that escort visitors to places of interest, introducing them to native Inuit and Dene communities, their crafts and wildlife knowledge as well as other aspects of Arctic life.

The North Pole

An escorted expedition to the North Pole is something to write home about. One of these once-in-a-lifetime happenings is an 11-night tour involving a flight from Montreal to the Northwest Territories' Resolution and a Twin Otter flight to the Magnetic North Pole. At the Geographic

Vehicles should be 'winterized' and emergency equipment carried for travelling in the Far North.

North Pole the party stands on thick ice at 90° North, toasting one another in champagne. The night is then spent at Ellesmere Island. Arctic clothing is provided in the price, which isn't cheap, but the trip provides a memorable experience for the fortunate few.

Private pilots flying in this region need to be experienced, with reliable communications and navigational aids, because of the proximity of the Magnetic North Pole. The NWT's Ministry of Economic Development and Tourism tells them: 'Our region is designated as an area of compass unreliability. When this is combined with a lack of visual aids to navigation, absence of radar coverage and lack of distinct landmarks, trips in our area call for cautious flight planning.'

Driving in the Far North

Major Highways

The **Alaska Highway**, built during World War II, goes from Dawson Creek, British Columbia, through the beautiful scenery of the Yukon's southwest corner to Fairbanks, Alaska. Whitehorse and Dawson City, of gold rush fame, are on the **Klondike Highway**. The **Dempster Highway** is a newer, unpaved route, with most of its 730km (450-mile) length remote from civilization. It branches off from the Klondike Highway east of Dawson City, passing through the Ogilvie Mountains and the Eagle Plains on its way

to Inuvik, in the Northwest Territories, about 375km (233 miles) north of the Arctic Circle. In the Yukon it is designated Highway 11 and in the Northwest Territories Highway 8. The **Liard Highway** provides access from British Columbia into the Northwest Territories. To the west are the Mackenzie Mountains.

Highway 3 skirts the western shore of the Great Slave Lake and passes through the Mackenzie Bison Sanctuary. The world's largest free-ranging herd of pure wood bison lives here. The **Mackenzie Highway** enters the Northwest Territories from Alberta. Highway 1 going west from Enterprise to the junction with Highway 3 is known as the **Waterfalls Route**. From the junction, Highway 1 continues west to Fort Simpson, the oldest continuously occupied trading post on the Mackenzie River. It was established in 1804 for the Hudson's Bay Company. The **Top of the World Highway**, an untreated route from Dawson City over the border to Alaska, provides terrific views, running along the top of a spine of mountains.

Highway Services

Work to upgrade roads can take place only in summer. Each year more stretches are paved. More than half the 528km (328-mile) route from the Alberta border to Yellowknife now has an asphalt surface. Services along northern highways have also improved. Most of the little communities along them have filling stations, restaurants and possibly a motel, but the communities are few and far between. Motorists are advised to take on fuel whenever the opportunity arises.

Driving in Winter

In winter the road system is extended by an estimated 50 percent by routes crossing land and frozen lakes and rivers. Off-highway communities and mine workings, cut off except by small plane transport in summer, can use trucks for a few months. Headlamps should be protected by grilles and speeds kept down on gravel or dust roads. All vehicles should be 'winterized' and emergency equipment should always be carried in winter.

River Crossings

Major rivers are crossed by toll-free car ferries in summer. In winter you can drive over bridges of ice up to 2m (6ft) thick. Inevitably there are a few weeks in the shoulder seasons when the ice isn't thick enough to drive over but there's too much of it in the rivers for the ferries to run, so trips have to be carefully timed.

Vehicle Hire

Cars, campers, recreational vehicles and 4WD vehicles can be rented at all major centres throughout the Yukon and Northwest Territories.

Towns and Cities

Yellowknife

Built on gold, Yellowknife is the Northwest Territories' only city. It has a population of around 15,000 and is in the Northern Frontier Country. Its Legislative Assembly meets in a new lakeside building of flying saucer-like design appropriate to the space age. The city's Prince of Wales **Northern Heritage Centre** is a museum chronicling the area's Native culture and the development of gold mining there. Yellowknife grew into a mining town out of the wilderness, by the Great Slave Lake. You see dog teams outside log cabins alongside high-technology

houses built with ecology in mind. Tied up at the lakeside are luxury yachts and freighter canoes used by trappers to reach remote camps.

Whitehorse

Whitehorse took over from Dawson City as capital of the Yukon in 1953. It developed from an encampment set up by gold prospectors nearly 100 years ago, quickly reaching a population of about 20,000. The town has a mix of log cabins and modern buildings, and its eestaurants may have Alaska king crab, Pacific halibut, Yukon River salmon and Arctic char on their menus.

Places to visit in Whitehorse include the **MacBride Museum**, with its reminders of the gold rush , the **Yukon Gardens**, with northern trees and wild flowers, and the **Old Log Church Museum**, showing pioneer architecture and telling of the work of early Anglican missionaries. The museum also tells the story of the bishop who ate his boots, which inspired Charlie Chaplin's film *The Gold Rush*.

The **SS** *Klondike* is on display in the town as a National Historic Site which can be toured. It is one of the sternwheelers which plied the Yukon River until the 1950s, and has been authentically restored.

First Nation skin boats, dogsleds and snowshoes are among the means of getting about featured in the **Yukon Transportation Museum** in Whitehorse. There is also a replica of the 1920s *Queen of the Yukon* aircraft. The city has a fine new

*Y*ellowknife, the capital, is the only city in the Northwest Territories. It's population is a mere 15,000.

The Gold Trail

The Klondike Highway, constructed in the 1950s, was extended to Skagway, Alaska, in the 1980s. The entire road follows the trail of the 1898 gold stampede. The Chilkoot Pass, popular with hikers, is a challenging trail from Skagway to the interior plateau of the Yukon. Hikers, who must take adequate supplies and anticipate harsh weather and terrain, take 3 to 5 days to negotiate the trail. It is bestrewn with evidence of the stampeders' trek – wagon wheels, picks and shovels and pot-bellied stoves.

gallery, the **Yukon Art Centre**, displaying the work of local and international Native and non-Native artists.

Many of the 1890s prospectors sailing the Yukon River in their quest for gold got no further than the Yukon Rapids at Miles Canyon, where their fragile boats broke up. Today the **Whitehorse Power Dam** allows safe navigation through the canyon aboard a 40-passenger trip boat.

Chinook salmon can be seen negotiating the fish ladder in late July and August from a viewing point below the dam.

One of the exciting annual events in the territory is the **Yukon Quest** in mid-February. It's a 1,600km (1000-mile) dogsled race, with viewing points at Dawson, Carmacks and Whitehorse.

Keno

Branching off the Klondike Highway at Stewart Crossing, the Silver Trail leads motorists to the Yukon's historic silver-mining region of Keno. Dating back to the turn of the century, some of the mines produced silver ore right up until the 1980s. **Keno City Mining Museum** has artefacts and memorabilia from the mines' heyday as North America's largest producer of silver.

Dawson City

Dawson City is the Gold Rush Capital. It lives and breathes the era, from displays

in the City Museum and the log cabins of poet Robert Service – 'Bard of the Yukon' – and Yukon writer Jack London, to the nightlife at Diamond Tooth Gertie's. She was a dance hall queen who made a fortune relieving the miners of their gold nuggets. Cancan dancers entertain at Diamond Tooth Gertie's Gambling Hall, with its roulette wheels, blackjack tables and slot machines, and the restored Palace Grand Theatre presents Gaslight Follies. At **Bonanza Creek** you can pan for gold – with success guaranteed!

About 30,000 of the 100,000 who followed the gold trail ended up where they intended at Dawson City by the end of the 19th century. Today the year-round permanent population number about 1,600. A number of Klondike National Historic

Sites in the area are open from mid-June to late August.

It was on 17 August 1896 that gold was first found in the Klondike, and a 4-day **Discover Days** celebration takes place at Dawson in mid-August every year. Another bit of annual fun in early September is the **Great Klondike Outhouse Race**, where people set their outhouses on wheels and race them 2.5km (about 1 1/2 miles) around the city.

Near the city is **Midnight Dome**, a summit which provides a panoramic view of Dawson, the Klondike and the Yukon River Valley. In mid-July the **International Midnight Dome Race** takes place, with Yukoners and visitors alike running from downtown Dawson to the Midnight Dome.

National Parks

The Yukon

The Yukon has two National Parks. **Kluane**, in the southwest, is Canada's largest, with the country's highest mountains. The highest of all, **Mount Logan**,

*P*olar bears and muskoken are among the permanent residents of the Far North.

is 6,107m (19,850ft).The park also has the world's most extensive non-polar icefield. It has abundant wildlife in its forests and tundra, including the sure-footed Dall sheep and mountain goats, which defy gravity on high peaks and narrow ledges.

Ivvavik National Park, in the northwest, was established in 1984. It is dedicated to wilderness preservation and the maintenance of aboriginal lifestyles. The nearest road ends more than 200km (125 miles) from the park boundary, and there are no visitor facilities. Aircraft access is limited to a few locations, and approval for landing has to be obtained in advance. There is some organized **whitewater rafting** in the park.

The Northwest Territories

National Parks in the Northwest Territories are: **Ellesmere Island** and **Auyuittuq Reserves**, which are prime examples of Arctic ecosystems; **Aulavik**, on Banks Is-

land in the western Arctic, which has the world's highest concentration of musk oxen, and has no visitor facilities; **Wood Buffalo**, on the Alberta border, with salt plains, caves and sinkholes; and **Nahanni Reserve**, a wilderness park reached by float plane or helicopter. There are no roads into the park. Day trips to 90m (292ft) **Virginia Falls**, in the park, are available by air from **Fort Simpson**, allowing for about 3 hours' hiking. Guided trips are also available.

A large area of the **Mackenzie Mountains** is in Nahanni Reserve, through which the South Nahanni River flows along deep canyons. Established in 1974, the park, which has some campgrounds, has been designated a World Heritage Area of Global Significance by UNESCO. **Nahanni Mountain Lodge** offers two well-equipped self-catering log cabins, each of which can sleep up to four people.

The Right Place at the Right Price

Hotels

The price range given for the following hotels should be regarded as a general guide. Room rates can vary greatly for the different seasons and there may also be a wide divergence in rates between properties offering similar standards. It is always worth asking whether any special discounts are operating. Be assured that any accommodation you choose, however inexpensive, will be clean and wholesome. As a basic guide, we have used the symbols below to indicate the price per night of a double room with bath, including breakfast.

  | up to $75
  || $75-$125
  ||| over $125

British Columbia

Victoria

The Empress |||
721 Government Street
Victoria, BC V8W 1WS
Tel. (604) 384-8111;
  fax (604) 381-4334
This world-famous Canadian Pacific property is the pride of Victoria and a legend in its own right. People stay here to say they've stayed here. The smooth service and elegant decor are as you'd expect from a hotel of this class. 481 rooms.

Ambleside Bed and Breakfast ||
1121 Faithful Street
Victoria, BC V8V 2R5
Tel. (604) 383-9948
Comfortable 1920s home, handy for downtown and sea, with pleasant antique furnishings.

Inner Harbour ||
412 Quebec Street
Victoria, BC V8V 1W5
Tel. and fax (604) 384-5122
The six-storey hotel has 65 attractively decorated rooms, each with its own kitchenette and electric coffee-maker. Other guest facilities include an indoor sauna, jacuzzi and heated outdoor swimming pool.

Stay 'n' Save Motor Inn |
3233 Maple Street
Victoria, BC V8X 4Y9
Tel. (604) 383-5111
Conveniently located for several noted attractions, this is a friendly place to stay and easy on the pocket.

Vancouver

Hyatt Regency Hotel |||
655 Burrard Street
Vancouver, BC V6C 2R7
Tel. (604) 683-1234;
  fax (604) 689-3707
In downtown Vancouver, this four-star, 644-room hotel is the city's biggest and one of the very best. Built over a vast shopping mall, and with a health club and heated swimming pool, guests need never venture outside. The soundproofed rooms are elegantly furnished, with plush bathrooms, digital clock radios and refrigerators. The hotel

also has two gourmet restaurants as well as a cosy bar.

Cambie Hotel ||
312 Cambie Street
Vancouver, BC V6B 2N3
Tel. (604) 684-6462
The hotel has no restaurant, and there are no extra trimmings, but it does provide a budget place to sleep in lively Gastown.

Holiday Inn Downtown ||
1110 Howe Street
Vancouver, BC V6Z 1R2
Tel. (604) 684-2151
Swimming pool, sauna, exercise room and 210 well-appointed rooms and suites in this modern, efficiently run hotel.

Alberta

Jasper

Jasper Park Lodge |||
Jasper, Alberta T0E 1E0
Tel. (403) 852-3301
Some of the accommodation is in luxurious individual lakeside cabins with open fireplaces. Elks and Canada geese graze in the extensive grounds.

Whistlers Inn ||
Connaught Drive
Jasper, Alberta T0E 1E0
Tel. (403) 852-3361;
  fax (403) 852-4993
Centrally located in a busy spot, the Whistlers provides 44 modern, airy rooms equipped with colour television, radio and good-sized bathrooms. The hotel also has a sauna and jacuzzi.

Banff

Banff Caribou Lodge |||
521 Banff Avenue
Banff, Alberta T0L 0C0
Tel. (403) 762-5887
Rustic decor and friendly staff at this hotel, just outside the downtown but with a free shuttle service. The vast lobby has an enormous fireplace. There are 207 rooms and suites, comfortably furnished and with spacious, brightly lit bathrooms.

Spruce Grove Motel |
545 Banff Avenue
Banff, Alberta
Tel. (403) 762-2112
Basic but comfortable rooms for very low rates, and you get a kitchenette.

Lake Louise

Château Lake Louise |||
Lake Louise, Alberta T0L 1E0
Tel. (403) 522-3511;
fax (403) 522-3894
A fairy-tale castle perched high up in the Rockies and surrounded by pine-clad snowcapped peaks, reflected in an emerald-green lake. The hotel's 531 rooms, some with spectacular views, are elegantly furnished in modern style. Other facilities include an indoor swimming pool, jacuzzi, boutiques and a rooftop restaurant.

Calgary

Westin Hotel |||
320 4th Avenue SW
Calgary, Alberta T2P 2S6
Tel. (403) 266-1611
High-class accommodation in the centre of Calgary. This high-rise hotel has a rooftop swimming pool and a reputation for good food. There are 525 rooms and suites, furnished in delicate pastel shades with excellent bathrooms.

Prince Royal Inn ||
618 5th Avenue SW
Calgary, Alberta T2P 0M7
Tel. (403) 263-0520; fax (403) 298-4888
A downtown all-suite property ideal for families. The suites are furnished for lavish living, with good-sized beds, comfortable armchairs, plenty of wardrobe space and fully equipped kitchens. Some of its 28

floors are non-smoking. There are also secretarial, fax and photocopying facilities for business travellers.

Edmonton

Cherrywood Inn ||
10010 104th Street
Edmonton. Alberta T5J 0Z1
Tel. (403) 423-2450;
fax (403) 426-6090
The Cherrywood's rooms have good, solid cherrywood furniture, and each has its own private balcony and remote-control television. A quiet location. Price includes buffet breakfast. Children stay free in parents' room.

Relax Inn |
18320 Stony Plain Road
Edmonton, Alberta T5S 1A7
Tel. (403) 483-6031
Handy for West Edmonton Mall, the hotel is comfortably furnished and has an indoor pool.

Saskatchewan

Regina

Plains Motor Hotel |
1965 Albert Street
Regina, Saskatchewan S4P 2T5
Tel. (306) 757-8661
This 60-room motel in downtown Regina has units for handicapped people, and nightly entertainment. Rooms are decorated in contemporary style.

Ramada Renaissance Hotel |||
1919 Saskatchewan Drive
Regina, Saskatchewan S4P 4H2
Tel. (306) 525-5255;
fax (306) 781-7188
A new 25-storey building with superb rooms and a three-storey water slide in its recreation complex. The Saskatchewan Trade and Convention Centre is within the building. Rooms are modern and well appointed, with colour television, sitting area and desk. Children under 16 stay free in parent's room. The hotel has two restaurants.

Saskatoon

Westgate Inn |
2501 22nd Street W
Saskatoon, Saskatchewan S7M 0V9
Rooms are attractive and comfort-

able. Some are equipped with kitchenettes. The modest price includes breakfast. Discounts are available for seniors.

Manitoba

Winnipeg

Hotel Fort Garry |
222 Broadway
Winnipeg, Manitoba R3C 0R3
Tel. (204) 942-8251
A 246-room hotel with 33 non-smoking rooms. It has a cocktail lounge, licensed restaurant and cabaret.

Sheraton Winnipeg |||
161 Donald Street
Winnipeg, Manitoba R3C 1M3
Tel. and fax (204) 942-5300
A good downtown location with all the facilities of a major group, including airport shuttle service. Children under 18 stay free in parents' room.

The Delta Winnipeg |||
288 Portage Avenue
Winnipeg, Manitoba R3C 0B8
Tel. (204) 956-0410;
fax (204) 947-1129
Centrally situated, with coffee shop and licensed restaurant, indoor pool and gift shop. The hotel's 272 comfortable rooms are fully equipped with television, hairdryer, radio and coffee-maker. Other facilities include a sauna, exercise room and a free Children's Creative Centre where youngsters can let off steam.

Ontario

Toronto

Holiday Inn on King |||
370 King Street W
Toronto, Ont M5V 1J9
Tel. (416) 599-4000;
fax (416) 599-7394
Light airy rooms with good views, and exceptionally helpful staff, make this a cheerful city base, whether on business or pleasure. Close to theatre district. Other facilities include two restaurants, guest lounge, indoor pool, sauna and fitness centre.

Alexandra Apartment Hotel |
77 Ryerson Avenue
Toronto, Ont M5T 2V4

Tel. (416) 350-2121
*Good budget accommodation in the
downtown, close to Chinatown.
Comfortable rooms.*

**Best Western Chestnut
Park Hotel** ▌▌▌
108 Chestnut Street
Toronto, Ont M5G 1R3
Tel. (416) 977-5000;
fax (416) 977-9513
*A large new 16-storey property
amid downtown Toronto's main attractions and amenities. Rooms are
well furnished with all modern comforts. A restaurant, indoor pool,
whirlpool, sauna and business centre are among the other facilities.*

SkyDome Hotel ▌▌▌
1 Blue Jays Way
Toronto, Ont M5V 1J4
Tel. (416) 360-7100
*Incorporated within the distinctive
SkyDome sports and entertainment
complex. The hotel's most expensive
rooms look out over the arena.*

Journey's End ▌▌
280 Bloor Street W
Toronto, Ont M5S 1V8
Tel. (416) 968-0010;
fax (416) 968-7765
*Plain and simple, but comfortable
and reliable, this new 194-room
downtown hotel is well placed, opposite the Royal Ontario Museum.
The hotel's 212 rooms are modern
and well equipped.*

National Capital Region

Elgin Business Inn ▌
180 Maclaren Street
Ottawa, Ont K2P 0L2
Tel. (613) 232-1121
*Low-cost accommodation with even
cheaper rates at weekends.*

Minto Place Suite Hotel ▌▌▌
433 Laurier Avenue W
Ottawa, Ont K1R 7Y1
Tel. (613) 232-2200;
fax (613) 232-6962
*Close to Parliament Hill, the hotel
has over 400 well-equipped suites
with one or two bedrooms. Kitchens
are fully equipped, with microwave,
electric stove, dishwasher, toaster
and coffee-maker. Children under
18 stay free in their parents' suite.*

Holiday Inn Crowne Plaza ▌▌▌
2 Montcalm, Hull, Quebec

Tel. (819) 778-3880
*A pool and a fitness centre, boutique
and coffee shop are among the
many amenities in this comfortable,
modern hotel.*

Quebec

Montreal

Best Western Europa ▌▌▌
1240 rue Drummond
Montreal, Que H3G 1V7
Tel. (514) 866-6492
*Close to many of Montreal's attrac-
tions, shopping and nightlife, the
Europa has a rooftop terrace and
an open-air swimming pool.*

Hotel Américain ▌
1042 rue St-Denis
Montreal, Que H2X 3J2
Tel. (514) 849-0616
*Well situated in the Latin Quarter,
close to Old Montreal, this 54-room
hotel offers very good value.*

Hotel du Parc ▌▌
3625 avenue du Parc
Montreal, Que H2X 3P8
Tel. (514) 288-6666
*A popular fitness centre, indoor
pool and underground boutique
help to make this a delightful downtown base.*

Quebec City

Château Frontenac ▌▌▌
1 rue des Carrières
Quebec, QC G1R 4P5
Tel. (418) 692-3861;
fax (418) 692-1751
*Quebec City's magical castle cele-
brated its 100th anniversary in 1993
with the construction of a new 66-
room wing, an indoor pool and gym.
Special packages and senior discounts are available.*

Hotel Manoir de l'Esplanade ▌▌
83 rue d'Auteuil
Quebec, QC G1R 4C3
Tel. (418) 694-0834;
fax (418) 692-0456
*This hotel has only 37 rooms but
that is twice as many as a lot of the
old hotel properties within the
walls. All rooms have private bathrooms. The hotel operates a ski bus
and is very conveniently placed for
the winter carnival festivities.*

Radisson Gouverneur Québec ▌▌▌
690 boulevard St-Cyrille Est
Quebec, QC G1R 5A8
Tel. (418) 647-1717;
fax (418) 647-2146
*There are 365 spacious rooms, a
fully equipped health club and a
substantial conference centre in this
modern, conveniently located hotel
not far from the old city walls.
There's also a restaurant and piano
bar on the premises.*

Hotel Château de la Terrasse ▌▌
6 Place Terrasse-Dufferin
Quebec, QC G1R 4N5
Tel. (418) 694-9472
*Facilities are fairly basic in this 18-
room hotel in the shadow of the
Château Frontenac, but it has a
good position within the city walls.*

New Brunswick

Saint John

Colonial Inn ▌
185 City Road
Saint John, NB E3L 3T5
Tel. (506) 652-3000
*With a licensed restaurant and
lounge bar, this 96-room inn offers
an indoor pool, wheelchair access
and some no-smoking rooms.*

Saint John Hilton ▌▌▌
1 Market Square
Saint John, NB E2L 4Z6
Tel. (506) 693-8484;
fax (506) 657-6610
*High-class accommodation and
great cuisine in a 200-room hotel,
perched at the harbour's edge. Excellent facilities include indoor
swimming pool, jacuzzi, saunas and
exercise room. The bedrooms are
furnished with New Brunswick pine.*

Prince Edward Island

Charlottetown

Rodd Hotel & Resort ▌▌▌
Pownel Street
Charlottetown, PEI
Tel. (902) 894-7371
*Special vacation packages include
golf and theatre themes at this hotel
in the business and shopping dis-
trict.*

South Rustico

Barachois Inn ▐▐
Church Road
South Rustico, PEI
Tel. (902) 963-2194
Restored 1870 house with antique furniture and bay views. A non-smoking establishment.

Nova Scotia

Halifax

Prince George Hotel ▐▐▐
1725 Market Street
Halifax, NS B3J 3N9
Tel. (902) 425-1986;
fax (902) 423-6048
This hotel, in the shadow of Citadel Hill, has more than 200 tastefully furnished rooms, and is excellently located for exploring the city's attractions. The hotel is connected by walkway to the World Trade and Convention Centre.

Waverley Inn ▐▐
1266 Barrington Street
Halifax, NS B3J 1Y5
Tel. (902) 423-9346;
fax (902) 425-0167
Oscar Wilde was a guest in this hotel of character, established in 1876. Today, its services include a free breakfast and snack room open from 6am to midnight.

Dartmouth

Concorde Inn ▐
379 Windmill Road
Dartmouth, NS B3A 1J6
Tel. (902) 465-7777
Modestly priced rooms with kitchenettes in a central location.

Newfoundland

St John's

Hotel Newfoundland ▐▐▐
Cavendish Square
St John's, NF A1C 5W8
Tel. (709) 726-4980;
fax (709) 726-2025
A long list of facilities in this luxurious Canadian Pacific Hotels and Resort property include indoor pool, sauna, whirlpool and gift shops. Among the 267 rooms and 19 suites are bedrooms designed for handicapped guests.

Captain's Quarters Hotel ▐
2 King's Bridge Road
St John's, NF A1C 6H4
Tel. (709) 576-7173
A 20-room property conveniently located near the downtown area, with restaurant and guest lounge.

Restaurants

Budget eating in major cities is easily available, as is ethnic food. Unlikely-looking bars often prove to have a long dining room menu of filling, low-cost food. Classier establishments pride themselves on presentation as well as fine cuisine, with seafood often to the fore. Just about everywhere at all price levels you're made to feel welcome and the staff are well trained. The prices below refer to a three-course meal for one, excluding service and wine.

▐ up to $20
▐▐ $20-30
▐▐▐ over $30

British Columbia

Victoria

Ming's ▐▐
1321 Quadra Street
Victoria, BC V8W 2K9
Tel. (604) 385-4405
The Cantonese menu includes Szechuan and vegetarian dishes, individually prepared.

Brady's Fish & Chips ▐
20 West Burnside Road
Victoria, BC V9A 1B3
Tel. (604) 382-3695
Victoria emulates the English way of life in more ways than one. There is a plethora of fish and chip establishments around the city, and this is one of the best, though fish and chips are obviously an acquired taste.

Antoine's Restaurant ▐▐▐
2 Centennial Square
Victoria, BC V8W 1P7
Tel. (604) 384-7055
Offering imaginative local and international cuisine in elegant surroundings, Antoine's is the perfect

after-theatre restaurant, with a four-course theatre menu which changes weekly.

**Parrot House
Rooftop Restaurant** ▐▐▐
740 Burdett Avenue
Victoria, BC V8W 1B2
Tel. (604) 382-4221
You may go for the splendid view, but the food is memorable, too.

Vancouver

1066 Hastings Restaurant ▐▐
1066 West Hastings Street
Vancouver, BC V6E 3X1
Tel. (604) 689-1066
Remember the name, and you remember the lot! There's a non-smoking section and wheelchair access.

Brother's Restaurant ▐
1 Water Street
Vancouver, BC V6B 1A1
Tel. (604) 683-9124
Probably the greatest value in Gastown – and you're welcomed by a monk. The monastery theme is reflected in the decor – stained glass, solid tables and frescoes – as well as in the rather cornily titled dishes (try Brother Julian's clam chowder or the Monastery burgers).

Hy's Encore ▐▐▐
637 Hornby Street
Vancouver, BC V6C 2G3
Tel. (604) 683-7671
A long-established steak and seafood house in the downtown area.

Cin Cin, Italian Wood Grill ▐
1154 Robson Street
Vancouver, BC V6E 1B5
Tel. (604) 688-7338
Fresh fish is the speciality of the house, while pasta, pastries and breads are cooked on the premises daily. Open to 1am.

Alberta

Jasper

Edith Cavell Dining Room ▐▐▐▐
Jasper Park Lodge
Jasper, Alberta T0E 1E0
Tel. (403) 852-3301
The very best of French cuisine is served in this elegant restaurant in a grand, lakeside setting.

Banff

Smitty's Family Restaurant I
227 Banff Avenue
Banff, Alberta
Tel. (403) 762-2533
The key word here is 'family'. The restaurant serves breakfast, lunch and dinner and for grown-ups there's wine by the glass.

Harvey's Restaurant I
304 Caribou Street,
Banff, Alberta
Tel. (403) 762-8115
Aficionados say Harvey's serves the best hamburgers in North America. This branch certainly measures up. Clean, efficient, courteous – and bang in the middle of town.

Lake Louise

Edelweis Dining Room III
Château Lake Louise
Lake Louise, Alberta
Tel. (403) 522-3511
The best of Canadian and Swiss cuisine is served here as diners drink in the spectacular view of the lake and glacier. There are other, less expensive, eating places in the Château Lake Louise complex.

Calgary

Cannery Row Restaurant III
317 10th Avenue SW
Calgary, Alberta
Tel. (403) 269-8889
Live jazz is sometimes served with the Cajun food in this converted warehouse. Pricey, but popular.

Buzzards Café I
140 10th Avenue SW
Calgary, Alberta
Tel. (403) 264-6959
More of a wine bar atmosphere here, but the food is good and tasty. There's a fine range of international beers to choose from, and the cuisine is similarly eclectic.

Edmonton

Chianti Café I
10501 82nd Avenue
Edmonton, Alberta
Tel. (403) 439-9829
Cheap and cheerful café brimming with young people. The extensive menu includes two dozen pasta dishes.

La Bohème III
6427 112th Avenue
Edmonton, Alberta
Tel. (403) 474-5693
The decor, like the cuisine, is pure French in this highly acclaimed restaurant. The wine list is extensive, and there's a good choice of vegetarian entrées, including provençale-style vegetables.

Saskatchewan

Regina

The Edgewater Café III
Beside the Kramer IMAX Theatre
Saskatchewan Science Centre
Regina, Saskatchewan
Tel. (306) 569-2233
Part of the old powerhouse complex that now houses the Science Centre, this dignified restaurant offers superb European cuisine in a relaxed lakeside setting.

Brewster's Brew Pub I
1832 Victoria Avenue E
Regina, Saskatchewan
Tel. (306) 761-1500
Very cheap casual eating at lunchtime and dinner – and they brew their own beer on the premises.

De Lat By Night I
1312 Broad Street
Regina, Saskatchewan
Tel. (306) 757-7291
Spring rolls and hotpot are the speciality in this licensed Vietnamese restaurant in the downtown area.

Saskatoon

Cousin Niks III
Grosvenor Avenue
Saskatoon, Saskatchewan
Tel. (306) 374-2020
If you're feeling peckish, try the eight-course gourmet dinner. Cuisine is predominantly Greek, and the open courtyard garden setting is soothingly conducive to fine dining. There's also a piano lounge which makes the perfect spot for cocktails before dinner.

Max's Diner I
Idylwyld Drive,
Saskatoon, Saskatchewan
Tel. (306) 934-0434
Saskatoon's young set meets here to

chat over hamburgers and ice cream in a 1950s ambience.

Manitoba

Winnipeg

The Golden Spike II
The Johnston Terminal
The Forks Market
Winnipeg, Manitoba
Tel. (204) 942-7745
Traditional Canadian favourites appear on the menu with contemporary dishes. The restaurant features turn-of-the-century railway artefacts and memorabilia.

Bistro Bohemia II
159 Osborne Street
Winnipeg, Manitoba
Tel. (204) 453-1944
Czech and Slovak cuisine and wines, as well as a wider selection of European fare, are served in this popular downtown location.

Eastside Exchange III
177 Lombard Avenue E
Winnipeg, Manitoba
Tel. (204) 943-2368
After a continental-style dinner, you may be taken to the theatre in the Eastside's chauffeur-driven limousine.

Ontario

Toronto

Herbs II
3187 Yonge St
Toronto, Ont
Tel. (416) 322-0487
Always imaginative, the menu changes daily according to the best available in the local markets.

Peter Pan I
373 Queen Street W
Toronto, Ont
Tel. (416) 593-0917
May the New York diner never grow up! This is a classic, serving grilled strip loin, pastas and seafood stir-fries. The work of local artists is on show – and for sale.

Il Fornello I
214 King Street W
Toronto, Ont
Tel. (416) 977-2855

Pizza-lovers will be delighted with this establishment, which is within walking distance of the theatres and SkyDome. The dining room has three wood-burning pizza ovens, and you can build your own pizza from more than 50 choices of toppings.

National Capital Region

Le Café ‖
National Arts Centre
53 Elgin Street
Ottawa, Ont
Tel. (613) 594-5127
A splendid canalside place to dine before or after an Arts Centre performance, this is also a popular place for lunchtime or teatime meetings. In summer it spills out onto a terrace.

Hy's Steakhouse ‖
170 Queen Street
Ottawa, Ont
Tel. (613) 234-4545
Reliable service in a place with a good reputation for steak and seafood.

Café Henry Burger ‖‖‖
69 rue Laurier
Hull, Quebec
Tel. (819) 777-5646
One of the best of a host of good restaurants on the Quebec side of the River Ottawa, the Café Burger overlooks the Museum of Civilization and beyond across the river to Parliament Hill. The food is predominantly French, and there's a choice of fixed price or à la carte menus.

Quebec

Montreal

La Reine Elizabeth ‖‖‖
900 boulevard René Lévesque Ouest
Montreal
Tel. (514) 861-3511
This long-established classic French restaurant is considered one of Canada's top ten.

Pizzédélic ‖
3509 boulevard St-Laurent
Montreal
Tel. (514) 282-6784

Creative staff here ensure that you'll remember the pizzas and the pizzeria.

Manonchka ‖‖‖
29 rue Laurier Ouest
Montreal
Tel. (514) 270- 0758
Caviar and music make for a memorable evening at this acclaimed Russian restaurant.

Quebec City

Auberge du Trésor ‖
20 rue Sainte-Anne
Quebec (QC) G1R 3X2
Tel. (418) 694-1876
The auberge's quick-service restaurant facing the Château Frontenac keeps local and visiting clients well fed from breakfast to dinner time.

Restaurant Louis Hébert ‖‖‖
668 Grande-Allée Est
Quebec (QC)
Tel. (418) 525-7812
An original and inspired touch is guaranteed at this delightful French restaurant on the ground floor of a 10-room inn. The menu changes frequently, and there's a choice of inside or al fresco dining.

New Brunswick

Fredericton

Pink Pearl ‖
343 Queen Street
Fredericton, NB
Tel. (506) 450-8997
Popular eastern buffet-meals at lunchtimes and evenings, as well as sturdier fare, attract an eager clientele.

Prince Edward Island

Charlottetown

Garden of the Gulf ‖‖‖
Prince Edward Hotel
Queen Street
Charlottetown, PEI
Tel. (902) 566-2222
This is a hotel dining room where you can rely on good seafood and other fare.

The Gainsford ‖‖
Water Street
Charlottetown, PEI
Tel. (902) 368-3840
The salads are a delight here, and delectable desserts are a speciality.

Nova Scotia

Halifax

O'Carroll's Restaurant ‖‖‖
1860 Upper Water Street
Halifax, NS B31 1S8
Tel. (902) 423-4405
Continental cuisine amid the Historic Properties. There's nightly entertainment in an adjacent lounge.

Thirsty Duck Pub ‖‖
5472 Spring Garden Road
Halifax, NS
Tel. (902) 422-1548
In a downtown neighbourhood, this pub is noted for its speciality beers and wines. Seafood, pastas and other dishes are served till late at night.

Newfoundland

St Anthony

The Lighthouse Keeper's Café ‖‖
Fishing Point Road
St Anthony
Tel. (709) 454-4900
Excellent seafood in a memorable location – a former lighthouse keepers' home with whales and icebergs likely to come into view.

Index

Discover the world

with **BERLITZ**®

Australia
Britain
Brittany
California
Canada
Egypt
Europe
Florida
France
Germany
Greece
Ireland
Israel
Italy
Kenya
Loire Valley
New England
Normandy
Portugal
Prague
Pyrenees
Rome
Singapore
Spain
Switzerland
Turkey
Thailand
Tuscany

IN PREPARATION
Scandinavia

BERLITZ DISCOVER GUIDES do more than just map out the sights – they entice you to travel with lush full-colour photography, vivid descriptions and intelligent advice on how to plan and enjoy your holiday or travel experience. Covering the world's most popular destinations, these full-colour travel guides reveal the spirit and flavour of each country or region. Use *DISCOVER* as a travel planner or as a practical reference guide. You'll find sightseeing information and suggested leisure routes, extensive full-colour maps and town plans, local hotel and restaurant listings plus special essays highlighting interesting local features. Colourful historical and cultural background is complemented by practical details such as what to visit and where to stay, where to eat and how much you should expect to pay.

No matter where you're going, make the most of your trip:

DISCOVER the world with **BERLITZ.**